D0946685

THE GEORGE GERSHWIN READER

READERS ON AMERICAN MUSICIANS

Scott DeVeaux, Series Editor

THE GEORGE GERSHWIN READER

EDITED BY

Robert Wyatt and John Andrew Johnson

OXFORD
UNIVERSITY PRESS

2004

OXFORD
UNIVERSITY PRESS

Oxford   New York
Auckland   Bangkok   Buenos Aires   Cape Town   Chennai
Dar es Salaam   Delhi   Hong Kong   Istanbul   Karachi   Kolkata
Kuala Lumpur   Madrid   Melbourne   Mexico City   Mumbai   Nairobi
São Paulo   Shanghai   Taipei   Tokyo   Toronto

Copyright © 2004 by Oxford University Press, Inc.

Published by Oxford University Press, Inc.
198 Madison Avenue, New York, New York 10016
www.oup.com

Oxford is a registered trademark of Oxford University Press

Library of Congress Cataloging-in-Publication Data
The George Gershwin reader / edited by Robert Wyatt and John Andrew Johnson.
p. cm. — (Readers on American musicians)
Includes bibliographical references (p.   ) and index.
ISBN 0-19-513019-7
1. Gershwin, George, 1898–1937—Criticism and interpretation.
I. Wyatt, Robert, 1948–.
II. Johnson, John Andrew. III. Series.
ML410.G288 G47   2004   780'.92—dc22   2003016160

Book design and composition by Mark McGarry, Texas Type & Book Works
Set in Monotype Dante

9 8 7 6 5 4 3 2 1
Printed in the United States of America
on acid-free paper

CONTENTS

Acknowledgments   IX

Introduction   XI

I. PORTRAITS OF THE ARTIST   I

1 Ira Gershwin: "In person, my brother was a good deal like his
   music" (1961)   3
2 Frances Gershwin Godowsky: "George Gershwin Was My
   Brother" (1962)   3
3 Kay Swift: "Did you ever feel that a composer resembled
   his music?" (ca. 1970)   6
4 Oscar Levant: "Variations on a Gershwin Theme" (1939)   7
5 Verna Arvey: "George Gershwin Through the Eyes of a
   Friend" (1948)   20
6 "Gershwin Bros." (1925)   25
7 Isaac Goldberg: "Childhood of a Composer" (1931)   27

II. THE GROWING LIMELIGHT (1919–1924)   37

8 George Gershwin: Letter to Max Abramson (1918)   39
9 Dolly Dalrymple: "Pianist, Playing Role of Columbus,
   Makes Another American Discovery: Beryl Rubinstein Says
   This Country Possesses Genius Composer" (1922)   41
10 George Gershwin: Letter to Ira Gershwin (February 18, 1923)   42
11 "Whiteman Judges Named: Committee Will Decide
   'What Is American Music'" (1924)   44
12 Paul Whiteman and Mary Margaret McBride:
   "An Experiment" (1926)   45
13 Olin Downes: "A Concert of Jazz" (1924)   49
14 Carl Van Vechten: Letter to George Gershwin (February 14, 1924)   52

15 James Ross Moore: "The Gershwins in Britain" (1994)   52
16 Ira Gershwin: "Which Came First?" (1959)   57

III. FAME AND FORTUNE (1924–1930)   63

17 Philip Furia: *Lady, Be Good!* (1996)   65
18 Ira Gershwin: Letter to Lou and Emily Paley (November 26, 1924) 72
19 Alec Wilder: "That Certain Feeling" (1972)   75
20 Carl Van Vechten: "George Gershwin, An American Composer
    Who Is Writing Notable Music in the Jazz Idiom" (1925)   77
21 Samuel Chotzinoff: "New York Symphony at Carnegie
    Hall" (1925)   82
22 Lawrence Gilman: "Mr. George Gershwin Plays His New Jazz
    Concerto" (1925)   85
23 "Paul Whiteman Gives 'Vivid' Grand Opera; Jazz Rhythms of
    Gershwin's '135th Street'" (1925)   87
24 George Gershwin: "Our New National Anthem" (1925)   89
25 George Gershwin: "Jazz Is the Voice of the American Soul" (1926) 91
26 George Gershwin: "Does Jazz Belong to Art?" (1926)   94
27 George Gershwin: "Mr. Gershwin Replies to Mr. Kramer" (1926)   98
28 Abbe Niles: "The Ewe Lamb of Widow Jazz" (1926)   101
29 Carleton Sprague Smith: "d'Alvarez-Gershwin Recital" (1927)   102
30 Allen Forte: "Someone to Watch Over Me" (1990)   103
31 "George Gershwin Accepts $100,000 Movietone Offer: Fox to
    Pay That Sum for Film Version of Musical Comedy—Composer
    Gets Bid of $50,000 for *Rhapsody in Blue* Rights" (1928)   107
32 George Gershwin: Letter to Mabel Schirmer (1928)   108
33 Deems Taylor: *An American in Paris*: Narrative Guide" (1928) 110
34 Olin Downes: "Gershwin's New Score Acclaimed" (1928)   112
35 George Gershwin: "Fifty Years of American Music . . . Younger
    Composers, Freed from European Influences, Labor Toward
    Achieving a Distinctive American Musical Idiom" (1929)   114
36 George Gershwin: "The Composer in the Machine Age" (1930)   119
37 Mary Herron Dupree: " 'Jazz,' the Critics, and American Art
    Music in the 1920s" (1986)   123

IV. MATURITY (1930–1935)   131

38 George Gershwin: "Making Music" (1930)   133
39 Robert Benchley: "Satire to Music" (1930)   137

40 John Harkins: "George Gershwin" (1932)   138
41 Arthur Ruhl: *Of Thee I Sing*, Kaufman-Ryskind Musical
    Comedy Satire at the Music Box" (1931)   143
42 "A Music Master Talks of His Trials" (1932)   145
43 Catherine Parsons Smith: From *William Grant Still: A Study in
    Contradictions* (2000)   147
44 Richard Crawford: "George Gershwin's 'I Got
    Rhythm' (1930)" (1993)   156
45 Allan Lincoln Langley: "The Gershwin Myth" (1932)   172
46 William Daly: "George Gershwin as Orchestrator" (1933)   175
47 Olin Downes: "George Gershwin Plays His *Second Rhapsody*
    for the First Time Here with Koussevitsky and Boston
    Orchestra" (1932)   177
48 George Gershwin: Letter to Rose Gershwin (June or July 1932)   178
49 Alexander Woollcott: "George the Ingenuous" (1933)   179
50 George Gershwin: Letter to Emily Paley (1934)   184
51 George Gershwin: Letter to Ira Gershwin (1935)   185
52 Frederick Jacobi: "The Future of Gershwin" (1937)   186

V.   PORGY AND BESS   191

53 Joseph Swain: From "America's Folk Opera" (1990)   193
54 George Gershwin and DuBose Heyward, Selected
    Correspondence (1932–1934)   201
55 "George Gershwin Arrives to Plan Opera on *Porgy*" (1933)   211
56 Brooks Atkinson and Olin Downes: "*Porgy and Bess*, Native
    Opera, Opens at the Alvin: Gershwin's Work Based on DuBose
    Heyward's Play" (1935)   213
57 George Gershwin: "Rhapsody in Catfish Row: Mr. Gershwin
    Tells the Origin and Scheme for His Music in That New Folk
    Opera Called 'Porgy and Bess'" (1935)   217
58 Todd Duncan: From an Interview by Robert Wyatt (1990)   221
59 Anne Brown: From an interview by Robert Wyatt (1995)   228

VI. LAST YEARS: HOLLYWOOD (1936–1937)   237

60 Edith Garson: "Hollywood—An Ending" (1938)   239
61 Isabel Morse Jones: "Gershwin Analyzes Science of
    Rhythm"(1937)   244
62 Nanette Kutner: "Radio Pays a Debt" (1936)   246

63 Alec Wilder: "A Foggy Day" (1972)   250
64 George Gershwin: Letters to Zenna Hannenfeldt (1936)   251
65 George Gershwin: Letters to Mabel Schirmer (1936–1937)   254
66 George Gershwin: Letter to Emily Paley (1937)   259
67 George Gershwin: Letter to Henry Botkin (1937)   260
68 George Gershwin: Letter to Rose Gershwin (1937)   261
69 George Gershwin: Letter to Rose Gershwin (1937)   263
70 George A. Pallay: Letter to Irene Gallagher (1937)   263

VII. OBITUARIES AND EULOGIES   269

71 Report in *Variety* (1937)   271
72 Arnold Schoenberg: "George Gershwin" (1938)   273
73 Olin Downes: "Hail and Farewell: Career and Position of
    George Gershwin in American Music" (1937)   274
74 Irving Berlin: "Poem" (1938)   278
75 Jerome Kern: "Tribute" (1938)   279
76 "Gershwin Left $341,089 Estate to His Mother; 'Rhapsody in
    Blue' Appraised at 'Greatest Value' and Opera Rights of
    'Nominal Interest' to the Residue" (1938)   280
77 Ira Gershwin: Letter to Rose Gershwin (1937)   281

VIII. AS TIME PASSES   285

78 "Music by Slide Rule" (1944)   287
79 Ira Gershwin: "Gershwin on Gershwin" (1944)   289
80 Vernon Duke: "Gershwin, Schillinger, and Dukelsky:
    Some Reminiscences" (1947)   289
81 Leonard Bernstein: "Why Don't You Run Upstairs and Write
    a Nice Gershwin Tune?" (1955)   293
82 Duke Ellington: "George Gershwin" (1973)   300
83 Wayne Shirley: "George Gershwin: yes, the sounds as well as
    the tunes are his" (1998)   301

Chronology   309
Selected Bibliography   325
Credits   333
Index   335

ACKNOWLEDGMENTS

A volume of this sort requires the patience, guidance, and support of many. Although only the most prominent are mentioned here, we are thankful to all. Our editors at Oxford University Press, Sheldon Meyer and Maribeth Payne, and the general editor of this series, Scott DeVeaux, each provided the tireless patience and support we required to negotiate and complete our task. We also want to thank those expert readers that Oxford asked to provide criticism of our plans early on and critiques of our manuscript as it developed. These specialists have helped to shape the book into one that will, we hope, be of use not only to the community of Gershwin scholars but to a general readership as well.

Needless to say, many libraries, archives, museums, and other collections were searched for the materials included in this volume. Myriad brilliant scholars and librarians afforded us invaluable assistance. Among them are Wayne Shirley, Ray White, and Walter Zvonchenko at the Music Division of the Library of Congress; Marty Jacobs, associate theater curator for Collections and Research Services at the Museum of the City of New York; Ned Comstock, a curator at the Doheny Library, Cinema and Television Archive, University of Southern California; Kendall Crilly and Suzanne Eggleston at Yale University's Gilmore Music Library; Vivian Perlis at Princeton University; and Nancy McAleer, a brilliant researcher who sleuthed copyright information.

Special words of profound gratitude go to writer Katharine Weber, one of Kay Swift's granddaughters, who has been a part of this project from the early moments. Her generosity with time, enthusiasm, priceless photographs, memories, introductions, and unfailing support has made her, in a sense, a silent author. Hats off to her and her mother, Andrea Kaufman, always Gershwin's favorite among Kay Swift's three daughters.

Edward Jablonski, author of so many Gershwin biographies, articles, and discographies that his credits overshadow all others, was enormously generous with his time and resources. No one has amassed such an array of Gershwiniana in the form of scores, letters, memorabilia, photos, timelines, videos, etc., and to inspect them with Ed's commentary is almost an extravagance.

An afternoon with Ed in his Manhattan apartment is, in itself, a Gershwin afternoon.

Hearty thanks are due to John Johnson's colleagues at Syracuse University who provided practical advice regarding editing a book of this sort. Wayne Franits, Gary Radke, and David Tatham all lent expertise similarly. Linda Straub deserves thanks for her administrative help. And Robert Jensen, dean of the College of Arts and Sciences, and Ben Ware of the University's Center for Research and Computing have John's deepest thanks for providing the support to travel and conduct some of the necessary research.

The copyright holders of the texts reproduced here likewise have been courteous to our requests. Without their support and generosity this book would have been impossible. We especially want to thank Adam Gershwin and the George Gershwin Family Trust as well as Mark Trent Goldberg and the Ira and Leonore Gershwin Trusts for allowing us to reproduce unpublished materials.

To Vicki Wyatt I owe my eternal gratitude for her unconditional support of this project and of me. Last, we note that closest of sustenance from our entire families. They deserve the greatest thanks of all.

INTRODUCTION

During his lifetime, George Gershwin (1898–1937) achieved an almost unprecedented level of success marked by an international reputation, massive wealth, celebrity status, and an uncanny means of attracting attention. He was sought after as a performing pianist and conductor as well as a composer of popular song, symphonic music, piano compositions, and opera. An almost childlike energy seemed to both surround and emanate from him throughout his entire life. Surely that energy was the personal quality that attracted reporters, an adoring public, and a nationwide audience of radio and phonograph listeners. During the 1920s and 1930s, the name "Gershwin" became a brand for the style of music that swept an eager public into theaters, movie houses, and any space where dancing occurred.

Yet no one, and certainly not Gershwin himself, could attach a name to the type of music that he was writing. Jazz was a much debated style during his lifetime. With the clarity provided by historical perspective, we can now state unequivocally that the music Gershwin composed was not jazz; during the 1920s almost any syncopated music received that label, regardless of the instrumentation or style. Gershwin was quick to cash in on the new fad, unafraid to be linked to the self-proclaimed "King of Jazz," Paul Whiteman, or to describe any of his own syncopated or blues compositions as jazz. During the 1930s, however, and especially during the time when he was composing *Porgy and Bess*, Gershwin began to separate himself stylistically from the jazz musicians who were quickly moving into the swing era.

Even today, over sixty-five years since his death, George Gershwin is a conundrum, both as a man and as a composer. Nor was it different while he was alive. Lambasted by his critics for a lack of formal compositional technique, he was able to attract audiences like no other composer of his era. Although many people and especially the press described Gershwin as a constantly vibrant man, many of his friends knew him as troubled and dark. Anne Wiggins Brown, the original Bess, described his complexity and his ability to shift moods quickly and drastically. With a pervasive folklore quality attached to the glamour of his life and the era in which he thrived, it is dif-

ficult to ascertain biographical fact and fiction, especially since it is possible
that at least some of the rich inheritance of spurious stories originated from
Gershwin himself.

This volume, like its model, Mark Tucker's excellent *The Duke Ellington
Reader*, was created as a source book, a compendium designed to sift through
the immense body of literature—biographies, interviews of the composer, his
friends, and colleagues, concert reviews, testimonials, letters both intimate
and business-like, feature articles, theoretical analyses of Gershwin's works,
poetry, and even comic books—in order to describe the composer not through
the perception of the biographer, but through reports by and about the composer selected for their authenticity and historical significance. The resulting
volume is intended to help to fill a void in Gershwin historiography by providing scholarly yet readable sources of information while tracing the short life
and career of a man, a musician, a celebrity, and, eventually, a legend.

Contained in this reader are six articles written by Gershwin between 1925
and 1930, during a time when he seemingly found it necessary to define his
music in print. Omitted are two other bylines—the "Introduction" to Isaac
Goldberg's *Tin Pan Alley: A Chronicle of the American Popular Music Racket*
(1930) and the "Introduction" to *George Gershwin's Songbook* (1932), both of
which were presumably ghostwritten by Goldberg. The article "Rhapsody in
Catfish Row: Mr. Gershwin Tells the Origin and Scheme for His Music in
That New Folk Opera Called 'Porgy and Bess'" is, as its subtitle suggests,
simply a report on and explanation of the opera. Other selections are mus-
ings of family members and close friends—his brother Ira, his sister, Frances
Godowsky, and his mother, Rose; Kay Swift, Oscar Levant, Mabel Schirmer,
Paul Whiteman, and others—contained within letters, formal interviews, or
biographical tributes to Gershwin's personality. Concert reviews of significant works are also included, reviews selected to include both criticism and
praise. Other entries are primary sources gleaned from magazines and newspapers of the time and articles taken from sources printed after Gershwin's
death in 1937 that either analyze his music or clarify his position in the chronicle of American music.

The George Gershwin Reader is divided into three main sections: Parts
I–VIII, which describe George Gershwin as a person and musician; a chronology or timeline that lists significant dates (births, deaths, premieres, concert
tours, vacations, personal details); and a selected bibliography, which presents
a portion of the massive literature on George Gershwin.

The main entries are prefaced by introductory headnotes and accompanied by descriptive footnotes to help situate and explain their contents. On
occasion, gentle editorial corrections were required in the articles, yet gram-

matical and spelling peculiarities usually have been retained without comment since these reflect the age in which the articles were written as well as the voice of their writers. In some cases, longer entries have been excerpted to remain pertinent to the specific topic or time period covered by the chapter.

The George Gershwin Reader supplements previous sources of primary and period information about Gershwin. In addition to the documentary produced by the BBC and aired on American television as part of PBS's *American Masters* series in 1987, these sources include most notably Merle Armitage's *George Gershwin* (1938), Edward Jablonski and Lawrence D. Stewart's *The Gershwin Years*, Robert Kimball and Alfred Simon's *The Gershwins* (1973), and Edward Jablonski's solo volume *Gershwin* (1987) and his edited compilation *Gershwin Remembered* (1992). While borrowing from their examples, this volume strives to supplement rather than supplant them since it cannot replace their special qualities. This is an edition, then, shaped by the objectivity fostered by distance of time and place if not benefiting, as did those previous readers, from direct contact with the subject.

One of the features of Kimball and Simon's anthology (as its title suggests) is its inclusion of lyricist Ira alongside composer George. And with this a word of explanation is in order. Although the present book focuses primarily on the work of the composer (as *its* title suggests), it can overlook neither Ira's crucial role in shaping the course of his brother's life and the style of his music nor Ira's extensive comments regarding the art they created together. Ira is not included in the title in part because he wrote his own reader in the form of the autobiographical *Lyrics on Several Occasions*, which was supplemented with the publication of additional notes in Robert Kimball's edition of the complete lyrics in 1993. Thus, here Ira's many roles (often as a collaborator in ways other than as a lyricist) are recognized, his unique perspective is included, but his work independent of George is not. Some scholarship in this direction has begun (e.g., Philip Furia's work or sections in some of the Gershwin biographies), but a volume devoted to Ira's total literary output remains to be written, along with the republication of his wonderful memoirs.

Beyond the previously available published sources, the 20-plus volumes of Gershwin Scrapbooks in the extensive Gershwin Collection at the Library of Congress (DLC [GC]) should be noted, for they constitute the most exhaustive of all readers, spanning the brothers' earliest years up to recent times. They will remain the place to go for serious archival work, although their highlights have found their way into this book.

Armitage's memorial volume stands as a valuable record of time and place, reflecting the views of prominent figures who knew the composer and recorded their thoughts around the time of his death. Given their great importance, several items from that book are reprinted here.

Jablonski and Stewart's volume and Jablonski's solo opuses likewise demonstrate an intimate biographical knowledge derived from decades of research and made many hitherto unknown sources (especially some informal recollections and less accessible articles) available to a wider public. Jablonski's *Gershwin Remembered* stands apart from the others and nearer to ours in its inclusion of editorial commentary. As there, we have tried to intrude as little as possible on the material we have chosen.

To the basic list of sources above, a few other items should be added. Perhaps more than any other single source, Isaac Goldberg's 1931 biography provides a timeless period glimpse of Gershwin during his lifetime, a uniquely valuable document given its dependence on the composer's own thoughts about his life and music that are contained in letters exchanged between the author and the composer. The 1958 reprint contains an excellent addendum by Edith Garson, expanding the original publication to include Gershwin's death in 1937. All of the many subsequent biographers, from Ewen to Schwartz, Rosenberg to Peyser, have departed from Goldberg's precedent yet interpreted the extant records in different ways, and each has organized, presented, and quoted from sources not excerpted elsewhere. So, in a sense, the bodies of Gershwin biographies likewise constitute a series of readers. And various articles since Gershwin's lifetime have sought to be biographical investigations, stylistic discussions, and interpretations of written commentaries. Throughout this volume, the headnotes refer to these books and articles, as their contributions seem relevant to the ongoing presentation of source readings.

So *The George Gershwin Reader* is part of several different kinds of series and strives to accomplish several tasks. Simply by its arrangement it offers a biographical sketch of the composer's life. This is presented in more exacting fashion in the chronology that follows the main body of the book, which, like the bibliography, updates the record based on current research. In sum, *The George Gershwin Reader* is really a handbook for specialist and general reader alike. For the former, it may act as a handy reference source, a place to consult often-used material efficiently with the benefit of the chronology and bibliography nearby. For the latter, this volume may be an introduction, interesting reading, or simply a place to learn more about Gershwin, his times, and his music.

I. PORTRAITS OF THE ARTIST

The following writings provide glimpses of Gershwin's multifaceted artistic persona from the perspectives of some of those who knew him best. His brother and alter ego Ira and his sister, Frankie, reflect personal views that speak to the reality of the man against the backdrop of his overall personal and artistic development. Close companions and friends Kay Swift and Oscar Levant speak with the spirit of knowing and seeing Gershwin on a daily basis. The balance of articles here present a recurring theme in this volume: namely, Gershwin's remarkably quick and steep ascendance onto and—once there—around the world's stage.

1 Ira Gershwin: "In person, my brother was a good deal like his music" (1961)

Not only was Ira Gershwin the composer's brother and closest collaborator, but following the composer's death he served as the spokesman for all
matters Gershwin. He carried out this responsibility with terrific aplomb,
as is apparent in the following concise reflection provided for a radio program by the Canadian Broadcasting Company in 1961. While speaking honestly and directly, Ira knows that when he talks about George he is also
talking indirectly about himself, thus he errs on the side of modesty.

In person my brother was a good deal like his music: vibrant, dynamic and
honest, and, if I may, charming. He was full of life and lived a full day.
Although most of it was devoted to the piano and his music, it was a contin-
ual source of amazement to me that he found time to engage in so many
other activities. He was a fine painter, a good golfer, a discerning and coura-
geous art collector, an excellent photographer, a wonderful dancer...
whether at a ballroom or taking a moment out of a show rehearsal to break
into a tap dance. And socially he was one of the most sought after young
men in New York or whatever city he happened to be in. George moved fast,
lived fast, studied hard, and learned fast.

2 Frances Gershwin Godowsky: "George Gershwin Was My Brother" (1962)

The younger sister of Ira, George, and Arthur, Frances Gershwin Godowsky,
or Frankie, after a brief career on the musical stage, married Leopold
Godowsky II, one of the inventors of the Kodachrome process. She speaks
about her brother at some distance, but echoes many of Ira's observations

SOURCE (1) Canadian Broadcasting Company radio commentary, on *Gershwin Remembered* (Santa Monica, Calif.: Facet 8100, 1987). The recording also features commentary by Fred Astaire, Oscar Levant, and
film composer Alfred Newman.
SOURCE (2) *Reader's Digest Music Guide* (November 1962): 4–6.

in the previous entry, notably George's abilities beyond music, as a dancer and painter. She also speaks to his reputation as a ladies' man. Unlike Ira, however, who was always somewhat guarded about more personal details, Frankie at least begins to reflect upon them. Despite his great success and surely the peer pressure of those around him, Gershwin never married, and was to some degree self-conscious or, as his sister says, "defensive" about aspects of his life and work.

George was surrounded with people and excitement all his life. Everyone in our family loved people and there was always something going on in our four-story house on 103rd Street, near Riverside Drive.[1] I would often come home and find a furious Ping-Pong game in progress on the main floor. On the second floor, mother would be having guests. On the third floor, Ira and his wife, Lee, might be entertaining friends. And George, who had the fourth floor to himself, would be playing and having a party of theater friends. I used to visit from floor to floor. It was always like that: games and friends and music. George played the piano constantly with a wonderful rhythm and virtuosity.

George loved to dance and he would show me the latest steps Fred Astaire was doing in *Lady, Be Good!* or *Funny Face*.[2] He danced beautifully in a broken rhythm, with grace and style. He was full of music and even at the dinner table would drum out a rhythm, asking: "Can you get this? Do you recognize this?" It was a game with him.

Success came early to George, who took it with disarming grace, despite the many people who spoiled him by catering to him. He also painted very well and could have been a successful professional artist, which brought him more attention and praise. Naturally, there were many women in his life.

But with all the people, the excitement, the success—and his absorbing interest in music—George was lonely inside himself. People didn't know him too well: he didn't let them get close to him. Ira, his collaborator on lyrics for most of his music, was closest. Of all of us, it was George who first spoke of getting married and having children. He loved a home, and yet it was George who never married. I suppose there was some unconscious fear which made it impossible for him to lose himself in a personal relationship. And, of course, music came first.

---

1 The family lived together in the arrangement that Frances describes here until 1929, by which time the quarters seemed cramped. George and Ira then moved to neighboring penthouses on Riverside Drive, at West 75th Street. In 1933, in their final move before settling in Hollywood, the brothers took up residences in apartments on the opposite sides of East 72nd Street.

2 Brother and sister team Fred and Adele Astaire starred in the Gershwins' *Lady, Be Good!*, the brothers' first complete score for a musical show, in 1924 and in their *Funny Face* in 1927.

George was a very open and frank person, without pretense. He was what he was, without apology, forceful and with great strength of character. He welcomed criticism of his work. For example, if he played something and I criticized the phrasing, or the melody, he would immediately try the song a new way, asking: "How about this?" He listened to suggestions, then made up his own mind about what he could use. But he was sensitive to personal criticism, which could make him defensive.

Because George was confident and believed in his talent, some people have called him self-centered. This is a misunderstanding. He simply knew what he could do and had no false modesty. He was definitely not conceited.

There was a big difference in our ages and I remember little of him as a brother when I was a child. I was the kid sister. He was grown up and often away on tour with Elsie Janis, Louise Dresser, Nora Bayes, or working on a musical. He would be in and out of the house, but he always brought some little gift for my mother and me—a pink felt doll's hat with a feather, a beautiful Japanese kimono. He would play for me and encourage me to sing. When I was about five, he played "By the sea, by the beautiful sea," and I recall how pleased he was that I carried the tune so well.

Years later, when Ira, Lee, George and I went abroad, I sang George's songs at Les Ambassadeurs, a Paris nightclub.[3] I could interpret his music because it was so much a part of me. All of us had good rhythm: it was a family pattern.

Of all George's music, the *Concerto in F* is my favorite. It is one of his most mature works and shows his musical development. As he grew older, George tended more and more toward serious music, although he had little classical training. His spontaneous melodic talent was so great that the French teacher Mlle. Nadia Boulanger refused to take him as a student, fearing classical discipline might harm his work.

I saw George last in Hollywood, where he was working on the music for *Shall We Dance* and *Damsel in Distress* with Fred Astaire. He was also giving a series of winter concerts, featuring *Rhapsody in Blue*, the *Concerto* and the *Suite from "Porgy and Bess,"* as well as conducting the Los Angeles Philharmonic. At that time, he told me he felt he hadn't scratched the surface on what he planned to do. He said he had so many ideas for the future: an American opera, string quartets, a symphony. Six months later, while I was in Vienna, I received a cable that he was dead.

George has not become a legend to me, despite his growing fame since his

---

3 The itinerary of the Gershwins' 1928 European trip is detailed in the Chronology at the end of this volume.

death. I remember his vitality, his charm, his excitement. He was a handsome man with beautiful brown eyes and wonderful coloring. After I grew up, there seemed no difference in our ages. I will always admire him for his extraordinary talent as a composer, as a pianist, and for his firm, but justified belief in himself.

3   Kay Swift: "Did you ever feel that a composer resembled his music?" (ca. 1970)

Perhaps no one beyond his immediate family knew Gershwin as well as Kay Swift (1897–1993). In addition to their romantic relationship, Swift, herself a composer of such hits as "Fine and Dandy" and "Can't We Be Friends," and Gershwin enjoyed camaraderie as creative artists. Swift knew Gershwin's music well and brought to their times together a schooled sense of musical mechanics that complemented Gershwin's gifts and seemingly voracious appetite for learning. She scored his *Preludes for Piano* as he played them in her Manhattan apartment, and it is clear that Swift helped, though not in a creative capacity, with the completion of some of the final scoring for *Porgy and Bess*. She also was near the composer during the time that he was studying composition with Joseph Schillinger, as is indicated by the appearance of some sketches in her hand in one of the composer's sketchbooks. Swift continued to lend her expertise to the perpetuation of Gershwin's legacy alongside Ira in the decades following the composer's death. The following reflection, while primarily concerned with a memory that predates their close involvement, includes the personal detail of the composer's height. It is evidence of her sharp sense, based on their many subsequent hours together, of the man and his music.

Did you ever feel that a composer resembled his music? I believe this can sometimes be possible, and in the case of George Gershwin, it was true. The man and his music seemed strongly alike.

This idea first became apparent to me at a rehearsal of his *Concerto in F*, in 1925. I had met Gershwin once, but did not know him well, and admired his songs. The rehearsal was in Carnegie Hall, and, although he did not, of course, run to the piano, he looked as though he might have liked to. Some of his excitement reached to the few of us who watched from the audience.

Being slim, long-legged and fast-moving, he always looked taller than his

SOURCE Unpublished typescript, Kay Swift Archive, Yale University, New Haven, Conn.

actual height, which was a couple of inches short of six feet. He sat erectly at the piano, with no needless gestures, but with an eagerness that made the first and last movements of the *Concerto* sound sparkling, while the slower, more wistful second movement never became too sentimental.

When he rose, at the end, to bow to the conductor Walter Damrosch, and the orchestra, it was apparent that the performance had given him just about the happiest experience a composer can have—to hear his composition, with the realization that the sound he has heard is as close as possible to the sound he hoped for while composing the work.

4   Oscar Levant: *"Variations on a Gershwin Theme"* (1939)

Famous for his quips and quick wit, Oscar Levant (1906–1972) went on to greater fame as a popular personality after Gershwin's death, appearing not only as a concert artist but also on radio, early television, and starring in Warner Brothers' Gershwin bio-picture *Rhapsody in Blue* in 1945 and MGM's classic Hollywood musical *An American in Paris* in 1951. As he describes below, Levant had known about Gershwin as early as 1918, when as a boy he attended a performance of *Ladies First* in his native Pittsburgh. Upon making his way to New York, he pursued a career as a concert pianist and occasional composer. But throughout his life he found himself in Gershwin's shadow, for the elder (by some eight years) musician had seemingly beat him to his aspirations. Yet, despite his sometimes acerbic comments, he respected Gershwin greatly, and the two men remained friends for the bulk of Gershwin's professional career. The most famous and often quoted essay on Gershwin that Levant wrote was published in 1940 in the form of his "My Life, Or the Story of George Gershwin," contained in his *Smattering of Ignorance*. The article below was an advance preview of that essay and appeared a year earlier in *Town and Country* magazine. As one of the first and still one of the best interpreters of Gershwin's piano music, Levant was uniquely positioned to offer a pithy view of the composer's style, tempered by his own élan. As a member of the Gershwins' inner circle, he provides a valuable glimpse of the man and his family beyond Gershwin's public image.

My first recollection of the theatre is of being a gallery spectator at a show called *Ladies First*, starring Nora Bayes. I was present in tribute to my uncle

SOURCE *Town and Country* 94 (November 1939): 58–61, 83–84.

Oscar Radin, who conducted the pit orchestra. I don't remember a thing about the performance (this was about 1918, when I was twelve) except that in the second act the show stopped and Bayes came down front to sing. Her treatment was highly personal and the piano accompaniment played a very subtle and important part, requiring almost constant improvisation. After one chorus of the first song my attention left Bayes and remained fixed on the playing of the pianist. I had never heard such fresh, brisk, unstudied, completely free, and inventive playing—and all within a consistent frame that set off the singing perfectly. I was jealous.

Thus, long before I ever met George Gershwin, or even heard of him, he began to impinge on my life. Like the first theme in an elaborate rondo, his was a discomfortingly insistent motif in my orbit. Later, when I reminded him of the show and his part in it, he remarked that Bayes was constantly complaining that his playing distracted her from what she was trying to do, and that she frequently threatened to get someone else.

When I was fifteen years old I left Pittsburgh, having realized that my chances of making the Pirates were something less than ephemeral (my legs had gone bad). I returned to the piano as my instrument of vengeance. Thus were established the two characteristics I have nurtured ever since as the dominant influences of my life—jealousy and revenge.

At this time music in New York was in a slothful, degenerate, undiscriminating, post-War enthusiasm for such pianists as Paderewski, Rachmaninoff, Hofmann, and Rosenthal. The public was content to be entertained rather than disturbed. Consequently, even though my scales were like a neurotic string of pearls, and my octaves, like the fabulous Zuleika Dobson, "Had no hips at all," I was forced into playing dance music.

I had an unhealthy contempt for most of the tunes we played. They had no qualities on which my jealousy-revenge hunger could feed. Soon, however, I began to notice a few songs which had merits sufficient to arouse my resentment—"Do It Again," "I'll Build a Stairway to Paradise," and several others. Here, I thought, was at last something worthy of envy; and I took note of the composer, George Gershwin, as a contemporary worthy of my most zealous dislike.

The thunderous shadow of George next fell on me with the febrile tornado of the *Rhapsody in Blue.* I recorded it with Frank Black for Brunswick early in 1925, when the regular pianist failed to show up. I was fond of the music and eager to make the recording, and afterwards called up the composer, "just to get his reactions," but mostly for approbation. I didn't get much for, contrary to the common impression that composers do not think highly of their abilities as performers, Gershwin was quite firm in his preference for his own version on Victor. At this distance I can acknowledge that it is much superior.

It was after this that I began to make infrequent, unprofitable appearances on the radio. I thought I might build up a following as a pianist in this way, but since I was never asked to play anything but the *Rhapsody*, I merely increased its vogue and added to my reputation as a mono-pianist. After my fourth appearance as soloist in the *Rhapsody* my mother suggested that there were other works for piano and orchestra, and also expressed the hope that she might sometime hear me play on an important program, like the Atwater Kent or the Roxy hour. I was able to fulfill her desire by appearing as soloist with Rapee on the Roxy broadcast, but when I called her up afterwards she exclaimed, "Again the *Rhapsody!*"[1]

So my joy at hearing that Gershwin had been commissioned by the New York Symphony to write a concerto could hardly have been exceeded by his. Now, automatically, my repertoire would be doubled. There was a growing concern in my mind about the progress of the work in which I had so definite a personal interest, and I beseeched an introduction to Gershwin.

I found him amazingly accessible at his apartment on 110th Street. He was working on the first movement of "our" concerto, with the late Bill Daly, his devoted friend and favorite conductor.[2] He was playing what he had written so far. In addition to the work itself, his swift and mettlesome playing so stimulated and excited me that the old dormant envy was revived. I was inarticulate and stammered some graceless remark. George mistook my confusion and admiration for disapproval and became involuntarily hostile. He returned to his work, and I left, having successfully made my usual bad impression. However, when the concert had its first performance in Carnegie Hall, I found that my esteem for the work and Gershwin's playing had not been vitiated by our angular meeting.

There followed an interim in which I began writing songs myself, some of them fairly successful. This led to a two-year stay in Hollywood, after which I returned to write a show for Fred Stone. I had begun to emerge somewhat from the Gershwin shadow and I now recognized him not merely as a subject of envy but, in my youthful bumptiousness, as a business competitor.

By coincidence *Ripples,* the Stone show, was housed in the New Amsterdam Theatre, opposite Gershwin's *Strike Up the Band* at the Selwyn. This juxtaposition renewed my old contrapuntal relationship with George, but with a

---

1 As a composer Arno Rapee would prove to be an important, and like Levant quick-witted, contributor to early film music.

2 Daly had a Harvard education and surely tutored Gershwin informally. He came to Gershwin's defense notably in 1933. See selection 46, p. 175.

more brassy timbre contributed by our mutual interest in a chorus girl in his show. In this competition, in addition to his ponderable advantage in being Gershwin while I was not, he had the extra weight-pull of a ducal fur-trimmed overcoat that gave him the appearance of a perpetual guest conductor. In my favor were a slovenly appearance, a certain rudeness, and a facility for creating anti-Gershwin propaganda, and my tactics were to appeal to the mother instinct that is latent in even a chorus girl.

For her part, she was devoted to *La Bohème* and swooned in ecstasy with each saccharine cadence. George had difficulty playing the Puccini score for her on the piano because it wasn't by Gershwin and he didn't read other people's music very well. It was no problem for me, however, and I eventually found myself dripping Bohemians from each ear. But despite my fluency, the race was not to the swift. I always felt that there was an element of wish fulfillment in her partiality for George: his fur collar had an association with Mimi's muff, which she always coveted.

During this contretemps I acquired a fondness for the score of *Strike Up the Band* and often found myself at the rear of the Selwyn resentfully transported by the fresh rhythms and humors of the lyrics and music. While in the spell of this discovery one afternoon I was tapped on the shoulder by a wraithlike figure. It was Leonore Gershwin, wife of George's brother and collaborator, Ira, whom I had met once before. She suggested that perhaps I would like to spend the evening with George and Ira.

I escorted her back to the apartment house on Riverside Drive where the Gershwins occupied adjoining penthouses. They were connected by a short passageway that facilitated their work together and the interchange of guests. The house was constantly filled with an element of parasites, both esthetic and gustatory, and I discovered I was their born leader.

Leonore was a gracious hostess and the first person to tolerate my unresolved social dissonances. Warmed in the sun of this amiable household, I flowered as a buffoon. From the first day's supper, I worked up to having four or five meals a day there, eating my way through the composition of the music and lyrics for *Delicious* and *Girl Crazy*. Out of sheer perverseness, I felt, George frequently cajoled me into leaving the wonderful dishes on Ira's table to share with him a menu suited to his favorite ailment, "composer's stomach." It consisted of gruel and such variations as oatmeal and farina, rusk, zweiback, Melba toast (only on festive occasions), RyKrisp, and Swedish bread. The pièce de résistance was stewed fruit or, when he was in a gluttonous mood, applesauce.

Between the two households I became a penthouse beachcomber. The two pianos in George's apartment made it possible for us to play his music together as it was written, for it was his custom to sketch his large works for two pianos before scoring them. The *Second Rhapsody* and the *Cuban Overture* were written in this way. There was also a great deal of singing and a sporadic stream of talk embracing prize-fighting, music, painting, football, and sex. The Gershwin enthusiasm for Ping-Pong was communicated to me, and we spent hours at the game. Amid this constant activity, there were frequent recesses for food variously disguised as lunch, dinner, supper, or midnight snack.

Once I had been admitted to George's friendship I took so much pleasure in the things he was writing and doing that I did nothing of my own. Listening to him improvise and play was enough for me. He had such fluency at the piano and so steady a surge of ideas that any time he sat down, just to amuse himself, something came of it. He got most of his ideas just by playing. Writing music was the thing he loved to do more than anything else, except perhaps to play the music he had written previously.

About this time he started to collect paintings and to develop his own considerable gift. Between his own paintings and the ones he purchased the accumulation covered the walls of several rooms. Each stray, less-than-femme-fatale visitor was escorted on a tour of the collection and treated to verbal annotations that eventually, through repetition, assumed the character of a guide's lecture. Included in his earliest collection were a Modigliani, a Derain, and a Rouault.[3] It is possible that his interest in painting was stimulated by a member of the family to whom he always referred as "my cousin Botkin, the painter." While Botkin was abroad one summer, with his usual commission to make purchases for George's collection, he discovered an obscure Picasso and had it shipped to New York. It was hung amid much ceremony and provided a welcome new subject for the lecture as an example of Picasso's "blue period."

Besides collaborating with George in private performances of his music, I also had opportunity occasionally to play his works in public. Our first association was in the summer of 1931 when the [Lewisohn] Stadium presented an all-American program in which Gershwin played the *Rhapsody* and I joined Russell Bennett in a performance of his *March* for two pianos and orchestra. The concert was postponed daily for almost a week because of rain. Each afternoon we dressed and had dinner together only to find the concert again canceled by an evening shower. I almost regretted the arrival of a clear day, for actually playing became an anticlimax to my most active season as a soloist.

---

3 With this comment, Levant confirms that works by these artists were indeed among the first that Gershwin purchased when he began his art collection.

The following summer the Stadium resumed its custom of presenting an all-Gershwin concert, and George flattered me by suggesting that I play the *Concerto*. (This was conditioned by the fact that he was playing both the *Rhapsody in Blue* and the *Second Rhapsody*, and decided that he could not undertake the *Concerto* as well.) My pleasure in appearing with George was exceeded only by that which I took in the little unpremeditated expressions of his reactions to the concert. It was hardly over when one of his truly well-disposed friends rushed back, wrung his hand, and said, "George, it was wonderful!"

"Is that all?" said George, with characteristic abstraction. "Just wonderful?"

The friend was in turn followed by others, plus a considerable accumulation of autograph-collectors. A cluster of talking, crowding persons marked the spot where Gershwin was. I was off to one side with not even one of George's myriad second cousins. At length, disturbed and embarrassed, I edged around and said, "You could send at least one of them over to me."

His reply was the generous offer to send over his younger brother, Arthur.

However, he did repay me with a warming and disarming gesture a few days later. I came up to the apartment and he greeted me with a small-boy smile, his hands clasped behind his back. "What would you rather have," he said, "money or a watch?" And he handed me a handsome wrist watch inscribed, "From George to Oscar. Lewisohn Stadium. August 15, 1932." It is by this watch that I have been late for every important appointment since.

These Stadium concerts were always singular events in Gershwin's year. They gave him contact with a larger audience than he ever experienced elsewhere, and it was an inexpressible satisfaction to hear his music played by such an orchestra as the Philharmonic. Owing, perhaps, to his background in the commercial theatre, where audience interest is the criterion of success—hence worth—he was keenly conscious of the drawing power of the all-Gershwin programs. I was not present at the concert in 1936, the last in which he participated. However, a friend relates that the concert was given on the evening of the hottest day in New York history, when the temperature went to 102.2. Despite the oppressive heat that lingered after sundown, a large crowd appeared for the concert, at which George both conducted and played. During the intermission the friend wandered backstage to exchange a greeting with George, and found him in conversation with Mrs. Charles Guggenheimer, director of the concerts. She was exuding enthusiasm, but George seemed detached and inattentive. When she paused for a moment he asked, "How's the crowd?"

"Grand," she answered. "More than 12,000."

With a shake of his head George observed, "Last year we had 17,000."

It was through my professional association with George that I made my re-entry into Pittsburgh musical life. This was in 1934 when George was invited to play the *Rhapsody* and *Concerto* with the orchestra there. Bill Daly was scheduled to conduct the orchestra but couldn't leave New York in time to do the rehearsal, so George suggested that I go out with him and play the solo parts while he got the orchestra into shape.

We took a late train for the overnight trip, sharing a drawing-room. A lengthy discussion of music occupied us for an hour or so, and I was actually in the midst of answering one of his questions when he calmly removed his clothes and eased himself into the lower berth. I adjusted myself to the inconveniences of the upper berth and reflected on the artistic-economic progression by which Paderewski had a private car, Gershwin a drawing-room, and Levant a sleepless night. At this moment my light must have disturbed George in his doze, for he opened his eyes, looked up at me, and said drowsily, "Upper berth, lower berth—that's the difference between talent and genius."

This was characteristic of a certain undertone in our friendship, a small element of nastiness, a fondness for putting the blast on each other. There was a party, several years later, in which, as always, an evening with Gershwin was a Gershwin evening. There were recurrent references to his piano-playing, his composing, his conducting, his painting—*marcato* monologues which George's audience absorbed with fascinated attentiveness. Finally there was a *luftpause*, and I enquired, "Tell me, George, if you had to do it all over, would you fall in love with yourself again?"

His discursiveness was merely a manifestation of his desire to share with the world the inexplicable phenomenon known as George. He was extremely gregarious by nature and gave frequent parties that served as a diversion from his work and a satisfaction of his need, as a bachelor, of companionship. He had a curious partiality for successful persons of the stock-broker type with whom he could play golf and go on weekends, but there were always others who were attracted by his enormous vitality and the worth and genuineness of his accomplishments.

He was tremendously fond of being amused and of exercising his own healthy humor. For months at a time we kept running inconsequential little phrases with no meaning for anyone but ourselves. Thus, his distrait "Just wonderful?" became a catch phrase of incredulity; and whenever somebody did or said something for the twentieth time, our comment was "Again, the *Rhapsody!*"

An important contribution to the sum of humor was that of "Papa" Gershwin, whose unpredictable reactions to any situation, however pat, supplied an endless fund of stories. Early in George's career, Papa accompanied him to the office of Harms, his publishers. When they were about to leave, Lou Hirsch, whose "Love Nest" was then the reigning hit, emerged from an inner office with a check in his hands. "Look at this," he exclaimed to George: "the first quarter's royalties—$26,000."

George made some properly incredulous remark, then, thinking that Pop would enjoy a glimpse of this historic document, he said, "Hey, Pop, take a look at this!"

Papa took the check and considered it for a moment. Then he seized Hirsch's hand, pumped it vigorously, and said, with brisk encouragement, "Good luck, Mr. Hirsch."

When the Gershwins ascended to the eminence of adjoining penthouses on West 75th Street, after successive moves downtown from 110th and 103rd, the décor of the apartments responded to the dominant tone of the day—so-called modern. Severe lines, black and white furnishings, chromium ashtrays, and all the rest abounded. One afternoon when a group of society women George had acquired in his expanding career were being shown through, Papa attached himself to the pilgrimage. George was called to the telephone and left the visitors engrossed in "functional lines" and "expressive angles." Papa edged up and, desiring to make some contribution to the discussion, blandly inquired, "Tell me, ladies, whatever became of Oh Fudge?"

George was broadening in many ways. Through his meeting, in Europe, such composers as Ravel, Stravinsky, Poulenc, and Tansman, he had become aware of shortcomings in his equipment. There was no lack of admiration for his writing, but his lack of schooling and of an acknowledged master put him in the position of a brilliant student from the East Side who had entered Harvard from night school instead of Groton. He once entertained thoughts of studying with Ravel, with whom he was very friendly, but after I had discovered traces of Gershwin's own influence in Ravel's piano concerto, I suggested that the results might be retroactive. However, in Joseph Schillinger, a theorist of Russian background living in New York, Gershwin found a musical analyst whose ideas and methods fascinated him. He was attracted by Schillinger's reduction of all musical procedures, from the most formidable to the least, to a mathematical system which he contracted to impart in a definite calendar period—the compositional equivalent of playing the piano in six easy lessons. Surprisingly enough, this was thoroughly efficacious if taken with the considerable mixture of application that George contributed.

His curiosity about things was further translated into a curiosity about himself. He reasoned that, having previously known himself only emotionally, he should also know himself scientifically, and this propelled him into psychoanalysis. It was a wholly unnecessary adventure, for it proved him to be enthusiastically un-neurotic. However, during the year and a half of analysis, it provided him with a fresh vein of after-dinner conversation, a laboratory variation, with clinical underscoring, on the theme, "Just wonderful?"

All this was a slightly frenzied counterpoint to one of the most ambitious undertakings of his life, the writing of *Porgy*. There always seemed to me in this score considerable evidence of his studies with Schillinger—not, of course, in the melodic writing, but in the working out of the rhythmic patterns, the planning of such episodes as the fugal background for the crap-game scene, and in some of the choral passages.

George was irresistibly drawn to the Guild Theatre each day during the rehearsal period. In addition to his music, the theatre offered the congenial atmosphere contributed by two men, Rouben Mamoulian and Alexander Smallens, both experts in their fields and sympathetic to Gershwin. His presence on one occasion doubtless saved one of the great performances of *Porgy*, the "Sporting Life" of Bubbles. Gershwin shared the opinion of Fred Astaire that the slim, dapper Negro was one of the great performers of the day and a dancer beyond compare. Moreover, he had shaped the part to fit Bubbles' talents.

But Bubbles' negligence about rehearsals and promptness almost overbalanced his abilities, and on one occasion Smallens' exasperation caused him to fling down his baton and shout to Mamoulian, "I'm sick of this waiting. We'll have to throw him out and get someone else."

Gershwin bounded from his seat. "Throw him out?" he said. "You can't do that. Why, he's—he's the black Toscanini."

This was my otiose period. Blooming with a deathlike glow, I had been lying fallow during the three long years in which *Porgy* was composed, sung, cast, rehearsed, discussed but never disparaged, relived, and finally produced. From time to time I appeared at George's magnificent duplex on East 72nd Street to find him absorbed not only in composition but also in the manipulation of his extensive arsenal of writing equipment. The desk in his workroom represented an incredible synthesis, in the pure Stokowskian sense, of carpentry and composition. It consisted not merely of the usual writing surfaces, but also of panels, drop-leaves, and other protruding appendages that made it possible for him to work without hunching over—in fact, almost without breathing. It had been made to his specifications and included racks for pens, drawers for rulers, triangles and T-squares, pigeonholes for erasers, pencils, and knives, built-in ashtrays, and a streamlined wastebasket. You absorbed the impression, in contemplating it, that in moments of extreme inspiration the desk would be psychically drawn to him.

For me the most remarkable feature of the apartment was its ingenious design: in a bachelor establishment of fourteen rooms George had managed to devise a layout that omitted even a single guest room.

It is an interesting commentary on Gershwin's talents that he never wrote a score in a strict musical form. The thematic fluency and easy-going rhythmic freedom of the rhapsody or unrestricted fantasy were his natural genre. You may ask for a slight exception in favor of the *Concerto*, but it is the Lisztian mantle draped loosely on the skeleton of sonata form. I think this was a natural consequence of his training as a song writer. It was a stroke of remarkable good fortune that his serious consideration of such a play as Ansky's *Dybbuk* for operatic purposes was set aside in favor of *Porgy*, in which his song-writing talent found a natural outlet through Negroid characters. But however songlike such sections as "Summertime," "It Ain't Necessarily So," and "I Got Plenty of Nuttin'" are, they were more consciously composed than his usual musical-comedy numbers. When *Porgy* was out of his hands a desire to work in his first vein reasserted itself.

Then too, once the fever of absorption in *Porgy* had been dispelled, Gershwin became aware that such men as Cole Porter and Richard Rodgers had made considerable advance into territory once indisputably his own, and he welcomed the assignment to write the score for *Shall We Dance* with [Fred] Astaire and [Ginger] Rogers.

Shortly before this I had been engaged to write the opera for *Charlie Chan at the Opera*, so I was already in Hollywood when the Gershwins arrived, in August, 1936. Among the greeting ceremonies was a dinner given them by Edgar Selwyn, who had produced *Strike Up the Band*. After the food and drink, George launched into a résumé of his music, old and new. Among the guests was Alexander Steinert, a Prix de Rome winner who had done much valuable work in preparing the chorus for *Porgy* and had conducted the road tour. In sheer politeness George finally suggested that Steinert play something of his own, believing that the surroundings would dissuade him. But Steinert responded with a whole piano concerto by himself, which George resented slightly as an excess of acquiescence.

For George, the attractions of California provided the atmosphere for a ceaselessly active life, both physical and intellectual. The backyard of his house held a swimming pool, a tennis court, and a Ping-Pong table. Tennis was second in his interest only to the piano. His pursuit of the sport permitted a transfer of the desk-motif to the outdoors, where it was represented by a dazzling array of shirts, shorts, slacks, shoes, and a repertory of beach robes of almost Oriental splendor. George played good tennis almost by ear, instinctively and in contradiction of all known theories of foot-position, swing, and timing. His absorption in the game was so complete that part of his man Paul's manifold duties was to volley with him in pre-game warm-ups.

George did not lack for competition. Ira was as devoted to the game as he was, and the court was open to all their co-workers from New York who were domiciled in Hollywood. Exceeding even George's passion for tennis was that of the great composer, Arnold Schönberg, who played with scientific intentness. The meeting of the two was affecting and resulted in, among other things, a standing invitation for the older man to use the court regularly.

On one occasion, after playing two vigorous sets, Schönberg and his opponents were driven off the courts by a sudden shower, and George and I joined them in their shelter. The sixty-year-old Schönberg wiped his brow and said, half to himself, "Somehow I feel tired. I can't understand it."

Then he suddenly added, "That's right. I was up at five this morning. My wife gave birth to a boy."

One of my most memorable experiences in music occurred during that California visit, when Elizabeth Sprague Coolidge sponsored the performance of the four Schönberg quartets and the last group of Beethoven, played by the Kolisch ensemble. George, Ira, and I were overjoyed and deeply impressed.

We were all together on the tennis court next morning and the talk turned to the concert. "I'd like to write a quartet some day," George said. "But it will be something simple, like Mozart."

Schönberg mistakenly interpreted this characteristically irrelevant reflection as a comment on his work. "I'm not a simple man," he answered, "and, anyway, Mozart was considered far from simple in his day."

Though George's acquaintance with formal music was rather scattered, he had pronounced likings both in classic and contemporary works. Rather curiously, since it was so opposed to the characteristics of his own work, he perceived the quality in Alban Berg's music when he first became acquainted with the *Lyrische Suite*. This was several years before Berg was known even as a name in America. He treasured the piano score of *Wozzeck*, and was deeply impressed by the opera when he journeyed to Philadelphia for the Stokowski performance in 1931.

Like many musicians, George found he could get more from phonograph records than from scattered performances. Among the albums that gave him particular pleasure were Stravinsky's *Symphonie de Psaumes*, the first symphony of Shostakovitch, the Milhaud violin concerto, and the complete Schönberg quartets privately recorded by the Kolisches. Somewhere, somehow, he had acquired a fondness for Honegger's lively operetta, *Les Adventures du Roi Pausole*. Also he greatly admired Duke Ellington records for their rich effects and fine tonal originality—mood pieces like the "Creole Love Song," "Swanee Rhapsody," and "Daybreak Express."

Among the modern works he studied in score were Stravinsky's *Les Noces*, the third piano concerto of Prokofiev, the Debussy preludes, and various orchestral works by that composer and Ravel. During the work on *Porgy* he referred constantly to *Die Meistersinger* as a guide to plotting the choral parts and for general precepts in vocal writing. Oddly, however, he refused throughout his career to study orchestration with a teacher; he preferred his pragmatic approach, bulwarked by Cecil Forsyth's *Orchestration*, which he regarded almost as a Bible.

As far as a partiality in older music was concerned, George leaned particularly to certain expansive moods of Brahms, whose string quartets we frequently played four hands at the piano. It was the long line and free development of melodic material that attracted him most. He identified certain expressions of his own with this composer, referring to the second theme of the *Second Rhapsody* as a "Brahms strain."

One of his favorite chamber-music works was the great C major quintet (with two cellos) of Schubert, with which he became acquainted during the period when he was writing *Of Thee I Sing* and *Let 'Em Eat Cake*. You can discern a slight influence of the second theme of the quintet's first movement in the tune, from *Let 'Em Eat Cake*, beginning "Two Hearts Are in Communion." He also liked the Mozart string quartets.

But we had constant gags about "favorite composers" for the sake of interviews: men like César Cui, Xaver Scharwenka, and, as a final blow, Ed Poldini, composer of "Poupée Valsante."

George played little concert music at the piano beyond certain Chopin preludes, for which he had no pronounced interpretative feeling. For technical purposes, when preparing to play his own music in public, endless repetitions of the first Cramer study sufficed.

On the whole, the playing of his music by others found him an enthusiastic audience, and he frequently expressed astonishment when I made some critical remark on flaws in some performances we heard together. There was one exception, however, when the concertmaster of the St. Louis Symphony, playing "Summertime" as a violin solo during a potpourri from *Porgy*, followed the orchestra at the respectful distance of one bar during the whole piece, with excruciating results. George's strongest reaction was, "You'd think anybody would know *that* tune!"

George made a most revealing remark on his own music one afternoon when we were playing over various scores and finally arrived at something by Manuel de Falla. In the midst of playing, George stopped and said, with a slight touch of disparagement, "He's a kind of Spanish Gershwin."

It was a particular source of pride for him that two movements of his piano concerto were included in the American program Fritz Reiner conducted at the Venice International Festival of Contemporary Music in 1932. The continuous applause prompted Reiner and Harry Kaufman, who was the piano soloist, to repeat the finale. This lingered in the back of George's mind; for in a casual conversation several years later a visitor mentioned that he had been present at that performance. George's interest immediately sharpened. "You were there?" he said. "Tell me all about it. I've never had a chance to speak to anybody who was there."

The visitor recalled his impressions of the occasion, and added, of course, that the last movement had been repeated. "They repeated the last movement!" George echoed, as though hearing it for the first time. Turning to another guest he said, "Think of that! The only other time in musical history it ever happened was when the Boston Symphony first gave the Tschaikowsky piano concerto in 1894."

No doubt his visitors were surprised at the elucidation of this odd bit of information, but George's reading on musical subjects was surprisingly wide.

This sketch has no pretense of being closely biographical. If it has an aura of impudence, that's the way it was. George once remarked, after a Don Quixote tilt with a blond windmill, "She has a little love for everyone, and not a great deal for anybody."

Whether this was true of the girl or not, I feel that George had unconsciously mirrored himself in those words. I myself can claim no special access to his feelings—we had merely a healthy, extrovertial intimacy born, to coin a phrase, of mutual interests. Excluding the members of his family, the only man who enjoyed his affection was the late William Merrigan Daly.

How pervasive his rich inventiveness and forceful spirit were is reflected in its effect on so alien a musician as Schönberg, who spoke these words at a memorial broadcast: "George Gershwin was one of this rare kind of musician to whom music is not a matter of more or less ability. Music to him was the air he breathed, the food which nourished him, the drink that refreshed him. Music was what made him feel, and music was the feeling he expressed. Directness of this kind is given only to great men, and there is no doubt that he was a great composer. What he achieved was not only to the benefit of a national American music, but a contribution to the music of the world."

No one could doubt how much Gershwin's music has meant to me, but I found small solace in the other panegyrics whose refrain was, "But his music lives on." No quantity of music could compensate for the loss of his corporeal presence, the cessation of his creative being.

5   Verna Arvey: "George Gershwin Through the Eyes of a Friend" (1948)

Wife of the dean of African American composers, William Grant Still, Verna Arvey knew Gershwin as a professional colleague and also as a friend. Her comments are important for several reasons. First, she provides a portrait of Gershwin's place in American music against the backdrop of its development in the two decades preceding her article, development that she witnessed firsthand. Arvey offers observations culled from Kay Swift, who, as Arvey explains, was often reluctant until much later to share her unique perspective on the man and his music. And while Arvey does not broach the subject of Gershwin's relationship or indebtedness to her husband, which recent scholarship has been investigating, she does describe the presence and importance of Will Vodery in Gershwin's career.[1]

Europe is objective about American music. The continent which is said to have held the roots of our own culture is still observing us with a critical eye, daring us to produce something that is genuinely interesting, musically speaking. A certain clique of American composers has made an attempt to foist its own atonal music on Europeans, and on Americans too!, as being America's most important product in the serious music field. What has been the result? The ironic and amusing fact is that all their efforts have had to come up against the music of George Gershwin. George Gershwin, writer of popular tunes and idealizer of Jazz! Our atonal friends look upon him with scorn. Yet there he is, right or wrong, accepted by Europeans as the American composer whose music finds greater favor with them! The reason may be that the atonalists in America are merely rewriting, and not too well, something that was done better in Europe by European composers many years ago, whereas George Gershwin's music says instantly that it is American in flavor. The atonalists may not consider Gershwin a serious composer, but many thousands of people, here and abroad, disagree with them.

Perhaps we didn't take George Gershwin seriously enough, while he was living, to probe deeply into his methods and ideals. Now that he has gone, we can do no more than to ask the people who knew him well. One of these, with a vast storehouse of unpublished memories, is Kay Swift.[2] She has been

SOURCE *Opera and Concert* 13 (April 1948): 10–11, 27–28.
    1 On Vodery, see Mark Tucker's article in *The Black Perspective in Music*. Questions exist regarding Gershwin's possible period of study with Still, the primacy of "I Got Rhythm," and the appearance of a similar theme in Still's later composition, the *Afro-American Symphony* (see selection 43, p. 147).
    2 See selection 3, p. 6.

asked to write magazine articles and a book about him, and hasn't done so. She was asked to contribute a chapter to Merle Armitage's book about Gershwin, but didn't. She feels that the latter was published too soon after Gershwin's death to have an adequate perspective.

She first met the composer when she was giving a party for musicians, among whom was Jascha Heifetz, at her home in New York some years ago. Around 10:30 or 11, when she and Chotzinoff were spelling each other at the piano, playing a work by Brahms, Marie Rosanoff of the Musical Arts Quartet walked in with a young man whom she introduced as George Gershwin.[3] He was new to the group, and soon he was asked to play the piano. He did so, very easily and competently. The guests were relaxed, listening to him, when suddenly he jumped to his feet, looked at his watch and said abruptly, "Oh, I have to go to Europe!" He rushed out of the house, ran like mad, and just made the boat.

There was never a doubt in anyone's mind after that George Gershwin had the artistic temperament.

It was the fall of the year when he returned from Europe. Miss Swift happened to attend a symphony rehearsal where he was playing his *Concerto*, then she met him afterward at a party at Walter Damrosch's home where Damrosch, a friendly, pleasant host, was joining his guests in parodying Wagner operas. Damrosch, in a strange costume, represented something. Miss Swift, in attire that was equally outlandish, represented something else. From then on, she and George Gershwin were friends.

To understand this friendship, it's necessary to know more about Kay Swift and her own gifts. For she is the composer of the music for *Fine and Dandy*, a musical show with book by Donald Ogden Stewart that played for a year in New York. From this show came the hit songs "Fine and Dandy" and "Can This Be Love." Not from the musical show but a standard hit tune nevertheless is Miss Swift's "Can't We Be Friends." She also wrote the ballet music *Alma Mater* for the American Ballet Company. In the years following Gershwin's death, her talents turned in several directions, one bringing forth a book called *Who Could Ask for Anything More?* which sold well, and was bought in Hollywood but is yet to be produced as a picture.[4] That sale brought her to Hollywood as a permanent resident. On the West Coast, she has written songs for a musical show that is still to come, and has dug up,

---

3 Samuel Chotzinoff, whom the Gershwins called Chotzie, was a family friend and a music critic. Chotzinoff eventually married Jascha Heifetz's sister, Pauline, who was a former Gershwin girlfriend.

4 Swift's book was adapted to film in the 1950 RKO movie *Never a Dull Moment*. It starred Irene Dunne as Kay Swift, Fred MacMurray as Kay's cowpoke husband, Fay Hubbard, Andy Devine, and a young Natalie Wood portraying one of Kay's three daughters by banker and sometime-lyricist Paul Warburg.

arranged, and transcribed a good deal of Gershwin's posthumous music for the film *The Shocking Miss Pilgrim* in collaboration with Ira Gershwin, whom she describes as having an extraordinary quality of musicianship for a man who isn't himself a musician. At present, she and her husband, Hunter Galloway, are collaborating on a book, the subject-matter of which came directly from her work for wounded soldiers during and after World War II.

Despite her own very special accomplishments, Kay Swift has the ability and the inclination to subordinate herself to someone else, provided she feels that that person is eminently worthy. So it happened that after George Gershwin discovered that she was capable of taking fast musical dictation, they very often worked together. When he was writing a piano piece, he used to work at the piano and let her write down what he played. She would notate, usually the melody, although she could and often did take down harmonies too. The *Spanish Prelude* was one she notated for him. Sometimes they would work at the two pianos he had in his home. When she first knew him he lived in a house with his entire family, later in a penthouse, still later in a duplex apartment that was his last New York home before leaving for Hollywood.

It's common knowledge that Ferde Grofé orchestrated the *Rhapsody in Blue*, but in later years Gershwin orchestrated his own serious works (not the music he wrote for the theatre). It was the *Concerto* that he orchestrated first of all. He didn't know a thing about orchestrating at the time, just picked up a book about it and went to work! The more he orchestrated, the more he enjoyed it and the more fascinated and thrilled he was by it.

It was the same with everything else he tried: golf, tennis, or painting. He had what might be called a "questing" mind. He was always finding something new and asking "How does this go? I'd like to try it." He would make one appointment to investigate. Then, the first thing he knew, he would have signed up for practice every day. Afterward, he never thought he had done well at these things, but he did. As Miss Swift expresses it, "Anything he wanted to learn, he hit with a terrific sock. He just tore into it." As a result, he wasn't learned in the "school" sense, but he had educated himself "like lightning." There was, in addition, an exciting quality to his very life. He woke up excited, eager to see what the new day would bring.

As a successful composer, the days very often brought to him other composers, some young, some old in the business, asking for advice and help. If it was an established song writer with an ailing tune, instantly George Gershwin would put his finger on the sore spot and explain how to remedy it. When aspiring youngsters came to him he was enthusiastic about and interested in their work so that, even if they had come in a discouraged mood, they were inspired when they left and eager to get to work. Singers who came to give auditions for him weren't nearly so nervous as they might have been, because his friendly, constructive and thoughtful manner had dispelled their fears in advance.

It was, in part at least, his tremendous interest in people, his desire to know what made them tick and to understand how they lived, ate, and conducted their business that gave his own music that human, common denominator quality. People are the same, basically, the world over. And Gershwin was not only one of the people, he was fascinated by his fellow-men. His music reflected this quality in him, just as any creator's self is mirrored in his creations.

"Believing" music is the way Kay Swift describes Gershwin's product. It was not bitter, as he was not bitter. Nor was it a preachment of any sort. Instead it showed his own inherent, fundamental faith in the rightness of all things and in ultimate justice. He had no formal religious affiliation, yet there is a strong religious quality in such a song as "Oh Lord, I'm On My Way" from *Porgy and Bess*.

At the time of his death, he had only scratched the surface of what he might have done. He had big, broad things planned. One of these, for which he already had sketched his ideas, was to have been a composition for orchestra and chorus about Abraham Lincoln, about whom he had thought and read much.

It's not startling to learn of Gershwin's interest in the Great Liberator, since there has been such a strong Negroid flavor in much of his music. This, recalls Miss Swift, was not at all accidental. She remembers going with him at 3, 4 and 5 A.M., after their respective shows were over, to little places in Harlem where there were recordings by Negro artists that couldn't be gotten downtown. There the composer would listen intently, making mental notes and absorbing the style. Besides that, Gershwin was certain to be present at any concert or show in which a Negro was doing something new in music. If getting there was difficult, he would make the effort somehow and arrive in time to hear it. He admired Ethel Waters' singing very much and was grateful for the extemporaneous "act" put on by Ethel Waters and Bill Robinson just for him before he left for Hollywood for the first time, in 1930. He attended the performance of William Grant Still's *Levee Land* at New York's Aeolian Hall, with Eugene Goossens conducting and the incomparable Florence Mills as soloist.

Many times Gershwin spoke to Miss Swift about a colored church in Charleston, S.C., where he had spent several months. He told her that she must not miss attending this church, and that she would enjoy hearing the spontaneous singing there. It was not until after he died that she went to

Charleston. There DuBose Heyward told her that the Macedonia Church, where the congregants were Gullah Negroes, was the one George had mentioned to her. The service in that church was unusually late at night, but despite the lateness of the hour, she went with a friend. Just as Gershwin had promised, she enjoyed the remarkable singing done by the congregation. She was so moved that she joined in the chorus. After the service she was asked to speak. She rose and inquired whether they remembered George Gershwin, and they replied that they did indeed, that he had come often to sing with them and that he always spoke to them when he came.

George Gershwin's name has sometimes been linked with that of the colored orchestrator, Will Vodery. The latter befriended the composer in the early days and once, when Gershwin was unknown, Vodery got him a job with a big publishing house. Gershwin never forgot that kindness and when he became famous he asked Vodery to orchestrate for him. This happening started the erroneous rumor that he had a colored ghost writer. No, says Miss Swift, Gershwin never claimed as his own any music that was not written by him. He did not take credit for the work of others. But it is true that he loved Negro music and deliberately saturated himself with it before writing his own music. He never hesitated to admit a debt to Negro music and to the artists who acquainted him with it, and he never employed someone else to do his work for him. His music is his own.

Anyone who listens to George Gershwin's music knows that it wasn't a chore for the composer to compose. This impression is corroborated, for we are told that he enjoyed every phase of it. His scores were good-looking, probably due to his innate sense of decoration and to his unexpected aptitude for painting, but more than that, due to his own pleasure in writing. Once Miss Swift was fussing because she had to make a piano copy of one of her own songs. Gershwin told her, "Never mind making a piano copy, because it's the only form of manual labor that goes with the creating of music. It's a good balance for other things, and it can be a most pleasurable occupation." After that, she too enjoyed making her own manuscripts.

It's interesting to speculate on what would have happened to Gershwin's music if he had lived, for in his later years he began to study Joseph Schillinger. For the first time, he began to realize that he had been throwing his musical material away! Too much, and not enough done with it. So he began to conserve material. The *Cuban Overture*, which Kay Swift considers a greatly underrated composition, was the first on which he consciously made use of his new knowledge of counterpoint, and of his desire to economize on his musical material. He also made use of Schillinger's teachings in the "Storm Music" in *Porgy and Bess*. However, he was too independent to become a slave to this system, except when he did his exercises for his lessons. He merely studied and digested it, then used it according to his needs, always subordinating it to his own personal idiom.

Where would this inner growth, this increasing awareness of the value of craftsmanship, this constant search for knowledge, have led a composer of such undoubted individuality?

Yes, he might have become America's greatest if he had lived and developed and continued to work hard. Certainly he succeeded in impregnating his music with the American spirit, and certainly his service to American music has been a great one.

6   *"Gershwin Bros."* (1925)

By the mid-1920s Gershwin was well on his way to lasting fame. The success of "Swanee," the growing list of popular songs, and the splash of *Rhapsody in Blue* had much to do with this, of course, but the American press also helped to shape Gershwin into a celebrity. *Time* founder and Gershwin's friend Henry Luce featured Gershwin in his magazine several times in 1925, most notably on the cover of the July 20, 1925, issue, the first time, and one of the few times since, that an American composer had received this notoriety. The following brief report not only updated the public as to Gershwin's activities; it introduced them to Ira as well.

Maneuvering around two grand pianos which took up most of the available floor space of a small Manhattan apartment, a young Jew last week went about the business of packing a suit-case. Old newspapers—the inseparable, useless adjuncts of this operation—lay here and there in crumpled disorder, but two, each containing an item which had been circled with a pencil mark, reposed on a table. The first item related how Composer George Gershwin, famed jazzbo, had recently returned from Europe; the second stated that this Gershwin, when he had finished the piano concerto which Dr. Walter Damrosch has commissioned him to write for the New York Symphony Orchestra (*Time*, May 4), will compose the score of a new musical comedy for the producers of *Lady, Be Good*. Soprano excitement abruptly galvanized the telephone at the young man's elbow: he began to address its black aperture. "Yes," he said, "this is Gershwin. . . . No, no, it's too hot. . . . I'm going away for the week-end. . . . I can't see anyone." Smiling, he hung up the receiver, tossed

SOURCE *Time* (July 20, 1925).

a last striped shirt into his bag. It was sometimes a nuisance, but he could not honestly pretend that it bored him, this growing public interest in his movements, his past, his plans.

George Gershwin, 27, was born in Brooklyn. At an early age, he contributed to the music of a rickety, rollicking, tenement street, at first with infantile mulling, later with a stout, pubescent chirrup. He skinned his knees in the gutters of this street; he nourished himself smearily with its bananas; he broke its dirty windows and eluded its brass-and-blue-clothed curator. When he was 13, his mother purchased a piano.

It was not that Mrs. Gershwin detected any seeds of musical talent in her grubby young son. She bought the piano because her sister-in-law had one. There it stood, big and shiny; it had cost a lot of money, and no one in the Gershwin family—not even Ira, the oldest, who was certainly a smart boy—could make music on it. George would have to learn. For some time the neighbors suffered; then they advised him to study in Europe. His first teacher died when he was still torturing Chopin's preludes. Max Rosen, famed violinist, told him he would never be a musician. When he was 15, he tried to write a song. It began decently in F, but ran off into G, where it hid behind the black keys, twiddling its fingers at Gershwin. Discouraged, he went to work as a song-plugger for a music publisher.

He plugged songs on tin-pan pianos—those renegade instruments that stay up late, every night, in the back rooms of cafes, in the smoky corners of thirdstring night clubs, till their keys are yellow, and their tone is as hard as peroxided hair. Gershwin's fingers found a curious music in them. He made it hump along with a twang and a shuffle, hunch its shoulders and lick its lips. Diners applauded.

"What's the name of that tune, honey?" asked a lady of Gershwin one night.

"No name," said Gershwin. "It has no name."

The ditty in question, afterward entitled "I Was So Young, and You Were So Beautiful," became Gershwin's first hit. Within a few years, he had written "Swanee," "I'll Build a Stairway to Paradise," "Yankee Doodle Blues," "The Nashville Nightingale," "Do It Again," "I Won't Say I Will," "Somebody Loves Me," "Lady, Be Good," "Fascinating Rhythm." Last year, he composed his famed *Rhapsody in Blue*, a jazz concerto constructed after Liszt. It took him three weeks to write it. He played it through twice with Conductor Paul Whiteman's celebrated jazz band. It was acclaimed at Carnegie Hall by a huge audience, hailed by daring critics as "the finest piece of music ever written in the U.S." Conductor Willem van Hoogstraten asked Gershwin to arrange it for a symphony orchestra. Next season he will play his concerto with the New York Symphony in Manhattan, Baltimore, Washington, Philadelphia. It is to be more serious than the *Rhapsody*, unconventional but in strict form. In the winter, he expects to write still another musical comedy, in collaboration with his brother.

Ira Gershwin writes the words to George's songs. Quieter than his more brilliant brother, he once tried to be an author. He spent two days polishing a poem, submitted it to a magazine. It was accepted. Ira Gershwin received a check for $1.00, abandoned literature, took to composing words for George.

7   Isaac Goldberg: "Childhood of a Composer" (1931)

In this entry, Isaac Goldberg (1887–1938) provides an overview of Gershwin's early years against the backdrop of America's coming of age at the beginning of the twentieth century. Taken from his landmark 1931 biography, Goldberg's portrait is shaped by and paraphrases liberally from letters he exchanged with Gershwin during the course of writing his book.[1]

The smiling irony of George Gershwin's career begins with his birth, on September 26, 1898, in Brooklyn, New York. For, whatever else is to be discovered in Gershwin's ancestry, one can unearth no traces of musical talent. No Talmudic geniuses blossom on his family tree; no wits sharpened by involved and erudite commentaries upon the Scriptures. No cantors.

The following day, in Brooklyn, was born a child who was christened Vincent Youmans.... Irving Berlin was ten years old; Rudolf Friml, fourteen, and still twenty-two years away from the United States; Will Handy was twenty-five; Charles K. Harris, about thirty-one; Paul Dresser, ten years the senior of Harris.... A fellow by the name of Theodore Dreiser was writing articles for the magazines on the importance of the barrel-organ in popularizing sheet music. He ought to know, for he is Dresser's brother, and had helped in making "On the Banks of the Wabash," two years before.... Deems Taylor and Jerome D. Kern were thirteen years old; Romberg was eleven, and would not see these shores until 1909.... Victor Herbert, in 1898, at the age of twenty-nine, was appointed conductor of the Pittsburgh Symphony Orchestra; during that year he wrote *The Fortune Teller*, and three other light operas... Ferde Grofé was minus four years old, and Zez Confrey, minus seven. Henry

SOURCE   Isaac Goldberg, *George Gershwin: A Study in American Music* (New York: Simon & Schuster, 1931).
   1 Isaac Goldberg was on the faculty at Harvard University as a lecturer in philology, and most of his correspondence with Gershwin is held by the University's Houghton Library in Cambridge, Mass.

Cowell would not appear on the scene for nine years; Aaron Copland, a Brooklynite, and George Antheil, from "over on the Jersey side," would wait two, and Dick Rodgers, four. De Koven, born in the same year as Herbert, had been famous for *Robin Hood* since 1890....

Ma Gershwin still retains suggestions of the striking beauty that was hers as a girl. This she has passed on to her only daughter. Rose Bruskin had come to New York from St. Petersburg; her future husband had followed from the same place and asked her hand in marriage. They were joined in wedlock in New York City on July 21, 1895; the bride was sixteen years of age.

"My mother's father," recalls George, "was a furrier. My paternal grandfather was some sort of inventor; his ingenuity had something to do with the Czar's guns. As for my father, he went to an opera occasionally, as most fathers do. He could sing fairly, and could whistle even better. He used to give excellent imitations of a cornet, and could coax music out of the silliest contraptions, such as combs and clothespins and pencils. But this was the extent of his musicality. As for my mother, she's what the mammy writers write about, and what the mammy singers sing about. But they don't mean it; and I do."

The line of Gershwin, then, was one rather of commercial acumen than of artistic dedication. Perhaps this helps to account for the directness of George's music; for his temperamental indifference to musical saccharine; for a certain spirit of satire and sophistication that very early begins to sing from his pages. If there was nothing saliently musical in his ancestry, neither were there any indications in his own childhood that he was to grow up into a musical prodigy. It was not until he had reached the age of confirmation that his household was to know what a piano, on the installment plan—looked like.

Ma Gershwin, though very loving, never pestered her children with excessive surveillance. She was set on having them educated.... Later, she would oppose George's desire to become a musician. She didn't want a son of hers to become a $25 per week piano-player. Yet when George was to determine upon the step from high school to Remick's, her resistance would crumble.

George, as he himself will remind you, was the rough-and-ready, the muscular type and not one of your sad, contemplative children. He was a merry nature, always on the go. He was the athletic champion of his gang. His real keyboard was the sidewalks—and, even more, the pavements—of New York; his family had moved across the Brooklyn Bridge when he was but a tot. Here he reveled in games of "cat" and hockey; here he achieved his first preeminence as the undisputed roller-skate champion of Seventh Street. Already he was George the First.

The clatter of rollers over asphalt.... The din of the elevated overhead.... The madness of the traffic below ... the cracked tones of the hurdy-gurdy....

The blatant ballyhoo of the honky-tonk. . . . The blare of the automatic orchestra as the merry-go-round traced its dizzy circles through Coney Island's penny paradises: The plaintive wail of the street singer across the obligato of a scraping fiddle. . . . These were the earliest rhythms to which young George awoke; these are the rhythms that sound not only from his first hits but from his most ambitious orchestral compositions. It is young New York, young America, seeking a voice for its holiday spirit, its crude exaltations.

On the whole, Gershwin as a child heard little music. Aside from the songs at school he recalls two or three concerts at the Educational Alliance on East Broadway. Coney Island and the carrousels contributed their squealing melodies. "One of my first definite memories goes back to the age of six. I stood outside a penny arcade listening to an automatic piano leaping through Rubinstein's *Melody in F.* The peculiar jumps in the music held me rooted. To this very day I can't hear the tune without picturing myself outside that arcade on One Hundred and Twenty-fifth Street, standing there barefoot and in overalls, drinking it all in avidly."

George's childhood, since he grew up in the early 1900s, so far as unconscious musical influence was concerned, was saturated in the unsophisticated ballads of those days. Morse, Von Tilzer, Charles K. Harris, Van Alstyne . . . these were the gods of the hurdy-gurdy, the stereopticon singer and the "coon shouter." Yet, out of all these popular tunes, Gershwin recalls but a few distinctly. "Strike Up the Band," "Here Comes a Sailor," and "Put Your Arms Around Me Honey, Hold Me Tight." . . . Where have vanished the saga of Bill Bailey and his dusky fellows? Yesterday it was the coon song, today it is the blues. The Negro is still in the ascendant, for between the Spanish-American War and the Great War that enclose like a parenthesis, Gershwin's coming-of-age, lies the evolution from ragtime to jazz.

Public school was much of a nuisance, and home work—when it came—drudgery. All that George remembers of school music, which was simply a nuisance within a nuisance, are such ditties as "Annie Laurie" and such belabored lesser classics as "The Lost Chord." He was especially haunted by the Sullivan song and by the Scotch tune, "I'll take the high road and you take the low road." ("Loch Lomond"). A time would come when the music of Sir Arthur Sullivan would fascinate him, since in essential spirit of jollity it so much anticipated his own. But in his years at Public School 20, and, later, at Public School 25, most tunes "meant nothing in my young life."

Nay, here is the crowning jest: In the days of the roller skate and the hockey stick it was George's firm conviction that there was something radically wrong with youngsters who went in for music. To scrape away at the fiddle, to wear out one's fingers on piano keys, was to be a "little Maggie," a sissy. Music was effeminate; it was taught by women to women and little girls, and if little boys submitted to instruction, they at once classified themselves.

Was there a trace of envy in this hostility? The piano, in the opening years of this century, was not a household necessity; it was, especially in Lower New York, much of a luxury and a symbol of relative affluence. A second-hand upright found its way into the Gershwin home because, chiefly, Mrs. Gershwin's married sister had got herself one.

"No sooner had it come through the window and been backed up against the wall," relates George, "than I was at the keys. I must have crowded out Ira very soon, for the plan originally had been to start him off on the instrument. You see, Ira is the eldest; I come next; then there is my brother Arthur and my sister Frances. Ira actually covered about thirty-two pages of Beyer's text before resigning to his fate. Words would come easier to him than music."

Time works its revenge. The keyboard began to fascinate George. Shortly he astounded the household by requesting, of his own accord, a piano teacher. The champion roller skater of Seventh Street had succumbed. He was to join—and not under compulsion—the ranks of the Maggies! What, besides a natural curiosity, had effected this sudden change in George?

He had been a "hard" kid. At six, it appears, he was almost as blasé and worldly wise as he is today. He had a girl at nine—the age of Dante's first encounter with Beatrice. He remembers now that he was fond of her because she played and sang. Perhaps the roots of his musical ambitions are to be discovered in this forgotten sweetheart. Certainly his parents held no high hopes for his future. He was, frankly, a bad child. He was guilty of petty pilfering; he ran the gamut of minor infractions. With a little less luck he might have become a gangster, for the neighborhood in which his father's first restaurant was situated was also the neighborhood that bred Lefty Louie and Gyp the Blood. The thugs liked Papa Gershwin for his congenial ways, but papa had no reasons for returning the compliment.

Pa Gershwin had the soul of the Wandering Jew. He was as restless as a modernist score, shifting residences and occupations as often as the Stravinskys and the Schoenbergs shift key and tempo. He has been a designer of fancy uppers for women's shoes—this, at $35 per week, was before George saw the light of lower Brooklyn; part-owner of a Turkish bath; proprietor of a cigar store; restaurateur, with a small chain of eateries... owner of a billiard parlor.... "For one eventful month," adds Ira, "he was even a bookmaker at Belmont Park, but too many favorites won." In moments filched from the stern business of lyric-writing, Ira has computed that, up to 1916, the Gershwins had been domiciled in twenty-eight different residences, twenty-five in

Manhattan and three in Brooklyn, owing "to the fact that the head of the house of Gershwin liked to live within walking distance of his place of business, and it seemed that every six months he had a new business."

Something of a jazzer himself, Pop Gershwin, stirred by the restless tempo of the new age, with its *nostalgie d'ailleurs*—its homesickness for elsewhere . . . The Dance of New York Life . . .

It was little Maxie Rosenzweig, now the noted violinist Max Rosen, who, without knowing it, had kindled the spark in George's vagrom soul. Rosenzweig, born in Dorohoi, Rumania, on April 11, 1899, had been imported to the United States at the age of eight months. He had received his first lesson in music from his father, a barber and a musical amateur, at the age of five. The child wonder attended the same school that George went to—Public School 25 at Fifth Avenue and Second Street. He had played at a school entertainment after the recess for lunch. George had not been interested enough to attend the performance, but the strains of the violin, floating down to him from the assembly hall, had suddenly thrilled him with Dvořák's *Humoresque*.

"It was, to me, a flashing revelation of beauty," he recalls out of those days. "I made up my mind to get acquainted with this fellow, and I waited outside from three to four-thirty that afternoon, in the hopes of greeting him. It was pouring cats and dogs, and I got soaked to the skin. No luck. I returned to the school building. Rosen had long been gone; he must have left by the teachers' entrance. I found out where he lived and dripping wet as I was, trekked to his house, unceremoniously presenting myself as an admirer. Maxie by this time, had left. His family were so amused, however, that they arranged a meeting. From the first moment we became the closest of friends. We chummed about arm in arm; we lavished childish affection upon one another in true Jean Christophe fashion; we exchanged letters even when only a week-end and some hundred blocks lay between us.

"Yes; Max opened the world of music to me. And he came near closing it, too. When we'd play hooky together, we'd talk eternally about music—that is, when we weren't wrestling. I used to throw him every time, by the way, though he was one of those chubby, stocky kids. He wasn't at all kind to my budding ambitions. And there came a climactic day when he told me flatly that I had better give up all thought of a musical career. 'You haven't it in you, Georgie; take my word for it, I can tell!'"

It was a bad guess. Today, however, Rosen is among the warmest admirers of the composer whose loftiest ambition it had once been to become his accompanist.

George's first teachers, of course, had been ladies. Twenty years ago the flat rate for piano lessons on the New York curb was fifty cents. George began to make up for lost time. He wore out his instruction books—he, too, had begun with Beyer's—and his instructors. The third lady within a short period was beginning to weaken when Gershwin met a musician named Goldfarb.

"Goldfarb," he recalls, "played the piano with great gusto and with a barrel of gestures. I learned that this fellow's teacher was none other than the former leader of a Hungarian band and of operetta. He gladly took me on as a pupil, at $1.50 per lesson. In those days that was a stiff price. He started me on a book of excerpts from the grand operas. In six months I had advanced as far as the Overture to *William Tell* when I fell in with a chap, Jack Miller, who was pianist of the Beethoven Symphony Orchestra."

The Beethoven Symphony Orchestra, it must have made a deep impression on Gershwin, for I find in his scrapbooks a yellowed clipping of a photograph that had appeared in the *New York World* magazine, April 27, 1913, was an amateur organization whose youngest member was about nine, and whose oldest was about fifty. "Miller spoke to me of his teacher, a certain Charles Hambitzer, and took me along with him one eventful day. Hambitzer, whose memory I revere, for he was the first great musical influence in my life, asked me to play something. I rubbed my fingers and dived into the Overture to *William Tell*. Hambitzer said nothing until I had finished. 'Listen,' he finally spoke, getting up from his chair. 'Let's hunt out that guy and shoot him, and not with an apple on his head, either!'"

It was a reciprocal discovery. In Hambitzer, Gershwin discovered the personality who was, for him, the ideal teacher. In Gershwin, Hambitzer found the ideal student. It was not long before he was writing to his sister, Olive, she is now Mrs. Ernest Reel, wife of the Milwaukee authority on chess, letters in which, with enthusiastic prescience, he predicted great things for his young star.

"I have a new pupil," he crowed, "who will make his mark in music if anybody will. The boy is a genius, without a doubt; he's just crazy about music and can't wait until it's time to take his lesson. No watching the clock for this boy! He wants to go in for this modern stuff, jazz and what not. But I'm not going to let him for a while. I'll see that he gets a firm foundation in the standard music first."

If any one person may be said, then, to have "discovered" George Gershwin, that person was Charles Hambitzer.

"Under Hambitzer," relates George with a gratitude that verges upon the sentimental, "I first became familiar with Chopin, Liszt and Debussy. He made me harmony-conscious. He wrote what I then considered the finest light music. Only the other day, by the merest accident, I got in touch with a woman who had the score of an unproduced light opera that he had written in his palmy days. It's not at all bad," he will add, forgetting his own music that he has been playing, and trying to work up your enthusiasm for the rediscovered Hambitzer score. "I was crazy about that man. I went out, in fact, and drummed up ten pupils for him."

"Harmony, up to this time, had been a secret to me. I've always had a sort of instinctive feeling for tone combinations, and many of the chords that sound so modern in my orchestral compositions were set down without any particular attention to their theoretical structure. When my critics tell me that now and then I betray a structural weakness, they are not telling me anything I don't know. I don't claim to be perfect; I hope I have too great a sense of humor for that. But I know where I'm going and I'm on my way!"

Hambitzer never taught George much harmony. Up to the time that he began work on the famous *Rhapsody*, in fact, Gershwin tells me, he knew, formally, about as much harmony as could be found in a ten-cent manual. Yet an imperious instinct guided him through the technical mazes, and though George could not name the things he was doing, he could do them or imply them with an uncanny skill that eludes the self-conscious quest of the Conservatory prizemen. Hambitzer died of tuberculosis at the tragic age of thirty-seven. With him was buried the primarily pianistic career of George Gershwin. He has since had lessons sporadically, from some of his famous friends, such as Ernest Hutcheson, but Hambitzer was his last teacher. As for harmony, henceforth Gershwin, after a course under Edward Kilenyi, and some instruction under Ruben Goldmark, would be, as he has been in instrumentation and orchestration, virtually self-taught.

From the early weeks with Goldmark, George smilingly remembers a telltale episode. The young student was eager to exhibit his prowess in the more important forms. He still is. Long before he had begun his harmonic researches under Goldmark, he had composed one movement of a Quartet. What would his teacher think of it? Should he take a chance and show it to this nephew of the famous Karl Goldmark, this pupil of Joseffy and Dvořák, ex-professor of piano and theory at the National Conservatory of Music in New York, ex-director of the Colorado Conservatory of Music? George took the chance. Goldmark weighed the music under his practiced eye. "It's good," he finally announced. "Yes, very good. . . . It's plainly to be seen that you have already learned a great deal of harmony from me."

George never kept a diary. He had few secrets from the world. He was, and remains, an open book; and, without trying to make a lily of him—George a lily!—it may be added that the pages are clean. I have seen copies of a magazine that he used to write and edit—for himself. It was—and this may not be without significance—a musical magazine, in travesty, heavy with the wordy, obvious humor of adolescence and of no use to anybody but himself. The subtle fun that he sometimes pokes at humorless popular writers in his music had already evidenced itself.

More interesting, for its light upon the influences that he was undergoing in his formative years, is an old ledger that he used as his earliest scrapbook. In it are pasted programs of the first concerts that he attended, clippings of the first articles on music that caught his interest. Times, in things other than music, have changed since those prewar days, as may be gathered from the advertisements of women's wear that used to flank the list of compositions. Music, like women's dresses, has acquired a boyish form, a minimum of material for a maximum effect. The spirit of an age manifests itself, with surprising fidelity, in the most disparate preoccupations of that age.

Who were the musical gods of Gershwin's youth? His scrapbooks show pasted photographs of Liszt, Hoffman, Bauer, Busoni, Bloomfield-Zeisler, Lhevinne, Ornstein, pianists all, pruned from a series on the great pianists and carefully indexed under the proper letter. The Russian school of composers was predominant, because of another magazine series. More than one of these names is still strange to the American music-lover: Liapounof, Ilyinsky, Sapelnikoff, Medtner, Balakirev, Glazounof, Mussorgsky, Glière. To this miscellany were added Wagner, Massenet, Sullivan, Gottschalk, Balfe, Raff. If the names show anything, they reveal the thoroughly fortuitous nature of George's earliest musical enthusiasm. It is doubtful that he ever heard, for example, much of the music by the rarer Russians. One name that does not appear in this list outweighs, for influence, the entire assemblage— Rimsky-Korsakoff.

For the rest, the concert halls of New York City completed his education; the improvised scrapbook abounds in programs of The Philharmonic Society—1913 is the great year for Gershwin's budding appreciation— Wanamaker's Auditorium, Cooper Union, New Aeolian Hall, Carnegie Hall . . . Gershwin treasures the program of a Sunday evening concert of the Waldorf-Astoria Orchestra, on April 13, 1913, at which Hambitzer, pianist of the band, played the first movement of the Rubinstein *Concerto in D Minor*. Five days later "Master Max Rosenzweig" gave a program at Cooper Union. George, in his enthusiasm, dragooned his entire family—unto the third generation—into the hall, having disposed of fifty dollars' worth of tickets.

I am inclined to think that in childhood days Ira exercised a certain influence over George. Not only as an elder brother but as a mentor. The club idea, just before the outbreak of the War, had reached its apex; Ira, as a student of unpretentious literary ambitions, had joined the Finley Club of New York City College, named after the college president. And what is a club without its annual entertainment? Accordingly, early in 1914, Ira found himself upon the arrangement committee, and George found himself upon the program. It is at this entertainment of the Finley Club, held in the reception hall of the Christadora House, 147 Avenue B, corner of Ninth Street, New York, that George makes his first public appearance as a pianist; and not only as a pianist, but as a composer.

George-I have the program before me-was down for two numbers: 3. *Piano Solo by George Gershvin* and 5. *Vocal Selections by Chas. Rose and George Gershvin.* This was Ira's spelling of the family name in those days; he appears on the arrangement committee as Isidore Gershvin. George must have been afraid to flaunt himself as a composer, for the tango that he wrote especially for this occasion is concealed behind the noncommittal designation, "Piano Solo." George remembers the piece perfectly, and smilingly plays it for you when he is in the mood. It is conventional and harmless enough, and bears testimony to assimilative rather than to creative powers. The tango was not the first piece he wrote; that distinction is reserved for a song entitled "Since I Found You." It was never published, and it is just as well. George was never a one-finger pianist, like so many of his brothers-to-be of Tin Pan Alley; but he went through the musical measles of harmonic groping. It cleared his blood and helped him to an understanding of what he was getting to want. He laughs as he recalls how, having begun the refrain of this song in G major he found himself suddenly at sea in F, unable to regain the shore.

It is easy to see, thus early in his career, that George is to be the product less of tuition than of intuition. His actual apprenticeship to instruction on the piano had lasted four years. He attributes his proficiency on the instrument not nearly so much to the teaching he received as to a habit that he cultivated consciously from his earliest teens. "I mean my habit of intensive listening. I had gone to concerts and listened not only with my ears, but with my nerves, my mind, my heart. I had listened so earnestly that I became saturated with the music.... Then I went home and listened in memory. I sat at the piano and repeated the *motifs*. I was becoming acquainted with that which later I would try to interpret, the soul of the American people."

George, then, born into one war, comes to maturity at the outbreak of another. He is born into ragtime; he evolves into jazz. The simplicity of the one and the complexity of the other form a graph of the trend in world affairs. The distance is not to be measured in years alone. It leaps from the armored cruiser to the airplane; from the crude kinetoscope of the penny and nickel arcade to the contemporary triumphs of the movie, the talkie, and television; from national naïveté to international sophistication. America and George come of age together.

II.   THE GROWING LIMELIGHT (1919–1924)

The 1920s witnessed Gershwin's emergence as a true star both at home and abroad. Just prior to the start of the decade, the success of "Swanee" had demonstrated his promise as a songwriter. This was repeatedly fulfilled in a string of hits from more than a dozen shows across the decade, from the leggy revues of George White's *Scandals* in the early years to the beginning of more sophisticated political satire in *Strike Up the Band* at the decade's close. During this time Gershwin wrote his first complete book musical score in *La, La Lucille*, began his collaboration with his brother Ira in earnest with *Lady, Be Good!* (1924), and started to experiment with higher-minded approaches to musical shows in the ill-fated *Blue Monday* (1922) and *Song of the Flame* (1925). And along the way, of course, he practiced his ever-present desire to compose music for the concert hall. While this actually had always been a part of his musical psyche, and brief, finished pieces such as the *Lullaby for String Quartet* even predate the decade, it came to fruition most notably and importantly with the premiere of *Rhapsody in Blue* in 1924. Other works in the later 1920s only confirmed what was already apparent—Gershwin and his music were durable. Trips to Europe tested and proved this further.

8 *George Gershwin: Letter to Max Abramson (1918)*

Here a young man, not yet twenty and not yet famous, Gershwin writes to a friend about his first tastes of success. He already speaks with a confidence that will recur in his writings. In this early letter Gershwin also demonstrates the directness of purpose that is among the strengths of his letters, truly remarkable given his lack of advanced formal education. Written from Cleveland while on tour with the show *Ladies First*, to newspaper reporter Abramson back in New York, this valuable letter documents Gershwin's activities and thoughts at that important time in his career, just prior to his breakthrough success with the song "Swanee," which occurred following its inclusion in Al Jolson's *Sinbad* about two years later. After out-of-town tryouts in Trenton, Pittsburgh, Cleveland, and Baltimore, *Ladies First* opened in New York at the Broadhurst Theater on October 24, 1918, where it ran for 164 performances, a modest success. Preceding *Half Past Eight* by a few months, and surely the one he intimates writing despite Jerome Kern's apparently discouraging advice, *Ladies First* was like much of Gershwin's work at this time as an aspiring songwriter in that he only provided a few songs for a score composed mostly by someone else, in this case A. Baldwin Sloane. The book and lyrics for the show were by Harry B. Smith. Essentially a star vehicle for ingenue Nora Bayes, the work glossed the then-current hot topic of women's suffrage albeit in the context of a feel-good musical revue, not a high-minded political satire.

Thursday 1:35 P.M.

Dear Maxie[1]

I was surprised to hear from you today. I wrote you a line yesterday and looked forward to a letter from you tomorrow. I surmise you wrote your letter before receiving mine, in fact I'm sure you did, therefore you are receiving this letter at such an early hour.

Max there are a whole lot of things I want to tell you about. I cannot put

SOURCE Gershwin Collection, Library of Congress (hereafter DLC [GC]).
    1 Abramson was closely associated with the Gershwins' inner circle, as he was the brother of George A. Pallay and a cousin of one of Gershwin's other close friends, Lou Paley, who married Emily Strunsky, sister of Ira's wife, Leonore.

them all into one letter very well without having it sent as a parcel post pack-age, so I'll divide them into chapters & mail them separately.

The first thing of interest to you is that the show is a very big hit here, the house being sold out for to-day's matinees. Go up to Izzy & read some of the criticizms [*sic*] I mailed him.

Baldwin Sloane told me he received $400 royalty from Trenton & Pittsburg [*sic*]. Zowie!!! Why didn't I write the show & let him interpolate? He gets 3 percent of the gross.

I think Miss Bayes is having my name put on the programme as the writer of interpolated songs. If she does, she'll be doing me a justice that I sorely need to get into that select circle of composers in New York.

"Something About Love" is in the show, sung by Fisher in place of "What's the Use," and it is showing up much better than the former song.[2] Last night he had to sing an extra verse & cho. The first time he sang it there were 14 or 15 requests for the song. It is not published yet. Nor is the Folk-Song.[3] Speaking of the Folk-Song, Miss Bayes told me yesterday of her confi-dence in the song. She said it was a great number, improperly put over, and a change in the singer would soon come. I think Jane Elliot is slated to do the song. I don't suppose she'll do it to my heart's desire but I'm sure it will be an improvement. I'm afraid no one will satisfy me after seeing Miss Bayes do it for Jane Elliot. Oh *Momma* what *she* does to it.

I gave Miss Bayes one big laugh the other day when Harry Smith was telling everybody of the cuts he made. Everyone was blue & a few were ready to quit. She yelled, and repeated it to the company. I have about 6 words in the play.

Seriously I am thinking of writing a show, Max. In spite of what J.K. told me. I am getting confidence & encouragement from this show, & B. Sloane. I'm going to make an attempt when I reach N.Y.

Miss Dean-Rosenbaum-Abramson sends her regards.

I enjoyed A. Charney's letter hugely & I will write her. I am enclosing her letter as per request.

How's everyone in N.Y. I wish you'd find out where S. Greene is. I wrote him twice without receiving an answer.

There are a few other things I'll tell you later.

Well, I think I'll ramble out & see that our bloody show goes well. Write

---

2   "Something About Love," with lyrics by Lou Paley, was reused the following year in *The Lady in Red* and was selected again for the London revival of *Lady, Be Good!* in 1926.

3   Gershwin refers to "The Real American Folk Song (Is a Rag)," a fairly early collaboration with his brother.

hard & heavy. Kiss everybody for me including Marilyn Miller.[4] Baltimore next week. I believe the Auditorium Thea[ter].

S'long,

George

9   Dolly Dalrymple: "Pianist, Playing Role of Columbus, Makes Another American Discovery: Beryl Rubinstein Says This Country Possesses Genius Composer" (1922)

More than simply a review of *Scandals of 1922*, Dalrymple's report, written for an English audience but quickly picked up by the *New York World*, is perhaps the earliest positive mention of Gershwin's merits as a composer and not merely as a songwriter. This in particular is what he sought in the one-act operetta *Blue Monday* that was included in the first performance of the 1922 edition of George White's revue. It is not clear whether Rubinstein actually heard Gershwin and lyricist B. G. DeSylva's "Opera Ala Afro-American" since there is no mention of it. Still, he is a few years ahead of the mainstream American press in pointing to Gershwin's aspirations to compose "an American opera along the lines of American popular music, but in a serious way," and to his ability to orchestrate, an ability that, beginning with the *Concerto in F*, would separate Gershwin from his songwriting brethren.

Beryl Rubinstein, the eminent young pianist who has appeared during the past season with a half dozen of the most renowned orchestras in this country, during his visit to Birmingham has revealed himself in an entirely different role.

He's a modern Christopher Columbus, for the reason he has discovered a real American genius-composer, and when he first mentioned to us who this genius is, we promptly felt that he was making sport of us just to see what would happen.

"I am absolutely in earnest," said Mr. Rubinstein, as he chatted about his visit to Birmingham, meeting old friends and enjoying the scenes where, as a youthful prodigy, he startled the music world with his talent.

"The man I refer to is George Gershwin, composer of the music of the *Scandals* in New York," said Mr. Rubinstein.

---

4 Singer-dancer Marilyn Miller would eventually star in the Gershwins' *Rosalie* in 1928.
SOURCE *New York World* (September 16, 1922).

Ejaculations. "Ohs! and Ahs! and whatever do you mean?" came quickly from the lips of the writer, who in other conversations with Mr. Rubinstein had been used to talking with him about such things as the Saint-Saëns *Concerto in F*, which he played several times with various orchestras the past winter, the Tschaikowsky concerto and the *Rhapsodie Espagnole* of Liszt, arranged by Busoni; so imagine the consternation when Mr. Rubinstein mentioned anything as "low brow" as the *Scandals*.

"I am absolutely in earnest," said Mr. Rubinstein, "not especially about the *Scandals* music although Mr. Gershwin's music is better than any of the rest in New York musical circles of that type.

"What I mean is that this young fellow George Gershwin, now only 25, has the spark of musical genius which is definite. In his serious moods he has written some very worthwhile things. I am including at a later date some of his compositions on my programs. So far, only one has been given to me, this in manuscript, the others now being in the hands of the publishers.

"This young American composer has the fire of originality, and he is preparing to write an American opera along the lines of American popular music, but in a serious way.

"Personally I loathe and despise the ordinary popular musical efforts of composers, that goes without saying, but with Gershwin's style and seriousness he is not definitely from the popular musical school, but one of the really outstanding figures in the country's serious musical efforts.

"Besides all this, Gershwin knows orchestration and will orchestrate his own compositions, which is a big thing. This young man has great charm and a most magnetic personality and I really believe that America will at no distant day honor this young man for his talent and his seriousness and that when we speak of American composers George Gershwin's name will be prominent in the list."

10   *George Gershwin: Letter to Ira Gershwin (February 18, 1923)*

Penned on Savoy Hotel stationery, Gershwin's wonderful letter to his brother back in New York was written the day after his arrival in London to begin work on *The Rainbow*, composed in collaboration with lyricist Clifford Grey. He writes full of energy and with a noticeably more mature voice

SOURCE DLC [GC].

than in his earlier letter to Abramson. Gershwin is excited about his new-found fame and anxious about his prospects during this, his first, trip abroad.

Sunday, noon.

Dear Iz.

Well, ol boy, here I am in London almost 24 hours, or rather only 24 hours & the rain is coming down in the manner we've heard about for years. It is not raining hard—but hard enough to keep one from going out. It will not however, keep me from going to C. Grey's house, in a few minutes to start on a show that begins music rehearsals Tuesday. Writing the *Scandals* in a month will seem an eternity compared to the time allotted us to write what will probably be called *Silver Linings*.

A funny thing happened yesterday which made me very joyful & for the moment very happy I came here. The boat was in dock at Southampton & everyone was in line with their passports & landing cards. When I handed my passport to one of the men at a table he read it, looked up & said, "George Gershwin writer of 'Swanee'?" It took me off my feet for a second. It was so unexpected, you know. Of course I agreed I was the composer & then he asked what I was writing now etc. etc. I couldn't ask for a more pleasant entrance into a country. When I reached shore a woman reporter came up to me & asked for a few words. I felt like I was a Kern or somebody.

Last night a man called me on the phone & said he was from the *Weekly Dispatch* & would like to have an interview. I met him & spoke a while to him. He asked my opinion about the possibility of a rag-time opera & when I thought it would come about. I told him my opinion & when it is published I'll send it along to you. Last night we went to see Jean Bodini's *You'd Be Surprised*. A review. It's a fast show with many scenes from burlesque & music by Melville Morris.[1] I wonder what he wrote as all I heard were popular American songs. George Robey, a famous comedian is in the show & I think he is a fine artist. He puts over a lyric song as good as anyone I've seen. The hit of the show is an orchestra. The Savoy Orchestra. And who do you suppose is the leader? Bert Ralston the sax player who recorded my "Mexican Dance" with me. He's got a great band and is a riot over here.

From what I can see America is years ahead of England theatrically, both in wealth of material & money. They're shy of ingenues, leading men, composers, etc. They have a half dozen good lyric writers however.

---

1 American composer and pianist Melville Morris, a charter member of ASCAP back in 1914, was head house pianist at Remick's when Gershwin arrived there in 1914.

The English are the politest people I've yet met. Even the taxi drivers are polite. How different from the Yellow Cabs of New York.

I'm finding a little difficulty in understanding the money system here. They go by 12*ves* instead of 10*s*. For instance a pence is equal to two cents. A six pence piece is, of course 12 cents. A shilling is 24. This is their par value. At present they are under par as you know. The cars drive on the left of the street which is also a bit befuddling.

I could go on & tell you more observations of my first 24 hours here but I must trot along to Grey's. Did you notice "trot along"?

Give my love to Mom & Pop & Frances & Arthur & tell them to drop a line to the br'er.

Am stopping at above Hotel but only for a few days. Until I can find a suitable apartment for Foster & myself. Address the mail to Chappell Mus. Pub. 50 New Bond St. London, until I find out where I shall definitely stay.

Give my regards to the "boys" individually.

Write heaps & heaps. (Notice? heaps & heaps?)

Your brother,

George.

11   "*Whiteman Judges Named: Committee Will Decide 'What Is American Music'*" (1924)

This first mention of Gershwin's most well known concert work, the *Rhapsody in Blue*, dates from little more than a month prior to the famous premiere. A popular story claims that this report reminded Gershwin of his commitment to Whiteman, making the premiere of the *Rhapsody* in early February a remarkable achievement since Gershwin would have needed to compose the work with amazing fluidity. There is nothing to suggest that he did not in fact do so.

Among the members of the committee of judges who will pass on "What Is American Music?" at the Paul Whiteman concert to be given at Aeolian Hall, Tuesday afternoon, February 12, will be Sergei Rachmaninoff, Jascha Heifetz, Efrem Zimbalist, and Alma Gluck.

Leonard Liebling, editor of *The Musical Courier*, will be chairman of the critics' committee, which is to be composed of the leading musical critics of the United States.

SOURCE *New York Tribune* (January 4, 1924): 11.

This question of "just what is American Music?" has aroused a tremendous interest in music circles and Mr. Whiteman is receiving every phase of manuscript, from blues to symphonies.

George Gershwin is at work on a jazz concerto, Irving Berlin is writing a syncopated tone poem, and Victor Herbert is working on an American suite.

12   Paul Whiteman and Mary Margaret McBride: "An Experiment" (1926)

Paul Whiteman's autobiography, written in collaboration with popular essayist Mary Margaret McBride, contains the following account of the *Rhapsody*'s premiere in the context of the concert as a whole.

Visions of playing a jazz concert in what a critic has called the "perfumed purlieus" of Aeolian Hall used to rouse me up at night in a cold perspiration. Sometimes a nightmare depicted me being borne out of the place on a rail, and again I dreamed the doors were all but clattering down with the applause.

That's the way I lived during waking hours, too, all the time I was planning the Aeolian Hall experiment—alternating between extremes of dire fear and exultant confidence.

We began to rehearse for the concert as soon as we came back from England. The idea struck nearly everybody as preposterous at the start. Some hold to the same opinion still. But the list of pessimists was a little shorter, I believe, when at half past five, on the afternoon of February 12, 1924, we took our fifth curtain call. . . .

If I'd been willing to wait a few centuries for a verdict on my work, I wouldn't have been so wrought up over the Aeolian Hall concert. But here I saw the common people of America taking all the jazz they could get and mad to get more, yet not having the courage to admit that they took it seriously. I believed that jazz was beginning a new movement in the world's art of music. I wanted it to be recognized as such. I knew it never would be in my lifetime until the recognized authorities on music gave it their approval.

My idea for the concert was to show these skeptical people the advance which had been made in popular music from the day of discordant early jazz to the melodious form of the present. I believed that most of them had grown so accustomed to condemning the "Livery Stable Blues" sort of thing

SOURCE   Paul Whiteman and Mary Margaret McBride, *Jazz* (New York: J. H. Sears, 1926).

that they went on flaying modern jazz without realizing that it was different from the crude early attempts—that it had taken a turn for the better.

My task was to reveal the change and try to show that jazz had come to stay and deserved recognition. It was not a light undertaking, but setting Aeolian Hall as the stage of the experiment was probably a wise move. It started the talk going, at least, and aroused curiosity. "Jazz in Aeolian Hall!" the conservatives cried incredulously. "What is the world coming to?"

I trembled at our temerity when we made out the lists of patrons and patronesses for the concert. But in a few days, I exulted at our daring, for the acceptances began to come in—from Damrosch, Godowsky, Heifetz, Kreisler, McCormack, Rachmaninoff, Rosenthal, Stokowski, Stransky. We had kindly response, too, from Alda, Galli-Curci, Garden, Gluck, and Jeanne Gordon. Otto Kahn and Jules Glaenzer agreed to represent the patrons of art on our roster and the prominent writers we asked were equally obliging. These included: Fannie Hurst, Heywood Broun, Frank Crowninshield, S. Jay Kaufman, Karl Kitchin, Leonard Liebling, O. O. McIntyre, Pitts Sanborn, Gilbert Seldes, Deems Taylor, and Carl Van Vechten....

That concert cost $11,000. I lost about $7,000 on it. The program alone, together with the explanatory notes, cost $900. We rehearsed for many weeks and since it was outside our regular work, every rehearsal meant extra pay for the men. Nine musicians were added for the occasion and their salaries also piled up the total.

I didn't care. It would have been worth it to me at any price. But never in my life had I such stage fright as that day. I had no doubt of the orchestra. But how would people take it? Would we be the laughingstock of the town when we woke the "morning after"? Would the critics decide I was trying to be smart and succeeding in being only smart-alecky? Or might I be able to convince the crowd that I was engaged in a sincere experiment, designed to exhibit what had been accomplished in the past few years with respect to scoring and arranging music for the popular band—that we were making a bona fide attempt to arouse an interest in popular music rhythm for purposes of advancing serious musical composition?

Fifteen minutes before the concert was to begin, I yielded to a nervous longing to see for myself what was happening out front, and putting an overcoat over my concert clothes, I slipped around to the entrance of Aeolian Hall.

There I gazed upon a picture that should have imparted new vigor to my wilting confidence. It was snowing, but men and women were fighting to get into the door, pulling and mauling each other as they do sometimes at a baseball game, or a prize fight, or in the subway. Such was my state of mind by this time that I wondered if I had come to the right entrance. And then I saw Victor Herbert going in. It was the right entrance, sure enough, and the next day the ticket-office people said they could have sold out the house ten times over.

I went backstage again, more scared than ever. Black fear simply possessed me. I paced the floor, gnawed my thumbs, and vowed I'd give five thousand dollars if we could stop right then and there. Now that the audience had come, perhaps I had really nothing to offer after all. I even made excuses to keep the curtain from rising on schedule. But finally there was no longer any way of postponing the evil moment. The curtain went up and before I could dash forth, as I was tempted to do, and announce that there wouldn't be any concert, we were in the midst of it.

It was a strange audience out in front. Vaudevillians, concert managers come to have a look at the novelty, Tin Pan Alleyites, composers, symphony and opera stars, flappers, cake-eaters, all mixed up higgledy-piggledy.

Beginning with the earliest jazz composition, "Livery Stable Blues," we played twenty-six selections designed to exhibit legitimate scoring as contrasted with the former hit-and-miss effects which were also called jazz. At that time I argued that all was not jazz that was so called. I still believe that "Livery Stable Blues" and *A Rhapsody in Blue*, played at the concert by its talented composer, George Gershwin, are so many millions of miles apart that to speak of them both as jazz needlessly confuses the person who is trying to understand modern American music. At the same time, in the course of a recent tour of the United States, I have become convinced that people as a whole like the word *jazz*. At least they will have none of the numerous substitutes that smart wordologists are continually offering. So I say, let's call the new music jazz.

This, then, is the jazz program we played that day:

True Form of Jazz
a. Ten Years Ago—"Livery Stable Blues"
b. With Modern Embellishment—"Mama Loves Papa" (Baer)

Comedy Selections
a. Origin of "Yes, We Have No Bananas" (Silver)
b. Instrumental Comedy—"So This Is Venice" (Thomas) (Adapted from *The Carnival of Venice*)

Contrast—Legitimate Scoring vs. Jazzing
a. Selection in True Form—"Whispering" (Schonberger)
b. Same Selection with Jazz Treatment

Recent Compositions with Modern Score

a. "Limehouse Blues" (Braham)
b. "I Love You" (Archer)
c. "Raggedy Ann" (Kern)

An Experiment

Zez Confrey (Piano—Accompanied by the Orchestra)

a. Medley Popular Airs
b. "Kitten on the Keys" (Confrey)
c. "Ice Cream and Art"
d. "Nickel in the Slot" (Confrey)

Flavoring a Selection with Borrowed Themes

"Russian Rose" (Grofé) (Based on the "Volga Boat Song")

Semisymphonic Arrangement of Popular Melodies

Consisting of:

a. "Alexander's Ragtime Band" (Berlin)
b. "A Pretty Girl Is Like a Melody" (Berlin)
c. "Orange Blossoms in California" (Berlin)

A Suite of Serenades (Herbert)

a. Spanish
b. Chinese
c. Cuban
d. Oriental

Adaptation of Standard Selections to Dance Rhythm

a. "Pale Moon" (Logan)
b. "To a Wild Rose" (MacDowell)
c. "Chansonette" (Friml)

George Gershwin (Piano—Accompanied by the Orchestra)
A Rhapsody in Blue (Gershwin)

In the Field of Classics
"Pomp and Circumstance" (Elgar)

A *Rhapsody in Blue* was regarded by critics as the most significant number of the program. It was the first rhapsody written for a solo instrument and a jazz orchestra. The orchestral treatment was developed by Mr. Grofé, Mr. Gershwin's manuscript being complete for the piano. It was a successful attempt to build a rhapsody out of the rhythms of popular American music. None of the thematic material had been used before. Its structure was simple and its popularity has been remarkable since we put it on the records. It is music conceived for the jazz orchestra and I do not believe any other kind of orchestra can do it full justice, though some have played it.

It seemed as if people would never let us go. We played all the encores we knew and still they applauded. My heart was so full I could hardly speak, as I bowed again and again. The spark that a responsive audience can always kindle in the performers had been glowing all afternoon and, as a result, we played better than I had ever hoped.

13   Olin Downes: "A Concert of Jazz" (1924)

> In probably the single most important review of the concert that included the *Rhapsody in Blue* premiere, Olin Downes is thorough and even-handed in his remarks in the *New York Times*. In them, Gershwin and his work clearly emerge as the most significant on the program.

A concert of popular American music was given yesterday afternoon in Aeolian Hall by Paul Whiteman and his orchestra of the Palais Royal. The stage setting was as unconventional as the program. Pianos in various stages of dishabille stood about, amid a litter of every imaginable contraption of wind and percussion instruments. Two Chinese mandarins, surmounting pillars, looked down upon a scene that would have curdled the blood of a Stokowski or a Mengelberg. The golden sheen of brass instruments of lesser and greater dimensions was caught up by a gleaming gong and carried out by bright patches of an oriental backdrop. There were also, lying or hanging about, frying pans, large tin utensils, and a speaking trumpet, later stuck into the end of a trombone—and what a silky, silky tone came from that accommodating instrument! The singular assemblage of things was more than once, in some strange way, to combine to evoke uncommon and fascinating sonorities.

There were verbal as well as programmatic explanations. The concert was referred to as "educational," to show the development of this type of music.

SOURCE *New York Times* 73 (February 13, 1924): 16.

Thus, the "Livery Stable Blues" was introduced apologetically as an example of the depraved past from which modern jazz has risen. The apology is herewith indignantly rejected, for this is a gorgeous piece of impudence, much better in its unbuttoned jocosity and Rabelaisian laughter than other and more polite compositions that came later.

The pianist gathered about him some five fellow performers. The man with the clarinet wore a battered top hat that had ostensibly seen better days. Sometimes he wore it, and sometimes played into it. The man with the trombone played it as is, but also, on occasion, picked up a bathtub or something of the kind from the floor and blew into that. The instruments made odd, unseemly, bushman sounds. The instrumentalists rocked about. Jests permissible in musical terms but otherwise not printable were passed between these friends of music. The laughter of the music and its interpreters was tornadic. It was—should we blush to say it?—a phase of America. It reminded the writer of someone's remark that an Englishman entered a place as if he were its master, whereas an American entered as if she didn't care who in blazes the master might be. Something like that was in this music.

There were later remarkably beautiful examples of scoring for a few instruments; scoring of singular economy, balance, color, and effectiveness; music at times vulgar, cheap, in poor taste, elsewhere of irresistible swing and insouciance and recklessness and life; music played as only such players as these can play it. They have a technique of their own. They play with an abandon equaled only by that race of born musicians—the American Negro, who has surely contributed fundamentally to this art which can neither be frowned nor sneered away. They did not play like an army going through ordered maneuvers, but like the melomaniacs they are, bitten by rhythms that would have twiddled the toes of St. Anthony. They beat time with their feet—lèse-majesté in a symphony orchestra. They fidgeted uncomfortably when for a moment they had to stop playing. And there were the incredible gyrations of that virtuoso and imp of the perverse, Ross Gorman. And then there was Mr. Whiteman. He does not conduct. He trembles, wabbles, quivers—a piece of jazz jelly, conducting the orchestra with the back of the trouser of the right leg, and the face of a mandarin the while. There was an ovation for Victor Herbert, that master of instrumentation, when his four *Serenades* composed for this occasion were played, and Mr. Herbert acknowledged the applause from the gallery. Then stepped upon the stage, sheepishly, a lank and dark young man—George Gershwin. He was to play the piano part in the first public performance of his *Rhapsody in Blue* for piano and orchestra. This composition shows extraordinary talent, just as it also shows a young composer with aims that go far beyond those of his ilk, struggling with a form of which he is far from being master. It is important to bear both these facts in mind in estimating the composition. Often Mr. Gershwin's purpose is defeated by technical immaturity, but in spite of that technical immaturity, a lack of knowledge of how to write effectively for piano alone or in combination with orchestra, an unconscious attempt to rhapsodize in the manner of Franz Liszt, a naïveté which at times stresses something unimportant while something of value and effectiveness goes by so quickly that it is lost—in spite of all this, he has expressed himself in a significant and, on the whole, highly original manner.

His first theme alone, with its caprice, humor, and exotic outline, would show a talent to be reckoned with. It starts with an outrageous cadenza of the clarinet. It has subsidiary phrases, logically growing out of it, and integral to the thought. The original phrase and subsidiaries are often ingeniously metamorphosed by devices of rhythm and instrumentation. There is an oriental twist to the whole business that is not hackneyed or superficial. And—what is important—this is no mere dance tune set for piano and other instruments. It is an idea, or several ideas correlated and combined, in varying and well-contrasted rhythms that immediately intrigue the hearer. This, in essence, is fresh and new and full of future promise.

The second theme, with a lovely sentimental line, is more after the manner of some of Mr. Gershwin's colleagues. Tuttis are too long, cadenzas are too long, the peroration at the end loses a large measure of wildness and magnificence it could easily have if it were more broadly prepared, and, for all that, the audience was stirred and many a hardened concertgoer excited with the sensation of a new talent finding its voice and likely to say something personally and racially important to the world. A talent and an idiom also rich in possibilities for that generally exhausted and outworn form of the classic piano concerto.

Mr. Gershwin's *Rhapsody* also stands out as counteracting, quite unconsciously, a weakness of the program—that is, a tendency to sameness of rhythm and sentiment in the music. When a program consists almost entirely of modern dance music, that is naturally a danger, since American dances of today do not boast great variety of step or character; but it should be possible for Mr. Whiteman to remedy this in a second program, which he will give later in the season. There was tumultuous applause for Mr. Gershwin's composition. There was realization of the irresistible vitality and genuineness of much of the music heard on this occasion, as opposed to the pitiful sterility of the average production of the "serious" American composer. The audience packed a house that could have been sold out twice over.

14   Carl Van Vechten: Letter to George Gershwin (February 14, 1924)

A native Iowan, Carl Van Vechten (1880–1964) first met George Gershwin at a Manhattan party in 1919 and, during the course of the next fifteen years, became his close friend. Entries in Van Vechten's diaries and appointment books during those years list frequent parties at his home at 150 W. 55th Street; his apartment became a standard meeting place for black and white artists and entertainers throughout the 1920s and 1930s. In later years the two friends would share a passion for photography and would own the identical camera, a small Leica. Gershwin was one of hundreds of famous personalities who sat for Van Vechten in his home studio.

Dear George Gershwin,

The concert, quite as a matter of course, was a riot, and you crowned it with what, after repeated hearings, I am forced to regard as the foremost serious effort by any American composer. Go straight on, and you will knock all Europe silly. Go a little farther in the next one and invent a new *form*. I think something might be done in the way of combining jazz and the moving-picture technique. Think of themes as close-ups, flash-backs, etc.! This is merely an impertinent suggestion; whatever you do, however, including playing the piano, you do so well that you need no advice.

Marguerite d'Alvarez, by the way, was reduced to a state of hysterical enthusiasm by the concert, especially your contribution. She wants to sing at the next one![1] You might tell Whiteman this: she would certainly give the audience a good time!

When you have an hour or two or an evening, telephone me. I want to talk with you.

Very sincerely,

Carl Van Vechten

15   James Ross Moore: "The Gershwins in Britain" (1994)

On July 8, 1924, George Gershwin boarded a liner at the West Side terminal to begin his second voyage to England. Staying in a London flat with Alex

SOURCE (14) DLC [GC].

1 D'Alvarez and Gershwin presented at least three joint recitals: at the Roosevelt Hotel in December 1927, with repetitions of the same program in Boston and Buffalo, N.Y., the following month.

SOURCE (15) *New Theater Quarterly* (February 1994): 39–43.

Aarons and his wife, Ella, Gershwin began working on his new show, *Primrose*, set to go into rehearsal only two weeks after his arrival. He brought with him seven polished songs, mostly with Ira's charming lyrics, and completed the musical by collaborating with newcomer Desmond Carter (d. 1939). He left shortly after the September premiere with a solid hit show, a truckload of gifts for his family and friends, and a prized photograph signed by Prince George, the Duke of Kent, with the inscription "From George to George."

George was in Britain now after the American premiere of *Rhapsody in Blue*, writing (now for [George] Grossmith, who had been rumoured to prefer [Jerome] Kern) his first book musical for the West End. On 8 July he wrote to his friend and collaborator Lou Paley and Paley's wife Em: "If the show is only half way decent it will be produced in America soon after its London presentation."

On 11 September 1924, *Primrose* opened at the Winter Garden [in London], where it ran for 255 performances. Heather Thatcher, who had already appeared in Kern shows at the same house, joined a characteristic Winter Garden troupe—Leslie Henson, Vera Lennox, Percy Heming, Claude Hulbert, and Margery Hicklin—in a show whose importance has been undervalued, especially in Britain, where it is a truly "lost" musical.

Guy Bolton, the Princess series nominally ended, had contracted with producers [Alex] Aarons and [Vinton] Freedley for a show featuring the Astaires, and for one more in Britain after [P. G.] Wodehouse's *The Beauty Prize* (for Kern). This was *Primrose*. In accordance with the practice of the time, Bolton shared his writing credit with Grossmith, who had apparently considered [Noel] Coward but decided on Bolton's track record.

Bolton and Wodehouse, both singly and together, were nearly as prolific as their highly inventive mid-career collaborative autobiography, *Bring on the Girls*, suggests. Wodehouse was the word-man and Bolton the expert constructionist (those hiring him were taking out play-doctor insurance). Together or apart, they never strayed very far from the plots they had invented for those Princess classics.

The plot of *Primrose* is such a contrivance and typifies the era's musical comedies. It suggests the task set for George, for Ira (finally writing under his own name—there was already a British Arthur Francis), and for [Desmond] Carter, a British lyricist Ira ranked with PGW [P. G. Wodehouse] as [William S.] Gilbert's authentic heir.

Aside from being the first score upon which the Gershwins collaborated under both their own names, *Primrose* was George's first score to be published in full (by Chappell in London and Harms in New York). Of special musical significance was George's orchestration of three songs—"Naughty Baby," "Isn't It Wonderful?" and "Berkeley Square and Kew."

Since *Primrose* came midway between *Rhapsody in Blue* and *Concerto in F* in 1925, these orchestrations are considered to settle a scholarly controversy— when did George learn orchestration? It seems now that he didn't orchestrate *Rhapsody* for the reason he gave: he was too busy. The first of many collaborations between the Gershwins and Bolton, *Primrose* was one of the first London musicals to be broadcast in part by the BBC. It also marked the first time an English reviewer said Ira was George's sister.

Claiming that in his score from *Primrose*, he had paid particular attention to English phrases and enunciation, George remarked that 6:8 was best suited to convey in music a mimetic sense of English conversation. And it is often suggested that why *Primrose* never transferred to the USA was because Gershwin had written such a perfectly "English" score—a myth perpetuated by remarks such as that attributed to Aarons: "Berkeley Square" (near which the Gershwins, Aarons, and his wife stayed while the show was taking shape) was "more English than anything Paul Rubens ever wrote." No English critic noticed this.

Now that the original score of the show has been recovered (part of the celebrated find in a warehouse in Secaucus, New Jersey, in 1982), performed (in Brooklyn) and in 1987 to a degree recorded ("Gershwin Overture": EMI 27 0575 1) this view should be reconsidered: Gershwin's score was, with exceptions, about as "English" as Richard Rodgers' for *The King and I* was authentically Siamese. But it is bracing, inventive, and tuneful. Perhaps the greatest significance of *Primrose*, as Edward Jablonski has said, is that it is "composedthrough," musical exposition setting the tone throughout. (Still, it was only three years later that George and Ira produced some deliberately Savoyard numbers for *Strike Up the Band*.)

Considering the practices of the time, the score of *Primrose* was startlingly original. Of its nineteen numbers (including an act-opening ballet) George recycled "American" material in only three. It's true, there was nothing particularly sweet-and-lowdown-jazzy about this score. But in the show's best songs, there is always a point where briskness eases and the melodic line becomes languorously saxophonic: Gershwin songs.

Desmond Carter received more lyric credit than Ira, whose name appeared in the published score six times—once with B. G. DeSylva (for "Some Far-Away Someone"). Ira's only solo credit was "Four Little Sirens We," a quartet for the beach scene at Le Bouquet obviously patterned upon *The Mikado* ("Four little Sirens, we / Making mermen fall for us / We never go in the sea/But we work as well as any Sirens mythology"). "Four Little Sirens We" had found its proper home. As "The Sirens," it was written by "Arthur Francis" to his brother's music for *A Dangerous Maid*, which closed in Pittsburgh in May 1921. The onstage *Primrose* sirens managed the inconsiderable feat of looking vaguely Viking.

Arguably the best, most recognizable Gershwin songs from *Primrose* were those George wrote with Ira. In "Wait a Bit, Susie," whose catchy melody falls trippingly down the scale, and (in the tradition of the era "plug" songs) becomes maddeningly embedded in the brain (a reviewer of the Gershwins' subsequent *Tell Me More* gave "Susie" a southpaw compliment: "nothing so easily remembered at first hearing as 'Wait a Bit, Susie'") there is more than a hint of the lyricist shortly to write "Looking for a Boy" in *Tip-Toes*:

> *There is Someone who*
> *Some fine day*
> *Will come and say*
> *He loves you*
> *Somebody who's lonely*
> *Someone who only*
> *Wonders what to do*
> *Watching waiting*
> *Hesitating, too.*

Though such safely saucy boy-girl cuteness was part of the musical comedy template and hardly specific to Ira, another preview of "Looking for a Boy" can be seen in "Boy Wanted"

> *To have the ghost of a chance*
> *He must be able to dance*
> *The sort of boy wanted*
> *Must have a smile.*
> *Boy wanted, lovable style.*

If you change its tempo, "Naughty Baby" ("Naughty baby, naughty baby who will tease you / I can show the way and know the way to please you") sounds startlingly like "Somebody Loves Me." And why not? In the golden years of musical theatre, just because you were writing one score didn't mean you weren't just—writing! The first eight bars of "Fascinating Rhythm" occurred to George while he worked on *Primrose*.

If George and Ira's songs are the best of *Primrose*, perhaps it is because their particular ability to work together, later celebrated in Ira's *Lyrics on Several Occasions*, was jelling. Talking of "A Foggy Day," he recalled: "All I had to say was 'George, how about an Irish verse?' and he sensed instantly the degree of wistful loneliness I meant." Guessing that their method was synthetic, Ira added, "When . . . I couldn't recall exactly the start of a particular song I wanted to discuss, I would visualize the vocal line and my forefinger would draw an approximation of its curves in the air. And more often than not he would know the tune I meant."

According to Britain's advanced practice, some of the songs from *Primrose*, including "Boy Wanted," "The Mophams," and "I Make Hay While the Sun Shines," were recorded by its original stars, Thatcher and Henson. As usual, other recordings were made by the Winter Garden Theatre Orchestra and the Mayfair Orchestra. On no recordings was Ira credited.

A footnote to *Primrose* was written in 1960 by the ubiquitous Wodehouse. With characteristic irreverence for tradition, including his own, he rewrote two of Carter's lyrics—"The Mophams" (now "The Pophams") and "When Toby Is Out of Town" (now "The Twenties Are Here to Stay") so they could be placed in a Broadway revival—of *Oh, Kay!*

By the time *Primrose* closed in 1925, London was awash with Gershwin, although critical acclaim was often withheld. One of his songs from *Little Miss Bluebeard* ("I Won't, I Will," with "Arthur Francis" and DeSylva), was warmly roasted ("of scarcely sufficient interest to justify what action there was"), as was just about everything else in showcase for Irene Bordoni. Ms. Bordoni changed costumes eight times and sang five songs (Irving Berlin and E. Ray Goetz were also victimized), and only Eric Blore's silly-ass Englishman won praise. "We do not often see a worse play," muttered one stunned reviewer of this show—which like its star had been very popular on Broadway.

It was an obvious coincidence, but while George never wrote another original score for London, he did now become a regular visitor. When the stars of *Charlot's Revue*, conquerors of Broadway, were feted, the Gershwins were there, and met Gertrude Lawrence. Within three years they would write two shows for her—one a classic and one a flop.

The Gershwins also now became even more regular participants in the transatlantic musical theatre of the era. Their series of New York successes began in 1924 (directly after *Primrose*) with *Lady, Be Good!*—their first complete collaboration to be produced on Broadway. Its success, which owed something to the reputations which the Gershwins and the Astaires had brought back from London, marked the first of Aaron's and Freedley's attempts to create a new, Princess Theatre-like series, substituting George for Kern (who no longer wanted to write on "such a small scale").

16　*Ira Gershwin: "Which Came First?" (1959)*

On the heels of the publication of his landmark *Lyrics on Several Occasions*, Ira ponders the collaborative process that yielded the Gershwins' huge bouquet of evergreens.

That certain question: "Which comes first?" When I was on jury service in New York many years ago there was a case found for the defendant. Afterwards, in the corridor, I saw the lawyer for the plaintiff approaching and thought I was going to be lectured. But no. Greetings over, all he wanted to know was whether the words or the music came first.

Every songwriter has been put this question many times, and by now nearly all interested know that no rule obtains: sometimes it's the lyric and sometimes the tune. And sometimes, more often than not these days, the words and music are written practically at the same time: this, when collaborators are at work together (in the same room, that is, though I have heard of collaboration on the telephone) and a song, sparked either by a possible title or by a likely snatch of tune, emerges line by line and section by section. (What comes first, according to show writers in demand, is the contract.)

With the great art-songwriters of the Elizabethan Age (John Dowland, Thomas Campion, half a dozen others), the words always came first, even though many of these highly talented men were also fine composers and wrote their own lute accompaniment. But already in that period were numerous instances where lyrics were fitted to music. This was done by satirists and parodists who, discarding the words of folk song and ballad, penned, quilled, if you like, new lyrics to the traditional tunes, lyrics which politicized, thumbed the nose, eulogized, or went in for out-and-out bawdry. (Lyric-transformation played quite a part also in early hymnody. In Germany, for instance, Martin Luther was a notable example of the hymnist who took many a secular song, well-known to the people and, retaining the tune, threw out the worldly lyric to substitute one of spiritual quality.)

The practice of putting new words to pre-existent song became more and more common, and led to the beginnings of ballad-opera. England's outstanding opus in this realm was Gay's *The Beggar's Opera*, London, 1728. This was so successful that it ran sixty-two nights, a new theatrical record that "stood unchallenged for almost a century." In the Heinemann edition (London, 1921) I count sixty-eight short "airs," chosen by Gay from the great store of English, Irish, and Scottish melodies, newly lyricized by the playwright.

SOURCE　*Saturday Review* (August 29, 1959): 31–33, 45.

Everyone knows that in the Gilbert and Sullivan operettas practically all the lyrics were written first. However, earlier in Gilbert's theatrical career he'd also had plenty of experience setting words to music. In the 1860s, many Extravaganzas and Burlesques of his, based on Continental operas, were produced in London. These were adapted by him into English with tricky lyrics and recitatives loaded with puns. Among them were Meyerbeer's *Robert le Diable*, which became *Robert the Devil; or The Nun, the Dun, and the Son of a Gun*, and Bellini's *Norma*, extravagandized to *The Pretty Druidess; or The Mother, the Maid, and the Mistletoe Bough*.

My favorite account of how songs are written was told to me second-hand many years ago. At a Christmas party in a music publishing house a shipping clerk was explaining to an impressed friend how hit-writer Walter Donaldson (who had just written both the words and the music of a hit) went about it: "Well, you see, he sort of gets the scope of the thing and then scopes it out."

The Babbitt and the Bromide. "It needs work" unquestionably applied to *Funny Face* when it opened in Philadelphia and looked like a failure. We were on the road six weeks, and everyone concerned with the show worked day and night, recasting, rewriting, rehearsing, recriminating, of rejoicing, there was none. "The Babbitt and the Bromide" was the final change. It went in on a Thursday or Friday night in Wilmington, when the audience consisted of no more than 200, mostly pretty and young and pregnant DuPont matrons (my wife's observation). The number was introduced at 10:50 and concluded with Fred and Adele Astaire doing their famous "run-around," to show-stopping applause, and suddenly, with all the other changes, the show looked possible. The week's business in Wilmington totaled $6,000. The following week we opened the new Alvin Theatre in New York and grossed $44,000.

Although our conception for performance of "Babbitt-Bromide" was that all the lines be sung in unison by Fred and Adele (as a dead-pan conversation carried on with neither listening to the other), they immediately felt it would be more effective nonsense to offer the phrases by turns:

FRED: Hello!
ADELE: How are you?
FRED: Howza folks?
ADELE: What's new?, etc.

Which presentation too was fine with us. Therefore the placement of this lyric in a duet category.

Fred and Vinton (Vinton Freedley, co-producer) won't recall this, but I made a mental note at the time: The day my brother and I demonstrated the song, Fred took me aside and said, "I know what a Babbitt is, but what's a Bromide?" Just about an hour later, in the Wilmington Hotel elevator, Vinton said to me, "I was brought up on Gelett Burgess and the Goops, so I know what a Bromide is, but what's a Babbitt?"

All through rehearsals Miss [Gertrude] Lawrence did "Jenny" most acceptably. But I kept wondering whether it would be as effective as the (deleted) Zodiac Song. This is what happened opening night in Boston. We were playing to a packed house, and the show was holding the audience tensely. It was working out. I was among the standees at the back of the house, next to me was one of the Sam Harris staff. In the circus scene when Danny Kaye completed the last note of "Tchaikovsky," thunderous applause rocked the theatre for at least a solid minute. The staff member clutched my arm, muttered "Christ, we've lost our star!," couldn't take it, and rushed for the lobby. Obviously he felt that nothing could top Danny's rendition, that "Jenny" couldn't compete with it, and that either Miss Lawrence would leave the show or that Danny Kaye would have to be cut down to size.

But he should have waited. The next few lines of dialogue weren't heard because of the continuing applause. Then, as Danny deferred to Miss Lawrence, it ended; and "Jenny" began. She hadn't been singing more than a few lines when I realized an interpretation was materializing we'd never seen at rehearsal. Not only were there new nuances and approaches, but on top of this she "bumped" it and "ground" it to the complete devastation of the audience. At the conclusion, there was an ovation which lasted twice as long as that for "Tchaikovsky." "Tchaikovsky" had shown us the emergence of a new star in Danny Kaye. But "Jenny" revealed to us that we didn't have to worry about losing our brighter-than-ever star.

It is easier to predict correctly what will happen to the stock market than what show numbers will do. One hopes for the best, but one best remain noncommittal. Not everyone does, though. Three or four nights after the Boston opening with "Lady" looking like a big hit, Kurt [Weill] told me he hadn't wanted to worry me but this is what occurred after the dress rehearsal. Hassard Short, a top revue man of excellent taste who was in charge of the show's physical production and lighting, took Kurt aside and said, "If you'll take my advice, you boys had better get two new numbers ready in a hurry. You'll find that 'Jenny' and the Russian number won't make it."

Re The Verse. All I had to say was, "George, how about an Irish verse?" and he sensed instantly the degree of wistful loneliness I meant. Generally, whatever mood I thought was required, he, through his instinct and inventiveness, could bring my hazy musical vision into focus. Needless to say, this sort of affinity between composer and lyricist comes only after long association between the two.

There was a different kind of musical communication between George and his earliest Broadway producer. Alex Aarons was quite musical himself and had faith enough to sign George at nineteen for *La, La, Lucille*. Alex was fond at the time of at least twenty of George's tunes which had not as yet been written up lyrically, so he had no means of calling for any one of them by numeral or title. But he could request what he wanted to hear this way: Whisking his hand across George's shoulder he would say, "Play me the one that goes like *that*." Or, "Play the tune that smells like an onion." Or, "*You* know, the one that reminds me of the Staten Island Ferry." And so on. Though this mutual musical understanding didn't develop between them at their first meeting it didn't take too long. I met Alex a few weeks after George did and at Aarons's apartment heard five or six requests in this oblique manner.

Later, when George had many tunes on tap for me and I couldn't recall exactly the start of a particular one I wanted to discuss, I would visualize the vocal line and my forefinger would draw an approximation of its curves in the air. And more often than not he would know the tune I meant.

Nice Work If You Can Get It. Somewhere, long ago, I read an illustrated article about a number of cartoons rejected by the humorous weeklies, cartoons and drawings not for the family trade. One submitted to *Punch*, I think, was, I'm pretty sure, by George Belcher whose crayon specialized in delineating London's lowly. In this one, two charwomen are discussing the daughter of a third, and the first says she's heard that the discussee has become a bore. Whereat the second observes it's nice work if you can get it. And that's all I remember about this title. It's all pretty vague and, on further reflection, it could be that I'm all wrong and that the phrase was around before I ever saw the Belcher two-liner. Anyway—

As I See It. Q.E.D.It. In lyric writing it's nice work when you get hold of a seemly title, for that's half the battle. But what follows must follow through in the verse and refrain, whether the development is direct or oblique. In brief:

> *A title*
> *Is vital.*
> *Once you've it,*
> *Prove it.*

Dummy Title. After my brother played me a sixteen-bar tune which he thought might be the start of something for Sportin' Life in the Picnic Scene,

I asked for a lead sheet (the simple vocal line); and to remember the rhythm and accents better, I wrote across the top a dummy title, the first words that came to my mind: "It ain't necessarily so." (I could just as well have written "An order of bacon and eggs," "Tomorrow's the 4th of July," "Don't ever sell Telephone short," anything, the sense didn't matter. All I required was a phrase that accented the second, fifth, and eighth syllables to help me remember the rhythm.)

Struggling for two days with the tune, I came up with no eureka notion. Then I remembered I had once written a dummy title to a Vincent Youmans melody when we were working on *Two Little Girls in Blue*, and a couple of days later when Youmans asked if I had finished the song, I told him I hadn't as yet got a title. Youmans: "What do you mean? It's called 'Oh, Me, Oh, My, Oh, You.'" Me: "But that was only my dummy title." Nevertheless, Youmans insisted that he was crazy about that particular title, which was fine with me, because I couldn't think of anything else, and the song turned out to be the most popular in the show.

So I began to explore the possibilities of this dummy title. At one point I decided that troublemaker Sportin' Life, being among a group of religious Sons-and-Daughters-of-Repent-Ye-Saith-the-Lord picnickers, might try to startle them with a cynical and irreligious attitude. And what would certainly horrify his auditors would be his saying that some accounts in the Bible weren't necessarily so. Once I had the rhymes "Bible/li'ble" and "Goliath/dieth," I felt I was probably on the right track. George agreed. He then improvised the scat sounds, "Wa-doo, Zim team bodd e-oo." Together, in a week or so, we worked out the rather unusual construction of this piece, with its limerick musical theme, the crowd responses, the lush melodic middle, and the "ain't nessa, ain't nessa" coda. Happily, in all the years that the song has been around, I have received only one letter remarking on its possible irreverence.

"Resistance Hymn." During World War II, *Porgy and Bess* was somehow permitted by the Nazis to be produced at the Royal Opera House in Copenhagen. This song came "to be something like a resistance hymn in Nazi-occupied Denmark, ever since the evening when, after the grimly boastful routine broadcast of the German arena's usual victory communique, the Secret Danish underground radio had cheerfully cut in with a significant "It Ain't Necessarily So."

"I Suggested." Whether to Kurt or George or others, there must be, without counting, at least half a dozen uses of "I suggested" among my "informative annotations." These aren't put in for any credit-claiming purposes. If, once in a great while in deliberations with the composer, a short musical

phrase came to me as a possibility and was found acceptable to my collaborator, that didn't make me a composer. More often than not, as in "Sing Me Not
a Ballad," my suggestion arose from some musical phrase of the composer's
own, which he had overlooked or whose potentiality he was unaware of.
Here is example number two.

Sometime in the middle Twenties, my brother and I spent three weeks or
so with librettist Herbert Fields on a musical to be called *The Big Charade*. I
forget now why this project was dropped. Anyhow, we did some work on it,
including a pseudo-medieval march called "Trumpets of Belgravia." Years
later, when *Of Thee I Sing* was being written, my brother was dissatisfied with
several starts he had made for the opening, a political campaign marching
theme, which inevitably had to be titled "Wintergreen for President." One
day, out of the blue, I found myself humming these seven syllables to the
exact rhythm and tune of the cast-behind "Trumpets of Belgravia, / Sing ta-
ra, ta-ra, ta-ra. . . ." When I suggested this tune to its composer, his approval
was nonverbal but physical. He immediately went to the piano and "Trumpets of Belgravia" became the serendipitous musical start of "Wintergreen
for President."

Conclusion? The lyricist needn't be a musician, but if he is musically
inclined he can sometimes be of help to the composer. (Not that the composer can't be of help with suggestions to the lyricist but, in my experience,
alas, rarely. Really.)

III. FAME AND FORTUNE (1924–1930)

It is difficult to imagine the exhilaration of an energetic twenty-five-year-old man of humble ethnic origins who is suddenly catapulted not only to the forefront of a musical society but also to the heights of national celebrity. With the release of the Victor recording of *Rhapsody in Blue* on June 10, 1924, followed successively by the opening of George White's *Scandals of 1924* in June, *Primrose* in September, *Lady, Be Good!* in December, *Tell Me More* in April 1925, and the premiere of *Concerto in F* and *Tip-Toes* in December 1925, Gershwin put together a string of triumphs unequalled in his too-short career. Along with the accolades came instantaneous wealth, icon status, and the adoration of the complete strata of American society. George Gershwin had become, at an early age, the American ideal: talented, prolific, dashing, and articulate. Writers began to script his story, and soon he followed their lead.

17 Philip Furia: "Lady, Be Good!" (1996)

Although George Gershwin had written complete musical scores for *La, La Lucille* (1919), *A Dangerous Maid* (1921), *Our Nell* (1922), *The Rainbow* (1923), *Sweet Little Devil*, and *Primrose* (1924), it was not until the opening of *Lady, Be Good!* on December 1, 1924, that the composer laid claim to a solid Broadway success. The synergy created by the combination of lyrics by Ira (their first exclusive collaboration), the production team of Alex Aarons and Vinton Freedley, the vaudeville siblings Adele and Fred Astaire, and the always-popular duo-pianists Phil Ohman and Victor Arden was unbeatable. The show set a record run for the Gershwins that was surpassed only by *Rosalie*, 335 (1928) and *Of Thee I Sing*, 441 (1931).

If the Jazz Age, as F. Scott Fitzgerald claimed, was born with the May Day riots of 1918, the era came to full-blown adolescence at 3 P.M. on February 12, 1924, at New York's Aeolian Hall. Until the wail of Ross Gorman's clarinet glissando opened the premiere performance of *Rhapsody in Blue*, the afternoon's program had been a stuffy sequence of "jazzed" classical and "concretized jazz," put together by Paul Whiteman, the self-anointed "King of Jazz." Once George Gershwin strode to the piano to perform his *Rhapsody*, however, the program turned electric. Originally entitled *American Rhapsody* (until Ira Gershwin suggested a change after gazing at Whistler's brooding blue "nocturnes" and "symphonies" at the Metropolitan Museum), *Rhapsody in Blue* captured the rhythmic vitality of New York at the height of the Roaring Twenties. By the end of that year George and Ira Gershwin had infused the same Jazz Age spirit into musical comedy when *Lady, Be Good!*, their first successful musical, opened at the Liberty Theatre on December 1.

Before *Lady, Be Good!*, the fortieth musical produced in 1924, Broadway productions had run the gamut from sonorous operettas, such as *The Student Prince* and *Rose-Marie*, to flippantly satirical revues like the *Greenwich Village Follies* and the *Grand Street Follies*. When the Gershwins teamed up to write songs for *Lady, Be Good!*, the American musical theater finally found its native idiom. George's score revealed his assimilation of blues and jazz, and Ira's lyrics regis-

SOURCE Philip Furia, *Ira Gershwin: The Art of the Lyricist* (New York: Oxford University Press, 1996). All footnotes in this entry appear in the original source.

tered his equally hard-won skill at setting such music to the American vernacular. The Jazz Age was, above all, an era intoxicated with its own language—*The American Language*, as H. L. Mencken had pugnaciously dubbed it with his volume of 1919. By 1927 it was clear to another linguistic innovator, Walter Winchell, coiner of "pfft" and "whoopee," that the "slang capital of the world" was the area around Broadway and Forty-second Street. There the worlds of music and theater, newspapers and magazines, sport and gambling, collided. Figures such as Ring Lardner and Damon Runyon, Ben Hecht and Charles MacArthur, Dorothy Parker and Robert Benchley mingled at the Algonquin Round Table, Jack Dempsey's Café, and Lindy's. Out of that Babel emerged a "talk of the town" that Jack Conway of *Variety* acclaimed as the "national slanguage": terms like "ballyhoo," "click," "hit," "fan," "flop," "baloney," "turkey," "cinch," "hooch," "phoney," "racket," and "squawk," as well as such phrases as "Sultan of Swat," "Yes, We Have No Bananas," and Tex Guinan's greeting to the "big butter-and-egg men" who frequented her "speakeasies": "Hello, Suckers!" In 1937, after having edited several editions of *The American Language*, H. L. Mencken looked back upon Broadway in the 1920s and proclaimed: "It is from this quarter that most American slang comes."[1]

In *Lady, Be Good!*, and a string of Jazz Age musicals that followed in its wake, Ira Gershwin set that language—its terms like "crush" and "mush," phrases such as "It's all bananas," and even " 's wonderful" way of clipping syllables from words—to his brother's music. The shows that provided the Gershwin brothers the opportunity to work their alchemy were produced by Alex Aarons and Vinton Freedley, two men who set out to resuscitate the Princess Theatre tradition but jazzed up for the new decade with larger-scale productions and greater emphasis on dancing. Originally, however, Aarons and Freedley planned to have P. G. Wodehouse supply the lyrics for their shows. In turning from Jerome Kern to George Gershwin, the producers felt they had given the Princess tradition enough of a Jazz Age face-lift and could retain Guy Bolton to write the book and Wodehouse the lyrics.

George, however, envisioned something beyond a resuscitation of the Princess shows. As he described it to his father one night, his ambition was to "write an absolutely new type of musical show, with modernistic words as well as modernistic tunes." "But where," he wondered aloud, "can I find a librettist? The well-known guys want the show written their way." "Try Ira," was Morris Gershwin's reply.[2] Whether it stemmed from fraternal (and pater-

1 William R. Taylor, "Broadway: The Place That Words Built," *Inventing Times Square: Commerce and Culture at the Crossroads of the World*, ed. William R. Taylor (New York: Russell Sage Foundation, 1991).
2 John B. Kennedy, "Words and Music," *Collier's* (September 28, 1928): 52.

nal) loyalty, George's decision was a fortuitous one, for the songs the Gershwins wrote for *Lady, Be Good!* and the other Aarons and Freedley musicals
that followed during the decade had a rhythmic "thrust" that was their hall-
mark. That overall pace was quickened with energetic dance numbers, black-
outs, and "crossovers" (brief musical scenes played in front of the curtain
while scenery was changed, keeping the "action in a state of nearly perpetual
motion."[3] Even the scenery, designed along sleek and gleaming Art Deco
contours by Norman Bel Geddes, was as streamlined as the Gershwins' songs
and reflected the world of the "smart set"—luxury hotels, country clubs, and
playboy mansions.

To achieve that all-important thrust a show had to be extensively doctored
throughout rehearsals—and sometimes even after opening night. Songs had
to be rewritten, shunted from scene to scene, thrown out or tossed in, all in
the interests of that magical rhythm. Since the book was constantly undergoing revision, a lyricist was well advised not to integrate his song too closely
into a dramatic situation or tie it to a particular character whose role might
be cut after the next rehearsal. It was rhythmic pace, rather than integration
between songs and story, that melded these shows into organic wholes. Not
only did the book not matter, the fact of its not mattering—its open display of
its own frivolousness—highlighted the energetic fusion of the other elements
of the show—the dances, the sets, and, above all, the songs.

When the stars of *Lady, Be Good!*, the brother-and-sister dance team of
Fred and Adele Astaire, first read the script, they thought it was "pretty stupid." Although it met their demand that they no longer be cast as lovers but
as brother and sister, Adele worried about the "tacky book" and "weak plot"
right up to the out-of-town opening in Philadelphia. Fred, however, reassured
her: "I told her that I thought this was one instance where it might not matter
because the whole thing had a new look to it, a flow, and also a new sound.
... This was no hackneyed ordinary musical comedy. It was slick and tongue-
in-cheek, a definite departure in concept and design."[4]

Fred Astaire's concerns about the book had been allayed from the moment
he first heard the song "Oh, Lady Be Good," which indicated to him how genuinely new—"smart and slickly paced"—this musical was to be. "Oh, Lady Be
Good" so epitomized the spirit of this musical that once Guy Bolton and Fred
Thompson heard it they changed the title of the show from *Black-Eyed Susan*
to *Lady, Be Good!* Years later, the sculptor Isamu Noguchi, who created a
streamlined, modernist bust of George Gershwin, marveled at the song's abil-

---

3 Lehman Engel, *The American Musical Theater* (New York: Macmillan, 1967), 30.
4 Fred Astaire, *Steps in Time* (New York: Harper, 1959).

ity to transfix the "timely, yet timeless image of an era"[5]—the heady, glistening aura of the Jazz Age. The title itself was a 1920s slang plea for sexual favors, which, Ira found, could serve as a ready-made fit for George's plaintive blue-note melody. The whole lyric is confected of tongue-in-cheek catch-phrases, from "I tell you I am so awf'ly misunderstood" to "I'm going to end it all." Together they form a seamless fabric, woven through with perfectly "singable" long vowels and even some clever light-verse rhymes:

> *I must win some*
> *winsome miss;*
> *can't go on like this.*

While it gave the show its title, "Oh, Lady Be Good" was not at all integral to the book. Sung not by a lover pleading for romance but by a lawyer beseeching the aid of the heroine in his latest scheme, even lines such as "please have some pity—I'm all alone in this big city" are completely unrelated to the setting—a country estate in Rhode Island.

Equally imbued with the energetic pace of *Lady, Be Good!* (and equally irrelevant to the book) was "Fascinating Rhythm," the biggest hit to emerge from the show. As a recent discovery has revealed,[6] George had previously written a composition called "Syncopated City" (another reflection of his fascination with the rhythm of New York in the Jazz Age). When he played it for the producers, Alex Aarons asked him to save it for a future musical. As the brothers Gershwin set to work on *Lady, Be Good!*, George played "Syncopated City" and suggested he and Ira adapt it into a song for the show. Frances Gershwin, their sister, recalled Ira's reaction to the music: "George, what kind of a lyric can I write for that?" Then, after a pause, he mused, "Still...it is a fascinating rhythm." While that bemused phrase, as Ira himself said, was not "the brilliant title," it "did sing smoothly."[7]

Not only was the title-phrase singable, it fit the asymmetrical pattern of George's melody. Another composer would have handled the rhythm much more conventionally, giving his lyricist a simple sequence of parallel four-bar phrases, such as:

> *Fas-ci-na-ting rhy-thm! (rest)*
> *You've got me on the go! (rest)*

---

5 Robert Kimball and Alfred Simon, *The Gershwins* (New York: Atheneum, 1973), 39.

6 In 1982, a treasure trove of scores and manuscripts from shows by the Gershwins, Kern, and other songwriters was discovered at the Warner Brothers warehouse in Secaucus, N.J.

7 Ira Gershwin, *Lyrics on Several Occasions* (New York: Alfred A. Knopf, 1959), 173.

> *Fas-ci-na-ting rhy-thm! (rest)*
> *I'm all a-qui-ver! (rest).*

George Gershwin repeats his melodic fragment, but each time on a different beat and at a different point in each bar:

> *Fas-ci-nat-ing rhy-thm! (rest) You've*
> *got me on the go! (rest) Fas-ci-*
> *na-ting rhy-thm! (rest) I'm all a-*
> *qui-ver (rest) (rest).*

It's the "fascinating" that begins on the downbeat in measure two that catches the singer and listener by surprise, then by stretching that second "fascinating" across "the boundary between measures two and three," the "downbeat falls in the third measure without any new word to announce it—a downbeat both felt and missed."[8] The surprises are compounded, when, almost magically, words and rhythm come out right by the end of the fourth measure.

Not surprisingly, Ira said that "Fascinating Rhythm" was "the hardest song I ever had to fit words to."[9] Once he had come up with a title that fit George's unusual music, Ira went back to a song he had written in 1923, "Little Rhythm, Go 'Way," and reworked some of its phrases. In the earlier song he had set a much more conventional melody by William Daly and Joseph Meyer with such simple words as

> *It's so persistent*
> *the day isn't distant, I know,*
> *when I'll go mad.*

Inspired by George's intricate rhythm, Ira now recast those lines into the more vernacular—and percussively alliterative—

> *so darn persistent*
> *the day isn't distant*
> *when it'll drive me insane!*

Ira found that contractions keep a lyric colloquial, providing a verbal equivalent for George's frequent syncopations. In the most common of American

---

8 Gerald Mast, *Can't Help Singin': The American Musical on Stage and Screen* (Woodstock, N.Y.: Overlook Press, 1928), 72. I am indebted also to singer Brian Kent for the analysis of "Fascinating Rhythm."

9 "Trying to Interview the Gershwin Brothers," *Boston Globe* (December 13, 1931).

catch-phrases Ira discovered verbal shards that perfectly fit the rhythms of George's musical phrases: "take a day off," "run along," and "make it snappy."

"It was a tricky rhythm for those days," Ira said, "and it took me several days to decide on the rhyme scheme."[10] When he showed his rhymes to his brother, however, George did not approve. "There was many a hot argument between us," George recalled, "over where the accent should fall."[11] Ira thought the last two notes of each phrase were accented equally and thus called for strong masculine rhymes (a rhyme on a single, accented syllable, such as *wake, quake, a-shake*). George maintained that since his downbeat fell on the next to the last note of the bar, the verbal accent should fall there as well and wanted Ira to provide feminine rhymes (two-syllable rhymes, with the second syllable unaccented, such as *hopping, stopping*). "The ear just didn't get it," Ira admitted, until George "had to explain it to me" by conducting it; once he saw his brother's hands describe that "funny beat—*Tah-tee-ta-ta-tah-ta*—" Ira realized the need for feminine rhymes:

> *What a mess you're making!*
> *The neighbors want to know*
> *why I'm always shaking*
> *just like a flivver.*

In *"flivver"* he found not only a match for the tremulously romantic *"a-quiver"* that dangled at the end of his opening phrase but a nickname for the automobiles that set the new pace of American life in the 1920s. "When one considers," observed composer Arthur Schwartz, that Ira "was required to be brilliant within the most confining rhythms and accents," "Fascinating Rhythm" is "a truly phenomenal feat."[12] Where "Oh, Lady Be Good" is a sly and slangy Jazz Age proposition, "Fascinating Rhythm" captures the plight of a doped-out addict of the nervous energy of the era. In a recording made by the Astaires and George Gershwin during the London run of *Lady, Be Good!*, it is clearly Fred who has seized that new rhythm. While Adele sings the tricky chorus in a traditionally strict tempo, Fred experimented with a "rubato approach" that indicated he was "beginning to explore a new genre."[13] As he would prove again and again in musicals and films, Fred

10 Ira Gershwin, *Lyrics on Several Occasions*, 173.
11 Robert Kimball, *The Complete Lyrics of Ira Gershwin* (New York: Alfred A. Knopf, 1993), 48.
12 Deena Rosenberg, *Fascinating Rhythm* (New York: Dutton, 1991), 91.
13 *American Popular Song: Six Decades of Songwriters and Singers*, ed. James R. Morris, J. R. Taylor, and Dwight Blocker Bowers (Washington: Smithsonian Institution Press, 1984), 38–39.

Astaire was the singer who best captured the intricate musical and verbal interplay of a Gershwin song.

Lady, Be Good! fulfilled a dream George Gershwin had had years earlier when he was a plugger on Tin Pan Alley and Fred Astaire a young hoofer in vaudeville: "Wouldn't it be great," George had said back then, "if I could write a musical show and you could be in it?"[14] Fittingly, *Lady, Be Good!* also gave Fred Astaire a number in which he could step out on his own. Ever since he was four years old, when his mother packed him and Adele on a train and left Omaha for New York and vaudeville, Fred had always danced with his sister. Now that he and Adele were playing siblings rather than lovers, Fred *got* to do a solo.

The dance evolved one day during rehearsals, when he embellished one of George's melodies with an impromptu tap routine. The melodic line echoed the clarinet glissando that opens *Rhapsody in Blue*, and Ira found a ready-made fit for it in another of the era's catch-phrases, "The Half of It, Dearie, Blues." According to Astaire, the title-phrase originated with a female impersonator in vaudeville, then quickly became part of the period's argot. F. Scott Fitzgerald had used it in "May Day," a short story about the birth of the Jazz Age, where the heroine muses about an upcoming dance:

> . . . she would talk the language she had talked for many years—her line—made up of the current expressions, bits of journalese, and college slang strung together in an intrinsic whole, careless, faintly provocative, delicately sentimental. She smiled faintly as she heard a girl sitting on the stairs near her say, "you don't know the half of it, dearie!"[15]

Taking that catch-phrase, Ira shrewdly couched it within the "I've got the . . . blues" formula to create a perfect "line" for George's melody, a line that keeps the syntax driving forward, piling up its sinuous modifier until it reaches "blues":

> *I've got the—*
> *you don't know*
> *the half of it, dearie—*
> *blues.*

On the recording of *Lady, Be Good!* Astaire sings the long-limbed line in an extended rhythmic curve as effortless as one of his dance moves, then throws

14 Astaire, *Steps in Time*, 55.
15 F. Scott Fitzgerald, *Tales of the Jazz Age* (New York: Charles Scribner's Sons, 1922), 85–86.

in other slang terms, such as "bunk" and "duffer," with the steely precision of his taps. What Astaire said of George Gershwin also went for Ira: "He wrote for feet."[16]

Such vernacular songs set the rhythmic pace of *Lady, Be Good!* right from the opening number. When the curtain rose, Fred and Adele, just evicted from their apartment, are pluckily setting-up housekeeping on the street. As Adele searches for an outlet to plug in a lamp, a rain shower begins, and Fred nonchalantly launches into "Hang On to Me," a syncopated and colloquial reworking of the formulaic pollyanna weather song. As one critic noted, *Lady, Be Good!* "started at such a lively and melodious gait that it did not seem possible that it could last for any great time"; nevertheless as song flowed into song, "speed and hilarity and the lilting music were continuous."[17] Another singled out Ira for his contribution to that overall pace: "There is a decidedly humorous poesy to Ira Gershwin's lyrics which stamp them as the most distinctive words to music we have listened to in the longest time."[18]

Lady, Be Good! inaugurated a series of streamlined musicals that ran through the rest of the decade. All had the same basic components—which usually came in twos: the two producers, Alex Aarons and Vinton Freedley; a book, by two writers; an orchestra that featured the twin pianos of Phil Ohman and Victor Arden, and, of course, songs by the two Gershwins. After *Lady, Be Good!* and *Tell Me More* (1925), George thought it brought good luck if a show's title was kept to two words: *Tip-Toes* (1925), *Oh, Kay!* (1926), *Funny Face* (1927), *Treasure Girl* (1928), and *Girl Crazy* (1930). All of these shows placed a premium on songs of romantic euphoria and other upbeat sentiments that were the perfect basis for Ira Gershwin's linguistic playfulness. What was taboo in these shows, however, were songs of romantic heartache or loss. Even when a ballad with just a touch of wistfulness, such as "The Man I Love," threatened to slow the frenetic energy of the production, it was cut.

18   Ira Gershwin: Letter to Lou and Emily Paley (November 26, 1924)

The Gershwins' first complete musical score together featured the talents of a young brother- and-sister team straight from vaudeville, Fred and

---

16 S. N. Behrman, *People in a Diary* (Boston: Little, Brown, 1972), 256.
17 *New York Herald Tribune* (December 2, 1924).
18 *New York Sun* (December 1, 1924).

SOURCE Reprinted in Robert Kimball and Alfred Simon, *The Gershwins* (New York: Atheneum, 1973), 39–40.

Adele Astaire. In Ira's letter to their close friends, he describes some of the events surrounding this important breakthrough work.

Hotel Sylvania
Locust and Juniper Streets
Philadelphia, PA.
Wednesday
Nov. 26, 1924

Dear Lou and Em,

It is Wednesday 3 A.M. in room 917 at the above hotel and I was just about to pop off to bed when I bethought me I ought to send you word and music of what was what—(thou I say it who shouldn't) what I mean is I have only received a couple of postcards from you), however—

I was down to 8th Street some three weeks ago, and all was and were well. They told me you had sent a long letter and all was and were well with you, to say the least. Details were lacking, but I'm guessing wrong if you're not having a good time. I hope that last sentence makes sense but I can't be bothered at this hour...

Well, *Lady, Be Good!* looks pretty good. I enclose a couple of clippings. We did great business last (our first) week—over $21,000, but the show needs lots of fixing, the first half hour being very slow. I don't think it can be remedied either, before we open in New York City next Monday Dec. 1, at the Liberty (sounds like little Jerry). Still, I think it will take for a nice few months anyway. We wrote about twenty-two or -three numbers and have about half that in now, as the show was an hour or more too long opening night. They are:

(I)
1. Hang on to Me (Fred & Adele)
2. End of a String (Scene Opening)
3. Fascinating Rhythm (Fred & Adele & Ukulele Ike)
4. So Am I (Adele & Alan Edwards—very cute number)
5. Lady Be Good (Catlett & Girls)
6. Finale

(II)
1. Opening Chorus (6 Little Rainy Afternoon Girls)
2. We're Here Because (2 minor people)
3. Half of It Dearie Blues (Fred & his girl)
4. Juanita (Adele & Boys)

5. Leave It to Love (A number which goes in tomorrow replacing "Man I Love")
6. Ukulele Ike's Speciality (He sings 3 or 4 numbers—the first 2, "Little Jazz Bird" and "Singin Pete" by the Gershwins)
7. Carnival Dance by Company
8. Swiss Miss (Yodel #)
9. Finale

My lyrics will be all right, I suppose, but it's too bad I couldn't get some of the niftier-lyric'd songs in, like "M.Y.T. Sascha," "Oil-Well," "Bad Bad Men," "Wonderful How Love Can Understand."

George played at Carnegie Hall Nov. 15 with Whiteman and ran away with the concert as far as the criticisms went. The critics suddenly discovered that they loved classical music again and proceeded to high-hat jazz in their reviews. But where the *Rhapsody* was concerned they were very enthusiastic. Ernest Newman knocked the concert but was delighted with the *Rhapsody* and expressed himself in no uncertain terms. Geo. plays it here in Philly tomorrow with P. Whiteman at the Academy of Music. Incidentally tomorrow is Thanksgiving Day and with the holiday matinee *Lady, Be Good!* should play to $9,000 on the day which means $90 for Ira which is not so bad ...

Be Yourself left for the road last week, not having done so well for 12 weeks. *Scandals* leaves next week after a six-month run. *Primrose* is doing well in London—*S.L. Devil* not so good on the road. George has several offers to do London shows, Saxe (English producer here now) insisting that he leave with him next week. But G. needs a rest and I don't think he will leave until the middle of January.

George is in New York at this writing attending to some new orchestrations for the show. He returns tomorrow for the Whiteman concert ...

Honestly you must forgive me: it is now 4:10 by my Waltham, and I'm not responsible for anything I've written.

I've been pretty busy here the past 10 days, writing songs and rewriting verses and choruses.

Well, old boy and girl, you see how it is. It is now 4:15 and they are probably preparing breakfast in the hotel kitchen.

Write me a long letter, telling me all sorts of things, and asking me all sorts of questions.

And with all sorts of love to you both, I pop off.

Iz.

19 Alec Wilder: *"That Certain Feeling"* (1972)

Tip-Toes opened at the Liberty Theater in December 1925, the third musical the Gershwin brothers had penned and premiered in one year.
Although *Tell Me More* (April 13, 1925, for one hundred performances) had
limited success, *Tip-Toes*, with its first-rate cast of Queenie Smith, Allen
Kearns, Harry Watson, Jr., Andrew Tombes, and Jeanette MacDonald,
showcased a bevy of memorable hit songs including "Looking for a Boy,"
"That Certain Feeling," "Sweet and Low-Down," and "Nice Baby!"

Now comes "That Certain Feeling," also from *Tip-Toes*. To me this is mint
Gershwin. It is A-B-A^1-B^1, a conventional thirty-two bars, only three of them
containing syncopation. This simple fact brings to mind the curious paradox
that though Gershwin is considered the great "jazz" song writer, his songs
show less syncopation than do those of many other contemporary writers.
This may imply that the native song is less distinguishable by its syncopation
than by other, more rarefied elements.

One of these is boldness; another is wit. Still another is unexpectedness.
Syncopation is only the obvious device. The others aren't as simply arrived at,
and rarely can be effectively employed by means of analytical imitation by
someone with a love or flair for the idiom. For example, it seems to me that
Kurt Weill often manages the astute imitation without the quality of self-
involvement.

The most effective song I know written in the manner of the opening
measure of "That Certain Feeling" is "Why Was I Born?". But the former
(forgetting for the moment the lyrics and their mood) pleases me more by
means of a single eighth note in the third and its imitative measures. This
eighth note is as unexpected as the quarter rest and repeated *c*'s in the first
measure are bold. And it is not only unexpected, it is sly in its function of
"kicking" the rhythm.

Yes, this song is neat as a pin. For example, in the last phrase of the *B* section, (the song is A-B-A^1B^1), the thirteenth measure repeats the initial idea of

SOURCE *American Popular Song: The Great Innovators, 1900–1950* (New York: Oxford University Press,
1972; repr. 1990), 132.

a quarter rest followed by repeated identical quarter notes. In this case, they are repeated *D*'s. The fourteenth measure imitates the second measure, but then completely fools me by returning to repeated *D*'s in the fifteenth measure, resolving in the last quarter not *B* flat, tied syncopatedly to a whole note in the sixteenth measure. And notice the alternate half-note chords under this passage: *B* flat major and *G* minor. This constitutes style. Though there were subsequent writers who revered Gershwin and, consequently, imitate him, I believe I would know these four measures were Gershwin even if they were played isolatedly and for the first time.

In the second half of the song, I admire the way he raises the repeated notes each time they occur, particularly the *unexpected* series of *E* naturals. But then I am disappointed that they don't proceed to their begged-for destination, *F* natural. Instead, they drop back to *E* flat.

The song is so direct and unbusy, so strong without being aggressive, that I am doubly disturbed by this curious lapse. It certainly isn't due to the problem of wide range—always a hazard in popular music because of the average singer's narrow range. For if the *E* natural had been raised *F*, the song would have had a range of only an octave, a less-than-average range for a popular song and very narrow for a theater song. "That Certain Feeling" is the first in a long line of songs in which Gershwin's obsession with repeated notes is evidenced.

20 Carl Van Vechten: "George Gershwin, An American Composer Who Is Writing Notable Music in the Jazz Idiom" (1925)

Perhaps no single article provided a bigger punch for Gershwin's career than Carl Van Vechten's important endorsement here. It came at just the right time, for the frenzy following the premiere of the *Rhapsody in Blue* had finally settled. It struck just the right tone too, balancing popular and serious, European and American concerns. And it came from probably the single most important social critic in New York at the time, a man who sought out and supported what was new, noteworthy, and deserving of being so next.

I cannot recall the time when I did not feel an instinctive interest in American popular music. Before I could play a note on the piano I was humming or whistling such tunes as "Down Went McGinty" and "The Man Who Broke the Bank at Monte Carlo." A little later, the execrable, sentimental ballads of the early nineties, "Two Little Girls in Blue," "After the Ball," and "Dairy Bell" were tried on my piano along with two-hand arrangements of the symphonies of Mozart, Haydn, and Beethoven. When "At a Georgia Campmeeting" and "Whistling Rufus" appeared in 1899, I appreciated this indication of a modest advance in the public taste. It is worthy of note that Debussy's sensibility to ragtime progress no farther. His "Golliwogg's Cakewalk" is an exact replica of the naïve rhythmic form employed in these pieces.

On the other hand, I gave a real welcome to Cole and Johnson's "Under the Bamboo Tree," which I admire to this day. I further enjoyed the primeval syncopations of "Bill Bailey," "Ain't It a Shame?," "Ma Blushin' Rosie," "All Coons Look Alike to Me," "When You Ain't Got No Money You Needn't Come Around," "Hiawatha," and "Bon-Bon Buddy," but when I heard "Alexander's Ragtime Band" (1911) I shouted.

Here, at last, was real American music, music of such vitality that it made the Grieg-Schumann-Wagner dilutions of MacDowell sound a little thin, and

SOURCE *Vanity Fair* 24 (March 1925): 40, 78, 84.

the saccharine bars of "Narcissus and Ophelia," so much pseudo-Chaminade concocted in an American back-parlor, while it completely routed the so-called art music of the professors. At the time, however, I was serving as assistant to Richard Aldrich, the music critic of the *New York Times*. In other words, I was a person of no importance whatever. Had I spoken, I should not have been heard.

Several years later, however, Irving Berlin's masterpiece having been succeeded by other popular airs worthy of attention, such as "Everybody's Doing It," "The Gaby Glide," "Ragging the Scale," and "Waiting for the Robert E. Lee," I wrote a paper, entitled "The Great American Composer," published in *Vanity Fair* for April 1917, in which I outlined the reasons for my belief that it was out of American popular music that American art music would grow, just as the idiosyncratic national line of so much European music has evolved from the national folksong. Nearly seven years passed before my prophecy was realized, but on February 12, 1924, a date which many of us will remember henceforth as commemorative of another event of importance besides the birth of our most famous president, George Gershwin's *Rhapsody in Blue* was performed for the first time by Paul Whiteman's Orchestra with the composer at the piano.

There is, however, an historical prelude to the *Rhapsody*. In the spring of 1923, Eva Gauthier, indefatigable in her search for novelties, asked me to suggest additions to her autumn program. "Why not a group of American songs?" I urged. Her face betrayed her lack of interest. "Jazz," I particularized. Her expression brightened. Meeting this singer again in September, on her return from Paris, she informed me that Maurice Ravel had offered her the same sapient advice. She had, indeed, determined to adopt the idea and requested me to recommend a musician who might serve as her accompanist and guide in this venture. But one name fell from my lips, that of George Gershwin, whose compositions I admired and with whose skill as a pianist I was acquainted. The experiment was eventually made, Mme. Gauthier singing the jazz group on her program between a cluster of songs by Paul Hindemith and Bela Bartok on the one hand, and an air from Schönberg's *Gurrelieder* on the other. This recital, given at Town Hall on November 1, 1923, marked George Gershwin's initial appearance as a performer on the serious concert stage.

The occasion did not pass uncelebrated. Newspapers and magazines commented at length on the phenomenon. Jazz, at last, it seemed, had come into its own. Presently, Paul Whiteman, weary of conducting for dancers more ready to appreciate a rigid tempo than variety in orchestration or the superlative tone quality of his band, had a pendent inspiration: he would give a concert to demonstrate the growth that jazz had made under ears too careless and indolent to distinguish the fine scoring and the intricate harmonic and rhythmic features of the new music from the haphazard, improvised performances of a few years earlier. His second idea was even more noteworthy: he commissioned George Gershwin to write a composition to be included in his first concert program.

As I had been out of the city when Mme. Gauthier gave her revolutionary recital, she very kindly invited me, late in January 1924, to hear a rehearsal of the same program in preparation for her Boston concert. It was at this rehearsal that Gershwin informed me of Whiteman's plan and added, in rather an off-hand manner, that he had decided to compose a concerto in fantasia form for piano and jazz band which he proposed to call *Rhapsody in Blue*. On that day, about four weeks before the date the composition was actually produced, he had only made a few preliminary sketches; he had not yet even found the now famous *andantino* theme! He played for me, however, the jazz theme announced by full orchestra, accompanied by figurations on the piano, and the ingenious passage, not thematic, which ushers in the finale (omitted from the phonograph record). At the first rehearsal of the program for the concert, the score was not yet ready. At the second rehearsal Gershwin played the *Rhapsody* twice with the band on a very bad piano. Nevertheless, after hearing that rehearsal, I never entertained a single doubt but that this young man of twenty-five (he was born in Brooklyn, September 26, 1898) had written the very finest piece of serious music that had ever come out of America; moreover, that he had composed the most effective concerto for piano that anybody had written since Tchaikovsky's B flat minor.

Enthusiasm rewarded the first performance of the *Rhapsody*, but general and adequate appreciation of the glamour and vitality of the composition, exhibiting, as it does, a puissant melodic gift in combination with a talent for the invention of striking rhythms and a felicity in the arrangement of form, did not come so rapidly, perhaps, as a ready admiration for the composer's obviously rare skill as pianist. After Gershwin had performed the concerto several times in New York and other cities (Whiteman undertook a preliminary tour with his organization during the spring of 1924), recognition of its superior qualities became more widely diffused; the abridged phonograph disk (even both sides of a twelve-inch disk offer insufficient surface to record the piece in its entirety) added to its fame; and the publication of the score, arranged for two pianos, in December, sealed its triumph. It has since been performed, although seldom with the composer at the piano, at nearly every concert given by the Whiteman Orchestra. Two causes have interfered with more general performances: first, the fact that the work is scored for a jazz

band; second, the fact that the piano part is not only of transcendent difficulty but also demands a pianist who understands the spirit of jazz. I have no
doubt whatever but that so soon as an arrangement is made for symphony
orchestra the *Rhapsody* will become a part of the repertory of any pianist
who can play it. Quite possibly, the work may have its flaws; so, on the other
hand, has *Tristan und Isolde*.

The story of this young man's career is worthy of attention. Born in
Brooklyn, George Gershwin was brought up on Grand Street in Manhattan.
Until he arrived at the age of thirteen he never even thought about music.
Shortly after his thirteenth birthday his mother bought a piano, for no other
reason than because her sister-in-law had bought one and it seemed a proper
thing to do. Once the piano was installed, somebody had to learn to play it
and young George was elected. After he had received four months' lessons he
already performed sufficiently well so that one of his father's friends advised
that he be sent to Europe to study. This advice, fortunately, was not followed.
Three neighbourhood teachers, in turn, directed the course of his fingers.
Then, by a fortuitous accident, he fell into the hands of a man who gave him
his first real reverence for music. This was Charles Hambitzer from whom he
received his first lessons in harmony. He was working on the Chopin *Préludes*
when this teacher died. Gershwin was as yet unfamiliar with the work of
Bach, Beethoven, Schumann, Schubert, or Brahms. A little later, he studied
harmony with Edward Kilenyi, but the full course of his instruction with his
several teachers occupied less than four years. In the meantime, George had
become acquainted with Max Rosen, for whose playing he felt a deep admiration, but Rosen offered him no encouragement. "You will never become a
musician. Give up the idea," was the violinist's candid advice.

Very early in his piano lessons he began to dabble in composition. A banal
"Tango" appears to be the earliest preserved example. "Ragging the
Träumerei," in 4-4 time, is written down in 2-4 and runs to twenty-one
mediocre bars. At this same period—he was about fifteen—he started a song
which began in F and wandered into G, from which region George found
himself utterly unable to rescue it.

At the age of sixteen, George went to work as a song plugger for Remick,
the music publisher, sometimes playing all day for vaudeville acts and until
two or three in the morning at cafés. His remuneration was fifteen dollars a
week. This irksome routine might have ruined his fingers for future concert
playing but Charles Hambitzer had instructed him to play with a "loose
wrist," a piece of advice which saved him his "touch." As a matter of fact, this
engagement did him a real service inasmuch as it taught him to transpose, no
two performers ever being able to negotiate a song in the same key. Further

vagaries of fortune led him to accept an opportunity to play the piano for the chorus rehearsals of Ned Wayburn's *Miss 1917*. It was here that he began to develop variety in his accompaniments, playing each repetition of a refrain in a different manner, a procedure which won encouragement from his employer, as it served to keep up the interest of the girls in their monotonous round of steps. It taught George the trick of lending individuality to the accompaniments of his songs. While he was playing for the chorus, Vivienne Segal sang two of his songs at a Sunday night concert at the Century Theatre. Harry Atkins, manager of *Miss 1917*, was so impressed with these tunes that he brought them to the attention of Max Dreyfus of the firm of T. B. Harms who, immediately recognizing the ability of the young musician, put him under contract. Eight months later, Gershwin wrote "I Was So Young and You Were So Beautiful" and found himself launched as the composer of a song hit.

Launched, but not satisfied. It usually happens that a manufacturer of jazz hits goes so far and no farther. Many popular composers are content to languidly pick tunes out with one finger on the piano, while an expert harmonizer sits by ready to step in. It is not even an infrequent occurrence for a man's first success in the field to be his last. Gershwin apparently determined not only to hold onto his success but to improve upon it. His friends and business associates advised him not to study harmony. He answered them by working with Rubin Goldmark from whom, he assures me, he received invaluable suggestions, especially in regard to form. He was warned that the *Rhapsody in Blue* would kill interest in his lighter music. It has had the opposite effect; he instinctively felt that it would have.

I first became acquainted with Gershwin's music through his "Swanee," written in 1919 for the revue which opened the Capitol Theatre. With "I'll Build a Stairway to Paradise," written for the fourth of George White's *Scandals*, I completely capitulated to his amazing talent and nominated him to head my list of jazz composers. In this vein he has added to his fame with the "Yankee Doodle Blues," "The Nashville Nightingale," "Do I Again," "Won't Say I Will," "Somebody Loves Me," and the present ubiquitous "Fascinating Rhythm."

The time has not come, of course, to appraise the fellow's work. One can only predict his future in terms of his brief past. His career up to date, it will be observed, has been a steady crescendo of interest. What he will do in the future depends on no one but George Gershwin, but it is fairly evident that ample opportunities will be offered him to do many things that he ought not to do. He is unusually prolific in melodic ideas; his gift for rhythmic expression is almost unique; he has a classical sense of form. His gay music throbs with pulse, a beat, a glamorous vitality rare in the work of any composer and already he has the power to build up a thrilling climax, as two or three passages in the *Rhapsody* prove. Even his popular music is never banal. There is always something—if it is only two bars, as in the case in "Rose of Madrid"—to capture the attention of even a jaded listener. Tenderness and passion are as yet only potential attributes of his published music—it might be stated in passing that the two are qualities that Stravinsky lacks—but some of Gershwin's finest inspirations have not as yet been either published or publicly performed. It is probable that the production of his twenty-four piano preludes and his tone-poem for symphony orchestra, tentatively entitled *Black Belt*, will award him a still higher rank in the army of contemporary composers.

Ernest Newman has remarked, in reference to jazz, that there are no such things as movements, there are only composers. Obviously, quite true. Nevertheless, I am just as certain that the *Rhapsody* came out of the jazz movement in America as I am that Weber's *Der Freischutz* came out of the German folksong. Negro spirituals, Broadway, and jazz are Gershwin's musical god parents. Whatever he does, or however far he goes in the future, I hope that these influences will beneficently pursue him.

21   Samuel Chotzinoff: "New York Symphony at Carnegie Hall" (1925)

Gershwin family friend Samuel "Chotzie" Chotzinoff wrote some of the best reviews of Gershwin's music in the 1920s. His view of the first performance of the *Concerto in F* is among the best he wrote and among the best considerations of the work.[1]

The long and eagerly awaited *Concerto in F* by George Gershwin jammed Carnegie Hall to its capacity yesterday afternoon when it was presented for the first time by Mr. Damrosch and the Symphony Society. Mr. Gershwin's concerto, like Deems Taylor's symphonic poem "Jurgen," was commissioned by the Symphony Society; but Mr. Taylor's poem, except for the interest of its title, did not cause the anticipatory excitement that followed the announcement of the commissioning of Mr. Gershwin's first attempt at symphonic form.

SOURCE   *New York World* (December 4, 1925): 16.
   1 For a well-wrought consideration of the work, see Charles Hamm's thoughts on the second movement in his "A Blues for the Ages," in Richard Crawford, R. Allen Lott, and Carol J. Oja, eds., *A Celebration of American Music: Words and Music in Honor of H. Wiley Hitchcock* (Ann Arbor: University of Michigan Press, 1990), 346–55.

Every day sees the presentation of some novelty and there are many organizations in New York for encouragement of new works; but so far, in spite of numerous alarms, nothing of any real value has emerged. Last year Mr. Gershwin came straight from Tin Pan Alley to a Whiteman concert of jazz at Aeolian Hall with a *Rhapsody in Blue*, which set everybody by the ears and gave to the future of American music an unexpected twist.

The excellence of the rhapsody was a bolt from the blue, for Mr. Gershwin was widely known as a good musical-comedy composer, a writer of fetching tunes and rhythms in the prevailing fashion. The piece was a lengthy flight compared to the composer's musical-comedy numbers, but there were those, even among his admirers, who considered the rhapsody one of those accidents which happen once in a lifetime—something that cannot be explained and certainly cannot be repeated.

When Mr. Damrosch rashly ordered the concerto there was a great deal of headshaking and inquiries about where Mr. Gershwin would get the knowledge required for the handling of a symphonic work, what would be the nature of his material, &c; and, as a matter of fact, Mr. Gershwin himself modestly disclaimed any knowledge of musical form. But, after all, there was the *Rhapsody in Blue*, which was as big an advance over his previous work as the concerto would be over the rhapsody. Mr. Gershwin intimated that he would trust to luck.

But it was not luck that carried the composer of the rhapsody to success, and luck alone would never have created the *Concerto in F* heard yesterday afternoon. The truth is that George Gershwin is a genius—perhaps the only one of all the younger men who are trying with might and main to express the modern spirit. You may cite his deficiencies as evidenced by his latest work—they are obvious. He is not a master of form; he is audaciously irresponsible and writes down, apparently, whatever he feels, indiscriminately. He lacks depth, and it seems that because of his lifelong environment he never will be able to rid himself of jazz, no matter how he sublimates it.

But all his shortcomings are nothing in the face of the one thing he alone of all those writing the music of to-day possesses. He alone actually expresses us. He is the present, with all its audacity, impertinence, its feverish delight in its motion, its lapses into rhythmically exotic melancholy. He writes without the smallest hint of self-consciousness and with unabashed delight in the stridency, the gaucheries, the joy and excitement of life as it is lived right here and now. But that is not all, since every jazz band in every night club in America does just this.

And here is where his genius comes in, for George Gershwin is an instinctive artist who has that talent for the right manipulation of the crude material he starts out with that a life-long study of form and harmony and counterpoint and fugue never can give to one who is not born with it.

The composition begins with a passage on the kettledrums exactly like the Beethoven violin concerto. But whereas Beethoven's drums intone their four beats modestly, Mr. Gershwin's drummers do not roast like sucking doves but smash away boldly and challengingly, as they should in this age. There follows a broad and insistent melody with shifting harmonies underneath it, and orchestra and piano break into a magnificent Charleston, and the Charleston, by the way, seemed last night as good and authentic material for symphonic treatment as anything that was ever used.

This first movement moved along almost always with broad fervor and genuine vitality, though at moments the composer's powers for thematic development dropped to zero. But it is to Mr. Gershwin's great credit that he didn't resort in these crises to padding, but calmly began on something else, so that the composition never lagged, but was continually revitalized.

The slow movement, a Blues whose themes closely resembled the fine Negro improvisations of that name, notably the "St. Louis Gal," is to my mind a masterpiece. I can recall nothing in modern music so beautiful, so haunting, so "kiddingly" melancholy. In it Mr. Gershwin revealed a delicate imagination and a remarkable sense for mood. I am not quite sure of the enduring quality of the concerto as a whole, but it seems to me that the Andante of Mr. Gershwin's concerto will remain beautiful for a very long time.

Mr. Gershwin played his concerto excellently and simply and disposed of its difficulties as if he had been a concert pianist all his life. He vitalizes his music with an inborn natural rhythm, and his flair for jazz playing and a peculiar languorous though rhythmic manner in the execution of Blues made his contribution to the performance a delight.

The same cannot be said of Mr. Damrosch and the Symphony Orchestra, who apparently didn't know exactly what to do with the strange work. Mr. Damrosch should have visited "Connies" in Harlem to find out just how to play a Charleston, and the only resemblance of the trumpet played yesterday to the same instrument in a good jazz band (which would have played the music perfectly) was the derby hat which covered it.[2]

Altogether the orchestral portion of Mr. Gershwin's work was hardly in the spirit of the composition. There was no finesse and a great deal of noise. Perhaps the right accompaniment could only have been supplied by Paul Whiteman, whose interpretative flair for just such music is akin to Mr. Gershwin's.

---

2 Connie's Inn, at Seventh Avenue and 131st Street, was owned and operated by George and Connie Immerman during the 1920s. Considered one of the top clubs in Harlem, it presented top entertainers to an all-white clientele.

22   *Lawrence Gilman: "Mr. George Gershwin Plays His New Jazz Concerto" (1925)*

Lawrence Gilman was another of the critics from the world of concert music who devoted attention to Gershwin's work fairly early on. Here he ponders Gershwin's "jazz concerto" by applying each of those terms to the work's content, concluding that the vitality of the former makes dependence on the latter burdensome.

Although both the program and the program notes at yesterday afternoon's Symphony concert austerely forbore to mention the fact, Mr. Gershwin's *Concerto in F* for piano and orchestra was, of course, none other than the already famous "Jazz Concerto" about which every one has been talking since it became known that Walter Damrosch had commissioned the illustrious composer of the *Rhapsody in Blue* to write a work of symphonic scope for performance under his direction. A crowd of almost Paderewskian proportions sloshed in out of the deluge to witness Mr. Gershwin's nuptials with the symphonic Muse. Mr. Gershwin was thunderously acclaimed. There was no doubt whatever of the popular delight in his achievement.

Mr. Damrosch, with his customary geniality, had welcomed the young lovers far down the street. Moreover, he had explained and justified the match to possibly dubious friends and relatives of the bride and groom.

"Various composers," he had told us, "have been walking around jazz like a cat around a plate of very hot soup, waiting for it to cool off, so that they could enjoy it without burning their tongues, hitherto accustomed only to the more tepid liquid distilled by cooks of the classical school. Lady Jazz, adorned with her intriguing rhythms, has danced her way around the world, even as far as the Eskimos of the north and the Polynesians of the South Sea Isles. But for all her travels and her sweeping popularity, she has encountered no knight who could lift her to a level that would enable her to be received as a respectable member in musical circles.

"George Gershwin seems to have accomplished this miracle. He has done it by boldly dressing this extremely independent and up-to-date young lady in the classic garb of a concerto. Yet he has not detracted one whit from her fascinating personality. He is the prince who has taken Cinderella by the hand and openly proclaimed her a princess to the astonished world, not doubt to the fury of her envious sisters."

We shall venture to amend Mr. Damrosch's engaging metaphor. Mr.

SOURCE   *New York Herald Tribune* (December 4, 1925): 19.

Gershwin has of course been keeping company with the lady whom we may call, not quite Cinderella, but Jazzerella, for quite a while. But now, desirous of moving in rather more genteel musical circles, and abetted by the excellent Mr. Damrosch, he seems to have stowed Jazzerella away in a flat in 135th Street, and to have sued successfully for the hand of a more patrician damsel further downtown—Euterpe, no less; and, unless we are a very poor reporter, it was Mr. Gershwin's marriage with this lady that we were privileged to witness yesterday.

To be sure, Jazzerella had left her mark on Mr. Gershwin (they usually do, the Jazzerellas of this world). A self-willed and strong-minded lady, she had not yielded him to gentility without a struggle; and Mr. Gershwin—a likable and manly Prince they say—has not attempted to conceal the fact that he owes her more than a little. But, to be quite frank, we cannot help wishing that the insidious Mr. Damrosch had left them alone, the Prince and Jazzerella. A handsome and congenial pair, they were self-sufficient, adequately contributive to their world. Mr. Damrosch, we fear, has succeeded only too well in his subtle scheme of uplift.

The trouble with Mr. Gershwin in this new phase of his is that in achieving respectability he has achieved also tameness and conventionality which, as he should know, so often happens. We need not discuss the question whether his *Concerto in F* is good jazz or not; that seems to us relatively unimportant beside the question whether it is good music or not; and we think it is only fairish music—conventional, trite, at its worst a little dull.

We listened with uncomfortably strained ears to catch a hint of that self-confident and untrammeled Young America which should long since have been striding over the hill. We wanted to hear a new sort of melodic line—far flung, daring, individual, full of tang and savor. We wanted to find an harmonic texture rich in new colors, fresh significations. Above all we wanted and hoped to discover a manipulation of characteristic rhythms which should emancipate them from the rigidity and monotony of the formulas of our time.

We wanted, in short, to hear a young American composer talking confidently, bravely, irrepressively, of himself. Instead we heard a facile and anxiously conformist youth stalking the stale platitudes of the symphonic concert hall—retailing exhausted clichés which were none too fresh when Rachmaninoff used them; remembering Tchaikovsky; remembering, discreetly, Stravinsky; not scrupling to relapse upon harmonic banalities, offering us the common coin of sentimental melody; using the old jazz meters in the familiar ways, and scoring all this for an orchestra singularly blatant, thick and inexpressive.

With Mr. Gershwin's desire to write what is called "serious" music (as opposed to what is called "popular" music) one has the liveliest sympathy. But we do not think that he has succeeded in demonstrating what is, after all, the essential difference between the two. The difference between "serious" music and "popular" music is not in any degree a difference in form or purpose or scope: it is nothing more portentous than a difference in the quality of the musical ideas involved. The waltz in *Die Meistersinger* is a far gayer and lighter thing than the waltz in *The Merry Widow*, which is heavy footed by comparison; yet Wagner's waltz is called "serious" music, and Lehar's "popular," for no better reason than because the first has distinction of musical thought and the second has merely adhesiveness.

If Mr. Gershwin is seeking what Mr. Damrosch calls "musical respectability," and what others call "recognition as a serious composer," he will not attain it merely by the seductively simple method described by Mr. Damrosch: by adopting "the classical garb of the concerto" or the symphony or sonata or suite. It is not so easy as all that. He can attain it, we think, only by paying no heed to those who warn him to be discreet and well mannered. He does not need a course in tonal etiquette. Learning which symphonic fork to use and what to say to the double basses while advancing toward your hat and coda, and when a perfect cadence is a little vulgar—these things will not suffice.

What Mr. Gershwin needs is to forget what other "respectable" composers have said before him in the conventional forms. If Rachmaninoff has used the fork on the extreme left, let Mr. Gershwin clamor for chopsticks, or use his knife. Let him forget to be polite, conformist. Let him build a cabin on some distant hilltop and soak his spirit in the wind and sun and rain, renouncing the ways of sophisticates and routiniers, listening for the voice that may, some day, speak to him out of the loneliness—his own voice, using his own idiom, which we like to think would be clear, and racy, and perturbing, and altogether welcome and reassuring.

23 *"Paul Whiteman Gives 'Vivid' Grand Opera; Jazz Rhythms of Gershwin's '135th Street' "(1925)*

One notable difference between the 1922 premiere of *Blue Monday* and its 1925 revival as *135th Street* (with the name changed to better reflect the story's Harlem locale) was simply that Gershwin's work was now the fea-

SOURCE *New York Times* (December 30, 1925): 10.

ture and not merely an afterthought. In fairness, this was part of Whiteman's aim, and in this way he was successful and helpful for Gershwin.
The concert performance (without sets and costumes) at Carnegie Hall
described here was an attempt to recoup the previous press garnered by
Whiteman's first "Experiment." This did not really happen.

Twenty minutes of as vivid "grand opera" as has yet been provided from
native and local materials by an American composer finished a two-hour concert of glorified "jazz" by Paul Whiteman's Orchestra last evening in
Carnegie Hall. The entire program is to be repeated in the same place on Friday night, when there will be opportunity for critical consideration both of
George Gershwin's one-act "135th Street" and of Deems Taylor's "Circus
Day" and other novel music that preceded it. Of the popular enjoyment last
night's first audience left never a doubt.

Mr. Gershwin's music, whether or not it proves the "grandest," was certainly the first in an opera première to be whistled within the hour on Broadway. On a stage dedicated once by Tchaikovsky, under the remembered
Paderewski lights and in the presence of a typical house, Blossom Seeley and
Charles Hart acted the swift tragedy of Harlem Mike's Saloon, with its "pro-
logue" by Jack McGowan, "just like the white man's opera."

An audience in which hundreds had stood for the two hours before, while
many restless feet kept time to the changing jazz rhythms, got its thrill at the
finale. Half a dozen short lilting songs, as many spoken retorts in the dramatic action, and then a pistol shot cracked noisily. Hart as the cheap gambler
died game, with the dancing chorus and the bar attendants, Benny Fields and
Francis Howard, taking up the tenor's refrain, "I'm goin' South in the
mornin'."

The song was sung by the crowd applauding out in front, it echoed later in
the lobbies and was still in the air when a street full of limousines came surg-
ing to the carriage calls. Mr. Gershwin bowed with Whiteman and the singers
from the stage. Mr. Taylor, whose "Circus" earlier set the house in a roar,
could not be found for a curtain call, and Mr. Whiteman made a speech for
him, saying, "I've no doubt he's just as unhappy and scared as I am."

Ferde Grofé, who arranged for jazz orchestra both the opera and the principal suite, had his own place first on the bill with "A Tone Journey," subtitled
"Mississippi." Individually there were encores for Chester Hazlitt's saxophone
solo, for Whiting and Kahn's ukulele song "Dust," for Perrella and Turner's
two-piano turn, which began with Chabrier's *Espagna*, and finally for an
unnamed violin juggler, who also played a tune with a bicycle pump before
the solos of "Meet the Boys."

Walter Damrosch, Henry Hadley, and other conductors and composers went backstage at the close of the concert to congratulate the virtuoso players and all concerned in their program.

24 George Gershwin: *"Our New National Anthem"* (1925)

The bulk of Gershwin's published writings concern the much-debated, ripe topic of his age: jazz and its current and possible future role in American music. Gershwin first explored this issue in print in the following essay from mid-1925.

The true importance of jazz in American music is a subject over which controversy has raged back and forth. There are those who condemn the new idiom, root and branch, and there are those who profess to see in it the new musical evangel. The former brand jazz as expressive of all that is ugly in modern life, condemning it as destructive of beauty, taste, and all that goes towards artistic progress; the latter hail it as the germ of a new school of music, a school essentially American. I myself tend more to the latter than the former, but I am far from going to the extreme limit of believing that jazz is going to revolutionize music or even American music. Jazz will in time become absorbed into the great musical tradition as all other forms of music have been absorbed. It will affect that music, but it will be far from being a predominant element. It will in short find its place.

Indeed, there are many signs that it is already finding its place. The blatant jazz of ten years ago, crude, vulgar, and unadorned, is passing. In my *Rhapsody in Blue* I have tried to crystallize this fact by employing jazz almost incidentally, just as I employ syncopation. I realize that jazz expresses something very definite and vital in American life, but I also realize that it expresses only one element. To express the richness of that life fully, a composer must employ melody, harmony, and counterpoint as every great composer of the past has employed them. Not of course, in the same way, but with a full knowledge of their value. It was in this belief that I determined to make a serious study of composition. Many of my friends advised me not to do this, saying that it would destroy my originality. I replied that every composer of the past who had added anything vital to music had been a well-trained musician and that I was convinced that the native talent which can be killed by study must be too frail to amount to much. I felt the rhythms of American

SOURCE *Theatre Magazine* (August 1925).

life, and in my music I had expressed them as best I could, but I knew I had gone as far as I could. To realize the richness of life, a knowledge of the past and of its technique was always needed. The future lies with the composer who, without forgetting the innate impressions of his youth, can employ in their expression the full resources of the masters of the past. It is only in this way that jazz can become of lasting value.

In speaking of jazz there is one superstition, and it is a superstition which must be destroyed. This is the superstition that jazz is essentially Negro. The Negroes, of course, take to jazz, but in its essence it is no more Negro than is syncopation, which exists in the music of all nations. Jazz is not Negro but American. It is the spontaneous expression of the nervous energy of modern American life....

The more one studies the history of jazz during the last fifteen years the more one realizes that it is following precisely the same course that all dances of the past have followed. Beginning with crudity and vulgarity, it has gradually been freeing itself and moving towards a higher plane. At first it was mere discord for the sake of discord, a simple reveling in animal vigor. But slowly the meaning of that discord, its color, its power in the depiction of American sentiment, has been brought to life. The discord of jazz is today no mere succession of meaningless and ugly grunts and wheezes. That these are still there is no doubt true, but then modern life is, alas! not expressed by smooth phrases. We are living in an age of staccato, not legato. This we must accept. But this does not mean that out of this very staccato utterance something beautiful may not be evolved. We all remember the ugliness of the early skyscraper architecture. We all remember the attacks hurled against this architecture, attacks justified in themselves yet oblivious to the beauty possible in the future. Today with such structures as the Woolworth Tower and the new Hotel Shelton we begin to realize that the skyscraper can be as beautiful as it is original. The same result will happen, I feel certain, in the case of jazz. Ugly at first, it is already feeling the touch of the beautiful. When at last it takes its proper and subordinate place in music, none of us will regret that it has come.

There is one great difficulty, however, in the employment of jazz that is extremely difficult for the composer to overcome. It is almost impossible to write down definitely, exactly, the effects wished, with the result that the musicians are only too apt to exaggerate their expression, and, if allowed to have their way, to twist the composition utterly away from the composer's intention. This is, of course, up to the conductor, who must be continually on the lookout and who must rule his musicians' fancy with an iron hand. Indeed, when a conductor undertakes to direct a work in which jazz plays an important part, he must be even more jealous of the composer's intention than if he were conducting a classical symphony. Once give the musicians their head with jazz, and in a short while they will evolve something which the author himself will fail to recognize as his own offspring.

It is then as useless to deplore the triumph of jazz as it is to deplore the triumph of machinery. The thing to do is to domesticate both to our uses. The present craze for dancing will pass as everything human passes. The evil which that craze brought in its wake will also pass, but a residuum of good will remain. The employment of jazz will no longer dominate but only vitalize. It is for the trained musician who is also the creative artist to bring out this vitality and to heighten it with the eternal flame of beauty. When this time comes, and perhaps it is not so far away, jazz will be but one element in a great whole which will at last give a worthy musical expression to the spirit which is America. Meanwhile we can but do our best by writing what we feel and not what we think we ought to feel. And no one who knows America can doubt that jazz has its important place in the national consciousness.

Just as the acrobatic country dances are the expression of the vigorous life of the peasants of central Europe, just as the minuet expressed the stately grace of the civilization centered at Versailles, the popular dances of today express the nervous, somewhat unthinking vitality of present-day America. There can be little doubt that we are in a transitory stage. It is inconceivable that the present tension can continue forever. With its modification jazz will probably gradually take its proper and subordinate place. Jazz is, in short, not an end in itself but rather a means to an end. What that end will be the future musical development of the country will determine.

25 George Gershwin: *"Jazz Is the Voice of the American Soul"* (1926)

Gershwin's use of the term "soul" is provocative but not in the way that a contemporary reader may first suspect. He surely has little sense of the term as much later applied to a fundamental aspect of black music; rather, here Gershwin uses the term more generally and literally.

The peak of my career was not, as my friends and the public think, when I played in my own *Concerto in F* in Carnegie Hall with the New York Symphony Orchestra, Walter Damrosch conducting. That was an event which

SOURCE *Theatre Magazine* (June 1926): 52B.

amiable contemporary biographers are recording as notable. And I may say, with gratitude and humility, it was.

But there are invisible peaks that anticipate the visible. There are spiritual fulfillments that precede the physical. The peak of my highest joy in completed work was when I listened to that concerto played by the fifty thorough musicians I had engaged for it. Two weeks before the evening when the *Concerto* was heard in Carnegie Hall, there was a reading of it on an afternoon in the Globe Theatre. Charles Dillingham had permitted the reading in his playhouse. I enjoyed it, not as one of my fair and mischievous friends said, as the mad king Ludwig enjoyed Wagner, being the sole audience in his theater; for Mr. Damrosch was there, and about a dozen others who I wished to hear it. Four of these were music critics. The rest were personal friends. That was the first time I heard my most serious work with my own ears. On this occasion I played the piano myself, and was listening, as it were, with the multiple ears of the audience. Another peak will be the evening of this day in which I am preparing these impressions for the *Theatre Magazine*, when I play my biggest composition with the New York Symphony Orchestra, for the radio and a million listeners.

When, last year at Carnegie Hall, I played my first concerto, I was twenty-seven years old. For eight years I had been writing compositions, so I was not totally surprised when great musicians came to the piano and paid me compliments upon my efforts as a composer. What caused a surprised smile, however, was that all of them—Rachmaninoff, Heifetz, Hofmann—complimented me upon my piano execution. For I had had but four years of piano study, and those not with teachers of celebrity. My facility had come not from tuition but from a habit I had consciously cultivated since I was in my early teens. I mean my habit of intensive listening. I had gone to concerts and listened not only with my ears but with my nerves, my mind, my heart. I had listened so earnestly that I became saturated with the music.

Then I went home and listened in memory. I sat at the piano and repeated the motifs. I was becoming acquainted with that which later I was to interpret—the soul of the American people.

Having been born in New York and grown up among New Yorkers, I have heard the voice of that soul. It spoke to me on the streets, in school, at the theater. In the chorus of city sounds I heard it. Though of Russian parentage, I owed no sensitiveness to melodious sounds from that source. My father was a businessman. No one in my family save my brother Ira and myself had an interest in music.

Wherever I went I heard a concourse of sounds. Many of them were not audible to my companions, for I was hearing them in memory. Strains from the latest concert, the cracked tones of a hurdy-gurdy, the wail of a street singer, the obbligato of a broken violin, past or present music—I was hearing within me.

Old music and new music, forgotten melodies and the craze of the moment, bits of opera, Russian folk songs, Spanish ballads, chansons, ragtime ditties combined in a mighty chorus in my inner ear. And through and over it all I heard, faint at first, loud at last, the soul of this great America of ours.

And what is the voice of the American soul? It is jazz developed out of ragtime, jazz that is the plantation song improved and transformed into finer, bigger harmonies. . . .

I do not assert that the American soul is Negroid. But it is a combination that includes the wail, the whine, and the exultant note of the old "mammy" songs of the South. It is black and white. It is all colors and all souls unified in the great melting pot of the world. Its dominant note is vibrant syncopation.

If I were an Asian or a European, suddenly set down by an aeroplane on this soil and listening with fresh ear to the American chorus of sounds, I should say that American life is nervous, hurried, syncopated, ever *accelerando*, and slightly vulgar. I should use the word *vulgar* without intent of offense. There is a vulgarity that is newness. It is essential. The Charleston is vulgar. But it has a strength, an earthiness, that is an essential part of symphonic sound.

When I realized beyond any possibility of error, or need of recantation, that the voice of America, the expression of its soul, is jazz, a determination to do the best possible in that idiom filled me.

Jazz is young. It is not more than ten years old. Ragtime is dead. It was dying when my ear began to be attuned to the voice of the spirit of America. I began to write songs. My first published one had the singular and unabbreviated title, "When You Want 'Em You Can't Get 'Em." I was seventeen when I offered it to an indifferent world. The publishing house for which I was working showed its estimation of the merits of the song by deciding to publish it. But the house of Von Tilzer was willing also to print my second song, with the title "You-oo, Just You." The first that pleased the sweetheart we all woo, that coy damsel, Miss Public, was "I Was So Young (You Were So Beautiful)." The melodious brother and sister, Mollie and Charles King, sang it in a musical version of *The Magistrate*, called *Good Morning, Judge*. When I was twenty my first show, *La, La Lucille*, was produced. It was at Henry Miller's Theatre.

The best song I have written, measured by its reception, was "Swanee," sung by Al Jolson. Mr. Jolson interpolated it in *Sinbad*. I have written the music for twenty-two musical comedies, the next to the last, now in its third year, being *Lady, Be Good!* and the last and most popular, *Oh, Kay!* Of my record for industry I am not ashamed. My average is about three musical comedies a year.

I shall go on writing them. They make it possible to flit away, as I shall do after writing this, to Lake Placid in the Adirondacks for a rest. My work is agreeable and remunerative. But to my compositions that most gratify the inward seeking, they are as numbers sung by Al Jolson and by a Caruso. That statement does not decry Mr. Jolson. In his realm he is king. But the creator longs to write what is worthy the voice of a master vocal musician.

My best works therefore are my *Rhapsody in Blue* and my *Concerto in F.* The *Rhapsody in Blue* represents what I had been striving for since my earliest composition. I wanted to show that jazz is an idiom not to be limited to a mere song and chorus that consumed three minutes in presentation. The *Rhapsody* was a longer work. It required fifteen minutes for the playing. It included more than a dance medium. I succeeded in showing that jazz is not merely a dance; it comprises bigger themes and purposes. It may have the quality of an epic. I wrote it in ten days; it has lived for three years, and is healthy and growing.

I do not know what the next decade will disclose in music. No composer knows. But to be true music it must repeat the thoughts and aspirations of the people and the time. My people are Americans. My time is today. Of tomorrow, and of my tomorrow, as an interpreter of American life in music, I am sure of but one thing: that the essence of future music will hold enough of the melody and harmony of today to reveal its origin. It will be sure to have a tincture of the derided yesterday, which has been accepted today and which perhaps tomorrow will be exalted—jazz.

26   George Gershwin: *"Does Jazz Belong to Art?"* (1926)

In a series of articles that brought Gershwin's comments about jazz in the concert hall to the forefront of a public debate, *Singing* magazine enabled Gershwin to posit the question simply. His reaction to the fallout from this article can be found in selection 27 in this book.

No student of singing can afford any longer to ignore jazz music or to sniff at it as a thing of low estate and of negative cultural value. The study and practice of jazz has a very important contribution to make toward the complete

SOURCE   *Singing* (July 1926): 13–14.

training of any modern disciple of the musical art. It can be of positive bene-fit to the vocalist in every department of his profession. The new understand-ing of rhythm which it imparts will simplify and amplify all his repertoire.

In the above sentences I have been bluntly dogmatic. Purposely so, because I believe the time has come when these statements can be made flatly and without apology, as matters of proved truth.

I have no intention of "defending" jazz. I am no propagandist, and I have no time to waste in "converting" those who hide their heads in the sand like the ostrich, and decline to see things as they are. Let jazz speak for itself. It is here, and all the tirades of our musical Jeremiahs cannot take it from us or abate its profound influence on the music of the present and future.

There has been too much argument about jazz—most of it from people who are not even clear in their terminology. To condemn jazz, for example, because there is much bad jazz in the world, is as absurd as to condemn all music because much bad music exists. I hold no brief for those compositions of the Dada school, which employ the instrumentation of electric fans or couple fifty synchronized electric pianos in a riot of noisy cacophony. That is not jazz; it is merely delirium.

But if you take the best of our modern serious jazz music and study it, you can come to only one conclusion—that it is, in the words of Madame d'Alvarez: "America's greatest contribution to the musical art."

The most vicious opponents of jazz bring the impartiality of complete ignorance to their judgment seat. "Of course I know very little about music," naïvely remarked Dr. John Roach Straton at the Town Hall Club, "but I am sure that jazz singing comes from the devil and will have no place in the heav-enly choir."

A few days later, a distinguished scientist, president of one of our greatest universities, ventured to deliver a commencement address before his Univer-sity School of Music. For the greater part of his address he stuck to his own bailiwick and talked paternally, but sensibly, about science. But finally he slipped into the abyss of trying to speak with equal authority on a subject outside his ken.

"My dear children," he said over his spectacles, "beware the dreadful jazz. Cultivate good music. While there may be art in these modern rhythms, it certainly is a different art than that portrayed in the established and recog-nized classics. Hold fast to that which has been proved by time." He contin-ued with a great deal more of the same kind of twaddle. Words, empty words, revealing nothing save a complete ignorance of his subject.

What would the learned Prexy say if a musician of note should rise before the commencement class in his Scientific School and declaim: "Boys and girls, beware the modern in science. Shun evolution and investigations of recent years. Give your time to Lucretius and the established classic of the golden age of King Tut. There is no such thing as progress. All that is good is old. All that is new is bad."

Every musician who has studied modern music knows that jazz already has made a real contribution to our art. How much this contribution will mean in the next decade nobody can predict, but assuredly its part will be large and important. Every composer of the present day has given a great deal of time and study to this musical development, although many of them cannot themselves write jazz successfully.

The successful jazz artist, whether he be composer, instrumentalist or singer, should get the rhythm into his blood early in life. Acquisition of the jazz art in one's riper years is always difficult and sometimes impossible. One of our most distinguished American singers, who has made a profound study of jazz and who sings a great deal of it, has never been quite able to get the genuine rhythm of it. He comprehends it intellectually, and it delight him, even though the complete thrill and abandon of the composition is somehow lacking. But he has deliberately specialized on the intellectual interpretation of jazz, and his contribution has been unique and important, because he has been able to show that there is a real musical soul in jazz, entirely apart from the powerful reaction of its native rhythms.

The late Amy Lowell, great New England poet and seer, was one of those who loved jazz, although she could neither sing it nor play it nor dance it. "I can only move my toe to it," she told me once, "but if I couldn't do that, I think I should burst with the rapture of it."

Jazz had a hard row to hoe in England for many years. The English are conservative to a fault, and they dislike to make even the slightest effort to comprehend anything which is new to their experience. But jazz has at last won its way to their hearts, and today I think the English understand its essential musical virtues better even than we do in America. Paul Whiteman last year packed Albert Hall fuller than it had ever been before in its musical history, and his audience was symptomatic of a change that pervades every stratum of English musical appreciation.

"Jazz is the music of the street," said a learned divine the other day, apparently feeling that this was the final word in condemnation. It is true that many of the street songs of today are jazz in character, but our best jazz is far too good musically to be popular in the street. Practically none of my own songs can boast of that wide popularity which entitles them to be called "songs of the street."

In the very dignified and sedate program which I shall give with Mme.

d'Alvarez in the Hotel Roosevelt recital series this fall, my own part will consist of selections from the *Rhapsody in Blue*, supplemented by two or three jazz "Preludes" on which I am now working and which will come before the public for the first time on that occasion. Later in the program, I shall accompany Mme. d'Alvarez in several songs selected from my later musical comedies, such as *Lady, Be Good!* and *Tip-Toes.*

Not one of the numbers on that program will be cheap or trashy in character, I am sure. They are all of sound musical value, and worthy of a place on any sober and dignified program. This partnership of Mme. d'Alvarez and myself in support of modern music comes as the result of her recent defense of jazz in a debate with the Rev. John Roach Straton. She sings jazz better, I believe, than any other great singer on our concert or opera stage today, because she interprets with fidelity and enthusiasm, not merely the notes, but the spirit and the rhythm of the music.

It is marvelous what a really great voice can do, musically speaking, with a good jazz air. The greater the voice, the greater its effectiveness in jazz interpretation, provided only that the singer has a superlative sense of rhythm. Rhythm is the very life of music. "Without perfect rhythmical feeling," we are told, "you can never move an audience to tears nor stir an arm to action."

Jazz is no child's play. Good jazz music needs as much effort and ability for its mastery as any other music. I suspect that many first-class musicians are forced to adopt an air of supercilious contempt toward it because they cannot master it. Perhaps they started too late; perhaps they never started at all; perhaps they lacked the "divine spark" which, after all, is an essential of good jazz performance. If you think that jazz is easy, try Kern's "They Didn't Believe Me" as a studio exercise; there are some passages in that song that will prove difficult hurdles for any voice.

I have been asked to recommend a list of jazz songs which a concert singer might study, either as an introduction to jazz rhythms or with a view to public performance. The appended list comes to mind as I pack my bag for a hurried trip to Europe, and is presented without any pretense that it is either complete or the best possible list for the purpose.

For any singer, an excellent training in jazz rhythms is the study of the phonograph records made by singers like Marion Harris, Al Jolson, and the Revelers. The quartet singing of the Revelers is marvelous, not merely in their perfection of rhythm, but also in their unique ability to get unusual and skillful orchestral effects with the voice.

There are some singers who will not find, in the present jazz vocal repertoire, anything which they will desire to add to their platform programs. But there are none of them who will not benefit greatly, in the broad sense of musical culture, from the serious study and practice of the rhythmic gymnastics which jazz supplies.

I close with the moral of this little tale: If you are a singer, don't ignore jazz music. Study it, love and cherish it, give it free rein in your heart. It will repay you a hundred fold. It will help you over many tough spots in your classics. It will add a new rhythmic meaning to your whole repertoire, old and new. It will be your good friend and companion through sunshine and shadow.

Don't condemn jazz on the say-so of any old fogy. Avoid musical snobbery. Think for yourself. Live in the musical present, and the past will be even more significant and precious.

27   George Gershwin: "Mr. Gershwin Replies to Mr. Kramer" (1926)

> During a time when the new musical style known as jazz was attached to almost any type of piece of syncopated music, the debate over what was and what was not jazz was waged in person, in print, and over the radio airwaves. The polite sparring between Gershwin and A. Walter Kramer, a well-respected composer of art song and symphonic music whose style was referred to as neo-romantic, produced intriguing information. First, it continued to fuel the rumor that Gershwin was not the orchestrator of his *Concerto in F* (see selections, 45, 46, and 83 in this volume). It also confirms, in retrospect, that Kramer had less foresight than Gershwin when he predicted, " . . . unless jazz should through some miraculous metamorphosis (of which now no one has even the slightest inkling) become the folk music of the United States, it will pass into memory before very many years have rolled around."

To the Editor of *Singing*:

I have just read Mr. A. Walter Kramer's article in the September issue of *Singing*. Mr. Kramer's sympathies are in no way anti-jazz; he merely feels, he says, that jazz ought to "stay in its place."

The most painful thing about any discussion of jazz is the seemingly inevitable confusion of terminology. The word "jazz" ought to be limited to a certain type of dance music. The word has been used for so many different things that it has ceased to have any definite meaning.

For instance, here are some of the widely different things that just now go under the heading of "jazz": popular songs like "Papa Loves Mama"; adapta-

SOURCE   *Singing* (October 1926): 17–18.

tions of the classics to dance rhythms; Negro spirituals; even a waltz number like Irving Berlin's "What'll I Do"; the *Rhapsody in Blue*. Some people go so far as to affix the jazz label to my *Concerto in F*, in which I have attempted to utilize certain jazz rhythms worked out along more or less conventional symphonic lines.

We need a new set of words for each of these widely divergent types, because much of the present discussion degenerates into a mere quibbling over words and definitions. The same word-trouble surrounds the colloquial use of the phrase "classic music." It means as many things as there are people who say it. A man writes a piece of music which he considers serious, but which really is pretty awful; he labels his work "classic" and an unsuspecting public accepts the label.

From any sound critical standpoint, labels mean nothing at all. Good music is good music, even if you call it "oysters."

Mr. Ernest Newman, who denounced jazz recently in no uncertain terms, was apparently speaking mainly about adaptations of the classics to dance rhythms. He heard the *Rhapsody in Blue* last year and wrote: "Mr. Gershwin's *Rhapsody* is by far the most interesting thing of its kind I have yet met. It really has ideas, and they work themselves out in a way that interests the musical hearer."

In other words, ideas are the things that count, not mere labeling of form. Mr. Newman continued: "But is this really jazz? The *Rhapsody* certainly begins as jazz, and every now and then in its later course it behaves as such. But it seems to me to forget to live up to its name for a great part of the time. Jazz, in fact, is now obeying a universal law of musical evolution. Why did so many passages in the *Rhapsody* sound so Brahms-like? I should not be surprised in five or ten years to find Mr. Gershwin writing classical music. What is at present certain is that he has written something for a jazz orchestra that is really music."

As long as there is such a thing as music known as "jazz," which is understood and appreciated by millions of people—some highbrow, but mostly lowbrow—the musician should at least know what it is, and what it is all about. His musical education is incomplete if he refuses even to recognize that it exists. When I recommended jazz studies to singers, all that I maintained was that certain numbers written in the jazz idiom would do them a lot of good from the standpoint of rhythm and accent. Here is a type of material which they can get in no other songs or vocal exercises.

There are one or two specific points in Mr. Kramer's article which I would like to correct. He is entirely right in saying that the song "They Didn't Believe Me" is not jazz.

I do not consider it jazz either, and the mention of it in my article was an error in the transposition of my dictation, which I did not have the opportunity to correct owing to my departure for England. The song which I had in mind was Irving Berlin's "Everybody Step," which because of its very interesting rhythmical qualities would help any singer who is at all interested in rhythmical variation for the voice.

Mr. Kramer does me an injustice in stating that my piano concerto was orchestrated by anyone but myself. The *Rhapsody in Blue* was orchestrated by Ferde Grofé, but this was done because the Whiteman orchestra is such a unique combination. And yet Mr. Grofé worked from a very complete piano and orchestral sketch, in which many of the orchestral colors were indicated. Even so fine an orchestrator as Deems Taylor gave his "Circus Day" to Grofé to orchestrate for Whiteman.

But the Concerto was orchestrated entirely by myself. I should be delighted to arrange a meeting with Mr. Kramer at his earliest convenience and go over with him the full score of the Concerto. It will perhaps interest your readers to look over a reproduction of a page of this original manuscript.

And, by the way, Mr. Kramer's point about the importance of orchestration seems to me a little over-stressed. He says: "It is the *arranger's* instrumental version that one hears. And instead of applauding *him*, one applauds the composer, who may have done little more than write the tune." Bach's *Passacaglia* was a great piece of music before Stokowski orchestrated it. Rimsky-Korsakoff reorchestrated in great measure Moussorgsky's *Boris Goudonov*. Chopin, although one of the world's greatest musicians, was a notably poor orchestrator.

The ability to orchestrate is a talent apart from the ability to create. The world is full of most competent orchestrators who cannot for the life of them write four bars of original music.

To sum up, a final quotation from Mr. Newman, slightly abbreviated to conserve space: "There is no virtue in any particular form of music. If the art of fugue writing had been discovered only a few years ago, there would probably have happened to it just what has happened to jazz; everybody would be writing fugues, and 999 out of every 1000 would be very bad fugues. There is no salvation for music in forms or fashion or coteries; there is salvation only in composers."

28 Abbe Niles: "The Ewe Lamb of Widow Jazz" (1926)

The Roosevelt recital series held at the popular hotel on 45th Street near Grand Central Station began in October 1926 with a recital by the Scottish lyric soprano Mary Garden and ended three months later with contralto Marguerite d'Alvarez and George Gershwin performing. Their mutual friend Carl Van Vechten, who thought they would produce a splendid team of diva and jazzer, had brought the two together in 1924. According to the many concert reviews, the only remarkable result of the program was the premiere of Gershwin's five preludes for piano. Although two or three had been announced in the July 1926 issue of *Singing*, a November 28 advertisement in the *New York Herald Tribune* promised six. After the Roosevelt program was repeated in Boston and Buffalo the following month with five preludes on each recital, the Harms edition of three *Preludes for Piano* was published later in 1927. This review of the New York recital and the following account of the Boston repeat performance (see selection 29) poses the continuing mystery: which of the piano preludes were published and which were discarded?

It is probable that the five new piano preludes which he played for the first time at the Roosevelt did not cost him an excessive amount of overtime, but were presented for what they are worth, recent by-products of his plenteous invention, and not to prove anything whatever. One was a frank salute to Chopin; one criticized the crudity of the ragtime in Debussy's "Golliwog's Cakewalk" in just the way one clog-dancer would choose to criticize another's step; one was built on a theme written but not used for the famous blues movement of the *Concerto in F*; one might be a song deprived of its words; one started on the docks in New Orleans to find itself shortly joyously footing it in Madrid. Yet every one should be published, none could have been written by another composer; the set exhibited the hard transparent surfaces, the fire-refracting facets and the cool blue depths of a circlet of well-cut aquamarines and diamonds. No evidence is lacking, in short, that if he chooses to go on Mr. Gershwin has only fairly started, that the end for him lies around a number of corners.

Just how many corners he may round cannot easily be prophesied. So far he has been faithful to his schooling, has put to new uses but yet retained the accents they like in the dance-halls. Were he utterly to drop those, what would remain? Certain of his peculiar brilliancies, if he were to tackle the larger musical forms again under such circumstances, would have less opportunity

SOURCE *New Republic* (December 29, 1926): 164–66.

to divert attention from the weakness in thematic development which he has thus far given reason to suspect, a weakness which, if remediable by further technical study, presents hardly less of a problem for the fact. And were that mountain surmounted, actual greatness is another matter. He has not attempted the loftiest heights, and perhaps he is waiting or perhaps he is wise; at any rate here we go beyond what one has the right to ask save from the admittedly greats. The immediately interesting if not exciting question is what possibilities he can point out in a despised argot, that we failed to suspect before he began using it. Mr. Ernest Newman sets jazz down as too feeble and limited a means of expression for anyone to touch who has anything to express. If it were to be pointed out to Mr. Newman that Gershwin's concerto was supposed to express something of considerable local interest, namely The Spirit of Young America, he might reply that according to the testimony of the composer that spirit must then be the Charleston and the blues—in which case it was most thoroughly expressed—but that the question remained whether, should one want to look at Young America from another angle, or look at quite something else again, one would seize anew on jazz. Foregoing available rebuttals to Mr. Newman's imagined comment (which from previous experience is milder than natural), one may yet observe that for any reasonable doubts on the question Gershwin is responsible. May he press his case.

29   Carleton Sprague Smith: "d'Alvarez-Gershwin Recital" (1927)

Marguerite d'Alvarez, contralto, and George Gershwin, pianist, gave a concert at Symphony Hall yesterday afternoon. Edward Hart was the accompanist for the singer, and William Daly played the piano arrangement of the orchestral part of Mr. Gershwin's *Rhapsody in Blue*.

The number of young people in the large audience lent it an unusual aspect. Evidently Mr. Gershwin and the promise of jazz had brought them, for they lingered to the end. Yet only a small portion of the program was devoted to jazz.

Mr. Gershwin's *Rhapsody in Blue* came first. The composer played the solo piano part with his accustomed light agility and keenly rhythmed phrases. Later he played five of his own preludes, hitherto unheard in Boston.[1] This music of comparatively recent composition shows a clear advance in the

SOURCE *Christian Science Monitor* (January 17, 1927): B-4.

1   The debate over the exact number of piano preludes was stimulated by an early biography which claimed that Gershwin played a sixth prelude in Boston the month following the New York debut. This review, as well as those in several other Boston newspapers, suggests that the repertoire was identical.

composer's abilities. The first exhibited clever manipulation of rhythms. The second proved unconvincing of anything. The third of these pieces was a flashing, spirited bit, effectively contrived. Fourth came a brief composition of amazing simplicity, yet widened scope. Last came a jerky, quivering musical sketch, full of the broken rhythms and syncopations of conventional jazz.

Mme. d'Alvarez deployed three French and three Spanish songs. She has a voice of velvety richness in its lower register and sharp brilliance in the upper part. She enunciates her words clearly and phrases her music and text in such a manner as to heighten meaning and musical import. But she also deviates from pitch rather disconcertingly and thereby obscures some of the listener's pleasure in her work.

For the closing group of songs, Mme. d'Alvarez joined with Mr. Gershwin in a performance of Jerome Kern's "Babes in the Wood" and Gershwin's own "The Nashville Nightingale," "The Man I Love," and "Clap Yo' Hands." One outstanding deficiency was revealed in Mme. d'Alvarez's interpretation of the popular music. She takes it all too seriously. Jazz is so much a kind of folk music that it must receive a performance like that generally accorded the old folk songs. It must be straightforward, sincere, and sung with a bit of humor and lightness. One should take it all quite lightly and carelessly, serious jazz composers (if there be such a thing) to the contrary notwithstanding.

30　Allen Forte: "Someone to Watch Over Me" (1990)

Whether listening to Gertrude Lawrence's upbeat recording of "Someone to Watch Over Me" or Dorothy Provine's sensual crooning atop a piano in a smoke-filled speakeasy on the short-lived *Roaring 20s* television show (1960–1962), this Gershwin tune has become one of the all-time favorites of jazz artists. Classic recordings by Ella Fitzgerald, Sarah Vaughan, Frank Sinatra, Teddy Wilson, Art Tatum, Lena Horne, and Oscar Peterson only begin to represent the field of renditions of a song perfectly crafted for improvisation. The ballad was fit into the second act of the zany P. G. Wodehouse and Guy Bolton book of *Oh, Kay!*, and Lawrence sang the song while cradling a gift given to her by the composer on opening night—the newly marketed Raggedy Ann doll.

The musical *Oh, Kay!* ran for either 246 or 256 performances.[1] In the show, which premiered on November 6, 1926, the glamorous actress Gertrude

SOURCE *American Popular Ballads of the Golden Era, 1924– 1950* (Princeton, N.J.: Princeton University Press, 1995), 153–56. All footnotes in this entry appear in the original source.
  1 *Oh, Kay!* was perhaps a reference to Gershwin's friend Kay Swift.

Lawrence introduced Gershwin's "Someone to Watch Over Me." It remains by far the best-known song from that musical.[2]

Alec Wilder raises the question of tempo in connection with this song, pointing out that the only tempo indication (in the sheet music) is "Scherzando," at the beginning of the verse.[3] If this is the true tempo, Wilder asserts, then the song is not a ballad. He also says that in the show the piece was performed at a fast tempo, but because we have no record of that we can never be quite sure. Nevertheless, the song is usually performed at ballad tempo. For example, both Frank Sinatra and Margaret Whiting, among other well-known performers, have recorded this song, Sinatra at a very slow tempo, replete with rubato, and Whiting at a moderate "fox-trot" tempo.[4]

Example 157 shows some of the major features of the first period of chorus 1. These include the pentatonic scale that ascends from e-flat^1 to e-flat^2 to arrive on apex pitch f^2 ("longing") and the slow, sequential descent, each bar of which presents a descending third.[5] Especially beautiful here is the last of these cascading thirds, c^2-b-flat^1-a-flat^1, in which each melodic note expands and has its own bass note.

Ex. 157

Indeed, expansion is the principal rhythmic affect here, for the long, slightly modified, titular lyric "Someone who'll watch over me" takes up an entire phrase (example 158). In this phrase the crux falls on the downbeat of bar 6, with e-flat^2, supported by the chromatic bass note A, setting "watch." In the most striking way the abrupt change of register to e-flat^2 refers back to apex

2 According to Joan Peyser, the sheet music for this song had sold 10,107 copies by the end of 1926, that is, in less than two months. Peyser, *The Memory of All That* (New York: Simon and Schuster, 1993), 124.

3 Alec Wilder, *American Popular Song: The Great Innovators, 1900–1950* (New York: Oxford University Press, 1972; repr. 1990), 136–37.

4 The Sinatra recording was made with the Tommy Dorsey Orchestra and dates from 1945, whereas the Margaret Whiting recording dates from a year earlier, 1944, and was made with trumpet player Billy Butterfield's group. Both recordings reflect the impact of big band performance practice on the popular ballad.

5 Duke Ellington's "In a Sentimental Mood" (1935) begins in exactly the same way, but the standard key is F major.

pitch f² at bar 2 ("longing"). The registral change is only momentary, however, for the melody drops back to e-flat¹, the song's nadir pitch, which then ascends to g¹ via f¹, setting "over me." Remarkably, this melodic gesture is identical in pitch to the first three notes of the song, and, as will be shown presently, it reflects a major event in the large-scale melodic design of the period.

Ex. 158

The careted numerals above the upper staff of example 158 indicate the scalar locations of pitches that govern larger areas of the melody and that serve as points of departure and goals of motion. As the careted numerals show, these reduce to scale degrees 1, 2, and 3. How these work as structural melodic foci is shown with greater precision and in more detail in example 159.

Example 159 takes the analysis in example 158 several steps farther. Perhaps its main feature at (b) is the long-range connection from e-flat¹ in bar 1 to g¹, the primary tone, at bar 7 via the passing tone f¹. As is apparent, exam-

Ex. 159

ple 159 has two parts: the upper (a) retains all the notes in register, while the lower (b) reduces the structure to a single register in order to reveal the long-range voice-leading connection clearly; the two displays are complementary. Thus f^1 at (b) represents f^2 above it at (a). By equating f^1 and f^2 as octave images, the long descending melodic motion of a sixth from f^2 (bar 2) to a-flat (bar 5) becomes the minor third from f^1 to a-flat^1 at (b). Similarly, the salient e-flat^2 at bar 6 ("watch") appears as e-flat^1 in the inner voice of (b). These analytical displacements disclose a linear feature of the design that is not immediately apparent from analysis of the surface of the music: the apex pitch f^2 at bar 2 is a displaced passing tone that connects the headnote of the song, e-flat^1, with the definitive occurrence of the primary tone, scale degree 3, in bar 7. What substantiates this connection is the harmonic under-pinning of f^2, headnote of the descending sixth, and that of the note of arrival, a-flat^1 (bar 5): the supertonic triad II supports both. We hear the sequential progression from bar 2 through bar 5 as a motion circumscribed by the supertonic triad, which then moves through a short chain of fifths to the tonic triad at bar 7, with its corresponding melodic goal, primary tone g^1 ("me"). The end of the phrase then brings with it the half cadence on the dominant, incorporating the jazzy chromatic (whole tone) chord in the sec-ond part of bar 7 as surrogate for the first inversion of the tonic triad. As will be apparent to the reader, the large-scale motion described in connection with example 159 at (b) is identical to the opening gesture of the song in bar 1: "There's a some-," a remarkable though perhaps entirely fortuitous correspondence.

The melody of the bridge (example 160) concentrates at first on e-flat^2, previously associated with keyword "watch" (example 158, bar 6). The bridge's opening three-note melody is vintage Gershwin: in bar 17 d^2 deco-rates e-flat^2 as lower adjacency, but beginning at bar 18, f^2 becomes the emphasized note, embellishing e-flat^2 three times. The persistent motivic allusion to bar 2 of example 157 ("longing") could hardly be clearer. At bar 21, e-flat^2 descends by step to d^2, completing the figure we first heard in bar 2. And at this point, the beginning of the second phrase of the bridge's period, the bass and harmony initiate a chain of fifths that leads inexorably to the dominant chord at the end of bar 24. Above this progression the melody in bar 22 leaps down from d^2, arpeggiating through b^1 to g^1 at bar 23 ("the key"). Because g^1 here is so strongly associated with the primary tone, I have assigned it a careted 3, enclosed in parentheses. Thus in its general contour the melody of the bridge clearly resembles that of chorus 1. The bridge's entire first phrase, however, is taken up with expressing the urgent f^2-e-flat^2 motive, so that the short descending arpeggiation d^2-b^1-g^1 in bars 22–23 now corresponds to the long stepwise descent of chorus 1. Following this arpeggiation, melodic attention focuses on the lower third of the pentatonic scale—the first three notes of the song, again—but now in reverse order, the order of closure to the tonic scale degree.[6]

Ex. 160

With the exception of the piano accompaniment in bars 31–32 (not shown), chorus 2 replicates bars 9–16 of chorus 1 to close melodically on scale degree 1 (the nadir pitch) at the end of a perfect authentic cadence, as before.

In my view, the main interest of this song lies in the opening ascending pentatonic gesture and the gradual return to the register of the onset of the song, a motion that (as shown in example 159) is governed by a large-scale melodic progression that operates at a deeper level. The bridge is developmental in the motivic sense discussed earlier, which represents an extraordinarily compelling and dramatic text-music association, albeit on of small scale, as befits the popular ballad idiom.

31 *"George Gershwin Accepts $100,000 Movietone Offer; Fox to Pay That Sum for Film Version of Musical Comedy—Composer Gets Bid of $50,000 for Rhapsody in Blue Rights" (1928)*

The remarkable size of the Gershwins' contract to compose the score for Fox's film *Delicious* speaks to their star power. While by traveling West they were following many of their compatriots who had left the boards of Broadway in the wake of the Great Depression, the Gershwins found their

---

6 Gershwin probably associated the pentatonic with what we now call "Black American" music. In *Oh, Kay!* "Clap Yo' Hands," a production number clearly intended for black performers, is also pentatonic. And "Maybe," the opening of which resembles "Clap Yo' Hands," also has strong pentatonic flavorings.

SOURCE *New York Evening Post* (August 14, 1928): 1–2.

first Hollywood experience distasteful since the composer, upon completing the requisite songs, played little role in fashioning the final musical
score. One of the Gershwins' songs for the film, "Blah, Blah, Blah,"
summed up his feelings perfectly. Gershwin returned to New York with, as
he once put it, "a Hollywood tan and a pocketful of motion picture money."

George Gershwin has been won over by the "talkies."

The jazz composer has accepted an offer of $100,000 from the Fox Movi-
etone Company to write a new musical comedy to be used exclusively for the
talking moving pictures, the *Evening Post* learned today from an absolutely
reliable source.

He is also considering two other offers, one of them for $50,000 for the
use for the "talkies" of his celebrated *Rhapsody in Blue*. If he accepts one of
these and this is considered likely, he will probably play the piano part of the
symphony.

Gershwin, who with Irving Berlin and Paul Whiteman sits upon the Olym-
pus of jazz, has already been working on a score of the new musical comedy,
while putting the finishing touches on the music of another new play for the
coming season, in which Gertrude Lawrence will be the leading woman.

The Movietone offer came to him shortly after his return here two
months ago from an extensive tour of Europe, during which he was accorded
enthusiastic receptions in musical circles in London, Paris, Berlin, and
Vienna. He also spent some time in Antibes on the French Riviera, working
on new songs with his brother, Ira, who writes the lyrics for many of his
numbers.

At first skeptical about the possibilities of the talking movies, Gershwin
then made a careful study of the new medium and finally decided that it constituted a good vehicle for jazz and other forms of modern music. His acceptance of the Fox offer, it is believed in musical circles, is likely to be the starting
gun of a race for contracts.

32   *George Gershwin: Letter to Mabel Schirmer (1928)*

Along with Kay Swift, Emily Paley, Kitty Carlisle (Hart), and a few others,
Mabel Schirmer was one of Gershwin's best friends. She was also the
recipient of some of his most genuine letters (see also selection 65). In
this letter he details for Schirmer, who is already in Europe, his upcoming

SOURCE   DLC [GC].

trip there, which resulted in *An American in Paris.* The famous taxi horns used in that work were purchased while shopping with Schirmer along the Avenue de la Grande Armée. He also refers to his desire to find a composition teacher during his visit.

February 28, 1928

Dear Mabel:

Received your letter, and glad you are going to be excited. This letter may not reach you until after I cable you the time of our departure, arrival, etc. But I thought I might let you know about some possibilities of our plans.

We sail on the Majestic on March 10th, going straight to London, and expect to stay in London from a week to ten days. Then we are coming to Paris, and from then on our plans are rather vague. I expect that we will stay in Paris for about two weeks and then go someplace where the climate is right, and where I can do some work. If, however, I find somebody to study with in Paris, I may take a place on the outskirts of Paris and stay there most of the time.

Ira and Lee are going to travel around more than I am and see some of the sights, but their plans are also indefinite. (Lee wants me to tell you that she is bringing over with her shoes, stockings, brassieres and records for you.)

If I go to the south of France, the kind of place I would like to take would be a house surrounded by a few cottages, where we could all live together and yet be separated if I wanted to work. In looking over some of the places, as you are doing, I wish you would keep this in mind. Also, I'd like to find, when I get to Paris, a valet who speaks several languages, and possibly drives a car.

I am looking forward to this trip more than any other I have ever taken, because it is the first time I have ever gone abroad without having to put on a show, and I will [have] much more time to myself.

We are all dying to see you and Bob, and can't wait till the day arrives.[1]

Love from all of us to you and Bob.

George

---

[1] "Bob" refers to Schirmer's husband, Robert Schirmer, of the music publishing house family. They later divorced.

33   Deems Taylor: "An American in Paris: Narrative Guide" (1928)

Fellow composer and critic Deems Taylor's programmatic reading of Gershwin's tone-poem, provided in the program for the premiere, likewise has helped to shape its popular interpretation.

You are to imagine...an American, visiting Paris, swinging down the Champs-Élysées on a mild sunny morning in May or June. Being what he is, he starts with preliminaries, and is off at full speed at once, to the tune of the First Walking Theme, a straightforward, diatonic air, designed to convey an impression of Gallic freedom and gaiety.

Our American's ears being open, as well as his eyes, he notes with pleasure the sounds of the city. French taxicabs seem to amuse him particularly, a fact that the orchestra points out in a brief episode introducing four real Paris taxi horns (imported at great expense for the occasion). These have a special theme allotted to them (the driver, possibly?), which is announced by the strings whenever they appear in the score.

Having safely eluded the taxis, our American apparently passes the open door of a café, where, if one is to believe the trombones, *La Maxixe* is still popular. Exhilarated by the reminder of the gay 1900s, he resumes his stroll through the medium of the Second Walking Theme, which is announced by the clarinetist in French with a strong American accent.

Both themes are now discussed at some length by the instruments, until our tourist happens to pass—something. The composer thought it might be a church, while the commentator held out for the Grand Palais, where the Salon holds forth. At all events, our hero does not go in. Instead, as revealed by the English horn, he respectfully slackens his pace until he is safely past.

At this point, the American's itinerary becomes somewhat obscured. It may be that he continues on down the Champs-Élysées; it may be that he has turned off—the composer retains an open mind on the subject. However, since what immediately ensues is technically known as a bridge passage, one is reasonably justified in assuming that the Gershwin pen, guided by an unseen hand, has perpetrated a musical pun, and that when the Third Walking Theme makes its eventual appearance our American has crossed the Seine and is somewhere on the Left Bank. Certainly it is distinctly less Gallic than its predecessors, speaking American with a French intonation, as befits the region of the city where so many Americans forgather. Walking Theme

SOURCE   *Program Guide, Carnegie Hall, New York* (December 13, 1928).

may be a misnomer, for despite its vitality the theme is slightly sedentary in character, and becomes progressively more so. Indeed, the end of this section of the work is couched in terms so unmistakably, albeit pleasantly, blurred, as to suggest that the American is on the *terrasse* of a café, exploring the mysteries of an Anise de Lozo.

And now the orchestra introduces an unhallowed episode. Suffice it to say that a solo violin approaches our hero (in soprano register) and addresses him in the most charming broken English and, his response being inaudible—or at least unintelligible—repeats the remark. The one-sided conversation continues for some little time.

Of course, one hastens to add, it is possible that a grave injustice is being done to both author and protagonist, and that the whole episode is simply a musical transition. The latter interpretation may well be true, for otherwise it is difficult to believe what ensues: our hero becomes homesick. He has the blues; and if the behavior of the orchestra be any criterion, he has them very thoroughly. He realizes suddenly, overwhelmingly, that he does not belong to this place, that he is the most wretched creature in the world, a foreigner. The cool, blue Paris sky, the distant upward sweep of the Eiffel Tower, the book-stalls of the quay, the pattern of the horse-chestnut leaves on the white, sun-flecked street—what avails all this alien beauty? He is no Baudelaire, longing to be "anywhere out of the world." The world is just what he longs for, the world that he knows best: a world less lovely—sentimental and a little vulgar perhaps—but for all that, home.

However, nostalgia is not a fatal disease—nor, in this instance, of overlong duration. Just in the nick of time the compassionate orchestra rushes another theme to the rescue, two trumpets performing the ceremony of introduction. It is apparent that our hero must have met a compatriot; for this last theme is a noisy, cheerful, self-confident Charleston without a drop of Gallic blood in its veins.

For the moment, Paris is no more; and a voluble, gusty, wisecracking orchestra proceeds to demonstrate at some length that it's always fair weather when two Americans get together, no matter where. Walking Theme Number Two enters soon thereafter, enthusiastically abetted by Number Three. Paris isn't such a bad place after all: as a matter of fact, it's a grand place! Nice weather, nothing to do till tomorrow. The blues return, but mitigated by the Second Walking Theme—a happy reminiscence rather than homesick yearning—and the orchestra, in a riotous finale, decides to make a night of it. It will be great to get home; but meanwhile, this is Paris!

34   Olin Downes: "Gershwin's New Score Acclaimed" (1928)

Not Wagner, not Cesar Franck, not Guillaume Lekeu, nor yet the conductor, Walter Damrosch, was the Personage of the concert given by the Philharmonic-Symphony Orchestra last night in Carnegie Hall. The evening's hero was a svelte and feted young man, who beamed from a box while the audience applauded rapturously his latest composition, and in vain endeavored to induce him to descend and bow from the stage. This young man—need it be said?—was George Gershwin, who, to the accompaniment of four automobile horns, saxophones, and other unhallowed machines of sound supposed to be taboo in serious musical circles, made his third bow as the composer of professedly symphonic intentions to a New York audience.

Mr. Gershwin's first score to be given critical attention was his *Rhapsody in Blue*. His second was his *Piano Concerto in F* based on jazz motives. The composition of yesterday evening might be assumed to be of an autobiographical color, since Mr. Gershwin has spent months composing in the French capital, and has called his latest effort *An American in Paris*. It contains many typical Gershwin melodies. It stirs the feet. It stirred players of the Philharmonic-Symphony Orchestra to effects of a kind they had seldom made, effects that emanated from the laboratory of Paul Whiteman rather than the traditions of Haydn or Mozart or the modern masters of counterpoint and orchestration in the city where Mr. Gershwin lately resided.

From them, or at least from modern music, he seems to have derived some useful suggestion, but however far he has wandered in the flesh, he has kept close in the spirit to Broadway. In that spirit intensified—"glorified," as Mr. Ziegfeld might put it—by the sonorities and technic of a great modern orchestra, his music was greeted last night and acclaimed. Mr. Damrosch, when the applause had subsided, turned with more sobriety of demeanor than he had previously shown, to conduct the concluding excerpt from Wagner's "Walkure." The audience recovered itself and Wagner's last chord sounded, and so to bed. It was Mr. Gershwin's evening.

Looking back on this hectic occasion, it is possible to relate certain impressions. Mr. Gershwin in the ideas of his new piece is nearer the style of the *Rhapsody in Blue* than he is to the more pretentious and less inspired piano *Concerto*. This American in Paris is less on his dignity in his last big score, but firmer on his feet. Mr. Gershwin has written a succession of tunes, some of them ingeniously couched in present-day musical terms, in his native patois, and has set them with telling orchestration. This is his natural and character-

SOURCE *New York Times* 78 (December 14, 1928): 37.

istic expression. He tells his story perhaps disjointedly in places, but at least with a becoming measure of jocosity, sentimentality, and humor. What is the story back of Mr. Gershwin's notes?

He admits a "program" for his music—or has Mr. Deems Taylor, whose explanation of the true meaning of *An American in Paris* is published by Mr. Gilman in the program note, provided him with one? The thing has been done before this. The "program" of Richard Strauss's *Tod und Verklarung* was supplied after the composition had been finished. Some say that one "program" for a piece of music will do as well as another, because music can be interpreted in so many ways by different listeners. This might well be true of the gay and pleasant tunes of Mr. Gershwin, which abound in his score. But we proceed with Mr. Taylor's verbal narrative.

An American strolls the Paris boulevard. A "walking theme" portrays the Champs-Élysées on a blithe May morning. French taxicabs amuse the American. Their calls, played on taxi horns, sound in the orchestra. From a café comes the sound (trombones) of "La Maxixe." A clarinet "in French with a strong American accent," announces another "walking theme." A third "walking theme"—we use Mr. Taylor's terminology. Has the American crossed to the Left Bank? Or is he "exploring the mysteries of an Anise de Lozo?"

Enter a solo violin, of a soprano sonority and address. But sentimental colloquy does not cure the American of his "blues." His "blue" tune is one of the most characteristic in the score. The blue tune and the violin solo do much to fill the later pages. And now a final gay theme (the American having, according to Mr. Taylor, met a compatriot), and the various motives, cheek by jowl, jostle each other to an uproarious conclusion.

If it is necessary to discuss this amusing piece analytically it may be recorded that it contains too much material, too many ideas, for its best good. But Mr. Gershwin has developed in his technical knowledge of compositions and orchestration too. He has woven into his piece some modern harmony and has now and again combined melodic fragments with genuinely contrapuntal results. It is still considerably easier, however, for him to invent ideas than to develop them. If this is easier, he might say, why "develop" them? Why not just provide more themes?

The music at least escapes pompous classic formulas. The composer seeks a new form of his own working, germane to the nature of his ideas. If these ideas are fragmentary, they are spontaneous, melodic, characteristic of Mr. Gershwin. He does not always join smoothly and resourcefully the different parts of his piece, but there is a material gain in workmanship and structure over the two earlier works that have been mentioned. Best of all, Mr. Gershwin is not dazzled by praise or misled by a desire to shine as a master of symphonic composition. He has returned to his native vein, which he seemed inclined to forsake in favor of "higher" or more "serious" ends in his jazz concerto. Because of the humor and snap of his music, aside from its defects of proportion and structure, he was warmly welcomed last night. His automobile horns were used conservatively, and in a really witty way. They did not bray discordantly as they do on Broadway, but sound as harmlessly as any sucking dove. The novel touches of orchestration are not exaggerated or sensational. If the work suggests a potpourri of popular airs rather than a symphonic fragment, its lack of formality excuses its manners, and if its hilarity is noisy, it is also contagious.

This performance, so far as could be judged of a work hitherto unknown, was one of true spirit and effectiveness. As much could hardly be said of the performance of Franck's symphony, woefully distorted in tempi, rhythms and the tearful sentimentality which frequently misrepresented the nature of the lovely and tender phrases. Technically this was one of the best of the performances Mr. Damrosch has led this season. On the interpretative side it was theatrical, showy and superficial in effect. Lekeu's Adagio for strings demonstrated anew the fact that for one great composer who lives a hundred lesser ones die in his shade. The excerpt from "Walküre," a short fragment, emphasized such disparity.

35   George Gershwin: "Fifty Years of American Music... Younger Composers, Freed from European Influences, Labor Toward Achieving a Distinctive American Musical Idiom" (1929)

Now among American music's leading figures, Gershwin was also emerging as its spokesman and demonstrated a growing maturity of outlook in the following piece. Moreover, its publication in *American Hebrew* magazine shows how Gershwin had become something more than a musical celebrity: he had become a true cultural icon, at once Jewish and American.

It is well-nigh impossible to speak about fifty years of American music, since it is my sincere belief that American music is not fifty years old. Of course, America has had its share of composers fifty years ago, just as it has them today—and we have had the profuse and sentimental outpourings of such composers as Cadman, Hill, Nevins, De Koven—but theirs is neither Ameri-

SOURCE *American Hebrew* (November 22, 1929): 46, 110.

can music nor good music and so we may dismiss their efforts with a wave of the hand. Even MacDowell—the first important musical voice that America has produced—I refuse to classify as an American composer. He is rather a pale shadow of Brahms, an echo of Brahms's intense and hyper-sensitive emotion—an American throat singing with a German voice. Listen to his *Piano Sonatas* or to his *Woodland Sketches* and you will immediately perceive that this, most emphatically, is not American music; one even fails to see wherein this music has come from the hand of an American.

For American music means to me something very specific, something very tangible. It is something indigenous, something autochthonous, something deeply rooted in our soil. It is music which must express the feverish tempo of American life. It must express the unique life we lead here—a life of weary activity—and our gropings and vain ideals. It must be a voice of the masses, a voice expressing our masses and at the same time immortalizing their strivings. In our music we must be able to catch a glimpse of our sky-scrapers, to feel that overwhelming burst of energy which is bottled in our life, to hear that chaos of noises which suffuses the air of our modern American city. This, I feel, must be in every American music.

And American music as such can hardly be said to be fifty years old. At most, it has been existing for only thirty years.

It was obvious from the very first that if America was to produce a music of distinction and individuality, it must first find a distinct idiom which it can use in expressing itself. Thirty years ago, we had many gifted composers fumbling in that direction. Some of them turned to the Indians for their inspiration and by use of Indian themes they hoped to find a native American musical idiom. But the fallacy is obvious. For the pale and fragile tenderness of Indian music can no more express the fret and chaos of our modern American life than can the music of Brahms or Schubert.

In the midst of this blundering there was found a prominent and significant Jewish composer, Rubin Goldmark, my teacher and friend. Goldmark sensed that it was futile to employ an Indian idiom to express America. But Goldmark, too, felt that America must have its individual idiom if it is to produce a music of distinction, and so he groped in another direction. And Goldmark's gropings were the first feeble steps towards the much-cherished destination. Not to the Indians did Goldmark turn but to the negro—with the negro's strong sense for rhythm, with his sad wails and pathetic groans. In the negro spiritual did Goldmark feel—just as Dvorak had felt—that he had found, at last, the American idiom.

His *Negro Rhapsody* is far from being American music. As we listen to it today—our ears trained to hear those strains and slides of the true American music of our time—this seems to be pretty feeble stuff. But as a pioneer work, its importance cannot be overestimated. Overlooking the fact that this is, at best, pretty thin music; that it resembles Dvorak more closely than it does anything American; that its fragmentary moments of beauty are as far removed from the American spirit as Rubin Goldmark himself was— overlooking these things the fact remains that Goldmark was among the very first to turn his eye towards the negro and to attempt to interpret America through the poignant strains of the spiritual.

And since jazz—certainly the most efficacious means, to date, for the creation of American music—has its roots deeply embedded in the negro spiritual, the importance of such a pioneer work as the *Negro Rhapsody* should not be disregarded.

Then came the age of jazz. Jazz, of course, has a long and varied history. It dates from 1890 when such simple and naïve songs as "All Coons Look Alike to Me" were in their heyday. But for the purposes of this essay we need go no further back than 1904—the date when Irving Berlin first began composing.

I want to say at once that I frankly believe that Irving Berlin is the greatest songwriter that has ever lived. He has that vitality—both rhythmic and melodic—which never seems to lose any of its exuberant freshness; he has that rich, colorful melodic flow which is ever the wonder of all those of us who, too, compose songs; his ideas are endless. His songs are exquisite cameos of perfection, and each one of them is as beautiful as its neighbor. Irving Berlin remains, I think, America's Schubert.

But apart from his genuine talent for song-writing, Irving Berlin has had a greater influence upon American music than any other one man. It was Irving Berlin who was the very first to have created a real, inherent American music. John Alden Carpenter—the composer of that intriguing jazz-ballet, "Skyscrapers"—said, not so long ago, that the next century will celebrate the birth of American music and the birth of Irving Berlin on the same day. I heartily agree.

Irving Berlin was the first to free the American song from the nauseating sentimentality which had previously characterized it, and by introducing and perfecting ragtime he had actually given us the first germ of an American musical idiom; he had sowed the first seeds of an American music. The first real American musical work is "Alexander's Ragtime Band." Berlin had shown us the way; it was now easier to attain our ideal.

I have learned many things from Irving Berlin, but the most precious lesson has been that ragtime—or jazz, as its more developed state was later called—was the only musical idiom in existence that could aptly express

America. And so, when I was eager to compose something larger and more permanent than mere songs, I did not for a moment think of abandoning the jazz idiom. My ideal was, first and foremost, to express myself, then, to express America. Somewhat vaguely I felt that it would be one and the same thing. And so, I wanted to use those mechanics of jazz—mechanics which I think are highly worthwhile and certainly worthy of the serious consideration and efforts of any composer—in larger forms, forms which had been handed down to us by the masters. My *Rhapsody in Blue*, my *Piano Concerto*, my tone-poem, *An American in Paris*—are all strivings in that direction. Of course, I do not feel that I have yet achieved my aim.

It is a difficult and treacherous task. But I shall certainly continue in that direction. And if I do not succeed myself I shall be happy, indeed, if I know that at least my efforts have inspired other composers to continue with this monumental labor.

But in all fairness to those other talented American composers who have attempted to create an American music in idioms other than jazz, let us glance at their efforts.

There is Leo Ornstein, for example, who came here at a tender age—having fled from the terrible darkness of a Russian persecution—and who, having arrived here, was so dazzled by the liberty and peace enjoyed here by everyone that he vowed, then and there, to dedicate his musical pen to this glorious country, with its sublime traditions. Everything Leo Ornstein has composed during his years in America—with the possible exception of his latest work, his *Quintet*, which is more Jewish in spirit than American—has attempted to express and interpret our country.

What is his idiom? Futurism—the chaotic sweep of rhythms which characterizes Stravinsky's music; the disjointed polytonality of Arnold Schönberg. Through these means has he composed some really felicitous music. There is a remarkable force to all of Ornstein's music—a burst of energy, a frenzy and a passion which are ever refreshing to the tired musical ear.

Leo Ornstein has given us a remarkable expression of the spirit of unrest and disquiet that is in the air, and his music has portrayed, more aptly than any other music I know of, the modern age, controlled as it is, by machinery. Leo Ornstein's music is an expression—colossal and effective—of the twentieth century. But wherein is this music American? The idiom is intrinsically a European idiom—and the music, despite its nympholeptic aims, is European music. It might just as well have come from a Schönberg as from the pen of an American.

Or take Ernest Bloch's very recent work, *America*. Here is really sublime music—sounding veritably heroic cadences and gargantuan phrases. This is, perhaps, the nearest approach to American music that anything which is not jazz has attained. There is a vastness of scope here, a grandeur, a breadth, a healthy vigor, one seems to feel the robustness of American pioneers, the nympholepsy of our early statesmen. One seems to feel the anguish, the pain, the heroism that has gone into the building of a nation. But if this is American music, it is rather music of early America—when America was yet in its youth—and not of our time. And therein is "America" an insufficient voice for our country.

During the past few years a few of the more gifted American composers —realizing, too, that jazz was the greatest and aptest musical idiom for America—turned to the composing of jazz. There was Aaron Copland—a very talented young man—with his *Music for the Theater* and his *Jazz Piano Concerto*; and there was Louis Gruenberg with such works as *Daniel Jazz*. Their efforts neatly epitomize the aims and achievements of all these younger composers.

I have been interested in their work because I knew that both Copland and Gruenberg are excellent musicians. Technically, they are masters of their trade—despite their youth—and their knowledge of matters musical is all-embracing. It is therefore worthwhile to observe how such consummate musicians would achieve their aim.

One finds, at the first hearing, that their music is highly agreeable: the melody is lyrical and decorated with ever original and striking harmonies. But there is something lacking in their music—something which is vital and significant, something inherently American. The tricks of jazz seem to be superimposed on their music rather than being a free, pliant, and sponta-neous part of it. Moreover, the American spirit is completely absent. And if the American spirit is not there what, pray, remains?

It seems that both Copland and Gruenberg have realized this sad lack in their music for both, in recent years, have abandoned the jazz idiom to com-pose their serious music in their own style.

I might be asked why it is that such consummate musicians as Ernest Bloch, Leo Ornstein, and Aaron Copland have failed in their attempts at American music. It can be easily explained. All of these musicians were trained by Europeans; they were rigidly raised in European musical tradi-tions. Once trained in such a tradition it is not the easiest thing in the world to shake it off. One becomes perpetually enslaved to it.

Men like Bloch and Ornstein have been taught to think in terms of idioms employed by Brahms and Richard Strauss; Copland has been trained to think along the lines of Stravinsky and Schönberg. The result, when they attempt to compose American music, is that their training sticks to them and their

American music becomes diluted with their European traditions. Fortunately, neither Irving Berlin nor I were taught by European masters—and so we were the free men whereas all others were slaves. We could plunge wholeheartedly into this new culture that is America, we could absorb the spirit and tempo of American life and, at last, we could express it, more or less, in our music because our music was as yet virgin and uninfluenced.

But fortunately more and more of the younger American composers are realizing the wisdom of freeing themselves from European influences—and so we have an increasing number of young men who, quietly and patiently, labor toward achieving American music. Their efforts are almost certain to bear fruit sooner or later. At any rate, we have gone a long way, during the past thirty years, in an attempt to find a musical idiom to express America. And, now that we have almost reached our destination, we realize that the goal is a glorious one, beckoning us resplendently: that it is infinitely worth striving for; and that all of our past efforts and labors have not been in vain.

36 George Gershwin: "The Composer in the Machine Age" (1930)

Unquestionably modern musical America has been influenced by modern musical Europe. But it seems to me that modern European composers, in turn, have very largely received their stimulus, their rhythms and impulses from Machine Age America. They have a much older tradition of musical technique which has helped them put into musical terms a little more clearly the thoughts that originated here. They can express themselves more glibly.

The Machine Age has influenced practically everything. I do not mean only music but everything from the arts to finance. The machine has not affected our age in form as much as in tempo, speed and sound. It has affected us in sound whenever composers utilize new instruments to imitate its aspects. In my *American in Paris* I used four taxi horns for musical effect. George Antheil has used everything, including aeroplane propellers, door bells, typewriter keys, and so forth. By the use of the old instruments, too, we are able to obtain modern effects. Take a composition like Honegger's *Pacific No. 231*, written and dedicated to a steam engine. It reproduces the whole effect of a train stopping and starting and it is all done with familiar instruments.

There is only one important thing in music and that is ideas and feeling.

SOURCE Oliver Saylor, ed., *Revolt in the Arts* (1930); reprinted in Merle Armitage, *George Gershwin* (New York: Longmans Green and Co., 1938; repr. New York: Da Capo Press, 1995), 225–30.

The various tonalities and sounds mean nothing unless they grow out of ideas. Not many composers have ideas. Far more of them know how to use strange instruments which do not require ideas. Whoever has inspired ideas will write the great music of our period. We are plowing the ground for that genius who may be alive or may be born today or tomorrow. If he is alive, he is recognized to a certain degree, although it is impossible for the public at large to assimilate real greatness quickly. Take a composer like Bach. In his lifetime, he was recognized as one of the greatest organists in the world, but he was not acclaimed as one of the greatest composers of his time or of all time until generations after his death.

I do not think there is any such thing as mechanized musical composition without feeling, without emotion. Music is one of the arts which appeals directly through the emotions. Mechanism and feeling will have to go hand in hand, in the same way that a skyscraper is at the same time a triumph of the machine and a tremendous emotional experience, almost breathtaking. Not merely its height but its mass and proportions are the result of an emotion, as well as of calculation.

Any discussion of the distinction between presentation and representation in music resolves itself into an attempt to determine the relative values of abstract music and program music. It is very difficult for anyone to tell where abstract music starts and program music finishes. There must have been a picture of something in the composer's mind. What it was nobody knows, often not even the composer. But music has a marvelous faculty of recording a picture in someone else's mind. In my own case, everybody who has ever listened to *Rhapsody in Blue*—and that embraces thousands of people—has a story for it but myself. An *American in Paris* is obviously a program piece, although I would say half of it or more is abstract music tied together by a few representative themes. Imitation never gets anyone anywhere. Originality is the only thing that counts. But the originator uses material and ideas that occur around him and pass through him. And out of his experience comes this original creation or work of art, unquestionably influenced by his surroundings which include very largely what we call the Machine Age.

It is difficult to determine what enduring values, esthetically, jazz has contributed, because jazz is a word which has been used for at least five or six different types of music. It is really a conglomeration of many things. It has a little bit of ragtime, the blues, classicism, and spirituals. Basically, it is a matter of rhythm. After rhythm in importance come internals, music intervals which are peculiar to the rhythm. After all, there is nothing new in music; I maintained years ago that there is very little difference in the music of different nations. There is just that little individual touch. One country may prefer a peculiar rhythm or a note like the seventh. This it stresses, and it becomes identified with that nation. In America this preferred rhythm is called jazz. Jazz is music; it uses the same notes that Bach used. When jazz is played in another nation, it is called American. When it is played in another country, it sounds false. Jazz is the result of the energy stored up in America. It is a very energetic kind of music, noisy, boisterous, and even vulgar. One thing is certain. Jazz has contributed an enduring value to America in the sense that it has expressed ourselves. It is an original American achievement which will endure, not as jazz perhaps, but which will leave its mark on future music in one form or another. The only kinds of music which endure are those which possess form in the universal sense and folk music. All else dies. But unquestionably folk songs are being written and have been written which contain enduring elements of jazz. To be sure, that is only an element; it is not the whole. An entire composition written in jazz could not live.

As for further esthetic developments in musical composition, American composers may in time use quarter notes, but then so will Europe use quarter notes. Eventually our ears will become sensitive to a much finer degree than they where a hundred, fifty or twenty-five years ago. Music deemed ugly then is accepted without question today. It stands to reason, therefore, that composers will continue to alter their language. That might lead to anything. They have been writing already in two keys. There is no reason why they will not go further and ask us to recognize quarter or sixteenth notes. Such notes, whether written or not, are used all the time, only we are not conscious of them. In India they use quarter tones and, I believe, consciously.

Music is a phenomenon that to me has a very marked effect on the emotions. It can have various effects. It has the power of moving people to all of the various moods. Through the emotions, it can have a cleansing effect on the mind, a disturbing effect, a drowsy effect, an exciting effect. I do not know to what extent it can finally become a part of the people. I do not think music as we know it now is indispensable although we have music all around us in some form or other. There is music in the wind. People can live more or less satisfactorily without orchestral music, for instance. And who can tell that we would not be better off if we weren't as civilized as we are, if we lacked many of our emotions? But we have them and we are more or less egotistic about them. We think that they are important and that they make us what we are. We think that we are an improvement over people of other ages who didn't have them. Music has become a very important part of civilization, and one of the main reasons is that one does not need a formal education to appreciate it. Music can be appreciated by a person who can neither read nor write and it can also be appreciated by people who have the highest form of intelligence. For example, Einstein plays the violin and listens to music. People in the underworld, dope fiends and gun men, invariably are music lovers and, if not, they are affected by it. Music is entering into medicine. Music sets up a certain vibration which unquestionably results in a physical reaction. Eventually the proper vibration for every person will be found and utilized. I like to think of music as an emotional science.

Almost every great composer profoundly influences the age in which he lives. Bach, Beethoven, Wagner, Brahms, Debussy, Stravinsky. They have all recreated something of their time so that millions of people could feel it more forcefully and better understand their time.

The composer, in my estimation, has been helped a great deal by the mechanical reproduction of music. Music is written to be heard, and any instrument that tends to help it to be heard more frequently and by greater numbers is advantageous to the person who writes it. Aside from royalties or anything like that, I should think that the theory that music is written to be heard is a good one. To enable millions of people to listen to music by radio or phonograph is helpful to the composer. The composer who writes music for himself and doesn't want it to be heard is generally a bad composer. The first incursion of mechanized reproduction was a stimulus to the composer and the second wave has merely intensified that stimulus. In the past, composers have starved because of lack of performance, lack of being heard. That is impossible today. Schubert could not make any money because he did not have an opportunity through the means of distribution of his day to reach the public. He died at the age of thirty-one and had a certain reputation. If he had lived to be fifty or sixty, unquestionably he would have obtained recognition in his own day. If he were living today, he would be well-off and comfortable.

The radio and the phonograph are harmful to the extent that they bastardize music and give currency to a lot of cheap things. They are not harmful to the composer. The more people listen to music, the more they will be able to criticize it and know when it is good. When we speak of machine-made music, however, we are not speaking of music in the highest sense, because, no matter how much the world becomes a Machine Age, music will have to be created in the same old way. The Machine Age can affect music only in its distribution. Composers must compose in the same way the old composers did. No one has found a new method in which to write music. We still use the old signatures, the old symbols. The composer has to do every bit of his work himself. Hand work can never be replaced in the composition of music. If music ever became machine-made in that sense, it would cease to be an art.

37   Mary Herron Dupree: " 'Jazz,' the Critics, and American Art Music in the 1920s" (1986)

It is notable that Gershwin capitalized on his connection to what was being called jazz during the 1910s and 1920s and then gradually began to disassociate himself from the term in the next decade. Certainly there was a shift in the style, especially as African American performers began to craft a music that was obviously different from the compositions Gershwin was producing. This condensed article allows us to understand the musical climate into which jazz arrived and flourished.

Music critics and social commentators in the 1920s expressed differing views on the relationship of jazz to American art music. The debate about jazz—about its origins and defining characteristics, its intrinsic worth, and its role in establishing a uniquely American musical style—was of paramount interest to those concerned with the present and future of American music and was waged with particular vigor in periodicals that regularly featured discussions of music: among music journals, the *Musical Quarterly*, *Modern Music*, and the omnibus music magazine *Musical America*; among more broadly focused political and literary periodicals, the liberal *Nation* and *New Republic*, H. L. Mencken's *American Mercury*, and the literary "little magazine" the *Dial*.

The above-named sources reveal that the term *jazz* once conveyed, broader meaning than it does today. In a general sense it sometimes referred to contemporary attitudes and modes of expression. The critic Waldo Frank, for example, in a 1928 article for the *New Republic*, grouped T. S. Eliot, Irving Berlin, H. L. Mencken, and Sinclair Lewis together in a "family of jazz" because "the trick in the jazz dance or song, the jazz comic strip, the jazz vaudeville stunt, of twisting a passive reflex to our world into a lyrical self-expression" was in all their arts.[1] British art critic Clive Bell used the term to signify any form of art or expression that demonstrated a preference for the short, obvious, and uncomplicated.[2] And musical definitions could be as vague as "music enjoyed by and large among the people of any country."[3]

Conceptions of what constituted jazz ranged widely in the twenties, and

SOURCE   Mary Herron Dupree, " 'Jazz,' the Critics, and American Music in the 1920s," *American Music* (Fall 1986), 287–301. All footnotes in this entry appear in the original source.

1   Waldo Frank, "The Rediscovery of America, XII: Our Arts," *New Republic* (May 9, 1928): 345.

2   Clive Bell, "Plus de Jazz," *New Republic* (September 21, 1921): 92–96.

3   George Gershwin, quoted in Hyman Sandow, "Gershwin to Write New Rhapsody," *Musical America* (February 18, 1928): 5.

few writers, in fact, sought to define jazz in musical terms.[4] Instead, they cited its most salient social characteristics and attempted to trace its genesis. While all writers acknowledged black roots for jazz, most were familiar only with jazz elements as performed by white musicians. Thus, for many, jazz signified dance music of groups like the Paul Whiteman band. Others identified jazz as a synthetic idiom—a commingling of Negro American and Jewish or Russian-Jewish elements. Isaac Goldberg wrote of jazz in the *American Mercury*: "In the course of its filtration from the South to a small but noisy point called Manhattan Island it has undergone something decidedly more than a sea change. It reaches from the black South to the black North, but in between it has been touched by the commercial wand of the Jew."[5] He identified the main practitioners of this synthetic music as Gershwin, Berlin, and Kern, thus equating jazz with the popular music of Tin Pan Alley.[6]

Hugo Riesenfeld, however, expressed a distinctly minority view that the popular syncopated music of the twenties was *not* jazz: "Jazz, as I understand it, describes only the first stage of development of modern syncopated music, when its outstanding feature was improvisation. Improvised noises of the slide trombones, cowbells, the train effects, shouting of negroes and all varieties of spontaneous exclamation—these embellishments, superimposed on the basic dancing tune, combined to create the early 'true jazz'."[7] Riesenfeld felt that what was often called jazz in 1924 was really just "popular syncopated music" with "one fixed form which is the fox trot, a slow march with rhythmic complications."[8]

The discussion of jazz and its relationship to art music began slowly in periodicals in 1921 and by 1924 was intense. Most often it took place in reviews of works by established composers who were obviously using jazz vocabulary and in accounts of some highly publicized concerts intended to introduce jazz as "serious music" to musically educated audiences in New York. Serious consideration of the subject reached a peak in 1926 and then waned in the late twenties.

Three events early in the decade seem to have focused concertgoers' attention on jazz as serious music. The first was a recital by Eva Gauthier[9] at

---

4 The qualifying quotation marks in the title of this article are meant to signal the varying meanings of the term that will be addressed in the course of this essay.

5 Isaac Goldberg, "Aaron Copland and His Jazz," *American Mercury* 12 (September 1927): 63.

6 Goldberg theorizes that the "musical amalgamation of the American Negro and the American Jew goes back to something oriental in the blood of both. The Nordic audiences of These States has always been content to take its musical pleasure at second hand." See ibid.

7 Hugo Riesenfeld, "New Forms for Old Noises," *League of Composers Review I* (June 1924): 25–26.

8 Ibid., 26.

9 Gauthier was a Canadian-born soprano who, after beginning a career in opera, turned to the concert stage and became a well-known proponent of modern music.

Aeolian Hall on November 1, 1923. In addition to traditional older composi-tions, Gauthier sang works by major European contemporary composers such as Schoenberg, Hindemith, Bliss, and Milhaud, and for her "American group" she performed ragtime numbers such as "Swanee" and "Alexander's Ragtime Band." George Gershwin accompanied her in these last works. Although there is no evidence that the program raised a storm of protest, an editorial in *Musical America* voiced reservations: "Jazz expresses merely the easy joy, insouciance, vulgarity and love of motion characteristic of Amer-ica's big cities.... Its natural place is scarcely in the concert room, yet its occa-sional introduction there should excite no indignant protests. What is bad will destroy itself. Time has a way of dealing wisely with all things."[10] Gau-thier was booked to repeat the concert in Boston the next week, but the sponsors canceled the event, evidently because "the place for jazz was Broad-way, not the concert hall."[11]

Three months later, on February 10, 1924, the League of Composers spon-sored a Sunday afternoon program devoted to jazz at the Anderson Galleries. Edward Burlingame Hill, then head of the music department at Harvard, spoke on "Jazz and the Music of Today," and Vincent Lopez,[12] with members of his orchestra, provided examples of popular tunes and jazzed excerpts from *Carmen* and *H.M.S. Pinafore*. The following Tuesday, on the afternoon of Lin-coln's Birthday, the most highly publicized of the three events took place: Paul Whiteman and his Palais Royal Orchestra played what Whiteman himself called the "first recital of typical American music."[13] "Quiet Aeolian Hall was all dressed up for the occasion. Across the back of the stage, and partly obscur-ing the rows of organ pipes, stretched a large screen, stippled in gold and con-ceived in the most advanced Longacre Square manner; while on either side towards the front, pasteboard pillars from the same exotic atelier shielded lanterns which threw beams of soft red and green lights upon the players."[14]

Whiteman organized the program historically, beginning with the "Livery Stable Blues," with which he intended to demonstrate the depths from which jazz had ascended and which the reporter for *Musical America* described as "exciting and *very* stupid."[15] The concert continued with contemporary, improved versions of jazz, including some Irving Berlin songs, a fantasy on

10 "Melting Pot Music," *Musical America* (November 10, 1923): 26.

11 Clair Reis, *Composers, Conductors, and Critics* (Detroit: Information Coordinators, 1972), 49.

12 Lopez is best remembered today for his popular radio show, which used the song "Nola" as its sig-nature tune.

13 "Capacity House Fervently Applauds As Jazz Invades Realm of Serious Music," *Musical America* (February 23, 1924): 32.

14 Ibid.

15 Ibid.

the "Volga Boatman's Song," MacDowell's "To a Wild Rose," Elgar's "Pomp and Circumstance," and some piano pieces by Zez Confrey.[16] A demonstration of the relationship of jazz to "good music" showed the thematic relationship between the "Hallelujah Chorus" and "Yes, We Have No Bananas." The high point of the concert was the premiere of two works composed especially for the event: *Four Serenades* by Victor Herbert and the *Rhapsody in Blue* by Gershwin.

Many well-publicized concerts followed, bringing jazz-inspired works before New York and eventually even Boston concert audiences, but, unlike the three earlier events, most did not attempt to "sell" or explain the modern popular idiom.

Works by European composers such as Stravinsky, Milhaud, Casella, and Krenek that showed jazz influence, particularly compositions predating similar American efforts, generated considerable interest in the periodicals, as did pieces by established and moderate (not "modernist") American composers like John Alden Carpenter. Two young American composers—George Gershwin and Aaron Copland—emerged as serious composers during the "jazz rage" and were proposed, to differing degrees, as eminent examples of American composers who had found their true compositional voice in an environment in which jazz was a major influence. Many compositions from the twenties used jazz style in parts or throughout. Deems Taylor's *Circus Day* for jazz orchestra, Frederick Converse's *Fliver Ten Million,* W. Franke Harling's opera *A Light for Saint Agnes*, and George Antheil's *Jazz Symphony* are just a few, but the works of Carpenter, Gershwin, and Copland generated the most extensive critical discussion of the issue of jazz and art music. . . .

The premiere of the *Rhapsody in Blue* at the famous Aeolian Hall concert in the winter of 1924 focused attention on George Gershwin as a serious composer of art music and elicited critical unanimity about the work: that it was the most significant work performed at the concert, that it raised important questions about the possible relationship between jazz and art music, and that Gershwin was an excellent songwriter who had managed to capture in this new work much of the spirit of the vernacular forms in which he excelled. Gershwin's "admixture of Liszt and pianistic rough stuff"[17] did not appeal to reviewers who considered intensive thematic development a *sine qua non* of art

16 "Kitten on the Keys" was Confrey's best-known work. Carl Engel, "Views and Reviews," *Musical Quarterly* 10 (April 1922): 299, described *Zez Confrey's Modern Course in Novelty Piano Playing* as a sort of twentieth-century continuation of Tartini's *Traité des agréments de la musique*. The Smithsonian Institution has released *An Experiment in Modern Music: Paul Whiteman at Aeolian Hall*, Smithsonian Collection R-028 (1981), an album that re-creates the concert, based on recordings made by Whiteman, Confrey, and others between 1919 and 1924.

17 Oscar Thompson, "Twilight Descends on the Gods of Tin Pan Alley," *Musical America* (August 16, 1924): 5.

music, but it did work for those who valued originality and unselfconscious use of vernacular speech over composers who, "hampered by early piety, invariably stick to the traditional spelling and lose all force in doing so."[18]

Gershwin's *Concerto in F*, first performed in December 1925, generated more specific discussion about the use of vernacular musical styles in art music, because in this work Gershwin chose to invest a traditional art form with his own jazz material. By writing a concerto, Gershwin entered the realm of "serious music" and opened himself to being judged as a serious composer. The concerto did not receive unqualified accolades, but most reviewers found something to praise: a lack of vulgarity, "startlingly genial" ideas, even "ideas of a bewitching shape, delicious and racy germs of music."[19] But Gershwin was seen to fail in the working out of ideas and in the lack of unity and of a feeling of style: "Opening choruses of musical comedies, closing choruses of musical comedies mix and mingle with Gershwin, Liszt, and Chaminade, all very smartly treated. Jazz beats and shuffles, Blues add the Yiddish to the darky wail."[20] The problem was that Gershwin did not know what to do with all these ideas. This weakness was seen as less problematic in the second movement, which was traditionally less developmental and often based on the straightforward presentation of melodic ideas.[21]

Observing this same flaw but seeing the problem as lying elsewhere, Abbe Niles, a frequent and sympathetic writer on jazz for the *New Republic*, wrote that jazz, and ragtime in particular, benefited most from episodic treatment and brief forms and that forcing it into the developmental modes of "good music" lessened its value.[22] An editorial in the same magazine identified the concerto's major problem as niceness, calling the work an example of the "vanilla epoch of jazz."[23]

Carl Engel, writing in his "Views and Reviews" column for the *Musical Quarterly*, took the opportunity while discussing Gershwin's concerto to point out that, contrary to the claims of some critics, jazz rhythms were perfectly appropriate for transformation into art compositions. "In themselves these rhythms have nothing that should bar them from marrying into the proud old family of the concerto and symphonies which are inclined to forget conveniently their early and somewhat low-born origin. An addition of a little red blood has often saved the weakened blue."[24] In particular he referred

18 Henry Osgood, "The Jazz Bugaboo," *American Mercury* 6 (November 1925): 329.
19 Carl Engel, "Views and Reviews," *Musical Quarterly* 12 (April 1926): 304.
20 Paul Rosenfeld, "Musical Chronicle," *Dial* 80 (February 1926): 174.
21 Ibid.
22 B.H. Haggin, "Two Parodies," *Nation* (January 13, 1926): 40.
23 Abbe Niles, "Lady Jazz in the Vestibule," *New Republic* (December 23, 1925): 138.
24 "Denatured Jazz," *New Republic* (May 11, 1927): 334.

to the minuet movement of the classical symphony and pointed out how contemporaneous objections to its use in works by Pleyel, Haydn, and others paralleled modern criticism of jazz.[25]

Three more Gershwin works followed in the 1920s: the one-act opera *135th Street* (which had been written earlier for George White's *Scandals* but was presented at a Whiteman concert in Carnegie Hall), the *Five Piano Preludes*, and *An American in Paris*. None of these, however, generated the extensive discussion of the jazz-art interface that the earlier works had. By the end of the decade, no work had appeared that won for Gershwin universal acknowledgment as a successful composer of art music, let alone a great one. The widely held opinion was that Gershwin was largely responsible for improving the quality of American popular music in general and had contributed brilliant works in that genre, but "that he will write great [art] music, his work to date does not promise. Its spirit is vital but not profound; not elevated, but humorous, witty, ribald; on occasion, pathetic or of a cool, blue melancholy, but not tragic."[26] Gershwin was "merely not the artist."[27]

Although a clear consensus about jazz and its relationship to art music did not exist among writers of the twenties, the majority view seems to have been on the negative side: jazz may or may not have intrinsic value, but jazz as art music usually did not work.

Some commentators felt that introducing the classics to unsophisticated audiences by using jazz versions could be an effective first step toward their gaining an appreciation of the original versions and becoming enthusiastic and knowledgeable concertgoers. This argument was probably a rationalization of a practice already well established, particularly when the new, jazzed version was not so much an original piece based on an old theme as a literal duplication of the classic work forced into a fox-trot rhythm and rescored for jazz orchestra. Paul Whiteman, the most vocal supporter of this kind of "musical slang,"[28] found it absurd that the musical public did not "rejoice to see music rising like a wave and engulfing America, to see people music-mad" when the "good music" proponents had only "been keeping good music barely alive...by artificial stimulation."[29] While abhorring the jazzing of the

    25 Carl Engel, "Views and Reviews," 304.
    26 Karl Spazier writing in the *Musikalisches Wochenblatt* (1791): "I furthermore hold that minuets are contrary to good effect because, if they are composed straight-forward in that form, they remind us inevitably and painfully of the dance-hall and the abuses of music, while, if they are caricatured—as is often done by Haydn and Pleyel—they incite laughter." Ibid.
    27 Abbe Niles, "A Note on Gershwin," *Nation* (February 13, 1929): 194.
    28 Paul Rosenfeld, "Musical Chronicle," *Dial* 80 (February 1926): 174.
    29 Oscar Thompson, "Twilight Descends on the Gods of Tin Pan Alley," *Musical America* (August 16, 1924): 5.

classics, critics B. H. Haggin[30] and Ernest Newman[31] did not even attempt to counter this perfectly reasonable argument. However, Oscar Thompson did: "The jazz arranger's course is to cheapen, to bring to the illiterate's level, and to destroy forever the bloom of beauty, as such popularizations almost inevitably do."[32]

With respect to more serious efforts to employ elements of jazz vocabulary in new works intended for the concert hall, most writers found that jazz contribute some positive qualities. These included an undeniable Americanness, vitality and energy, and specific musical characteristics such as unique rhythmic qualities and scoring.

Beyond the discussion of what individual composers had done with jazz, of what it was and was not, had and had not, three more general ideas dominated the debate about the relationship of jazz to art music in the twenties. The first was that jazz is best in its natural state, and that forcing it to conform to the demands of art music through development, expansion into long, organic forms, and so forth, robs it of essential charm and force. The result is a "blight of politeness...pernicious sameness" and "smooth, sophisticated vacuousness."[33] Proponents of jazz in its natural state even found Gershwin guilty of what they saw as an emasculation of jazz, the only composer who seems to have avoided this condemnation was Copland, probably because of the abstract quality and essentially "sour," angular style of his music. Those few writers who held the view that true jazz was the earlier, black, improvisational style considered Paul Whiteman the prime culprit behind the "vanilla epoch of jazz." Carl Engel felt that the Victor recording of "When Buddah Smiles," for example, was infinitely preferable to the watered-down versions of jazz concocted for "the silly wriggling of neurotic simps."[34]

A second commonly voiced opinion also addressed the failure of the jazz-art interface but blamed it on jazz's lack of susceptibility to the procedures necessary to transform it into successful art music. This point of view was most frequently espoused by those who disapproved of jazz in any form and has been encountered already in this article, particularly in the criticism of Gershwin's music. Jazz was essentially dance music; it could never quite be

30 Quoted in B. H. Haggin's review of Whiteman's book, *Jazz*, "Add Americana," *Nation* (September 22, 1926): 276.

31 Ibid.

32 Editorial, "Newman Excoriates Jazz," *Musical America* (September 18, 1926): 16.

33 Oscar Thompson, "Jazz, as Art Music, Piles Failure on Failure," *Musical America* (February 13, 1926): 3.

34 Carl Engel, "Views and Reviews," *Musical Quarterly* 8 (October 1922): 626.

liberated from the demands of dance for the regular two-four or four-four meter with predictable, short phrases and periodic structure. It was fundamentally episodic and not susceptible to developmental procedures. Jazz was "an art of embellishment, based on a limitation—limitation to one subject matter, the four quarters of the fox-trot measure; and embellishment of this (also limited) by rich, ingenious scoring, by a not unrestrainably syncopated melody, and more recently, by chords borrowed from serious architecture."[35] Clive Bell, discussing jazz in the sense of a general cultural phenomenon, felt that short-windedness was its prime characteristic: "An accomplished jazz artist, whether in notes or words, will contrive as a rule to stop just where you expect him to begin. Themes and ideas are not developed; to say all that one has to say smells of the school, and may be a bore.[36]

35 B. H. Haggin, "The Pedant Looks at Jazz," *Nation* (December 9, 1925): 687–88.
36 Bell, "Plus de Jazz," 93.

IV. MATURITY (1930–1935)

By 1930, when the United States was in the throes of the Great Depression, Gershwin was comfortably on his way toward immortality. The first part of the decade saw him completing a trilogy of political satires with the book-writing team of Morrie Ryskind and George S. Kaufman. The first of these shows, the reworked *Strike Up the Band* (1930), was a moderate success, running for 191 performances at the Times Square Theatre. The second musical, the blockbuster *Of Thee I Sing* (1931), received the first Pulitzer Prize for a musical work, although not for the music per se, since such a category was not yet established. Running for 441 performances, this show set an attendance record for a Gershwin production. And the final political satire, *Let 'Em Eat Cake* (1933), was a decided flop with a mere 90 performances to its credit. Gershwin followed up or answered the *Rhapsody*, *Concerto*, *Preludes*, and the tone poem *An American in Paris* with similar but more mature, experimental works during this time in the *Second Rhapsody*, *"I Got Rhythm" Variations*, the *Songbook*, and the *Cuban Overture* respectively. By the middle of the decade, then, he finally felt qualified to bring the two strains of his musical life—popular music for the theater and art music for the concert hall—together in one work in the form of his, as he put it, "labor of love," the opera *Porgy and Bess*. Gershwin matured in other ways now as well, as he became more comfortable with his fame and the responsibility he faced as a leading figure on the American musical scene. The following essays detail these musical and personal developments.

38 George Gershwin: "Making Music" (1930)

In the following piece the composer deals with the larger issues of inspiration and compositional productivity.

"There are so many songwriters today that if placed end to end, it wouldn't be a bad idea!"

This futile but perhaps sage suggestion, presented the other day by a well-known Broadway wag, is being echoed up and down the Great Blight Way. And with no little reason. Never, in all our history of popular music, has there been such a plethora of composers—professional, amateur, and alleged—as we have today. Responsible, of course, are those two fresh hotbeds, the coniferous cinema and the radio. The merciless ether, by unceasing plugging, has cut down the life of a popular song to but a few weeks, with the result that anyone who thinks he can carry a tune—even if it's nowhere in particular—nowadays takes a "shot" at music-making. "I care not who makes the nation's laws, if I may make its theme songs" appears to be the general attitude. One music publisher facetiously declares that songwriting may someday displace the anagram!

With this enormous increase of interest in songwriting I find that I am being asked more often than ever by laymen as well as by aspiring composers for my formula, if any: just how, where, why, and when I write my music. In placing it all on the record here, I only wish to correct a few of the many popular misconceptions about songwriting.

Often I am given to understand that composing a song is an easy affair. All a number needs for success, it seems, is thirty-two bars: a good phrase of eight bars used to start the refrain is repeated twice more with a new eight-bar added which is much less important. It sounds simple, of course, but personally I can think of no more nerve-wracking, no more mentally arduous task than making music. There are times when a phrase of music will cost me many hours of internal sweating. Rhythms romp through my brain, but they're not easy to capture and keep; the chief difficulty is to avoid reminiscence.

SOURCE *New York World Sunday Magazine* (May 4, 1930).

Inspiration, commonly considered the main spring of composition, is as elusive as it is illusive. I might call it an unconscious something that happens within you which makes you do a thing much better than if it were done self-consciously. When it does come, it may be truly called a gift from the gods. Out of my entire annual output of songs, perhaps two—or at the most, three—come as a result of inspiration. When I want it most, it does not come, so I never rely on it; that is, I don't sit around and wait for an inspiration to walk up to me and introduce itself. What I substitute for it is nothing more than talent plus my knowledge. If a composer's endowment is great enough, the song is made to sound as if it were truly inspired.

After all, making music is actually little else than a matter of invention. What causes me to write is only my inventiveness, aided and abetted by emotion. I combine what I know of music with what I feel. I see a piece of music in the form of a design. With a melody I can take the whole design in one look; with a larger composition, like a concerto, I have to take it piece by piece and then construct it so much longer. No matter what they say about "nothing new under the sun," it is always possible to invent something original. The songwriter takes an idea and adds his own individuality to it; he merely uses his capacity for invention in arranging bars his own way. Though it can hardly be said that I come from a musical family, my grandfather really was an inventor in Russia, while my father at one time was a devotee of opera and showed an authentic love for music, I think, by being able to imitate a trumpet almost perfectly and to whistle very beautifully.

Just as a creator of fiction or of poetry, a composer of music smells symphonic ideas in every fact. To me they are represented by both abstract and concrete ideas. Though I am a great lover of nature, none of my music comes from viewing detached scenes, no matter how beautiful or "inspiring" they may be; most of my ideas arise from contact with people, from personalities and emotions of men and women I meet.

The idea for the *Rhapsody in Blue*, for example, came to me quite suddenly. The vivid panorama of American life swept through my mind—its feverishness, its vulgarity, its welter of love, marriage, and divorce, and its basic solidity in the character of the people. All of the emotional reactions excited by contemplating the American scene, with all its mixtures of races, . . . were stuffed into the first outline of the *Rhapsody*, with a dominant theme derived from the fashionable "blue" or melancholy rhythm.

I really prefer writing serious music. A serious composition is either a success or a failure because of what the composer does to it. I may write a good score for a musical comedy, but if the book or cast is poor my work registers a flop. A symphony, on the other hand, lives or dies according to its real worth. While popular music may be tricked very easily, serious music offers so many more interesting problems in construction, in orchestration, in other details. For a long time—as far back as my eighteenth year—I have wanted to work at big compositions. I am glad I can do it now. Nor will the contention of Madame Galli-Curci that opera is old-fashioned deter me from writing my opus.

Of extreme importance to the concocter of tunes is his mood. Without the proper mood it is almost impossible to compose satisfactorily. Frequently I have to force myself into a mood. Although, to write a happy song, for example, I do not actually have to be happy, I must try to feel like one who is happy. To get into the proper frame of mind I sit at the piano and play. Thus I find myself most frequently at the piano while composing.

Composing at the piano is not a good practice. But I started that way and it has become a habit. However, I give my mind free rein and use the piano only to try what I can hear mentally. The best method is one which will not permit anything to hold you down in any way, for it is always easier to think in a straight line, without the distraction of sounds. The mind should be allowed to run loose, unhampered by the piano, which may be used now and then only to stimulate thought and set an idea aflame. The actual composition must be done in the brain. Too much, however, should not be left to the memory. Sometimes, when I think the phrase is safe in my mind, I will find that I have lost it the next day. So that when I get a phrase which I am not sure I will remember the following day, I set it down on paper at once. Occasionally I dream a composition, but rarely can I remember it when I wake. On one occasion I did get out of bed and write a song. That number, incidentally, is one of my recent compositions, "Strike Up the Band."

What comes first, the words or the music? Odd, how this question is the first which enters the mind of most people when the art of writing songs is under discussion. In my own case most frequently the music is written first. Often, however, my brother Ira will write the lyric first, but always in a definite rhythm. These songs are mainly of the comedy variety.

Like the denizens of the prize ring, the songwriter must always keep in training. He must try to write something every day. I know that if I don't do any writing for several weeks I lose a great deal of time in catching my stride again. Hence I am always composing.

My creative work is done almost exclusively at night, and my best is achieved in the fall and winter months. A beautiful spring or summer day is least conducive to making music, for I always prefer being out than at work. I don't write at all in the morning, for the obvious reason that I'm not awake at that time. The afternoon I devote to physical labor—orchestrations, piano copies, etc. At night, when other people are asleep or out for a good time, I can get absolute quiet for my composing. Not that perfect peace is always necessary; often I have written my tunes with people in the same room or playing cards in the next. If I find myself in the desired mood, I can hold it until I finish the song.

"To be a songwriter you must live a songwriter," a famous popular composer once remarked. I can think of no more apt dictum for those who are seriously contemplating composing music as a profession. You can't be something else—a butcher, a baker, or a broker—and then suddenly write a successful song. One must write, rewrite, and then write again. Knowing Tin Pan Alley, living in the atmosphere of words and music, tells the beginner what not to do. The outsider looking in will find it extremely difficult to break through to recognition.

I learned to write music by studying the most successful songs published. At nineteen I could write a song that sounded so much like Jerome Kern that he wouldn't know whether he or I had written it. But imitation can go only so far. The young songwriter may start by imitating a successful composer he admires, but he must break away as soon as he has learned the maestro's strong points and technique. Then he must try to develop his own musical personality, to bring something of his own invention into his work.

For some songwriters it is not even absolutely essential that they know anything about music. Many of the composers with the greatest number of successes to their credit—among them Walter Donaldson and Irving Berlin—can't read a line of music. What they have is an innate sense of melody and rhythm; all they seek is to write a simple tune that the public can easily remember. In order to write longer compositions, the study of musical technique is indispensable. Many people say that too much study kills spontaneity in music, but I claim that, although study may kill a small talent, it must develop a big talent. In other words, if study kills a musical endowment, it deserves to be killed. I studied piano for four years, and then harmony. And I shall continue to study for a long time.

Above all, the aspiring composer should write something every day, regardless of its length or quality. Continued writing offers greater chances for achieving something original and important. Perhaps the tenth—or the hundredth—song will do the trick.

39   Robert Benchley: *"Satire to Music"* (1930)

Writer Robert Benchley (1889–1945) approached the second, more high-minded incarnation *Strike Up The Band* (the flawed 1927 version died after a two-week try-out in Philadelphia) in the following piece in the more high-minded *New Yorker* magazine.

There is a great deal more to *Strike Up the Band* than comical gags and nice music. For one act, at least, it is about as devastating satire as has been allowed on the local boards for a long time. I say "allowed' because only a little over eleven years ago it would have landed Messrs. Ryskind, Gershwin, and Selwyn in Leavenworth. Kidding war and war-makers is a sport for which there is an open season and a closed season. The open season is only during those intervals when nobody happens, for the moment, to be wanting to make a war.

The story (originally written by George S. Kaufman and now revised by Morrie Ryskind) of a musical-comedy war with Switzerland over the use of Grade B milk in chocolate involves the presence of several types of super-patriot who were much in evidence in these parts during 1914–1918. There were plenty of them in the audience on the opening night and some of the lines spoken for comedy must have sounded vaguely familiar to them. All members of the National Security League should be made to attend *Strike Up the Band*—and not laugh. In fact, those who have a right to laugh are only those who laughed (or cried) at the same things in the days when we were planning a war of our own. Oddly enough, Mr. Ryskind himself is one of the few who come under that heading, having had some trouble at Columbia University for saying much the same things that he is now drawing down royalties for.

Mr. Ira Gershwin's lyrics, too, would have been matter for heavy conferences among the patriotic societies of an earlier day. Any man who would write: "We don't know what we're fighting for, but it really doesn't matter" would bear watching. And incidentally, Mr. Ira Gershwin will bear watching, or listening to, today, for his lyrics are consistently literate, correct, and amusing. I need hardly call attention to the merits of his brother George, who has written for *Strike Up the Band* some of the best things he has done. It is too bad that the show did not come into town when it was first written two years ago, for the score at that time contained "The Man I Love," which later came in all by itself and won more than a passing popularity. But Mr. Gershwin's finale to the first act is fine enough to carry a show without help.

SOURCE   *The New Yorker* (January 25, 1930): 27–28.

I have left until the last any mention of Bobby Clark because I am told that I made something of a display of myself at the opening by laughing so loudly. If many more newspapers in their play-reviews comment on the noise I make when I laugh, I shall begin to think that there is something in it. I have now in my scrapbook four personal notices of my laugh, not all of them complimentary but all very clearly printed, and I am thinking of having them put on my personal stationery. ("Mr. Benchley's guffaws rising as a sort of overtone over the general merriment."—Arthur Ruhl in the *Herald Tribune*.)[1]

Perhaps after this I need only add that I thought Bobby Clark funny. He has turned from his old-time hand-to-hand encounters with cigar and stick (although he still carries them) and is funny without them. Some time I shall have to sit down and think out the reason why he is so funny. Right now I don't know. But to see him, in a Confederate general's coat and an admiral's hat, executing maneuvers which he counts on to make him physically attractive to a lady, is something very definite in emotional experiences. Mr. McCullough, the only straight-man in the business who dresses up like a comic, is also present, and our old love, Blanche Ring, adds her sure touch to a picture which is already pretty darned good. The second act runs downhill quite a bit, but, having started so high up, it doesn't have time to get very far.

40   John Harkins: "George Gershwin" (1932)

George Gershwin always accommodated the press, especially for feature stories in significant publications. From Carl Van Vechten's March 1925 article in *Vanity Fair* and the cover story in *Time* on July 20, 1925, through myriad interviews both feeble and fantastic until almost the time of his death, it is obvious that Gershwin enjoyed having reporters in his home to entertain and enjoy them. He was especially fond of showing off his furniture, paintings, sculptures, wardrobe, and athletic equipment. Usually from these interviews one can ascertain a relaxed and jovial Gershwin, the persona he always displayed to the press.

It is George Gershwin's notion that most great composers have suffered from indigestion as a consequence, rather than a cause, of creative work and its accompanying nervous strain. He himself has it. In Gershwin's instance the ailment is due partly to this strain of labor and to the tension attendant upon

1   See Ruhl's review of *Of Thee I Sing* (selection 41, p. 143).
SOURCE   *Life* (August 1932): 13–16.

opening nights of shows and first performances of concertos, and partly, no doubt, to the syncopated life he leads.

Gershwin preaches the benefits of a regular, routine existence. He must "feel fresh" to create and he believes his best work can be done before noon. Indeed, he hopes, some day, to become a member of the early-to-bed, early-to-rise school for the sake of his health as well as his work. At present, however—and the present places him at the head of its music class—he accomplishes nothing in the morning, and no one leads a more uncertain, unsystematic life.

The only brief he might present on behalf of his personal regularity is that he spends seven or eight hours a day in bed. There is little telling which seven or eight hours of the day or night they will be, and not all seven or eight will be spent in sleep; but he forces himself to remain in bed that long, even when he is awake, for he believes the relaxation does him good.

If Gershwin goes to bed at one o'clock he is retiring early. It is much more likely to be three or four o'clock, or later, in the morning before his day is done. So that part of the morning that comes after dawn is pretty much a thing of the past by the time he rises.

A room in Gershwin's home has been fitted out in a semi-professional gymnasium manner but a few kicks and a simple back exercise or two, performed by the bedside, are all that the young composer will undertake in an athletic way before breakfast.

Unlike so many of the late-rising stars of the theatre, Gershwin dresses before the first meal of the day, pulling on a shirt, flannel trousers, white wool socks and house slippers cut out to resemble sandals. Dressing, he believes, puts him in a mood for composition. If he eats in his pajamas, he is in a mood for lounging through the day.

His informal, comfortable attire of the home is removed far from his dress of the street. In Broadway's fashion, he is a "snappy" dresser. Rather tall, tending to slightness, handsome in a tanned way, the pleated trousers and wasp waists of his suits, the brightly checked scarf over his shoulders, make him appear just one of the crowd in Times Square. In winter he makes his home in a huge fur coat. After dark, he appears in full dress, never a dinner jacket.

Because of his composer trouble, or indigestion, Gershwin's breakfast is a light, quick repast of orange juice, occasionally a cereal, toast, eggs, and coffee.

Immediately afterward, he is ready for work, or for painting, an avocation that in the last few years has come to be only slightly subordinate to his music.

Gershwin is a prolific and prodigal composer, as well as one of distinction and talent. He works with such concentration and rapidity that he is inclined to fret at the comparative slowness of those working with him. When working with his elder brother Ira, upon a musical show—and generally they are working on one—George constantly is vexed because Ira, an even later riser, never is ready to start the day's stint before one o'clock in the afternoon.

Gershwin's methods of composition vary with the work at hand. Engaged upon a musical show, brief refrains that will have a popular appeal are the first objective. Form and structure are secondary, to be undertaken later. In the more pretentious field of suites and concertos, form and structure are the basic elements. The filling, sweet as it may be, is put in afterward.

Within his musical show scores there is another division. In most shows, where the simple demand is for a song for a spot, the music is written first, the words will follow. But in lyrical scores like that of the now popular *Of Thee I Sing*, where the words tell a part of the story, brother Ira writes the words first, then music is fitted to them.

Luncheon does not interrupt work in the Gershwin household until midafternoon. After that come more working hours until dinner, at eight o'clock in the evening, and generally at home. The evening, if possible, will be a quiet one. Gershwin, who will be 31 on the 26th of September, feels that he no longer can maintain the night life pace, with its speed of every night out, at which he went in the twenties.

Rehearsals, of course, absorb many nights. Then there are certain social obligations imposed upon a composer whose admirers regard him as a genius and insist upon feting him. But Gershwin, one of the first-rank artists of the theatre, rarely goes to a playhouse except for the premiere of one of his own shows, when he conducts. And Gershwin, composer of much of the most popular dance music of the last fifteen years, does not dance, unless dancing is an accomplishment that he carefully has concealed from his friends.

When he does go out, it is in a restrained way, for he feels that he should uphold the dignity of his position in music. He rarely takes anything to drink. Until recently, he smoked long, black cigars in an unceasing procession. But a year ago, during an examination, his doctor suggested that he might be smoking too much. Gershwin had a cigar in his mouth at the time. It was the last one he smoked. Since then, except to light a cigarette for a woman, he has not touched tobacco. He thinks he feels better for it, and he has gained four pounds. If he ever smokes again, it will be to make honest men of the caricaturists who continue to draw him with cigars in his mouth.

Gershwin rarely entertains, except on Sunday evening, when he regularly is host to a group of friends that include Winnie Sheehan, the motion picture executive; Buddy DeSylva, Bill Daly, and Oscar Levant, the songwriters; and Bob Garland, the drama critic.

He is a gracious host, exceptionally gracious to women, with a knack of making them feel of comparative importance.

He passes expensive cigars to his guests. Then, inevitably, someone suggests that he play. He sits down before the piano, and it is hours before he rises. He always plays his own compositions. The only greater offender—if so harsh a word may be used—in that way was Debussy. While George is playing, Ira sometimes sings. As a guest once remarked: "An evening at the Gershwins' is a Gershwin evening."

George and Ira have separate penthouses on the seventeenth story of an apartment building at Riverside Drive and Seventy-fifth Street in New York. They share the whole side of the terraced roof that stretches between their apartments, facing down the Hudson River.

A visitor, passed along by the building doorman who has instructed the elevator man that the call is for "Georgie Gershwin," not Ira, might believe, and with reason, that he was wandering by mistake into a painter's studio as he enters the home of the man who led the jazz parade from Tin Pan Alley to Carnegie Hall.

Paintings hang all over the walls. They stand on the floor, resting against tables and chairs. It is true that a grand piano, with some show of importance, fills nearly one-quarter of the living room. But it is an easel, upholding a half-finished portrait, that occupies the center of the floor space.

Gershwin's assembly of paintings is a notable one of French works, that frequently is drawn upon for gallery exhibits. He started it almost as casually as he began his hobby of painting. He had had both in mind from early youth, but it was only a few years ago that he did anything about either.

He was sitting one day on the roof outside his penthouse, thinking of some water colors that his brother had obtained a few days before, when he decided that it might be amusing to attempt to copy one. The copy was so successful that he has been painting ever since, sometimes for as long as eight hours a day. Just now he is working on a fair-sized portrait of his grandfather, a remarkable likeness enlarged on canvas from a yellowed snapshot that measures no more than two inches by three. The grandfather stands against a background drawn out of Gershwin's memory of his boyhood in the East Side of New York.

The collection of French pieces had what must seem at first glance to have been a haphazard start. At the end of his only invasion of Hollywood's motion picture studios, Gershwin had in a California bank what sometimes is called curiously a "round sum" of money. He left it there and wrote to his cousin, Henry Botkin, a painter mostly resident in Paris, that it was time to start assembling paintings. Soon photographs of possibilities arrived by mail. The composer chose those that appealed to him and they were purchased for him from the California art fund.

Botkin still is sending paintings from Paris, and they sprawl all over

Gershwin's six-room home, an elaborate establishment as penthouses go in New York. Matters, and paintings, have reached a point of congestion where the collector is complaining continually that he will have to move into larger quarters. Perhaps he will, some day. He already has invested a large portion of his income in paintings, and in expensive cigars.

The penthouse is furnished with an ultra-modern touch. In the living room, at the other end from the piano, is a deep couch, set under terraced bookcases. On the lowest terrace top is a bronze head of the composer, done by a Japanese sculptor. The bookcases are filled, for the musician's interest in literature is more than casual. He carries on an intimate correspondence with John Galsworthy, and they exchange manuscripts and scores. Galsworthy, in his play *Escape*, used a refrain from Gershwin's show *Lady, Be Good!* as a whistling signal.

Around the walls of the combination gymnasium-office, where Gershwin exercises and his secretary works, hang tiers of photographs, including one of Prince George of England that is inscribed "From George to George." The floor once was padded like a wrestling mat, but Gershwin has abandoned that grunting sport. But the room has foils that he still uses and houses a Ping-Pong table upon which he plays with a measure of skill. His other indoor sports are dice, poker, and indoor golf. He gambles at all three as often as possible.

He spends his weekends at golf course or beach in Westchester, Long Island, or New Jersey. Until the pressure of work became too great he went to Europe at least once a year. In fact, he wrote *An American in Paris* while he was making a hectic but triumphant tour abroad a few years ago. Now, for longer vacations, he goes to the Adirondacks, Lake Placid, Saranac, to Saratoga for the racing, and to Canada for the open golf tournament there.

Today he is involved in a tremendous amount of work. There is at least one new musical show for next season, with two others in the offing. There is the soon-to-be-published *George Gershwin's Songbook*, that will carry the arrangements of his pieces not only as they first were published but also as he plays them at home. In the back of his head are plans for a grand opera he is building upon the drama *Porgy*, a project looking five or six years ahead.

Gershwin is a self-made musician. He had to beg his family for permission to take music lessons when he was a child. His first teachers were neighborhood girls who charged fifty cents an hour. Then a male teacher charged three times as much. He played for the fatherly Max Dreyfuss, of the Harms music house, who encouraged him to go on with his studies, until he was convinced that he wanted more and more music. Again over the opposition of his parents, he quit high school and joined the piano players at the Remick music publishing corporation. For $15 a week he plugged songs for twelve hours a day for dizzy blondes seeking something new for their acts. He studied under Rubin Goldmark, distinguished orchestrator. And that was his musical education until he composed "Swanee," the song that brought first popularity.

The opposition of his mother and father to his career never changed his respect and fondness for them, and he points out that they did not object so strenuously that they discouraged him. He thinks now, however, that parents should encourage children in whatever they may want to do. But then, Gershwin is a bachelor.

41   Arthur Ruhl: "Of Thee I Sing; *Kaufman-Ryskind Musical Comedy Satire at the Music Box*" (1931)

Within the Gershwin political trilogy, *Of Thee I Sing* was clearly the most successful. The first musical show to be awarded the Pulitzer Prize (although not for its music since that category was not yet created), the challenges of the work seemed ideally suited for the Gershwins at this point in their career.

The favorable reports which followed the road tryout of the new Kaufman-Gershwin musical comedy, *Of Thee I Sing*, were amply confirmed a the Music Box on Saturday night when this very amusing satire on American political life made its first appearance in New York. An audience, including former Governor [Alfred E.] Smith, Mayor [James J.] Walker, Miss [Ethel] Barrymore and many others similarly able to pass expert judgment, received the piece with more than routine first-night enthusiasm—with a spontaneous relish, in fact, which greeted the torchlight procession and chorus, "Wintergreen for President," with which the story began, and continued until the final curtain.

The entertainment provided by the Messrs. Kaufman and Ryskind and the Gershwin brothers is a good deal more than conventional musical comedy. Although routine musical comedy methods are followed more or less, including "girls" in the usual musical show connotations of that word, there is a coherent story, definite satirical intent, displayed both in music and lines, a complete absence of vaudeville and interpolated "specialties." In short, satirical operetta rather than the historical jumble of the routine musical show.

Beginning with a scene at national committee headquarters ("Let's

SOURCE   *New York Herald Tribune* (December 28, 1931): 9.

see—which party are we?" as one of the committee asks), the story follows
John P. Wintergreen's campaign through until his triumphant election on the
slogan "Put Love in the White House." No other issue seemed available,
although the committeemen combed carefully the party's record from 1776
through the early decades of the last century. As the chairman explained,
what you need for an issue is something that everybody can get excited about
and yet something that doesn't really make any difference. Love was just the
thing—especially for the handsome but otherwise wholly undistinguished Mr.
John P. Wintergreen.

Have a bathing beauty contest, the winner of which will marry the new
President. All that the candidate needs to do is to fall in love with the successful girl. Wintergreen will become the Great Lover. He will propose to his
future bride in every state in the Union. The pictures of John and Mary will
hang on every wall in the land, each step in their romance will be accompanied by answering throbs in the Great American Heart. Love will sweep the
country and carry John P. Wintergreen into the White House on a rose-
decked tidal wave.

So much for the first act. In the second part, the satirists tackle Washington and there are scenes in the White House, in the Senate, Supreme Court,
and so on, in the course of which pretty much everybody comes in for a rap,
especially the unhappy vice president. Beginning with their first scene in the
national committee room, when the unfortunate Alexander Throttlebottom,
venturing to visit his colleagues, is thrown out as an intruder whose name
they don't even know, until he comes in, toward the end, with a little shirt he
has knitted with his own hands for the White House baby, the authors have
no mercy whatever for the second man on the ticket, and what shreds of self-
esteem they might have left him are undone effectually by the very amusing
acting of the self-abasing Victor Moore.

The piece is funny all through, with scarce a moment that hasn't its
double-edged or barbed point, either implicit in the situation or expressed in
the lines. But perhaps the high spot was reached in the election rally scene in
Madison Square Garden, where William Gaxton, as the presidential nominee,
gave his deliciously accurate imitation of Jimmy Walker's platform manner
(with the Mayor himself looking up at him from a second-row seat); the garden's loud-speaking announcer drowned out the unhappy vice-presidential
candidate every time he started to speak; and when one of the senatorial
bores began his thunderous harangue, a mat was hastily unrolled directly in
front of the speaker's platform, and two enormous Turkish wrestlers began a
burlesque wrestling match. The senator's sonorous periods, mercifully
squelched by the audience's rapturous applause of the "muscle merchants,"

proceeded in unison with the ridiculous antics of the mat behemoths (excellently carried off by Tom Draak and Sulo Hevonpaa) and made an episode both hilariously funny in itself and characteristic of the author's ruthless handling of politicians in general.

Messrs. Gaxton and Moore, and pretty Miss Lois Moran, with her unusually crisp and agreeable diction and speaking voice, are the principals of an all-round excellent cast, including June O'Dea, Dudley Clements, and Florenz Ames. It would be as difficult to compare the unsentimental, cerebral style of Mr. Kaufman's wit and Mr. Gershwin's music with Gilbert and Sullivan as to compare a floral decoration on a city skyscraper's façade with a primrose by the river's brim, yet the Gilbert and Sullivan analogy was suggested frequently during the evening. There was no question, in any case, of the piece's brilliant success.

42 *"A Music Master Talks of His Trials"* (1932)

It has long been supposed that some—if not most—of the anecdotal accounts of George Gershwin's escapades originated with the composer himself. One such story, concerning Gershwin's proposed studies with Ravel ("How much do you earn per year, Mr. Gershwin?" [answer] "Well, if that is the case, it is I who should be studying with you!"), was attributed to Igor Stravinsky as well. Both Ravel and Stravinsky denied the conversation. The following story appeared in several newspapers with only minor episodic variations. Whether partially or completely factual, it is, nonetheless, a delightful tale.

Last Saturday night when the shouting in connection with the triumphant premiere of *Of Thee I Sing* had died down George Gershwin, the composer of its score, stood on the stage of the Music Box surrounded by a knot of personal friends and admirers and recalled an incident in his early life which was in striking contrast to the scene which he had been surveying all evening from a balcony seat. He said:

"Back in what are generally called the 'old days' I got fed up with working as a song plugger for fifteen dollars a week and decided to seek a broader field of activity. I wanted to write music for the theatre and I felt that I should be in and of the theatre, if you know what I mean. I got myself a job at Fox's City Theatre on Fourteenth Street as a piano player. The pay was to be twenty-five dollars for a seven-day week.

SOURCE *New York American* (January 3, 1932).

"I was to play during the 'supper show' while the orchestra musicians were out to dinner. I sat through a matinee performance watching the acts go through their routine and felt that I could make good when the time came to take up my task. And I did make good for the first two or three acts. My Waterloo and the most humiliating moment of my life arrived simultaneously when a 'tab revue' took the stage.

"It was a typical small time vaudeville act with a leading juvenile, a soprano, six chorus girls, and a comedian who was terrible. It carried so-called special music and when I fussily turned to the sheets on the piano rack I discovered that they were in manuscript form and that the musical symbols on them bore a more than marked resemblance to the hieroglyphics on a Babylonian funeral urn. There were penciled notations and smudges and blots and life suddenly became unbearable.

"I went bravely on, however, and struggled through the opening chorus. Then, suddenly, I found myself playing one thing while the prima donna was singing something else. I tried to find the right cue, but failed and gave up trying to play.

"The comic—I can still see his leering face—came down to the footlights and began to jeer at me. 'Who told you you were a piano player?' he bawled out. 'You ought to be driving a truck.' The audience howled, the chorus girls giggled and I died a thousand deaths.

"I struggled through the show and then looked up the house manager. He was out to dinner so I explained things to the head usher. 'I'm quitting,' I told him. 'I can't face that comic again. If I did there would be bloodshed.' I left without collecting my salary.

"I got that, however, about twelve months [years] later. The Fox company sent for me to write the music for a picture and it was agreed that I was to receive a hundred thousand dollars. When it came time for signing the contract I changed the figure to read $100,003.13 and when eyebrows were raised I told the story.

"'You see I've got an eighth of a week's salary coming on the basis of twenty-five a week,' I remarked, and the revised figure was solemnly agreed to."

43 *Catherine Parsons Smith: From* William Grant Still: A Study in Contradictions *(2000)*

When asked what his favorite tune was, George Gershwin would always respond, "I Got Rhythm." Not only was it used as the theme song of his radio show "Music by Gershwin," it received the most developed treatment in his *Songbook* and was the subject of the 1934 piano and orchestra variations. Yet, musicians of his day and modern scholars have questioned the origin of this sensational tune.

The initial presentation of the minstrel tune (theme 1A) in the Scherzo [of Still's *Afro-American Symphony*] is accompanied by a countermelody identical to the opening of the chorus of a hit pop tune of the day. Gershwin's show *Girl Crazy*, featuring the infectious "I Got Rhythm," opened October 14, 1930, as Still was preparing to travel to Rochester for the performance of *Africa* and just two weeks before he began to compose the *Afro-American Symphony*. The quotation appears once, immediately after the introduction, in the horns, in a spot where it is intended to be heard, meant to be a reference listeners would clearly understand. A second, following statement is broken up by octave displacements and changes in instrumentation; then the fragment of this catchy tune is heard no more. It seems entirely possible that Still changed his initial conception of this movement (as shown in ex. 1) specifically to accommodate this quotation. Indeed, he made more revisions from his original outline of the symphony in this movement than he did for any of the others, scrapping both the original main theme and his initial outline for the movement. He went back to his 1924 theme book to borrow an early tune he had labeled "Hallelujah!" years earlier [ex. 2].

Why does this current pop tune appear in the Scherzo of this symphony? The question puzzles modern performers, even seems to embarrass them; in one recent recording, the quotation is all but inaudible, seemingly deliberately made so.[1] I believe that Gershwin's "I Got Rhythm" reinforces the meaning of that first statement of theme 1A, in its major/minstrel form in which the African American presence is perceived solely through the eyes of white interpreters, thereby speaking to the meaning Still intended for the movement and for the symphony as a whole. We hear the start of "I Got Rhythm" intact only

SOURCE Catherine Parsons Smith, *William Grant Still: A Study in Contradictions* (Berkeley, Calif.: University of California Press, 2000), 136–144. All footnotes in this entry appear in the original source.

1 Detroit Symphony, Neeme Järvi, conductor, Chandos CHAN 9154, 1993. The tenor banjo is also almost inaudible on this otherwise excellent recording. The horns, which are assigned the first "I Got Rhythm," and banjo are very clear, however, in the performance by the Cincinnati Philharmonic Orchestra, Dinching Cai, conductor, Centaur CRC 2331, 1997.

Ex. 1

Ex. 2

once; then the movement goes on to its real business, the transforming shift toward a black-influenced, modally inflected minstrel tune with the very political "Hallelujah" and "Emancipation" themes folded through it.

Why did Still choose this particular tune to make his point? Where did the "I Got Rhythm" melody come from in the first place? Here the answer grows more speculative. Modern listeners more familiar with Gershwin's song than Still's work assume that Still borrowed Gershwin's melody, but some older African American musicians believe it was Still's to begin with. Evidence from the theme book supports them—partly. The story about Still, Gershwin, and "I Got Rhythm" also draws on anecdotal evidence, all collected well after the fact. There are several versions. Judith Anne Still tells of her father walking down a New York City street with Eubie Blake and hearing the tune as they walked past an open door. Blake asked wasn't that Still's tune from *Shuffle Along* days, and Still acknowledged that indeed it was. Blake expressed anger at the theft; Still's response was more sanguine. In a published interview from 1973, Blake went into much greater detail:

Do you know William Grant Still? . . . He's a personal friend of mine. [Eubie darts to the piano.] Do you know this tune? [He plays Gershwin's "I Got Rhythm."] . . . All of the fellows in my orchestra would be playing around, having a good time, but Still would be playing this little tune over and over. [Eubie hums the melody.] So I heard the darn thing so much that one day I said to him (not while we were playing in New York, but later when we were in Boston), "What's the tune you're playing?" Still answered me, "One day you'll hear it in a symphony, an American symphony!" . . .

Now, one day Dooley Wilson . . . comes up to me and says, "Boy, have I got some music; this is swell music!" I played the music for him—it was all Gershwin music—and when I got to the piece "I Got Rhythm," I didn't have to look at the music. I knew it! You know, once I hear a tune—if it's a good tune—I don't forget it. . . . Now, one day I was walking down 56th Street, and I saw Still standing in front of the Carnegie Hall entrance. . . . I said, "You know that tune you used to play?" I hummed it for him. "Is that your tune?" He looked at me but didn't answer. So I said, "I saw the music to 'I Got Rhythm' and it's the same as your tune." Still said, "Yeah? Well, I'll see *you* later." He would not say that Gershwin stole the tune; he is just that kind of man.

[Interviewer] How do you explain it?

Oh, that's easy. Still used to teach Gershwin orchestration. He had to go to Gershwin's place on Park Avenue to give the lessons, and while he was waiting for Gershwin to come down—Gershwin was always late—he would play this darn tune on his oboe. Gershwin heard the tune and took it. Now Gershwin probably didn't mean to take it or steal it because he didn't have to. The man was a genius! But that tune was Still's tune. It could happen to anyone.[2]

2 "Conversation with Eubie Blake: A Legend in His Own Lifetime," ed. Bobbi King, *BpiM* I-2 (1973): 155–56. In a 1977 interview, Blake lists this among unacknowledged white "borrowings" from black musicians. Eubie Blake, taped interview with Lorraine Brown, Research Center for the Federal Theater Project (George Mason University), January 9, 1977, Eubie Blake Collection.

Blake's version is demonstrably inaccurate on at least one point. In a section of the interview not cited here, he has Still conducting his own symphony at Carnegie Hall. Actually, the New York premiere of Still's symphony (which must have been the *Afro-American*) took place in late 1935, long after *Girl Crazy* had closed. Still did not conduct, nor did he conduct any of his concert works in New York City. (He was living in Los Angeles by then and probably did not attend the performance.) In fact, Blake's association of the theme with the Boston run of *Shuffle Along* argues against Gershwin having heard it in the theater, for Gershwin is much less likely to have attended performances outside of New York.[3]

In October 1996, Dominique-René De Lerma wrote of interviewing Still about this when the two met in 1969:

> Still told me (I was also an oboist) that he doodled from the pit before *Shuffle Along* performances [i.e., in 1921 or 1922] with this little figure—
> . . . and knew that Gershwin was in the audience. The figure, of course, generates the Gershwin tune. . . . The same figure with the same rhythm appears in the third movement of the *Afro-American Symphony* in the horns, with the statement of the theme. Still had an expression on his face when we talked about this which clearly suggested he felt Gershwin had appropriated his doodle. I don't think it is extended enough to justify a copyright violation, but it is a strange coincidence and Still's reaction might be symptomatic of his vigilance.[4]

Gershwin was well known to seek out performances by black musicians, and *Shuffle Along* would have been an obvious show for him to have attended, maybe more than the one time Still mentioned to De Lerma.[5] Affirming once more that Gershwin was interested in Still's work, Verna Arvey notes that Gershwin attended the performance of Still's *Levee Land* at a concert pre-

---

3 Judith Anne Still reports that her father and Blake went at least once to Gershwin's apartment to help him with orchestration. But in his 1973 interview Blake was probably confusing Still with Will Vodery, who orchestrated for Gershwin, most notably Gershwin's 1922 one-act opera, *Blue Monday*.

4 Manuscript Reading Report, Dominique-René De Lerma, University of California Press, September 29, 1996. De Lerma and Still met at a conference organized by De Lerma at Indiana University, June 18–21, 1969. Subsequently De Lerma edited a collection that included a Still speech drawn from the conference: *Black Music in Our Culture: Curricular Ideas on the Subjects, Materials and Problems* (Kent, Ohio: Kent State University Press, 1970).

5 Still's recollection of Gershwin in the audience of *Shuffle Along* (De Lerma, n. 4 above) dates Gershwin's acquaintance with African American jazz and blues earlier than assumed by Charles Hamm in "A Blues for the Ages," in Crawford, Lott, and Oja, *A Celebration of American Music*, 346–55. Hamm was unable to document Gershwin's acquaintance with African American music making before 1925, the year of Gershwin's *Concerto in F*.

sented by the International Composers' Guild at Aeolian Hall, January 24, 1926. In the same essay, probably from the late 1960s, she wrote of Gershwin's attendance at a performance of *Shuffle Along*.

> One Negro musical show which took New York by storm in the early Twenties was *Shuffle Along*. George and Ira Gershwin and most of the other Broadway celebrities attended it, some more than once. . . . As the show went on and on, the players in the orchestra began to get tired of playing the same thing over and over again, so very often they would improvise. Most of them had a special little figure that they added, as they felt so inclined. Still's figure was melodic. Later, when he was composing the *Afro-American Symphony*, he used the small little figure, wedded to a distinctive rhythm which he had originated in the orchestration for a soft-shoe dance in the show *Rain or Shine*.[6]

Arvey was reporting what Still had told her. The awkwardness of her telling betrays her unfamiliarity with a milieu outside her own experience, but it also reflects a struggle to get the story as Still remembered it. Her words seem to amplify De Lerma's report about what happened. Later, Still wrote generally about musical borrowings in American music, though not in detail about his own experiences. In "The Men Behind American Music" (1944), Still writes with a certain ambivalence, mainly about plagiarism in commercial music:

> As for George Gershwin, who wrote so much in the Negroid idiom, there are many Negro musicians who now claim to have done work for him, arranging or composing. I have no way of knowing whether any of these claims are justified. I do know that Gershwin did a great deal of unconscious borrowing from several sources (not always the Negro) and that he did some conscious borrowing which he apparently was generous enough to acknowledge, for he gave W. C. Handy a copy of the *Rhapsody in Blue*, autographed to the effect that he recognized Handy's work as the forerunner of his own . . .
>
> Quite often colored musicians claim to have had their creations or their styles stolen from them by white artists. In many cases these tales

---

6 Verna Arvey, "Memo for Musicologists," reprinted in *Fusion* 2, 21–25. This essay first appears under this title in the first edition of *Fusion* (ed. Robert Bartlett Haas; Los Angeles: Black Sparrow Press, 1972, 88–93). To judge from the citation in the *Bio-Bibliography* (A30), which quotes a sentence reproduced in the quotation here, it is probably an expansion of Arvey's "Afro-American Music Memo," *Music Journal* 27 (November 1969): 36, 68. Arvey goes on to discuss Dvořák's use of "national American melodies" in the symphony *From the New World*, so strongly influenced by the singing of "Plantation songs and Hoe-downs" by Harry T. Burleigh.

may be dismissed as baseless rantings. But there have been so many
instances in which they are justified that one cannot ignore all of them.
I have learned this from my own experience and from the experiences
of my friends in the world of music.[7]

In support of his statement, he describes hearing an arrangement of his own
over the radio that was ascribed to another arranger.[8]

Still never claimed "I Got Rhythm" for himself, at least in writing. Yet
the 1924 theme book and the 1926 "Rashana" sketchbook offer evidence that

Ex. 3

partly supports the claims to precedence made in his behalf. The theme
book shows several themes that begin with the tune's opening four pitches,
sol, la, do, re (see ex. 3). In every case, the opening melodic contour is similar, but the tempos are slower, syncopation is not notated, and the melodies
go off in other directions rather than (or before) turning back on them-

---

7 William Grant Still, "The Men behind American Music," *Crisis* (January 1944): 12–15, 29. Reprinted
in Spencer, *Reader*, 114–23.

8 In June 1938 Still wrote to Willard Robison to complain, "While listening to a local radio station last
Thursday night, I heard some transcriptions [implied: from Robison's "Deep River Hour," for which Still
had arranged] made by the Associated Music Publisher Inc. [Still was later to correct this to "Associated
Recorded Program Service"] . . . All of them sounded like my own arrangements, although they were credited to Walter Remson. Do you think that it is fair to me to do a thing like that?" In a later letter he notes
that the Associated Recorded Program Service had informed him that " 'Walter Remsen' [*sic*] is a pseudonym for Willard Robison." Carbon copies of letters, Still to Robison, June 12, 1938, and August 1938, Still-
Arvey Papers.

Still also wrote very generally about white borrowings of the music of African Americans, again distin-
guishing between unconscious borrowings and conscious imitation, in "A Symphony of Dark Voices,"
Opera, Concert and Symphony (May 1947): 18–19, 36, 38–39 (reprint, Spencer, *Reader*, 136–43).

selves. Most memorable is its use as shown in example 4, "From the Land of Blues," the "melodic sketch" in the "Rashana" sketchbook not otherwise identifiable.

Gershwin's "I Got Rhythm" depends for its impact on three musical elements in addition to its text: a four-note gap-scale figure that turns back on itself, a syncopated rhythmic pattern, and a drive to a cadence that rounds it off. Still's themes, as they are notated in the examples we have, all lack the syncopation that is associated with Gershwin's tune. A handwritten notation

Ex. 4

on a draft of the Arvey essay quoted above, very likely made at Still's behest, reinforces Arvey's reference to the 1928 musical *Rain or Shine* as the place where Still, in one of his orchestrations, used both the melodic pattern and the syncopated rhythmic figure.[9] At least for now, this clue leads to a dead end. Only two songs from *Rain or Shine* are deposited in the Library of Congress; six more were returned to the claimant several years after they were deposited for copyright, and another six were never deposited.[10] One cannot know which (if any) of the fourteen might have quoted the "soft-shoe dance" to which Arvey refers, or whether the pattern occurred only in a section that never reached print or copyright. We are left with what appears to be Still's word—which is reliable in other cases but which cannot be verified in this one. Blake, who seems to have embroidered his story in order to make his broad point about unacknowledged borrowing, went out of his way to acknowledge that Gershwin's use of Still's idea was inadvertent: "it could happen to anybody."

It is obvious that the ascending gap-scale figure *(sol, la, do, re,* or *do, re, fa, sol)* fascinated Still. How Still improvised on it from the orchestra pit during the run of *Shuffle Along* (or in Gershwin's living room), we cannot know. Comparison of Still's and Gershwin's treatments of it shows both their similarity and where they parted company. Still's failure to claim the song as his own may simply represent his acknowledgment that he used it differently from the way Gershwin did, and/or that the distinction between something improvised and something written down was very important to him. Perhaps he feared that any serious claim on his part would be dismissed as "baseless ranting." Since the melodic motive we know about is not used in the same way by both composers, at least in the surviving written versions, the question of primacy becomes less relevant. The difference in their use of the same basic melodic material seems far more interesting than the similarity. For Still, it was a brief blues gesture to be extended at will; for Gershwin, a snappy, open-and-closed eight-bar song-and-dance phrase. The contrast points to the operation of different sensibilities powerfully influenced by the cultural position of each composer, the specific tasks in which each was involved, and the unpredictably vagaries of individual talents and predilections.

Despite his lack of action, Still must have known that, one way or other, he had helped Gershwin reach that melody. Perhaps Still could see the interaction on a broader scale. For him the melodic figure belonged to the blues,

9 Unsorted biographical papers at WGSM.
10 Wayne D. Shirley to the author, June 24, 1997. Short excerpts from the choruses of four of the returned songs appear on the back covers of the two deposited songs. None shows the characteristic rhythm.

Ex. 5

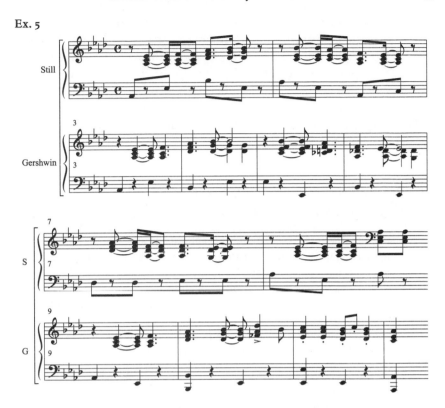

and to the African American past. By quoting Gershwin's version where he did, as part of the whites-in-blackface minstrel representation with which the Scherzo begins, he suggested where Gershwin's tune fitted into his fusion aesthetic with a subtlety appropriate to the mythical Trickster. Moreover, the appearance of "I Got Rhythm" along with *Girl Crazy* in mid-October 1930—assuming that date is when Still first heard it—must have pushed Still to begin writing the symphony he had contemplated for so long.[11] It might even have provoked him to rethink the Scherzo, to abandon for something far richer his initial idea of portraying the "janny sect" that he had laughed at when his mother had taken him along during the summers she taught rural African Americans without access to regular schools. One imagines his thought that Gershwin's use of that material aptly demonstrates the "minstrel mask" of the past, the one imposed from "outside." His own treatment

11 Still was not the only musician to quote "I Got Rhythm," although he was probably the first to use it in concert music, in a written score. Richard Crawford, in *The American Musical Landscape* (Berkeley and Los Angeles: University of California Press, 1993), devotes a chapter to "I Got Rhythm." He describes its subsequent use as a song, as a jazz standard, and as a chordal structure for jazz improvisation . . .

pointedly addresses the "real" past: slavery, Emancipation, the blues. He felt secure, perhaps, in his own sense of the "authenticity" of his own application, with the scale, with his constantly changing thematic "treatments" that modern commentators may think of as "signifying." If Still stimulated Gershwin from the pit in the *Shuffle Along* production or as the orchestrator of *Rain or Shine*, Gershwin's commercial adaptation in turn provoked Still to sit down and compose the symphony he had contemplated for so long, and even to add this tricksterish layer of meaning.

44   Richard Crawford "George Gershwin's 'I Got Rhythm' (1930)" (1993)

Another analysis of "I Got Rhythm," this abbreviated article speaks of the genesis of the work, its initial treatment, and its use as a master subject for scores of jazz composers and instrumentalists. In this chapter, Crawford includes a table listing 79 recordings of this song.

"I Got Rhythm" occupied a special place in Gershwin's work. It was the song he himself singled out as best suited for embellished instrumental performance. In *George Gershwin's Songbook* (1932), which contained eighteen Gershwin songs in his own arrangements for piano, "I Got Rhythm" was one of only two songs—"Liza" was the other—for which he supplied two choruses rather than one. In its strict observance of the notated rhythm, Gershwin's arrangement pays tribute to the song's instrumental pedigree. Singers have tended to loosen the declamation to something closer to a half note and quarter note: ♩♩|♩♩ . The *Songbook* version, however, centers on a series of dotted quarter notes in duple time—a standard way of creating instrumental syncopation that dates at least as far back as Scott Joplin's "Maple Leaf Rag" (1899), whose second strain achieves that effect through figuration rather than accented chords.[1] In 1934, Gershwin returned to "I Got Rhythm," using it as the basis for a set of variations for piano and orchestra. This gave him something new to play along with the *Rhapsody in Blue* and the *Concerto in F* on a concert tour he took that year with the Leo Reisman Orchestra.[2] The work contains six character variations in which the tune appears as a

SOURCE Richard Crawford, "George Gershwin's 'I Got Rhythm' (1930)," in *The American Musical Landscape* (Berkeley, Los Angeles: University of California Press, 1993), pp. 217–35, 336–44. All footnotes in this entry appear in the original source.

1 I am grateful to James Dapogny for this suggestion.

2 Jablonski, Edward, *Gershwin* (New York: Doubleday, 1987), 258–59. In Jablonski's opinion, "much of the wit and charm of this work is smothered in the reorchestration by William C. Schoenfeld published in 1953" (260).

hot Broadway number, a waltz, and in other guises as well, including one Gershwin called a "Chinese variation." On his radio show, he told his audience that variation was inspired by Chinese flutes, "played out of tune, as they always are."

Now let's go back to October 1930. Within ten days of the opening of *Girl Crazy* on the 14th, three significant recordings of "I Got Rhythm" were made. On the 20th, Freddie Rich, conductor of the CBS Radio Orchestra, recorded it with a group under his own name. On the 23rd, Red Nichols and His Five Pennies—all thirteen of them, and including Goodman, Krupa, Miller, and other members of the *Girl Crazy* pit band, plus vocalist Dick Robertson—made their own version. And on the 24th, one of New York's best black bands, Luis Russell and His Orchestra, recorded another version. Each can be taken to represent the beginning of a different approach to Gershwin's number: (1) "I Got Rhythm" as a *song* played and sung by popular performers; (2) "I Got Rhythm" as a jazz standard, a piece known and frequently played by musicians, black and white, in the jazz tradition; and (3) "I Got Rhythm" as a musical *structure*, a harmonic framework upon which jazz instrumentalists, especially blacks, have built new compositions.

Let's begin with the song. I noted Ira Gershwin's struggle to find a rhyme scheme fitting George's tune. But I said nothing about the words he finally wrote. William Austin has pointed out that the Gershwin brothers used the word "rhythm" in several of their songs. In 1918 Ira called ragtime "a rhythmic tonic for the chronic blues."[3] In 1924 he wrote: "Fascinating rhythm, it'll drive me insane";[4] in 1928, "Listen to the rhythm of my heart beat";[5] in 1930, "I Got Rhythm"; and in 1937, "Today you can see that the happiest men/All got rhythm."[6] Austin adds: "I believe the Gershwins are largely responsible for [the word] rhythm entering the vocabularies of millions of people for whom it had previously been too technical."[7] The two Gershwin songs with

---

3 The song was "The Real American Folk Song (Is a Rag)," written under Ira's pseudonym, "Arthur Francis," with music by George. It was interpolated into the Broadway musical comedy *Ladies First*, whose music was mostly by A. B. Sloane. Its refrain begins: "The real American folk song is a rag—A mental jag—A rhythmic tonic for the chronic blues." See Ira Gershwin, *Lyrics on Several Occasions* (New York: Knopf, 1959), 180.

4 "Fascinating Rhythm" was sung by Fred Astaire in *Lady, Be Good!* and led into a dance number. See Jablonski, *Gershwin*, 83.

5 The line comes from a verse of "Embraceable You," written originally for "an operetta version of *East Is West*" (1928), a show that was never completed, then put into *Girl Crazy*. See Gershwin, *Lyrics*, 30–31.

6 The quotation is from "Slap That Bass," another Astaire number, seen in the film *Shall We Dance?* See Gershwin, *Lyrics*, 221.

7 William Austin to Richard Crawford, 23 February 1985. My own unsystematic but fairly extensive search through song lists confirms Austin's point. "Rhythm" became a kind of catchword in the 1930s, as "syncopation" had been earlier. But the only prominent use I found before the Gershwins' "Fascinating Rhythm" (1924) is the name of a well-known white jazz group that began recording in August 1922 under the name of the Friar's Society Orchestra, changed by March 1923 to the New Orleans Rhythm Kings. A

TABLE 6
Recordings of "I Got Rhythm" and Contrafacts to 1942[a]

Performer[b]	Date	Recording Company
Fred Rich & Orch (v)	20 Oct 1930	Columbia
Red Nichols & Five Pennies (v)	23 Oct 1930	Brunswick
Luis Russell & Orch (v)	24 Oct 1930	Melotone
Fred Rich & Orch (v)	29 Oct 1930	Harmony, Okeh
Ethel Waters (v)	18 Nov 1930	Columbia
Cab Calloway & Orch (v)	17 Dec 1930	ARC; rej[c]
Adelaide Hall with piano (v)/London	Oct 1931	Oriole
Louis Armstrong & Orch (v)/Chicago	6 Nov 1931	Okeh
Billy Banks (v; medley)	13 April 1932	Victor test
Bobby Howes (v)/London	10 May 1932	Columbia
Roy Fox & Band (v)/London	19 May 1932	Decca
Blue Mountaineers (v)/London	18 June 1932	broadcast
Don Redman & Orch	30 June 1932	Brunswick
Ray Starita & Ambassadors (v)/London	12 Aug 1932	Sterno
*New Orleans Feetwarmers (v): "Shag"	15 Sept 1932	Victor
*Joel Shaw & Orch (v): "Yeah Man"	Oct 1932	Crown
Arthur Briggs & Boys (v)/Paris	ca. June 1933	Brunswick
*The King's Jesters/Chicago: "Yeah Man"	29 July 1933	Bluebird
*Fletcher Henderson & Orch: "Yeah Man"	18 Aug 1933	Vocalion, Brunswick
Spirits of Rhythm (v)	29 Sept 1933	ARC; rej
Five Spirits of Rhythm (v)	24 Oct 1933	Brunswick
Freddy Johnson & Harlemites/Paris	ca. Oct 1933	Brunswick
Freddy Johnson & Harlemites/Paris	7 Dec 1933	Brunswick
Casa Loma Orch	30 Dec 1933	Brunswick
*Jimmy Lunceford & Orch: "Stomp It Off"	29 Oct 1934	Decca
*Chick Webb's Savory Orch: "Don't Be That Way"	19 Nov 1934	Decca
Joe Venuti & Orch	26 Dec 1934	London (LP)
Stéphane Grappelli & Hot Four/Paris	Oct 1935	Decca
*Nat Gonella & Georgians (v)/London: "Yeah Man"	20 Nov 1935	Parlophone
Garnet Clark (piano)/Paris	25 Nov 1935	HMV
Fats Waller & Rhythm (v)	4 Dec 1935	HMV
*Chick Webb & Orch: "Don't Be That Way"	Feb 1936	Polydor (LP)
Red Norvo & Swing Sextette	16 March 1936	Decca
The Ballyhooligans (v)/London	2 April 1936	HMV
Joe Daniels & Hot Shots/London	15 July 1936	Parlophone
*Count Basie & Orch: "Don't Be That Way"	ca. Feb 1937	Vanguard
Jimmy Dorsey & Orch/Los Angeles	3 March 1937	Decca
Lionel Hampton & Orch[d]	26 April 1937	Victor
Benny Goodman Quartet	29 April 1937	MGM
Glenn Miller & Orch	30 June 1937	Brunswick

TABLE 6 (*continued*)

Performer[b]	Date	Recording Company
Count Basie & Orch	30 June 1937	Coll. Corner
Dicky Wells & Orch/Paris	7 July 1937	Swing
Valaida [Snow] (v)/London	9 July 1937	Parlophone
Chick Webb & Little Chicks	21 Sept 1937	Decca
Emilio Caceres Trio	5 Nov 1937	Victor
Scott Wood & Six Swingers (medley)/London	12 Nov 1937	Columbia
Benny Goodman Quartet	16 Jan 1938	Columbia
*Benny Goodman & Orch:		
"Don't Be That Way"	16 Jan 1938	Columbia
Bud Freeman Trio	17 Jan 1938	Commodore
*Lionel Hampton & Orch:		
"Don't Be That Way"	18 Jan 1938	Victor
*Benny Goodman & Orch:		
"Don't Be That Way"	16 Feb 1938	Victor
*Ozzie Nelson & Orch/Hollywood:		
"Don't Be That Way"	5 March 1938	Bluebird
*Mildred Bailey & Orch (v):		
"Don't Be That Way"	14 March 1938	Vocalion
*Jimmy Dorsey & Orch:		
"Don't Be That Way"	16 March 1938	Decca
*Teddy Wilson & Orch:		
"Don't Be That Way"	23 March 1938	Brunswick
Larry Adler with Quintette of Hot Club of		
France/Paris	31 May 1938	Columbia
*Gene Krupa & Orch: "Wire Brush Stomp"	2 June 1938	Brunswick
*Johnny Hodges & Orch:		
"The Jeep is Jumpin'"	24 Aug 1938	Vocalion/OKeh
Louis Armstrong & Fats Waller (v)	19 Oct 1938	Palm Club
Clarence Profit Trio	15 Feb 1939	Epic
*Erskine Hawkins & Orch: "Raid the Joint"	8 April 1939	Bluebird
*Earl Hines & Orch: "Father Steps In"	12 July 1939	Bluebird
*Tommy Dorsey & Orch: "Stomp It Off"	20 July 1939	Victor
*Count Basie's Kansas City Seven:		
"Lester Leaps In"	5 Sept 1939	Vocalion
*Earl Hines & Orch/Chicago: "XYZ"	6 Oct 1939	Bluebird
Benny Goodman Sextet (medley)	24 Dec 1939	Vanguard
Caspar Reardon (v)	5 Feb 1940	Schirmer
Count Basie & Orch/Boston	20 Feb 1940	Coll. Corner
Fletcher Henderson & Horace	27 Feb 1940	Vocalion
Henderson's Orch (v)/Chicago		
*Duke Ellington & Orch/	4 May 1940	Victor
Hollywood: "Cotton Tail		
(Shuckin' and Stiffin')"		
Sid Phillips Trio/London	6 May 1940	Parlophone
*Count Basie & Orch: "Blow Top"	31 May 1940	Epic
Max Geldray Quartet/London	26 July 1940	Decca

TABLE 6 (*continued*)

Performer[b]	Date	Recording Company
*Coleman Hawkins & Orch: "Chant of the Groove"[e]	summer 1940	[LP reissue]
Felix Mendelssohn & Hawaiian Serenaders/London	28 Oct 1940	Columbia
*Johnny Hodges & Orch/Chicago: "Good Queen Bess"	2 Nov 1940	Bluebird
*Duke Ellington & Orch/Fargo, N.D.: "Cotton Tail"	7 Nov 1940	Palm
*Johnny Hodges & Orch/ Hollywood: "Squatty Roo"	3 July 1941	Bluebird
Metronome All-Star Leaders	16 Jan 1942	Columbia

[a] Contrafacts—i.e., newly titled tunes with new melodies based on the harmonic structure of "I Got Rhythm"—are indicated by an asterisk; their titles are listed with the performers' names.
[b] Unless otherwise indicated, location is New York; *v* denotes inclusion of vocal.
[c] Here and elsewhere, "rej." identifies a rejected take: a recording that was not commercially issued.
[d] As "Rhythm, Rhythm."
[e] Not listed in Rust. See John Chilton, *The Song of the Hawk: The Life and Recordings of Coleman Hawkins* (Ann Arbor, Mich.: 1990), 180.

"rhythm" in the title are both built on syncopation. "Fascinating Rhythm" from 1924, sung by a character obsessed with an off-center rhythmic pattern, divides its first four bars, in effect, into measures of four, three, five, and four beats. As for "I Got Rhythm," of the seventeen lines in the lyrics of its chorus, thirteen are set to the same four-note figure, a rhythmic cell that hits only one of the four strong beats in the two bars it covers. For Ira Gershwin the lyricist, "rhythm" in this song was tied up with aggressive, accented, syncopated groupings of beats.

But Ira's lyrics are not really about rhythm in the way that those of "Fascinating Rhythm" are. They're an expression of general well-being. Rhythm and music are linked with "daisies in green pastures," with "starlight," "sweet dreams," and being in love. The message here is that "the best things in life are free"—incidentally the title of a hit song from the Broadway show *Good News* (1927). Merman's performance was an outpouring of high spirits, saying, most of all, "I feel *wonderful!*" Her sustained "high C" through the A sec-

search through Brian Rust, *Jazz Records, A–Z, 1897–1942*, rev. 5th ed. (n.p., [1983]), turned up no other groups that recorded between the NORK and three who began to record in 1925; the St. Louis Rhythm Kings (April), Paul Fried and His Rhythmicians (September), and the Blue Rhythm Orchestra (October). Rust's index yielded only one tune with the key word in its title that circulated before "Fascinating Rhythm" was published (December 1924): "The Rhythm Rag" by Willard Robison, recorded in September 1924 by Robison and his Deep River Orchestra.

tions of the second chorus—we can imagine outstretched arms and a multi-kilowatt smile—is the opposite of a celebration of rhythmic trickiness.

As a show-stopping song and vehicle for a new and vibrant theatrical talent, "I Got Rhythm" could hardly have been more successful. But as a popular song independent of the show, its success was more modest. "I Got Rhythm" called for a kind of vocal energy that few popular singers of Gershwin's day possessed. The first "jazz" recording, made by Freddie Rich with Paul Small as vocalist six days after *Girl Crazy* opened on Broadway, follows the sheet music straightforwardly and attempts neither to match Merman's exuberant interpretation nor to bring out the snap of Gershwin's syncopation. Its emotional blandness is matched by that of a version recorded the same day by Victor Arden and Phil Ohman, a duo-piano team whose orchestras had played in the pit of many Gershwin shows. (Frank Luther sang on this recording.)[8] A 1938 performance by singer Jane Froman reinstates the full-throated, high-spirited Merman approach with the help of a Schubertian running figure in the violins.[9] There is a 1943 recording, from a film version of *Girl Crazy*, in which Judy Garland restores "rhythm" as an issue by conscientiously singing the syncopations that Gershwin wrote.[10] And when Mary Martin sang "I Got Rhythm" for a reconstruction of the show in the 1950s, the accompaniment in her second chorus was reduced to percussion, supporting the text's first line literally as well as figuratively.[11]

Now let's consider "I Got Rhythm" as a jazz standard. We've already noted that jazz performers were among those who first played Gershwin's song in public, and Red Nichols's recording shortly after the show's premiere was the first of dozens in the jazz tradition.

In the jazz tradition, we usually speak of tunes, not songs. A jazz tune is defined first and foremost by its structure: by the pattern of repetition and contrast in its melodic phrases and the harmonic framework underlying them. Second, it is defined by its ethos: by the mood it projects and the

---

8 Victor V22558. See Brian Rust, *The American Dance Band Discography, 1917–1942* (New Rochelle, N.Y., 1975).

9 Brian Rust and Allen G. Debus, *The Complete Entertainment Discography from 1897 to 1942*, 2nd ed. (New York, 1989), 328, dates this recording (Victor 12332) 10 July 1938, New York City. It is part of a medley of "Vocal Gems" from *Girl Crazy*.

10 Decca 23310; the LP reissue on Decca is numbered DL 5412.

11 In his discographical supplement to Goldberg, *George Gershwin*, 366, Allen Dashiell criticizes the recording as evidence of "star trouble." "Miss Martin," he complains, "chose to bend the songs to her will (and style) so that there is as much Martin here as Gershwin." "I Got Rhythm" is one song said to be marred by the singer's "coy mannerisms." Jablonski, *Gershwin*, 404–5, follows suit. He writes: "*Girl Crazy* is spoiled a little (not enough to hurt) by the mannered singing of Mary Martin who, as A Star, was assigned songs that could have been better sung by others, i.e., hear Louise Carlyle do 'Sam and Delilah' and then wish she had done the other Merman songs from the show."

tempo at which it is played. Only third does its melody come into play, for in
the jazz tradition the melody is often little more than an entrée into the performance; after being heard, it is usually discarded for free melodic invention
by the performers. The chorus of "I Got Rhythm" follows one of the most
common Tin Pan Alley song forms: statement, restatement, contrast, and
return, with the contrast being called the "bridge" or "release." We could dia-
gram the form as AABA[1], the first three phrases filling eight bars and the
fourth ten, by virtue of the two-bar extension. Gershwin's harmony is as ele-
mental as his melody. The latter is cast in two-bar units, with the four-note
syncopated cell moving up, then down, then up again, and then breaking the
pattern with a cadence. The harmony supports these gestures with a parallel
pattern: three I-ii[7]-V-I loops followed by a I-V-I cadence. Or perhaps it would
be better to describe Gershwin's harmonic *framework* that way, as Gunther
Schuller does,[12] noting that the published song actually employs a more varied and colorful sequence of chords:

$$B\flat \ B\flat_6 \ Cm_7 \ F_7 \ | \ B\flat_6 \ Edim \ | \ Cin_7 \ F_7|$$
$$B\flat \ B\flat_6 \ Cm_7 \ F_7 \ E\flat m_6 \ | \ B\flat \ F_7 \ | \ B\flat \ C\sharp dim \ F$$

Ira Gershwin liked George's tune's ability to "throw its weight around."
The "weight" of "I Got Rhythm" as Gershwin wrote it stems partly from
tempo and syncopation but perhaps even more from economy of
material—from the song's avoidance of tonal complexity or variety. The
song's first melodic statement (A) dwells on B-flat; its restatement (A), in
what is virtually a note-for-note repetition, does the same; the release (B)
jumps to the relative minor, then wends its way back through the circle of
fifths; and the return (Al) restates the beginning, again note-for-note, soften-
ing the austerity a bit with a concluding tag. The classic simplicity of the
song's harmonic design summoned jazz performers' inventiveness, both
melodic and harmonic, to a degree matched by only one other structure in
the history of jazz: the twelve-bar blues. But even before discussing jazz performances, it is well to recall the impression George Gershwin's music for "I
Got Rhythm" made upon Ira Gershwin and Ethel Merman, two people far
removed in sensibility from the world of jazz. Ira's response as a lyricist was a
list of abrupt, colloquial claims ("I got . . ."); Merman found as a singer that

---

12 Gunther Schuller, *The Swing Era: The Development of Jazz 1930–1945* (New York, 1989), 127, out-
lines the "traditional way" jazz musicians harmonize "I Got Rhythm." In the A section, the harmonic progression is
  $$B\flat \ Gm7 \ | \ Cm7 \ F7 \ | \ B\flat \ Gm7 \ | \ Cm7 \ F7 \ |$$
  $$B\flat \ B\flat 7 \ | \ E\flat \ E\flat \ | \ B\flat \ F7 \ | \ B\flat \ [F7].$$

one sustained note could replace the Gershwin brothers' first six bars, to the vast delight of the *Girl Crazy* audience. Both, in short, discovered in George's music a certain bare, even abstract quality—one that an Alec Wilder might consider as a weakness in a popular song[13] but that, within the genre of the up-tempo instrumental number, proved astoundingly able to unlock jazz musicians' inventiveness.

From the many available jazz-style performances of "I Got Rhythm," I've chosen three for brief discussion here. The first, from 1937, is played by the Glenn Miller Orchestra (ex. 32). This is Miller's band before it settled into the formulas that were to make it a huge commercial success; and since Miller had known the tune when it was brand new, his arrangement from seven years later carries special interest [recorded 9 June 1937, Brunswick 7915].

Ex. 32. George Gershwin, "I Got Rhythm," bars 1–8

If one accepts the premise that a jazz arrangement is a commentary upon—even a kind of analysis of—the original tune, Miller's first chorus confirms his view that Gershwin's melody line leaves something to be desired. Melodic interest here lies more in the reed countermelody composed by Miller than in Gershwin's original, played staccato in the brass. Miller's recording suggests how most jazz instrumentalists performed "I Got Rhythm": as an up-tempo flag-waver, a piece consistently played fast, and hence a kind of test piece, putting the group, and especially the improvising soloist, on trial.[14] Later in Miller's arrangement is a striking effect that shows his band at the peak of its rhythmic drive. Discarding not only Gershwin's melody but his harmony too, Miller here reduces the first six bars of Gersh-

---

13 A comment Virgil Thomson made about Aaron Copland may apply to "I Got Rhythm," though certainly not to many other Gershwin songs. In 1932, in a discussion of his colleague's "American" side, Thomson wrote that Copland, for all his fondness for displaced accents, "never understood that sensuality of sentiment which is the force of American popular music" (quoted in Minna Lederman, *The Life and Death of a Small Magazine* [*Modern Music, 1924–1946*], I.S.A.M. Monographs no. 18 [Brooklyn, 1983], 22). "Sensuality of sentiment" is not a conspicuous trait of "I Got Rhythm."

14 Jazz being a music in which the status of players and singers rests upon the judgment of their peers, the literature is full of stories of performers having to prove themselves.

win's A section to virtually nothing but rhythm and sound. Twice the band crescendos on one note, played on alternate eighths by the brass and reed sections and sweeping listeners (or dancers) ahead like a canoe in white water.[15]

A notable recording from the mid-1940s testifies to the place of "I Got Rhythm" in the jazz repertory by that time. The scene was New York's Town Hall on the evening of 9 June 1945. The audience had gathered, but by concert time only two musicians had shown up, tenor saxophonist Don Byas and bass player Slam Stewart. What to do? Give the customers back their money and send them home? Not that night. Byas and Stewart set out on a voyage over some jazz standards, and "I Got Rhythm" was the second number they played. Their performance, up-tempo and obviously unrehearsed, confirms our sense of Gershwin's song as a vehicle for virtuosic melodic play over familiar harmonic ground. After paraphrasing Gershwin's melody (without the original two-bar extension), Byas improvised four fluent inventive choruses, stood by while Stewart soloed in his patented style of bowing the bass and singing (through clenched teeth, an octave above), then followed with four additional choruses that explored Gershwin's tune further.[16] Also noteworthy is a recording made by pianist Art Tatum with guitar and bass accompaniment at around the same time, and at breakneck speed. Tatum is known for technical virtuosity and unmatched harmonic imagination. He is also known as a melody player—one who respected the original tune and tended to keep it within earshot even during his improvised choruses.[17] In "I Got Rhythm," however, Tatum flashes only a hint of Gershwin's melody, then gives it up completely in the second chorus. Tatum's recording, from the mid-1940s, also confirms a trend that had already begun in the 1930s in performances of "I Got Rhythm": that of embellishing the ii-V-1 chord progressions in Gershwin's A sections with richer harmonies. In his last two choruses, Tatum begins each of the eight-bar A sections on an F-sharp seventh chord—enharmonically G-flat, or the flat sixth degree—and then moves downward through the circle of fifths in a succession of half notes until, at the beginning of the fifth bar, he reaches the B-flat tonic in which the piece is rooted. (The harmonic progression is: F-sharp$_7$, B$_7$, E$_7$, A$_7$, D$_7$, G$_7$, C$_7$, F$_7$, B-flat.)

15 Miller's performance is reissued in *Big Band Jazz: From the Beginnings to the Fifties*, selected and annotated by Gunther Schuller and Martin Williams (Smithsonian Recordings, 1983).

16 First issued on Commodore Records, Byas and Stewart's performance is included in the *Smithsonian Collection of Classic Jazz*, edited and annotated by Martin Williams, revised ed. (Smithsonian Recordings, 1987).

17 Martin Williams, *The Jazz Tradition*, new and revised ed. (New York: Oxford, 1983), 94–94, puts it in a somewhat different way. "Art Tatum's capacities for melodic invention were limited," Williams writes. "He was basically an artist of the arabesque, true, but he also functioned in that middle ground which André Hodier has called paraphrase, where fragments of the original theme take their place beside invented phrases, to form allusive structures in variation. . . . Tatum's best harmonic and melodic adornments help us discover what is potentially beautiful in a popular song; his invented, passing phrases subdue what is not." By that standard, Tatum found little that was beautiful in the melody of "I Got Rhythm."

Tatum's recording, which drapes Gershwin's scaffold with fresh harmonic material, brings us to the third approach performers took to "I Got Rhythm."[18] As early as 1932, with Sidney Bechet's recording of a tune he called "Shag," black jazz musicians had begun to invent new melodies on the structure of Gershwin's song, abandoning his tune entirely and renaming their versions as new compositions.[19] Fletcher Henderson's "Yeah Man" from August 1933 is another example, as is "Stomp It Off," recorded by Jimmie Lunceford in October 1934.[20] And so is Chick Webb's "Don't Be That Way," from November of the same year.[21] This tune, by the way, adds to the story of Benny Goodman's relationship with Gershwin's song, for he and Edgar Sampson are named as co-composers. The melody of "Don't Be That Way," a tune that Goodman played at his Carnegie Hall concert in January 1938, and that began the recording issued long after the events, is shown in example 33.[22]

Ex. 33. Edgar Sampson and Benny Goodman, "Don't Be That Way," bars 5–12, melody only, played by Chick Webb and His Orchestra (19 November 1943, Decca 483)

The long list of tunes based on the chord progression of "I Got Rhythm" includes recordings by the best swing bands, such as Count Basie's "Blow Top" from 1940 and Woody Herman's "Apple Honey" from 1945.[23]

In "Cotton Tail"[24] (1940), Duke Ellington wrote three memorable strains to Gershwin's chords. First, the lean explosive melody of the first chorus,

18 On 30 June 1932, Don Redman and His Orchestra made the first wholly instrumental recording of "I Got Rhythm"—an early example of many black musicians' tendency to omit Ira Gershwin's lyrics.

19 Williams, *Jazz Tradition*, 49, identifies Bechet's "Shag" as "the first non-thematic use on records of the 'I Got Rhythm' chord progression." "Shag" is attributed to Bechet on the record label, but I was unable to find in the Library of Congress copyright records any evidence that it was published or even copyrighted.

20 "Yeah Man," a song with words by Noble Sissel and music by J. Russel Robinson, was copyrighted as a published item on 27 May 1932 (entry no. 30349) and published by DeSylva, Brown, and Henderson, Inc. Joel Shaw made the first jazz recording in October of that year, just after Bechet and the New Orleans Feetwarmers recorded "Shag." "Stomp It Off," with a melody attributed to Sy Oliver and Jimmy Lunceford, was copyrighted as an unpublished piece of 1 April 1936 (entry no. 121547) by Denton and Haskins Music Co. Lunceford had recorded it in October 1934.

21 "Don't Be That Way," attributed to E. M. [Edgar] Sampson, was copyrighted as an unpublished piece on 16 May 1935 (entry no. 104261). Webb had recorded it on 19 November 1934. As table 6 indicates, it seems to have had the most active independent life of all "I Got Rhythm" contrafacts during the swing era.

22 Schuller, *Swing Era*, 24, attributes Goodman's arrangement to Edgar Sampson and calls it "one of the band's most popular successes." He also finds Webb's 1934 recording far superior to Goodman's two versions of 1938.

23 *Good Morning Blues: The Autobiography of Count Basie*, as told to Albert Murray (New York, 1985), 239, confirms that "Blow Top," recorded by Basie and his orchestra on 31 May 1940, was composed and arranged by Tab Smith.

24 Ellington's first recorded "Cotton Tail" on 4 May 1940. On 29 July 1940, it was copyrighted as an unpublished piece (entry no. 225831) by Robbins Music Corp.

played by saxes in unison and one muted trumpet (ex. 34a). Second, a sixteen-bar statement for the brass in which Ellington manages, without establishing a predictable pattern, to create a powerful sense of rhythmic coherence (ex. 34b). Finally, Ellington composes a thirty-two-bar melody—not Gershwin's AABA but ABCD for the sax section in full harmony (ex. 34c).[25]

Ex. 34.   **(a) Bars 1–8**

(b) Chorus 4, bars 1–16, rhythm only

(c) Chorus 5, bars 1–8, melody only

---

25 Ellington's composed variations on Gershwin's tune are striking.

The so-called bebop revolution of the early 1940s broke decisively with the swing era in many things. But one tradition it carried on and even intensified was the practice of making new tunes on the chord progressions of older ones.

Each of the most prominent black swing bands—Count Basie, Duke Ellington, Erskine Hawkins, Fletcher Henderson, Earl Hines, Jimmie Lunceford, Chick Webb, as well as groups featuring major soloists like Johnny Hodges and Lester Young—had its own version of "I Got Rhythm" as a standard vehicle for up-tempo "blowing." So too did many bebop musicians. The reasons were partly artistic, partly social, but they were also economic. Drummer Max Roach has been quoted as saying:

> Of course there are about ten million tunes written on the changes of "I Got Rhythm." . . . This wasn't pilfering. In cases where we needed substitute chords for these tunes, we had to create new melodies to fit them. If you're gonna think up a melody, you'd just as well copyright it as a new tune, and that's what we did. We never did get any suits from publishers.[26]

Few bebop musicians after World War II played "I Got Rhythm" as a jazz standard. But as a key, a tempo, a structure, and an occasion for virtuosic improvisation, it was deeply engrained in the jazz repertory, even when its harmonic scheme was embellished with remote chords. And bebop musicians, like their predecessors, sought ownership in the tradition that Gershwin's show song had begun.

No one in the jazz tradition was more closely identified with the "Rhythm changes" than alto saxophonist Charlie Parker, who returned again and again to the structure of Gershwin's tune throughout his career, composing at least seventeen different pieces based upon it, many of which were picked up, played, and recorded by other jazz performers (table 7). The harmonic structure of "I Got Rhythm" won a place in Parker's imagination, much as the theme of the *Eroica* Variations or perhaps Diabelli's *Waltz* had in Beethoven's—though Beethoven concentrated his efforts on lengthy, integrated compositions, while Parker's "I Got Rhythm" variations are scattered widely among many performances. Following is a quick trip through Parker's *SaxÜbung*, pieced together from recordings made between 1944 and 1950.[27]

Gershwin's "Rhythm changes" inspired Parker to compose several different kinds of variations upon them. The most old-fashioned of the three

---

26 Quoted from Dizzy Gillespie with Al Fraser, *To Be, or Not . . . to Bop: Memoirs* (Doubleday and Company: Garden City, N.Y. 1979), 207.
27 Note also that none of Parker's versions uses the two-bar extension at the end of Gershwin's tune.

TABLE 7

Parker's Compositions on "I Got Rhythm"

Name	Recording Date[a]	Copyright Date	Copyright Entry[b]
"Red Cross"	15 Sept 1944	17 Sept 1945	EU439039
"Shaw 'Nuff"[c]	11 May 1945	11 Nov 1948	EP32267
"Thriving from a Riff"	26 Nov 1945	1 Dec 1945	EU449251
"Anthropology"[c]	March 1946	13 Aug 1948	EP29445
"Moose the Mooche"	28 March 1946	1 Nov 1946	EU51928
"Bird's Nest"	19 Feb 1947	20 April 1961	EU656872
"Chasing the Bird"	8 May 1947	20 Jan 1948	EU112914
"Dexterity"	28 Oct 1947	21 April 1961	EU65181
"Crazeology"	17 Dec 1947	21 Aug 1961	EU672281
"Constellation"	18 Sept 1948	15 Nov 1948	EU148835
"Ah-Leu-Cha"	18 Sept 1948	15 Nov 1948	EU148840
"Steeplechase"	24 Sept 1948	15 Nov 1948	EU148831
"Passport"	5 May 1949	1 June 1953; 1956	EU318785
"An Oscar For Treadwell"	6 June 1950	20 March 1967	EU431242
"Swedish Schnapps"	8 Aug 1951	26 March 1956	EU431248
"Kim"	30 Dec 1952	1956; 3 Jan 1967	EU431245
"Celerity"	none given	19 March 1958	EU517086

[a]Recording dates from Brian Priestley, *Charlie Parker*, Jazz Masters series (Tunbridge Wells, England, 1984).
[b]EU means unpublished copyright; EP means published copyright.
[c]Co-composer with Dizzy Gillespie.

employs the riff style, in which a melody is built up by repeating one brief melodic motive (ex. 35)—Parker's process of abstraction here reduces the A section's harmony, except for bar 6, to a B-flat tonic chord. (In the release, however, a new riff based on Gershwin's chord changes appears.) In 1948 Parker composed a new riff for the A section, leaving the bridge free for improvisation. He called this piece "Steeplechase" (ex. 36).

Ex. 35. Charlie Parker, "Red Cross," bars 4–12 (15 September 1944, Savoy 532)

Ex. 36. Charlie Parker, "Steeplechase," bars 1–8

The riff approach establishes a context of regular predictability as a launching pad for the improvisation that follows. But Parker's second approach does the opposite. "Moose the Mooche," for example, is an invention for unison duet—alto sax and muted trumpet—that is rhythmically asymmetrical, broken into irregular phrases by rests in unexpected places (ex. 37). And "An Oscar for Treadwell" (ex. 38) is built in a similar way, with phrases of four beats, eight beats, fifteen beats, and five beats in its first eight bars. Its bridge is free.

Ex. 37. Charlie Parker, "Moose the Mooche," bars 9–16 (28 March 1946, Dial 1003)

Ex. 38. Charlie Parker, "An Oscar for Treadwell," bars 8–16 (6 June 1950, Verve MGV 800)

Finally, Parker employed the "I Got Rhythm" chord changes to create a kind of obstacle course that only the best players could negotiate. Bassist Milt Hinton once explained how Parker, Dizzy Gillespie, and other bebop pioneers would discourage players who wanted to join their after-hours jam sessions at Minton's in Harlem during the early 1940s.

> "What're y'all gonna play?" [they'd ask.] We'd say, "I Got Rhythm," and we'd start out with this new set of changes and they would be left right at the post. They would be standing there, and they couldn't get in because they didn't know what changes we were using, and eventually they would put their horns away, and we could go on and blow in peace and get our little exercise.[28]

"Shaw 'Nuff" (ex. 39) shows this approach. Played at top speed, it also changes harmony every two beats. Intimidation is the name of the game here—intimidation of any neophyte with the gall to try to join such a performance.

Ex. 39. Charlie Parker and John "Dizzy" Gillespie, "Shaw 'Nuff," bars 24–32 (11 May 1945, Guild 11002)

From Parker's heyday in the years just after World War II, many bebop players—Thelonious Monk, Art Pepper, Miles Davis, Sonny Rollins, Sonny Stitt, Bud Powell, and Fats Navarro among them—created their own new tunes on Gershwin's chord changes.[29] And some of these new tunes themselves became standards. Ellington's "Cotton Tail" totaled more than thirty recordings in the years 1943–68, and Parker and Gillespie's "Anthropology" logged nearly twenty more in the same period.[30] Moreover, the steady stream

---

28 Gillespie, *To Be*, 143.

29 Examples include the following, whose dates are the earliest date of copyright deposit. Clifford Brown, "Brownie Speaks" (27 December 1956, EU453249); Al Cohn, "The Goof and I" (26 March 1948, EU122626); Tadd Dameron, "Delerium" (copyright information not looked for); Miles Davis, "The Theme" (28 March 1966, EU918852; unattributed in some other sources); Dizzy Gillespie, "Anthology" with C. Parker (10 December 1947, EU107329).

30 Jorgen Grunnet Jepsen, *Jazz Records, 1942–[1969]: A Discography*, 8 vols. (Copenhagen, 1963–70), lists the chronology of "Anthropology" recordings.

of "I Got Rhythm" variants that flowed through the 1950s had the effect of updating the tune so that when, for example, drummer Art Blakey featured the young trumpeter Wynton Marsalis in a performance of "The Theme" in 1981, half a century after "I Got Rhythm" first saw light of day, it did not sound anachronistic.

Gershwin's song "I Got Rhythm" is an especially good example of what I've referred to earlier as "performers' music": music composed and published with the expectation that performers, rather than being bound by a composer's score, will change melody, harmony, tempo, or mood as they see fit, thus putting upon it the stamp of their own musical personalities.[31]

"I Got Rhythm" attracted an unusually wide range of treatments from performers, flourishing in several different traditions of performance. These traditions are documented not in musical notation but in commercially produced phonograph recordings.

It seems appropriate to end this chapter with a comment on a performance that combines elements of the different traditions that made Gershwin's song their own. The singer is Ella Fitzgerald, accompanied by a sizable orchestra.[32] The presence of the verse, which is seldom sung, and a string section, helps to remind us that we're dealing, after all, with a *song* from a

Ex. 40. George Gershwin, "I Got Rhythm," Chorus 2, bars 1–16, melody only, sung by Ella Fitzgerald with orchestra conducted by Nelson Riddle (1958–59, Verve VE-2-2525)

31 There are many more "I Got Rhythm" contrafacts than the ones on which I have gathered information here. But to provide a statistical summary of the ones I've dealt with: Between 1930 and 1968, a total of 280 jazz recordings of "I Got Rhythm" and 45 of its contrafacts have been traced. The count is based on pieces listed in Rust and Jepson's discographies.

32 Ella Fitzgerald, *The George and Ira Gershwin Songbook* (Verve recording VE-2-2525).

Broadway *show* by Gershwin. The introduction in the first chorus of a swinging beat and big band sound celebrates the song's pedigree as a jazz standard.
But what kind of jazz standard? Ella Fitzgerald, a big band singer since 1935,
knew full well the tradition of instrumental performance that lay behind "I
Got Rhythm" when she made this recording in 1959. And the beginning of
her second chorus (ex. 40) with sixteen bars of wordless scat-singing—clearly
the musical climax of this performance[33]—can be heard as a tribute to the
countless trumpeters, pianists, sax players, and guitarists, from the time of
Red Nichols and Luis Russell, through Ellington, Parker, Gillespie, and
beyond, for whom Gershwin's song, or his tune, or his harmonic structure,
or all three, marked out a territory in which artistic capacities were tested
and honed and realized—a territory in which artistic truth was to be sought
and found.

45   Allan Lincoln Langley "The Gershwin Myth" (1932)

> Violist Allan Lincoln Langley's pejorative use of the term "myth" is unset-
> tling and warrants some investigation. Simply, fueled by anti-Semitism, he
> uses the term to denote that Gershwin's success was a by-product of some
> sort of deception intended to conceal his real abilities. William Daly's
> response in the entry following is a convincing and truthful answer to
> Langley's charges.

Prior to the premiere by Paul Whiteman of the *Rhapsody in Blue*, Gershwin
was the most striking and original figure in the Broadway musical galaxy. He
had turned out show after show, and was enjoying increasing réclame and
popularity. This was deserved; in Gershwin there was, in addition to song and
jazz fecundity, a peculiar emotional consanguinity with the gaiety, daring and
double entendre that characterized the theatre in the boom decade. Jazz,
both rhythmical and sentimental, was in its heyday and Gershwin wrote
superlatively in its limited vein.

Gershwin continued to write show after show with no noticeable deterioration. But the *Rhapsody in Blue*, an immediately exciting ambassador to
musical ports, divided its composer's field in two. Shortly afterward appeared

---

33 As I hear it, a melodic quotation follows the semitone hike after bar 8. Bars 9–10, plus the first
three notes of bar 11, sound to me like a reference to "The Parade of the Wooden Soldiers" by Léon Jessel,
first published in Germany in 1905.

SOURCE   Allan Lincoln Langley, "The Gershwin Myth," *American Spectator* 1 (December 1932): 1–2.

in succession the *Piano Concerto, An American in Paris,* and more recently the *Second Rhapsody* (in Rivets).[1] Gershwin rapidly achieved the sanction of the concert hall and the consideration of some of the important conductors and critics. The world in general was informed that America at last had a great and original composer. Appropriately enough for the concert entrepreneurs, the new genius had the additionally laudable faculty of packing auditoriums. His works were produced, through interesting patrons, in Europe; they performed wonders in reducing Stadium deficits. The new genius had worked an extraordinary miracle; he could make Art pay dividends. History was made.

But, one asks, actually by whom? And for whom? It must be emphasized that in America equilibrium in artistic estimates is still a rare occurrence. Any meteoric rise of a composer to fame in our orchestral fields is, in these days of symphony budgets and critic-box-office liaisons, partly suspect. On another front, it is always observable that popular acclaim itself exerts an influence, at least temporarily, on press comment, often causing hilarity for dispassionate historians and playing havoc with critics' reputations for consistency and penetration. Thirdly, the immediate inertness of general musical judgment, accompanied by its singular scarcity of authoritative analysis, allows inordinate periods to pass before mature appraisals are widely reached. These factors, as well as others too involved to discuss here, have contributed enormously to the building of the Gershwin myth.

Demonstration is simple. The Whiteman premiere of the *Rhapsody in Blue* was a mild sensation. The *Rhapsody* was legitimate jazz, orchestrated in jazz tradition and played by a legitimate jazz orchestra in a professedly jazz concert. So far, so good. There the matter would ordinarily have ended. For while many distinguished persons were attracted by the *Rhapsody,* no cultivated musician, from the very beginning, was fooled for a minute by its lack of constructive distinction, nor by the self-conscious, artificial connective material which linked its different melodies.

But the New York Symphony was then approaching the end of an unequal struggle with the Philharmonic for prestige. It had, through the success of Mengelberg, been forced long before this to introduce guest conductors. What better than to discover a great American composer? The Philharmonic's preliminary indifference to the Gershwin comet afforded an

---

1 A naming nightmare, the *Second Rhapsody* grew initially from music written for a scene in the 1931 Fox Film Corporation production *Delicious,* starring Janet Gaynor and Charles Farrell. His starting point, the "rivet theme," convinced him that the extended work for piano and orchestra should be titled *Rhapsody in Rivets.* When the film was aired, however, it was credited as *New York Rhapsody.* The title page of the score provides a fourth moniker, *2nd Rhapsody for Orchestra with Piano.*

excellent point of departure. The New York Symphony caused it to be bruited about that Gershwin, at the behest and with the encouragement of Dr. Damrosch, would compose a jazz piano concerto which would presumably establish once and for all the existence of an indigenous genius and incidentally heap new laurels on his patron who, as has already been observed, was then badly in need of fresh publicity. It worked like a charm. Carnegie Hall was sold out, and all the way from the highest critics to *The New Yorker* the matter was taken with an unprecedented seriousness. Fully established as the most significant figure in American symphonic music, past or present, Gershwin departed for France. Thence he returned with *An American in Paris.* The merger of the two major New York orchestras brought its premiere under the auspices of the hitherto Philharmonic, as the high spot of Mr. Damrosch's final active year. Widespread introductory ballyhoo; another sold-out house; generous and voluminous program notes by Deems Taylor—what more could a composer ask?

After this there was a considerable hiatus; but two years later appeared in quick succession the *Second Rhapsody* and the *Rumba.* All five were on an all-Gershwin program which last summer broke the Stadium attendance record. No other American composer had so far achieved the dignity, even in a summer series, of confining a major orchestra to a program entirely of his own works. Victor Herbert was popular in the past, as is Jerome Kern at present. And the former at least wrote his own effective orchestrations (in passing it is only fair to mention that Kern has his Bennett and that Gershwin in earlier days at least, had his Grofé and later, his Daly). But no one has put either Herbert or Kern in Carnegie Hall as a popular symphonist, nor given all-Herbert or all-Kern programs in the Stadium, nor yet transported any of their work to Italy for American music festivals.

It was the *Concerto* that made fools of the critics. Mr. Chotzinoff rhapsodized that Gershwin was a great genius. Mr. Gilman, viewing with natural alarm the anachronism of jazz tortured into classical forms, yet committed the naïve blunder of advising Gershwin to take to the mountains and find his soul. One would have thought it fairly obvious that the Gershwin sound was already endemic to Broadway. In justice to Gilman, it should be recorded that he lived to atone for this particular sentimentality by condemning roundly last season the *Second Rhapsody.* But for a long time no single commentator of repute had either the honesty or courage to announce boldly that, both as inspirational or mechanical invention, the *Concerto* was a profoundly amorphous and meretricious work. It undoubtedly, in the first and second movements, contains the best semi-serious jazz music of all Gershwin's attempts of symphonic size; but when these themes run out, and spurious Chopinesque padding is resorted to, the effect to any discriminating ear is first absurd, and then disgusting.

Except for the crudest and most elementary structural contrasts, there is not in a single one of the "symphonic" Gershwin works even a pretense of spontaneous form, nor any inherent resourcefulness in development. With the exception of a few particular orchestral tricks (such as the clarinet glissandos in the *Rhapsody in Blue* and various other routine jazz attributes) the orchestrations are blatant, involved and ordinary, with constant alternation of straining for effect with genuflection to traditions foreign to the composer's motivation. Transparent anachronisms prevail throughout. There is no such thing as a characteristically Gershwinian orchestration; no repetitive idiosyncrasies, such as are found in all composers of stature, no recognizable habits. (Fritz Reiner, an admirer of the *Rhapsody in Blue*, once said to me that he wished someone would tell Gershwin to have a competent composer entirely reorchestrate it and remove its instrumental clumsiness and self-consciousness.) Themes, no matter how good, are stated, naïvely, *forte, piano*; fast, slow; the closing sections (except in the *Concerto*) are mainly but palpable and inept restatements, bald, and without a trace of balance or inevitability.

It is only too evident that Gershwin's entire march to fame has been conducted on a piecework basis. The *Rhapsody in Blue* required the services of Grofé. In a controversy with Walter Kramer, Gershwin published a facsimile page of score to prove that he orchestrated the *Concerto* himself. How proof is thus established remains a moot question. As for *An American in Paris*, the genial Daly was constantly in rehearsal attendance, both as répétiteur and adviser, and any member of the orchestra could testify that he knew far more about the score than Gershwin. The point is that no previous claimant to honors in symphonic composition has ever presented so much argument and controversy as to whether his work was his own or not.

46 William Daly: "George Gershwin as Orchestrator" (1933)

As Gershwin had responded to Kramer, here Gershwin's close friend William Daly responds to Langley for him, in the more prominent venue of the *New York Times*.

In the *American Spectator* for December appears an article by Allan Lincoln Langley, entitled "The Gershwin Myth," in which the author definitely tries

SOURCE *New York Times* (January 15, 1933): I, 6.

to convey to the reader the idea that Gershwin is not the orchestrator, and probably not the author, of the works attributed to him. I am signally honored by being mentioned as a probable "ghost writer," as attest the following:

"As for *An American in Paris*, the genial Daly was constantly in rehearsal attendance, both as répétiteur and adviser, and any member of the orchestra could testify that he knew far more about the score than Gershwin. The point is that no previous claimant to honors in symphonic composition has ever presented so much argument and so much controversy as to whether his work was his own or not."

I thank Mr. Langley for the compliment, but I neither wrote nor orchestrated the *American*. My only contribution consisted of a few suggestions about reinforcing the scoring here and there, and I'm not sure that Gershwin, probably with good reason, accepted them. But, then, Gershwin receives many such suggestions from his many friends to whom he always plays his various compositions, light or symphonic, while they are in the process of being written. Possibly Mr. Langley feels that we all get together (and we'd have to meet in the Yankee stadium) and write Mr. Gershwin's music for him.

I would be only too happy to be known as the composer of *An American in Paris*, or of any of Gershwin's works, or as the orchestrator of them. But, alas! I am by trade a conductor (and because Gershwin thinks I am a good one, especially for his music, maybe Mr. Langley has been thrown off the scent). It is true that I orchestrate many Gershwin numbers for the theatre; but so does Russell Bennett. And I have reduced some of his symphonic works for smaller orchestra for use on the radio. And it is true that we are close friends—to my great profit—and that I use that relationship to criticize. But this is far from the role that Mr. Langley suggests.

In fine, the fact is that I have never written one note of any of his compositions, or so much as orchestrated one whole bar of any one of his symphonic works.

Mr. Langley's asseverations are of importance only through the fact that they are now published and are sent abroad in the world to influence those who have no means of checking up on the facts, and to give comfort to those who want to think that Gershwin is a myth.

I suppose I should really resent the fact that Langley attributes Gershwin's work to me, since Langley finds all of it so bad. But fortunately for my amour propre, I have heard some of Langley's compositions. He really should stay away from ink and stick to his viola.

47   Olin Downes: *"George Gershwin Plays His* Second Rhapsody *for the First Time Here with Koussevitzky and Boston Orchestra"* (1932)

Surely the performance of a new Gershwin concert work, and the much-awaited follow-up to the *Rhapsody in Blue*, in the venerable confines of Carnegie Hall with Koussevitzky's Boston Symphony from out-of-town made for news. Coverage of the event in the *New York Times* by Olin Downes evaluated not only the performance but made a comparison to Gershwin's previous rhapsody.

The program offered by Serge Koussevitzky and the Boston Symphony Orchestra last night in Carnegie Hall was refreshing for its catholicity and interest. Mr. Koussevitzky is one of the very few conductors today who appear to realize that music was not made exclusively in Germany, Italy, or France, either; who examines scores of all kinds and schools with curiosity and a singular appreciation, whatever their contents may be; who can be relied upon to supplement the routine sort of program which, in the main, New York City still receives.

The novelty of last night's concert was George Gershwin's *Second Rhapsody*, scored for piano and large modern orchestra, with the composer as solo pianist. The originality of the Gershwin *Rhapsody in Blue*, first heard in this city February 12, 1924, was the cause of Mr. Gershwin's later adventures in the symphonic field, with his *Concerto in F* (1925) for piano and orchestra and *An American in Paris*, a score which will probably remain the best constructed and most effective of Mr. Gershwin's present "period"—this though certain of the ideas of the *Rhapsody in Blue* are more original.

The score performed last night is the expansion of a five-minute sequence inserted into the picture *Delicious*, a screen comedy-drama, based on a story by Guy Bolton, with lyrics by Ira Gershwin and music by George, produced in 1931. The rhapsody was written in California in the spring of the same year and later somewhat revised. Some of the comedy scenes showed the streets of New York, and for the five-minute orchestral sequence Gershwin conceived a "rivet theme" to echo the tattoo of the skyscrapers. The *Second Rhapsody* had originally the title of *Rhapsody in Rivets*.

This rhapsody has more orchestration and more development than the *Rhapsody in Blue*. Its main motive is reasonably suggestive of rivets and racket in streets of this metropolis; also, if you like, of the bonhomie of inhabitants.

SOURCE   *New York Times* 81 (February 6, 1932): 14.

There is a second theme, built into a contrasting section. Thus, jazz dance rhythm and sentimental song are opposed and juxtaposed in this score. The conception is wholly orchestral. The piano is not so prominent as in the *Rhapsody in Blue*; it is, in fact, merely one of the instruments of the ensemble.

But with all its immaturities, the *Rhapsody in Blue* is more individual and originative than the piece heard last night. In fact, the *Second Rhapsody* is imitative in many ways of the *Rhapsody in Blue*. One of the figures of the first part, and certain harmonic cadences, and the song theme of the middle part, have all quite direct derivations from the earlier work. Furthermore, the *Second Rhapsody* is too long for its material.

The work was superbly performed. Mr. Koussevitzky, who conducts it for the second time this afternoon, led the orchestra as earnestly as if he had been introducing a new symphony by a Roussel or a Miaskovsky, and patiently labored to obtain from the players the last ounce of their energy. It was a virtuoso performance. Mr. Gershwin played a modest piano part simply but with the composer's authority. There was royal welcome for the composer, the performers, the music. Nevertheless, we have had better things from Mr. Gershwin, and we expect better in time to come.

Mr. Koussevitzky also figured on this occasion as the one conductor who has seen fit to honor in New York the memory of a great French composer, the late Vincent d'Indy, with a performance of one of his representative works. The second item of the program was the *Istar Variations*. . . . Mr. Koussevitzky read the music with realization of its poetical and sensuous quality. . . .

Throughout the evening the glorious orchestra responded with the utmost bravura and sensitiveness to every wish of the leader, and Mr. Koussevitzky was on particularly favorable ground. He played not only d'Indy and Gershwin for the middle of his program, but Prokofiev of the *Classic* Symphony for a beginning and Scriabin of the *Poème de l'Extase* for an end. . . .

A refreshing program and a brilliant concert, which caused the audience to admire anew the conductor and the band, and to applaud all participants with an enthusiasm deserved by their achievements.

48   *George Gershwin: Letter to Rose Gershwin (June or July 1932)*

There are but a few extant letters between the Gershwins and other family members, but those from Ira and George to their mother, Rose, reveal the tone of their relationship with her. The sometimes matter-of-fact tone of

SOURCE   DLC [GC].

Gershwin's first letter here contrasts with his warm closing salutation ("your loving son") in his later letters (see selections 68 and 69).

Saturday—

Dear Mom—

I think it was very bad luck that you should come to Palm Springs during a cold spell & while all southern California was the center of a storm. That really is unusual & I hope by this time the warm healthful sun in Palm Springs has rewarded you for your patience.

We had a fine trip south on the Augustus. Beautiful boat, beautiful weather, calm sea. We got off the boat in Havana as we decided not to take the cruise. We've been here now for about 2 weeks & we look like new people. Ira & Lee love it here. All day we relax on the beach & at night we go places & do things, sometimes staying up later than is good for us. But it is really grand & especially as they are having a terrific cold spell up north are we lucky to be here.

Ask Golly [1] to get you that diet book "Health via food" by Dr. Hay. I read it & believe that if you follow it you will never be ill again. In fact when you get back I will go with you to his health farm & together we will take his cure. I am sure it will be beneficial to us both.

I hope you & Golly are having a perfect time, meeting the right people, eating the right food, doing the right things, so that you will come back in *right* condition.

When I get home, which will be in about 2 weeks I will write you about everything of interest in New York. Much love to you from us all & give Golly a kiss for us.

George

49 Alexander Woollcott: *"George the Ingenuous"* (1933)

Noted reviewer and social critic Alexander Woollcott (1887–1943) had known Gershwin's music at least as early as 1922, when he provided a review of the *Scandals* of that year. In this piece, he offers anecdotes based on firsthand contact with the composer that not only echo those found elsewhere in this volume in similar personal recollections, they help throw into sharper relief a sense of what Gershwin was truly like.

---

1 Golly, short for "Gollywog," was the nickname of Cecelia Hayes, a family friend. She was depicted by George in a pen and ink drawing and by Ira in an oil painting playing backgammon with Leonore Gershwin.

SOURCE *Hearst's International-Cosmopolitan* 95 (November 1933): 32–33, 122–23.

The first time I ever met George Gershwin he came to dine with me at my hotel in Atlantic City. I saw before me a slim, swarthy, brilliant young man who, with his dark cheeks that can flood with color, his flashing smile and his marked personal radiance, does, when serving at the altar we call a piano, achieve a dazzling incandescence. But this was a mere dinner-table and his fires were banked, his light curtained with melancholy. He began by apologizing for the eccentric dinner he would have to order.

"You see," he explained, "I have terrible trouble with my stomach."

Small wonder there was born in me then and there a suspicion that skill and fertility in these strange new rhythms of American music are somehow mysteriously derived from fermentation in the alimentary tract.

Since that day I have heard a good deal about the Gershwin stomach, and learned to understand its proper place in this thumbnail sketch. Like you and me, Master Gershwin is profoundly interested in himself, but unlike most of us he has no habit of pretense. He is beyond, and, to my notion, above, posing. He says exactly what he thinks, without window-dressing it to make an impression, favorable or otherwise. Any salient description of him must begin with this trait. All the stories told about him derive from it.

When, shortly after the French and Indian wars, I was an undergraduate at Hamilton College, I introduced to a snow-bound group in the dormitory one afternoon the game of choosing for each person in our class the one adjective which fitted him more perfectly than any other. I even ventured the dogmatic assertion that, if we made our selections well, someone should be able to identify the men from the list of adjectives. I even hastily suggested that my own adjective should be "noble," but this was voted down in favor of another which reduced the whole episode in my memoirs to the proportions of a disagreeable incident. Well, if I were thus rationed in this article and could have but one adjective for George Gershwin, that adjective would be "ingenuous."

Ingenuous at and about his piano. Once an occasional composer named Oscar Levant stood beside that piano while those sure, sinewy, catlike Gershwin fingers beat their brilliant drum-fire—the tumultuous cascade of the *Rhapsody in Blue*, the amorous languor of "The Man I Love," the impish glee of "Fascinating Rhythm," the fine, jaunty dust-spurning scorn of "Strike Up the Band." If the performer was familiar with the work of any other composer, he gave no evidence of it. Levant (who by the way, makes a fleeting appearance in the new Dashiell Hammett book under the guise of Levi Oscant) could be heard muttering under his breath, "An evening with Gershwin is a Gershwin evening."

"I wonder," said our young composer dreamily, "if my music will be played a hundred years from now."

"It certainly will be," said the bitter Levant, "if you are still around."

Now all musicians like to be asked to perform, but tradition bids them do so with a feigned reluctance. Surely you are familiar with the embarrassment of the tenor who, though he has been careful to bring his music roll to a party, must nevertheless affect a pretty surprise at being asked to sing. The late James K. Hackett used to compose orchestral music of singular aridity and, in the days of his affluence, keep a sixteen-piece orchestra on tap, day and night, to play it to him in his moments of despondency.

It was no easy job to take this orchestra with him to parties and yet evince a bashful and touching surprise when asked by his reckless hostess to vouchsafe a sample of his melodic art. Indeed, his nasty predicament called for rather more acting than he would have needed for an entire performance of *Macbeth*. But he used to manage it. Now Gershwin would recognize no such silly necessity. He is not merely a good pianist. He is a great one. No one knows this better than he does. Then he likes to play his own music. He could not possibly be bothered with a ritual of behavior which called for his pretending otherwise.

However, such willingness to perform at the drop of a hat is characteristic of songwriters. Indeed, George Kaufman, who has gone into a fruitful partnership with Gershwin in the evolving of such works as *Of Thee I Sing* and *Let 'Em Eat Cake*, is now arranging an interesting event for the next Olympic games. Twelve composers are to be lined up behind a tape. At a distance of a hundred yards, a tempting grand piano is to be wheeled into position, opened, set. Then, while myriad spectators sit tense, a pistol is to be fired and the race begun.

It is generally conceded that Gershwin will win, hands down. Hands down, that is, on the keyboard. Such artless readiness irks Kaufman only when they are at work on a new show and Gershwin the Ingenuous will insist on playing the score in every drawing-room for weeks and months in advance. By the night of the anxious New York premiere, everyone in the audience already knows it by heart. Even the critics hurry to their typewriters and, after describing the insouciant gayety of the new score, cannot help adding, "To be sure, much of the music is reminiscent," being vaguely conscious, poor dears, that they have heard it before somewhere.

Sometimes the sheer candor of Gershwin's self-examination more than ruffles his colleagues. Sometimes it maddens them. There was the instance of the rift with Harry Ruby, himself no mean songwriter but even so, of course, no Gershwin. They were playing ball together at Gershwin's country place one summer when the game grew so rough that Gershwin withdrew. His hands, he explained, were too valuable to be thus risked.

"Say," said Ruby, "what about *my* hands?"

"Well," Gershwin replied, "it's not the same thing."

Over this disconcerting reply Ruby brooded in silence for a long time, and in the process developed a reluctance to visit his erstwhile crony. Indeed, they did not see each other again for two years. When they did meet, it was by chance on the boardwalk at Atlantic City.

Gershwin was overjoyed at the reunion. Where had good old Ruby been keeping himself? What was the matter, anyway? Had he, Gershwin, said anything, done anything, to offend? After a moment's meditation, and seeing that candor seemed *de riguer*, Ruby decided to tell him, and did so, relating the forgotten incident just as I have told it to you. "And then," he wound up, "you said, 'It's not the same thing.'"

Gershwin received this in silence, took the story into the council-chambers of his heart, examined it, and then replied, "Well, it isn't."

And of course he was so right. A similar habit of honest appraisal, I understand, complicated some of his romances. He is personable, free and thirty-five, and there are ever lovely ladies along his path. There was one girl he had rather meant to marry, but he never got around to telling her so. Meanwhile, she eloped with someone else. Gershwin was dining with friends when the news reached him. His head sank on his breast. In their respect for his manly grief, they let him be the first to speak. "I'd feel terrible about this," he said, "if I weren't so busy just now."

Then there was the girl who rather meant to marry *him*. The trouble was that she had twice his musicianship. From the cradle she had learned to walk with Bach and the great ones. Inevitably she thought of him as less than Bach. He could scarcely quarrel with that, but he knew that such a point of view at close range was likely to keep him in an unproductive state of discouragement. Better get him a helpmeet on a lower musical plane, one who did not know enough to realize his limitations. Gershwin's contribution to this familiar decision was to recognize the source of his discomfort, confess it cheerfully, and rest upon it.

This ingenuousness is not finding its most frequent expression in relation to his painting. He has taken up the graphic art in a big way, spending long hours at his easel, looking up only to gaze meditatively over the rooftops of the magical city and wonder out loud whether he might not do well to give up music altogether in favor of oil and canvas. Since painting presented the more interesting problems, why not divert his indisputable talent from the one art to the other?

Meanwhile, there are many of his own works to be seen in his new home, affably sharing the wall space with little things by Utrillo, Renoir, and Cézanne, who are good painters, too. On the merits of these early Gershwins, I would not feel qualified to speak. My instinctive notion that they are godawful is tempered by a humbling knowledge that I feel the same way about many modern paintings for possession of which our malefactors of great wealth pay through their respective noses.

I would say only this. Anyone who tells you George Gershwin can't draw simply has not seen the multitude packing the Stadium when it is announced that he is going to play.

That new home is a penthouse on East Seventy-second Street, New York City, a bachelor apartment of fourteen rooms (counting a trunk room). Its items include a great paneled reception hall, three pianos, and a bar that is a rhapsody in gayly colored glassware. A private telephone connects his work-room with the apartment across the street occupied by his brother, Ira Gershwin, who writes the words for his music. There is a sleeping porch quipped with strange jalousies. There are mysterious gadgets devised as substitutes for will power in setting-up exercises. There are flights of stairs that fold up and vanish at a touch.

To this richly upholstered eyrie, it is a far cry from the days when old man Gershwin ran a six-table restaurant up near the car barns, and this small, tough street Arab of his begetting used to come around hopefully on roller skates and, as a special treat, have a dish of mashed potatoes. One day, bare-foot, grimy, and astonished, he came to a halt in 125th Street, in front of a penny arcade. To tempt patrons, a mechanical piano, its hammers visible behind the glass, was banging away ceaselessly at something the young passer-by later learned to identify as Rubinstein's "Melody in F." For an hour it riveted George Gershwin, aged six, to that spot, holding him in a spell which has not yet been broken.

The sheer drive of his advance through the purlieus of Tin Pan Alley can be described in terms of vitality, in terms of that unmistakable incandes-cence heretobefore attested to. But why in this one instead of another—in George instead of Ira Gershwin, for instance—this gift should have flowered, I do not pretend to know. Of all talents, that for the invention of music is to me the most mysterious. A great singer is visibly constructed by nature for his life work. "Himmel!" cried Svengali, peering in wonder at the architec-ture of Tribly's throat. "Himmel, the roof of your mouth!" But in what pre-disposition and grouping of faculties lies the gift for the creation of melody, I cannot guess.

I have even read a clotted and humorless monograph on Gershwin by one Isaac Goldberg, which, while it made me a trifle seasick, left me none the wiser.

As I finished my inspection of his luxurious new home one evening last summer, I found myself struggling with a mischievous impulse to say, "Ah, if instead of dying of starvation in a garret, Franz Schubert had a place like this to work in, he might have amounted to something." I did suppress the impulse, but on my way home I fell to wondering what there was about Gershwin that incited me to such teasing—what, indeed, there was to make faintly derisive, in intention at least, all the characteristic anecdotes people tell about him, of which I have here given only a sample handful. And it dawned on me that if we were all thus moved at times to a little urchin pebble-shying in his direction, it might be because of our knowledge—our uncomfortable, disquieting knowledge—that he is a genius.

That is a term I have not heretofore had occasion to employ in this series of articles. Gershwin is a genius, and perhaps the rest of us instinctively snatch at and magnify any little failing of his so that we can console ourselves with the reflection that he is just like the rest of us, after all.

50　*George Gershwin: Letter to Emily Paley (1934)*

In mid-June 1934, George Gershwin, his cousin, the painter Henry (Harry) Botkin, and Gershwin's valet, Paul Mueller, boarded a train in Manhattan to carry them south to Charleston. The plan for the five-week stay in South Carolina was twofold: to allow Gershwin to compose without the constant interruption of friends and social engagements; and to permit him to sample the inflections of the native Gullah dialect and the ambience of Charleston and environs. Renting a house on Folly Beach next to the summer home of Dorothy and DuBose Heyward, the creators of the play and book versions of *Porgy* respectively, George worked harmoniously with DuBose and, during their brief time together, they produced a significant portion of the opera. This poignant letter to his childhood friend Emily Strunsky Paley portrays a relaxed, content, and contemplative George Gershwin.

I've thought about you a good deal, also. In fact we probably exchanged thoughts. Mental-telepathy fashion. Your letter which arrived yesterday was so welcome. It really set me up. So sweetly worded, so sincerely felt, your letter was like seeing and talking to you. The trip down here was a very good thing in many ways. Firstly, I've thought a great deal about my present & future plans & have come to a few decisions. Secondly, the place itself is very different from anything I've seen or lived in before & appeals to the primitive man in me. We go around with practically nothing on, shave only every other

SOURCE DLC [GC].

day (we do have <u>some</u> visitors, you know), eat out on our porch, not more than 30 feet from the ocean at high tide, sit out at night gazing at the stars, smoking our pipes, (I've begun on a pipe) the 3 of us, Harry, Paul & myself discuss our two favorite subjects, Hitler's Germany & God's women. We are in truth, Yankees from the No'th, always suspected a little by the southerner as being a bit slick. Lonesomeness has crept in and bit me quite a few times, but that is to be expected. Paul & Harry have also been bitten, so I suppose that should be a bit consoling.

I've finished one scene of the opera & am now working on the second. It's been very tough for me to work here as the wild waves, playing the role of a siren, beckon to me, every time I get stuck, which is often, and I like a weak sailor turn to them, causing many hours to be knocked into a thousand useless bits.

I've seen and heard some grand Negro sermons & when I see you I shall tell you all about them. Also remind me to tell you how we found ourselves in an auto in 4 feet of the Atlantic. Also, how we discovered a turtle's eggnest & found it to contain 164 eggs about the size of a silver dollar. Also, about the beauty contest which takes place Sat. night when I will be the judge.

Give all my best to dear Lou & tell him I've only played golf twice and shot an 85 the second time. My regards to your family & the gang.

Love,

George

P.S. We are driving home starting Monday. Stopping off various places. Home Saturday.

51   *George Gershwin: Letter to Ira Gershwin (1935)*

Monday

Hello Ira,

How are you big brother? It seems funny writing to you & not being in a foreign country. Palm Beach is once more itself after a few days of cold weather. I'm sitting in the patio of the charming house Emil has rented, writing to you after orchestrating for a few hours this morning. Expect to finish scoring Scene II Act I this week. It goes slowly, there being millions of notes to write.

DuBose, whom I saw in Charleston, was very pleased with your lyrics &

SOURCE *Modern Music* 15 (November–December 1937): 3–7.

thought it would be agreeable to him to split the lyric royalties with you. He is coming north for a few weeks around the first of April.

Wrote Munsell of taking 25% of the opera & told him how it would be split, namely 4 thousand for me, 4 thousand for Emil and 2 thousand for you. Just received his answer in which he says he'd rather not have any outside money in the property meaning of course Emil's interest. That 10 thousand represents 25% based on a 40 thousand dollar production. The cost may go higher in which case I think if we took 15% between us it would not be risking too much % yet we'd have a good interest in the undertaking. What do you think?

Spoke to Mom on the phone last night. She seems quite well. I think I'll run down to Miami to dine with her some night this week.

Flash! Mrs. Dodge Sloan is naming a horse after me. By Sir Galahad out of Melodia.

Flash! I needed a 4 to break 80 yesterday. Oh I forgot to mention—a 4 on a par 5 hole.

Write, big boy & let me know what goes on. One of those old fashioned newsy letters of which you are an undisputed king. Send my love to Lee & Arthur. Hope you are well & happy.

George

52   *Frederick Jacobi: "The Future of Gershwin" (1937)*

Editor Minna Ledermann's short-lived "little magazine," *Modern Music*, is among the most important in the history of American music historiography, for in its pages virtually every important figure on the scene from the mid-1920s through the mid-1940s is covered by and for a well-read, knowledgeable readership. Among other things, here was a journal by composers for composers. Frederick Jacobi (1891–1952), a learned observer, after the composer's death wrote what could be seen now as a dubious epitaph.

The music of George Gershwin has, during his lifetime, suffered from inadequate critical appraisal. His admirers have lauded him fatuously, with little of that quiet detachment which should go into the written consideration of even those works which one loves best. Current Broadway productions frequently blaze out with a highlight from the criticism of some contemporary Ace: "Swellest Show I Have Ever Seen." This is not criticism. Similarly, the

SOURCE *Modern Music* 15 (November–December 1937): 3–7.

late Henry Finck did not really appraise the performances of ladies such as Geraldine Farrar and Mary Garden. He had obviously fallen for their charms and merely allowed the cup of his adolescent infatuation to spill over into his critical column.

And so it is with Gershwin; his music has that high attribute of making people fall in love with it. The overwhelming affection which it is held by hundreds of thousands of Americans testifies to its glamour and the thousands are never entirely wrong. Yet the large public is indiscriminating and love is blind; Gershwin deserves more than the thoughtless fealty of the many who see no further than today. He also deserves more than has been afforded him by many in High Places. There a lack of suppleness has frequently prevailed and a lack of the realization that our muse may, and does, assume garbs of marvelous and infinite variety. Gershwin appeared as a novelty and he threw a certain amount of confusion into both camps.

Like his illustrious predecessors, Jacques Offenbach and Sir Arthur Sullivan, Gershwin wanted to burn the candle at both ends: to be both Sinner and Saint, a sort of Madonna of the Sleeping Cars. And, what is still more difficult—and here he found no precedent in the works of the author of the *Lost Chord* nor in those of the composer of the *Synagogical Service*—he wanted to be both at the same time. The effort is commendable but it rarely works! Different moods, different styles and different technics; and the man who is capable of the one can rarely also master the other. It is true that Rossini has written a *Stabat Mater* and that the style of the *Barber of Seville* is amazingly different from that of *William Tell*; that Verdi has composed not only a *Requiem* but also works as widely divergent in mood as *Il Trovatore* and *Falstaff*; that there is in many respects a far cry between the *Finale* of the *Ninth Symphony* and that of the *Sixth* and that *Götterdämmerung* and *Die Meistersinger* represent two different psychological worlds. These are cases of immense and breath-taking versatility but there is no lack of unity of purpose nor singleness of approach. And there was, in each case—whether in church or in the theatre—but one type of similarly minded and similarly educated audience to be pleased. With Gershwin it was, perhaps, the reverse. He wanted to talk both to the Winter Garden and to Carnegie Hall—"Swanee" for the one and for the other the *Concerto in F*: different pieces, it is true, with different textures and different outward forms. But the message, jazzy and glowing, was to remain about the same. And it must be remembered that the Masters were men whose technic and whose intellectual approach were distinctly of another order: that it is considerably easier to unbend gracefully than to strain beyond one's reach.

For, though a master within his own small forms, Gershwin was completely beyond his depth in a phrase more than sixteen or thirty-two bars long, in one not regularly constructed on the last on which all such phrases are constructed. If Rachmaninoff had only come to his help in bringing "around the curve" the illustrious second theme in the *Rhapsody in Blue!* If he had only been able to extricate himself from the meshes of his own creation in the over-sweet and ill-formed "Bess, You Is My Woman Now!" These are but fundamentals of phrase structure. For the longer intellectual effort required to sustain a symphonic movement Gershwin was wholly inadequate; nor is there any indication that he realized his shortcomings as an architect. And with his failing craftsmanship so also vanished his sense of style. How otherwise explain the laborious and old-fashioned recitatives in *Porgy and Bess* and the indiscriminate and ill-fused mixture which constitutes so large a part of the idiom of that work? Gershwin who, at his best, not only has his own individual style but who also possesses that supreme thing called: style! The effectiveness of those parts of *Porgy and Bess* which are effective is for the most part based on well-known theatrical and musical clichés.... "It Ain't Necessarily So!" How that small piece, lean and wiry, stands out in its place, like a black diamond in the fog! Here Gershwin is himself again with no lapses into the vulgar, no departures from his usual good taste. How strange that Gershwin should, in his larger and more pretentious works, lack precisely those qualities which are otherwise so much his own: style, shape, and that indefinable thing called authenticity, that sense of something freshly felt rather than of something heavily reconstructed!

But in each of Gershwin's works there is some genius. Who has not been rocketed aloft into some jazzy sky on the wings of the opening phrase of the *Rhapsody?* Whose feet have not twitched to the initial strains of the *American in Paris*: each of us a Bill Robinson in his own mind and floating down an imaginary Champs Elysées to the sound of celestial taxicabs? What is this and who are you, George, to have done this thing to us: to have changed our world, to have made our ordinary comings goings to become things unreal, light and sweet, and ourselves disembodied and carefree as a kite in air?

The *Preludes for Piano* show Gershwin in his less favorable light. As in most of his serious efforts, the ideas are essentially short of breath; he lacks the ability to draw them out, to make them unfold, so to speak, from within themselves. Such a thing as a long, consecutive thought is scarcely known to Gershwin and on such long, consecutive thoughts great music is built. Whether it be in science, philosophy, or art, human beings lose interest in even the most attractive fragments and are ultimately held only by those ideas which, clearly conceived, are followed through to a well-formed and logical conclusion. This was not for Gershwin. In the *Concerto in F* the themes are fresher and he does best with those, like the second theme in the first movement, which are rounded, closed-off and complete entities in themselves. Otherwise he is helpless in his attempts to carry along—to spin out—his ideas. Repetition, foreshortening (stretto) and climax; then a new idea or the return to an old one; that is his usual formula and it finally becomes wearisome almost to the point of exasperation. The piano writing is adroit and rather personal: "stencilled . . . snappy . . . and cackling," to quote from his own excellently written little foreword to the Alajalov-Schuster-and-Simon *Songbook*. And the *Concerto*, as a whole, has an obvious, Russian effectiveness. But its charming material is marred, for some of us at least, by the lack of skill, the lack of modesty with which it is presented. I believe that the *American in Paris* will live longer than either the *Rhapsody* or the *Concerto* and that, of the more pretentious works, *Porgy and Bess* will be the first to go.

It is not in his "larger" works that George will live. It is in the great number of his songs, almost every one of which is a gem in its own way. Within the confines of his small structure he was able to mold phrases of considerable variety and in the best of these there is the perfection of an expert craftsman. They are supple, balanced, and expressive. His harmony here is equally perfect: the sensitive choice of his simple chords gives perhaps even more pleasure than his excursions into the realm of those more elaborately "barbered." His rhythms are lively and amusing and in this field he was undoubtedly a real innovator. In all of these things he never once oversteps the boundary of the best taste and each of his songs has "character:" George's and its own. His melody, though perhaps more instrumental than vocal, is warm and lithe and all the qualities are so fused as to make a really perfect whole. Who can forget the insinuating melodic line of the "You Don't Know the Half of It Dearie, Blues"? The perfection of harmony and form which is in "The Man I Love"? The subtlety of that masterpiece: "Mine" from *Let 'Em Eat Cake*? The bawdy and really marvelous little climax in "Sam and Delilah"? The dry, pulsating surge of "Fascinating Rhythm," "Clap Yo' Hands" and "High Hat"—off-center and fantastically poised, as a moment in a dance by Fred Astaire? "Liza!" "Lady Be Good!" "Who Cares!" Who of us has not felt their glow and the exhilarating sense of careless, high enjoyment with which they are suffused?

Most of these songs are no longer young, as songs of this kind go. But they are still fresh and their undimmed vitality augurs well for the future. George was undoubtedly very fortunate in having his brother, Ira, a marvelous collaborator. The most perfect wedding of their talents was, perhaps, in *Of Thee I Sing* which, as a whole, is unique in the annals of the Gershwins and of the American stage. One need not underestimate the importance of

Ira in bringing to fruition the talents of George. But the music of George is something in itself and in his tragic and premature passing America has lost one of its brightest stars. He shone during his day and was not, God knows, unacclaimed. And I believe that his future is equally assured. He belongs in the company of those blissful demigods, Sullivan, Offenbach, and Johann Strauss; men who have evoked immediate response in the hearts of their contemporaries, men who have been the articulate expression of their age and who have, to an extent granted to few, molded their age and become a symbol of what it was. Their vein has been rich and complete.

And so it has been with George. If my criticism has been more detailed than my praise, the intention has in no sense been to belittle him as a composer: rather to define his scope and to place him firmly in a category where, among our contemporaries in any event, he unquestionably stands supreme. His memory must be guarded and cherished, his music frequently performed so that the unique and brilliant flame with which he illuminated our scene may carry on for many years to come.

V. PORGY AND BESS

The literature on *Porgy and Bess* is immense. To appreciate the scholarly dialogue about the work, the reader may wish to see Hollis Alpert's work, *The Life and Times of Porgy and Bess* (1990); two contributions by Richard Crawford ("It Ain't Necessarily Soul: Gershwin's 'Porgy and Bess' as a Symbol" [1972] and "Gershwin's Reputation: A Note on *Porgy and Bess*" [1979]); Charles Hamm's article "The Theatre Guild Production of *Porgy and Bess*" (1987); two articles by Wayne Shirley ("Porgy and Bess" [1974] and "Reconciliation on Catfish Row: Bess, Serena, and the Short Score of *Porgy and Bess*" [1981]); and Lawrence Starr's articles ("Towards a Reevaluation of Gershwin's *Porgy and Bess*" [1984] and "Gershwin's 'Bess, You Is My Woman Now': The Sophistication and Subtlety of a Great Tune" [1986]); details for all are in the bibliography.

In short, *Porgy and Bess* was and is a phenomenon. Although the employment of an all-black cast had become commonplace by 1935, the standard operatic setting, with recitative connecting arias, ensemble numbers, and chorus sections, was anything but ordinary. Nor was the treatment of the play, the authenticity of the dialect used, the quality of music and libretto, and the excellent professional cast that was assembled. Every aspect of the production was first-rate with an ample budget allotted to bring the show to its tryout run in Boston and later to the Alvin Theater. Yet, the production was controversial and, owing to the controversy, ran for only 124 performances. The following articles will address the factors that determine the ultimate question: Was *Porgy and Bess* a successful or a failed experiment?

53 Joseph Swain: From "America's Folk Opera" (1990)

By one of those curious coincidences of history, George Gershwin was inspired to compose *Porgy and Bess* at about the same time and in just the same way that Jerome Kern got his idea for *Show Boat*. After a trying rehearsal of his newest musical comedy *Oh, Kay!* in the fall of 1926, Gershwin tried to fall asleep by reading DuBose Heyward's recent novel, *Porgy*. Instead, as Heyward's wife, Dorothy, recounted later, "he read himself wide awake" and became enthralled with the dramatic prospects of the story. By four o'clock in the morning the composer was writing to Heyward, inquiring if he might be interested in turning *Porgy* into an opera.[1]

DuBose Heyward was an early figure in the Southern Renascence of American literature and the foremost author of the so-called Charleston writers.[2] *Porgy* was his first novel, published in 1925, and ultimately his best-known work. It portrays a black community in Charleston during a summer around the turn of the century. The principal character, Porgy, a crippled beggar who transports himself in a goat-drawn cart, was modeled after a somewhat notorious figure of Heyward's native Charleston known as "Goat Sammy." The plot of the book is extremely loose, "seemingly little more than a series of vignettes in structure."[3] One of its most unusual features is the recurrence of songs and spirituals sung by the community at large. For Heyward, these songs were the most economical means to his end of expressing the collective spirit of the community:

> The spiritual said everything for him (the black man) that he could not say in the new language that he found here—awe in the presence of death—his racial terror of being left alone—his escape from bondage into the new heaven—everything.[4]

SOURCE Joseph Swain, *The Broadway Musical: A Critical and Musical Survey* (New York: Oxford University Press, 1990), 51–57. All footnotes in this entry appear in the original source.

1 This story is recounted in Dorothy Heyward, "Porgy's Goat," *Harper's* (December 1957), 37–41, and in Stanley Green, *The World of Musical Comedy* (New York: Ziff-Davis, 1960), 120.

2 William H. Slavick, *DuBose Heyward* (Boston: Twayne, 1981), 9.

3 Ibid., 57.

4 Letter from DuBose Heyward to Kathryn Bourne, December 21, 1931. Cited from Frank Durham, "DuBose Heyward's Use of Folklore in His Negro Fiction," *The Citadel: Monograph Series No. 2* (Charleston, S.C.: The Citadel, 1961), 18–19.

It could have been these spirituals that attracted Gershwin, or perhaps Heyward's apparent success in getting at the heart of the black community, for Gershwin was already interested in black culture. In 1922, as part of a revue he was writing for George White's *Scandals*, he composed a twenty-minute one-act music drama called *Blue Monday*, with a libretto by G. B. "Buddy" DeSylva. The story, set in Harlem, involves two young men vying for the love of a woman and ends with the woman shooting her lover on suspicion of infidelity. The number was roundly criticized and White withdrew it after a single performance. A revival by Paul Whiteman in 1925 under the title *135th Street* proved no more successful. The critical consensus is that Gershwin, trying to set a soap-opera libretto, had too little experience in serious dramatic composition.[5]

Despite Gershwin's and Heyward's initial enthusiasm for the new project, there was a hiatus of nine years between Gershwin's first reading of *Porgy* and the premiere of the opera in Boston in September 1935. The first obstacle was Dorothy Heyward, a playwright with several works to her credit, who told her astonished husband that she had already begun to turn the novel into a play, which eventually became a successful production of Broadway's Theatre Guild. This seemed to upset Gershwin not in the least. Dorothy recalls that "It was a great moment when George said there was plenty of room for both play and opera. And plenty of time. He wanted to spend years in study before composing his opera."[6] The last statement reveals no polite assurance on Gershwin's part. His detached estimation of his own talents and of his own music is a characteristic that recurs in almost all Gershwin biographical writing, and in 1926 the failure of *Blue Monday*, his only other attempt at serious music drama so far, could not have been far from his mind.

A second obstacle was Gershwin's own busy career. The late 1920s saw him engaged to write a series of musical comedies for the production team of Alex Aarons and Vinton Freedley, along with his brother Ira as lyricist and Guy Bolton as librettist.

> At first, it was the producers' intention to have these shows follow the bright, witty pattern of the old Princess Theatre attractions, only, according to Guy Bolton, on a larger scale. . . . Despite these intentions, the shows soon became star vehicles rather than closely coordinated book-and-music shows.[7]

---

5 See Charles Schwartz, *Gershwin: His Life and Music* (Indianapolis and New York: Da Capo, 1973), 60–61, for more details on this piece.

6 Heyward, "Porgy's Goat," 37.

7 Green, *The World of Musical Comedy*, 111.

However, a much more significant series of Gershwin musical plays opened in 1930, in collaboration with librettists George S. Kaufman and Morrie Ryskind, beginning with *Strike Up the Band*, and continuing with *Of Thee I Sing* (1931) and *Let 'Em Eat Cake* (1933). These are often called "satirical operettas" and in these works Gershwin makes a significant advance integrating the music with the story.

The most successful of the three was *Of Thee I Sing*. A story about a fictitious political campaign and presidential administration in which the main issue is "Love," the play successfully lampooned "hush-hush scandals, nonsensical debates, party politics, under-the-counter deals, political campaigns, and ridiculous bids for votes."[8] The play is undoubtedly an important landmark in the history of the American musical, running for 441 performances at the Music Box Theater, winning the 1932 Pulitzer Prize for Drama, becoming the first musical comedy to be published as a book, and attracting praise from all quarters for its musical and dramatic innovations. Despite all this, it has not survived in the repertoire, and critics are equally agreed about the reason, best explained by Lehman Engel:

> In *Of Thee I Sing* (1931) most of the comedy comes out of contemporary political situations. It worked well enough in its own time to win the Pulitzer Prize.
>
> Today it is meaningless, and the show, because it is built squarely on comedy, cannot be revived. It is significant that—and this is surely an important indication of modern-day artistry—the songs, *including* the lyrics, are not dated. The lyrics are universal and therefore enduring. Only the "comic" dialogue is entirely dated, and *Of Thee I Sing*, once funny because of it, is now impossible to revive because of it.[9]

Because of these shows, Gershwin did not begin work on *Porgy and Bess* until 1933. In retrospect, however, the delay must be considered most fortuitous, and the time between the initial inspiration and his actual composition well spent, for surely the satirical operettas constituted the most important part of the "study" he told DuBose Heyward that he wished to make. It should not be forgotten, too, that Gershwin was only twenty-eight years old when he read the novel, and that the gain in artistic maturity in those busy years was probably significant. Indeed, Stanley Green sees Gershwin's com-

8 Abe Laufe, *Broadway's Greatest Musicals* (New York: Funk & Wagnalls, 1969), 32.

9 Lehman Engel, *The American Musical Theatre: A Consideration* (distributed by Macmillan, 1967), 112. For similar assessments, see Laufe, *Broadway's Greatest Musicals*, 33, and Schwartz, *Gershwin*, 219–20.

positional *oeuvre* as an uninterrupted progression that, had he not died in 1937 of a brain tumor, was quite unlimited in its promise:

> His entire career had been the most steady, step-by-step advance of any theatre composer. There was some overlapping, but it is remarkable that his rise was so chronologically systematic—from revues (1920–1924), to musical comedies (1924–1930), to satirical comic operas (1931–1933), to an American folk-opera (1935).[10]

Gershwin himself seems to have realized that *Porgy and Bess* was to be his most important composition to date, representing an unprecedented attempt by a Broadway composer to write a serious music drama. As Heyward converted *Porgy* from stage play to opera libretto, along with certain lyric contributions from Ira Gershwin,[11] George spent eleven months composing the music (from February 1934 to January 1935), and nine more laborious months orchestrating it (from January to September 1935), a prodigious length of concentrated effort for any Broadway composer.[12] Because he refused to have the blackface, black professional singers were recruited from all over the country. There was even a special rehearsal in order to test the orchestrations, an aspect of Gershwin's compositions that had attracted criticism, and still does. Critic Irving Kolodin observed the intense preparations:

> Watching this American folk-opera grow to perfected performance as a theatre work through months of careful rehearsal aimed to unify the drama and the music, the singing and the acting, has been an illuminating experience to a musician accustomed to the perfunctory and uncorrelated rehearsal generally accorded to the productions prepared for the conventional opera.[13]

After a triumphant tryout at the Colonial Theatre in Boston on September 20, 1935, the Theatre Guild presented *Porgy and Bess* to Broadway at the Alvin Theater on October 10, 1935, exactly eight years after the premiere of *Porgy* the stage play.

Except for an intensely symbolic analysis by Wilfrid Mellers,[14] almost all

10 Green, *The World of Musical Comedy*, 123.

11 It is very difficult to know precisely what Ira contributed to the whole text of *Porgy and Bess*. See Schwartz, *Gershwin*, 261–62, and Slavick, *DuBose Heyward*, 81.

12 See Schwartz, *Gershwin*, 258ff., for a detailed chronology of the composition.

13 Irving Kolodin, "*Porgy and Bess*: American Opera in the Theatre," *Theatre Arts Monthly* (November 1935): 853.

14 Wilfrid Mellers, *Music in a New Found Land* (New York: Hillstone, 1964), 392–413.

serious dramatic criticism of *Porgy and Bess* has been blunted and forestalled by preoccupation with three other matters.

The first is a concern over exactly what is the "authentic" version of the opera. This is a relatively recent concern, brought about by a history of revival that recorded various cut versions and spurred by a steadily growing appreciation of the opera's value. The first revival, a very successful production for Broadway by Cheryl Crawford in 1942, deleted many of the recitatives. Subsequent revivals in the 1950s restored much of this music, but often altered the order of numbers given in Gershwin's piano-vocal score published in 1935. Thus, when in 1976 Lorin Maazel and the Cleveland Orchestra recorded all the music in Gershwin's original 1935 score, and the Houston opera produced a "complete" stage version, these events were hailed as events that, for the first time, revealed the true greatness of the opera.

As is often the case with matters of authenticity, however, especially in opera, the issue is rarely so simple. Ironically, the original production at the Alvin, under Gershwin's constant and direct supervision, was cut. Rouben Mamoulian, the production's director, wrote three years later that *"Porgy and Bess* as performed in New York was almost forty-five minutes shorter than the original score,"* which was sent to the publisher six months in advance of the premiere.[15] Excluded were the opening piano solo, known as the Jazzbo Brown music, the "Buzzard Song," Maria's denunciation of Sportin' Life in Act II, much of Porgy's solo and the following trio in Act III, and many other snippets from the score.[16]

Why did Gershwin cut music from his original score? Was the opera cut to make it conform to the normal length of a Broadway show, as *Show Boat* was, or were there deeper dramatic reasons? Was Gershwin convinced that they would improve the opera, or simply increase its chances for profit? David Ewen writes, unfortunately without citation, that "these cuts hurt Gershwin, who loved every note; but, showman that he was, he accepted them willingly and often insisted on them."[17] But Todd Duncan, the original Porgy, recalls:

He was upset in Boston. My God, that opening night was killing. I think it was four hours. We performed the whole opera and we didn't get out until one o'clock or something. George didn't want one beautiful blessed note cut. He and [stage director] [Rouben] Mamoulian and

15 "I Remember," in Merle Armitage, *George Gershwin* (New York, London: Longmans, Green, 1938), 52.

16 For a complete list and discussion of cuts, see Charles Hamm's recent "The Theatre Guild Production of *Porgy and Bess*," *Journal of the American Musicological Society* XL, No. 3 (Fall 1987): 495–532.

17 David Ewen, *A Journey to Greatness* (New York: Henry Holt, 1956), 266.

[musical director] [Alexander] Smallens walked in the Boston Common all night long, fighting and fussing and talking about it.... all that last part that I sang, George Gershwin wrote for my voice. He wrote that after he met me and after he heard me. But it was just too much for one man to sing at the end of an opera....[18]

Charles Hamm's study reveals that cuts were made from the time of the first rehearsals, through the tryout in Boston, up to the New York premiere in October. According to rehearsal scores, they seem to have been the direct result of stage experience, and since Gershwin was in constant attendance during rehearsals, they must have had his approval, painful though they may have been to make.[19]

Such a multiplicity of versions places *Porgy and Bess* in the same confusing situation that obtains with a great many classical operas. There is a certain amount of authentic music that was removed or added at one time or another for one reason or another, usually with the composer's consent. One thinks of the cuts Beethoven made in the later versions of *Fidelio* and the extra solo arias Mozart put into his operas at the behest of irate singers. Knowing the precise reasons for such changes might make performance decisions today easier, but will never remove entirely the need to make them. As with these other operas, the "complete" score of *Porgy and Bess* is somewhat of a fiction. Naturally, the critic must be wary of this state of affairs, as it would be embarrassing to analyze some number as the key to the opera, only to find that Gershwin had cut it. On the other hand, the pre-cut score is Gershwin's first attempt to solve the dramatic problems, and as such must be considered a critical resource.

Is it an opera or a musical? This question was the focus of the reviews that followed the premiere and has not yet been dismissed. Olin Downes and Brooks Atkinson, writing for the music and drama columns of the *New York Times* of October 11, 1935, make typical comments:

The style is at one moment of opera and another of operetta or sheer Broadway entertainment. Why commonplace remarks that carry no emotion have to be made in a chanting monotone is a problem [I] cannot fathom. Turning "Porgy" into opera has resulted in a deluge of casual remarks that have to be thoughtfully intoned and that amazingly impede the action.[20]

18   "Todd Duncan," in Robert Kimball and Alfred Simon, *The Gershwins* (New York: Atheneum, 1973), 181.
19   Hamm, "The Theatre Guild Production," 505–7, 514–21.
20   *New York Times*, October 11, 1935, 30.

Generally, the drama critics objected to recitative per se and the music critics to "Summertime," "I Got Plenty o' Nuttin'," and other tunes which seemed "too popular" for opera. Gershwin replied to both in the *New York Times* of October 20, 1935, writing that his recitatives were composed to the natural speech accents of blacks, and that "Nearly all of Verdi's operas contain what are known as 'song hits.' *Carmen* is almost a collection of song hits."[21]

Since it has been shown time and again that dramatic action can be created from any of the various genres subsumed under the various titles of "opera," "music drama," "operetta," "musical," and so forth, the classification of *Porgy and Bess*, as far as its dramatic artistry is concerned, is truly a trivial issue. As Engel so sensibly remarks:

> It has always seemed to me that this annoyance with *Porgy* is far more the product of semantics than of anything Gershwin put into his score. It is as if just calling *Porgy* by the name "opera" serves to assail the sensibilities of those who believe that such a classification is a slur on the dignity of Wagner, Verdi, and Mozart.[22]

An issue much more serious than the mere classification of *Porgy and Bess*, but related to that matter, has been the quality of its declamatory vocal writing, including accompanied recitative, arioso, and the like. Opinions on this vary wildly, perhaps because there is little theory or consensus about what makes good recitative. At one end of the controversy there is Irving Kolodin, writing in 1935 that the declamatory writing is one of Gershwin's "most impressive accomplishments, for its adherence to the characteristics of the persons in the drama,"[23] and at the other end David Hamilton, in a review of the 1976 Cleveland recording, insisting that "in much of the scene music, there isn't any consistent idea of how to get from one place to another."[24] Even strident critics admit, however, that some of the most moving and dramatically important passages in the opera—such as Porgy's first speech, his subsequent invocation to the dice, and Bess's final plea to Crown in Act II—are composed in the declamatory style. If there are other awkward moments, if the entire declamatory music is not perfect, it is still absolutely necessary to set up the most striking moments:

> In *La Boheme, Otello, Louise, Die Meistersinger,* and all the others, there are many passages of recitative that in themselves might seem dull to

21 *New York Times,* October 21, 1935, Sec. X, p. 1.
22 Engel, *The American Musical Theatre,* 143.
23 Kolodin, *"Porgy and Bess,"* 858.
24 Quoted in Andrew Porter, "Musical Events," *New Yorker* 61 (February 25, 1985): 93.

this listener or that; but without the musical texture they create, many
lyric passages that are not songs or arias would be impossible
because—if there were no musical continuity—they would become
small, isolated islands of music, unconnected, rootless, and even silly.[25]

And such passages in *Porgy and Bess* are essential not only for their lyricism
and intrinsic beauty but for what music they contribute to the dramatic
development.

Lastly, there is the most complex and politically sensitive question of the
three: is *Porgy and Bess* a fair representation of black music and black culture?

Generally, the reaction of the black community has not been favorable
through the years.[26] "The times are here to debunk Gershwin's lampblack
Negroisms," said Duke Ellington after the premiere, and Ralph Matthews
seconded this opinion: "The singing, even down to the choral and ensemble
numbers, has a conservatory twang."[27] As listeners have become more aware
of the sensibilities of racial minorities, the undeniable stereotypical features
of the opera have become even more glaring.

It is difficult to fault Gershwin for any conscious misrepresentation of the
culture he tried to portray. He stayed for a month on Folly Island off the coast
of South Carolina, close to a Gullah community, to hear their music and
observe their religious celebrations, and he refused to accept a prestigious
contract from the Metropolitan Opera for the premiere of the opera because
a black cast would not have been allowed. These are not the actions of a
dramatist who is interested in stereotypes. That the opera is in some ways
still stereotypical shows not that Gershwin was racist but that he was a child
of his time, subject to its cultural prejudice and ignorance.

In the end, Gershwin did what any opera composer must do: he recast
raw material into a unified musical-dramatic idiom. Hall Johnson, a black
composer writing for *Opportunity* magazine in 1936, realized this even as he
described characteristics that bothered him:

> [Gershwin] is an individual artist, as free to write about Negroes in his
> own way as any other composer to write about anything else. The only
> thing a really creative artist can be expected to give us is an expression

25 Engel, *The American Musical Theatre*, 144–45.
26 For a fine introduction to this complex issue, see Richard Crawford, "It Ain't Necessarily Soul:
Gershwin's *Porgy and Bess* as a Symbol," *Yearbook for Inter-American Musical Research* VIII (1972):
17–38.
27 Robert Garland, "Negroes Are Critical of *Porgy and Bess*," *New York World-Telegram* (January 16,
1934), 14.

of *his own* reaction to a given stimulus. We are not compelled to agree with it or even like it.[28]

The social and political implications of *Porgy and Bess* for the black community are very real and quite complex, and require discussion, but ultimately they are irrelevant to any dramatic appraisal of the work. This may be difficult to swallow for some, and, indeed, Gershwin's opera has been unjustly criticized on these terms. "Folk-lore subjects recounted by an outsider are only valid as long as the folk in question is unable to speak for itself, which is certainly not true of the American Negro in 1935," wrote Virgil Thomson in that year.[29] "Nor was it true of Spaniards and Spanish gypsies 60 years earlier, but one is grateful that such fine scruples did not keep Bizet from composing *Carmen*," retorted William Youngren.[30] There may not be a single opera that does not distort some social truth held today (one wonders how feminists would receive *The Magic Flute*!), but such defects lie apart from the musical-dramatic issues with which the composer is wrestling, and modern opera lovers forget politics as part of their suspension of disbelief that allows them to enter into the medium in the first place.

54   *George Gershwin and DuBose Heyward: Selected Correspondence (1932–1934)*

Although the record of portions of the ongoing dialogue between Heyward and Gershwin concerning the development of their opera is incomplete due to their in-person meetings and telephone conversations, they did leave behind a sizable sequence of seventeen letters (ten from Gershwin and seven from Heyward) that, over their course, explicate their long-distance working relationship.[1] Eleven of the letters are presented here.

March 29, 1932

My dear Mr. Heyward:

I am about to go abroad in a little over a week, and in thinking of ideas for new compositions, I came back to one that I had several years ago—namely,

28 Hall Johnson, "Porgy and Bess—A Folk Opera," *Opportunity* (January 1936): 26.
29 Virgil Thomson, "George Gershwin," *Modern Music* (November–December 1935): 13.
30 William Youngren, "Gershwin, Part IV," *New Republic* 176 (May 14, 1977): 25.

SOURCE DLC (GC). Copies of this correspondence, along with much else regarding the novel (1925), play (1927), and opera versions of the *Porgy* story, can be found in the Heyward Collection at the South Carolina Historical Society in Charleston (SCHS[HC]).

1 An eighteenth letter, from Gershwin to Heyward, dates from 1937, well after the initial run of *Porgy and Bess* was over.

PORGY—and the thought of setting it to music.[2] It is still the most outstanding play that I know, about the colored people.

I should like very much to talk with you before I leave for Europe, and the only way that I imagine that would be possible would be by telephone. So if you will be good enough to either telephone me collect at Trafalgar 7–0727—or send me your telephone number by telegram, I will be glad to call you.

Is there any chance of your being abroad in the next couple of months?

I hope this letter finds you and your wife in the best of health, and hoping to hear from you soon, I am

Sincerely yours,

George Gershwin

Sept. 3rd, 1932

My dear Gershwin:

I attach a letter just received from my old *Porgy* agents. I cannot see brother Jolson as Porgy, but I have heard that he was casting about for something more artistic than his usual Sonny Boy line, and what his real potentialities are, I have very little idea.

Of course, this does not shake me in my desire to work with you on the story, only it reminds me that I evidently have an asset in *Porgy*, and in these trying times that has to be customary agreement with your producer, with whom, I presume, you have been already discussing the matter. With this attended to I will withdraw the rights from the Century Play Co., and will also withdraw from sale the picture rights, which are at present on the market. It seems to me that this is very important for both of us, as certainly neither of us would wish to put our time on it without this protection.

Will you please at earliest possible moment wire me whether your associates are prepared to enter into a definite agreement at this time, so that I may know how to handle the Jolson matter. I will then leave promptly for New York so that we may get that settled, and also have our first conference on the rewriting of the book.

Please do not construe this letter as an attempt to force a decision upon you in the matter. I understand perfectly that you want to do the play. So do I. It is, however, very important for me to have some definiteness as to dates, and that would be the principal value of a contract to me. I am always having a hard time adjusting my work to my time. Perhaps you have not yet taken the matter up with a producer. All that I would ask then would be your definite assurance that you would plan for production either this spring or early next fall.

---

2 Gershwin is referring to his trip to Havana, which yielded the *Cuban Overture*. Originally they planned to continue to cruise to Europe but left the boat in Cuba.

Would it be possible to use Jolson, and arrange some sort of agreement with him, or is that too preposterous?

Please let me hear from you at your very earliest possible convenience, and I must act at once in this Jolson matter.

All good wishes,

Sincerely,[3]

September 9th, 1932

My dear Heyward:

I have just returned from a short vacation in the Adirondacks and found your letter.

I think it is very interesting that Al Jolson would like to play the part of Porgy, but I really don't know how he would be in it.[4] Of course he is a very big star, who certainly knows how to put over a song, and it might mean more to you financially if he should do it—provided that the rest of the production were well done. The sort of thing that I should have in mind for *Porgy* is a much more serious thing than Jolson could ever do.

Of course I would not attempt to write music to your play until I had all the themes and musical devices worked out for such an undertaking. It would be more a labor of love than anything else.

If you can see your way to making some ready money from Jolson's version I don't know that it would hurt a later version done by an all-colored cast.

If you are planning to come north I shall be most anxious to see you to discuss various aspects of the opera. I expect to be here until February. I have not planned with any producers yet as I should like to write the work first and then see who would be the best one to do it. I know that Shumlin, the producer of *Grand Hotel*, is very much interested in the idea.

I hope that you and Mrs. Heyward are well.

Best wishes,

George Gershwin

November 12, 1933

Dear George:

I enclose two copies of first scene which I have worked over for you to start on.[5]

---

3 The extant copies of Heyward's letters, in either SCHS (HC) or DLC (GC), do not contain signatures.

4 The project discussed here, with Al Jolson starring in a show written by the *Show Boat* team of Jerome Kern and Oscar Hammerstein II, never materialized.

5 Along with the rest of the manuscripts for the opera, Heyward's libretto, sent to Gershwin in installments, is in DLC (GC). Gershwin worked directly from this document.

I have cut everything possible, and marked a couple of possible further cuts in pencil on ms. As a matter of fact, this is now a very brief scene considering that it carries all of the exposition necessary for the play.

I have been thinking a lot about this job and have a pretty definite feeling about the treatment which I submit for your consideration. I feel more and more that all dialog should be spoken. It is fast moving, and we will cut it to the bone, but this will give the opera speed and tempo. This will give you a chance to develop a new treatment, carrying the orchestration straight through the performance (as you suggested) but enriching it with pantomime and action on the stage, and with such music (singing) as grows out of the action. Also, in scenes like the fight, the whole thing can be treated as a unified composition drawing on lighting, orchestra, and the wailing of crowd, mass sounds of horror from people, etc. instead of singing. It can be lifted to a terrific climax. That fight was treated with a great deal of noise in play. That is not my idea of best art in handling it.

I am offering a new idea for opening of scene as you will see from the script. The play opened with a regular riot of noise and color. This makes an entirely different opening, which I think is important. What I have in mind is to let the scene, as I describe it, merge with the overture, almost in the sense of illustration, giving the added force of sight and sound. I think it would be very effective to have the lights go out during overture, so that the curtain rises in darkness, then the first scene will begin to come up as the music takes up the theme of jazz from the dance hall piano. The songs which I have written for this part will fall naturally into the action and mood of the separate flashes of negro life.

You may have entirely different ideas about this, but we will be able to discuss all that when we meet in Charleston.

I probably will not be able to do anything more until after we meet as I shall be terrifically busy winding up here and moving my family to Folly Beach near Charleston. I expect to get there by the first. My address there will be, Mail: Folly Beach, S.C. Telegraph: Care Folly Operating Company, Broad St., Charleston.

Be sure to get a set of pictures from Munsell, then you can visualize the set and action.[6]

I shall send you a picture in a day or so, and you must not forget to let me have one with your autograph for my study here.

It was a great pleasure seeing you in New York. All good luck to you until we meet.

As ever,

---

6 Warren Munsell represented the Theatre Guild, producers of the opera who had also produced DuBose and Dorothy Heyward's play version of the story.

25 November 1933

Dear DuBose:

I am leaving with my friend, Emil Mossbacher [sic], the night of December second—next Saturday—for Charleston, arriving there sometime on the third.

I expect to stay two or three days and then leave for Florida.[7] I hope you can arrange it so as to spend most of the time with me. I would like to see the town and hear some spirituals and perhaps go to a colored café or two if there are any.

I have been reading through the first scene which you sent and think you have done a swell job, especially with the new lyrics. There may be too much talk, but I can't tell until I start composing just how that will work out.

On account of the many things I have to do at the present I haven't actually started composing. I want to do a great deal of thinking about the thing and the gathering in of thematic material before the actual writing begins. So, until my tour is ended I don't expect I will have much finished but after that I shall devote all my time to "Porgy."

Looking forward to seeing you, I am

Very sincerely,

George Gershwin

Feb. 6. 34

Dear George:

You will soon be getting back from your tour, which I hope has been a huge success in every way.

I know you will be eager to see some more of the script, so am sending the next two scenes herewith. I have about completed the next scene also, but it is not yet typed, and I want to do a little more work on it.

Act 2, scene 1 may still seem a little long to you, but I have reduced it from 39 pages in the talking script to 18 for the opera, and it is strong on humor and action. Let me know how you feel about it and if you think it needs more lyrics.

Act 2 scene 2 ought to be good. I have cut out the conventional negro vaudeville stuff that was in the original play and incorporated material that is authentic and plenty "hot" as well. I have discovered for the first time a type of secular dance that is done here that is straight from the African phallic dance, and that is undoubtedly a complete survival. Also I have seen that native band of harmonicas, combs, etc. It will make an extraordinary introduction to the primitive scene of passion between Crown and Bess.

I think maybe the composition on the lyrics I have done better wait until

---

7 Gershwin completed "Summertime" during this vacation with the Emil Mosbachers in Palm Beach.

we get together. I have in mind something for them that I cannot well suggest by writing, especially the boat song. But don't let that stop you, if you feel moved with ideas of your own.

I have a letter from Munsell asking how we are getting on. He says that they want to get out subscription announcements for next season before long, and want to have some assurance from us before mentioning the opera, and saving its place on the schedule. I will write him, but I suggest you drop in there some time. Get yourself, also, a set of the pictures, they will help you to visualize the sets.

I am afraid, after careful consideration, that we are not going to be able to go to Florida—much as we would like it, and appreciate Mr. Mosbacher's invitation. The baby is not very well, and we could not leave her. Then too, I find my creative ability practically paralyzed in a new environment. I am just getting into my stride here now, and I do not want to risk breaking it.

Please let me know your plans as soon as you perfect them, and I cannot urge you too strongly to plan to come to Charleston at the earliest convenient moment for your visit. You really haven't scratched the surface of the native material yet. This secular stuff, for instance.

Thanks for the picture, especially for the inscription.

Affectionate greetings and all good wishes from us all.

26 February 1934

Dear DuBose:

Well here I am, back again after an arduous but exciting trip of 12,000 miles which took 28 days.[8] The tour was a fine artistic success for me and would have been splendid financially if my foolish manager hadn't booked me into seven towns that were too small to support such an expensive organization as I carried. Nevertheless, it was a very worthwhile thing for me to have done and I have many pleasant memories of cities I had not visited before.

I received your Second Act's script and think it is fine. I really think you are doing a magnificent job with the new libretto and I hope I can match it musically.

I have begun composing music for the First Act and I am starting with the songs and spirituals first.

I am hoping you will find some time to come up North and live at my apartment—if it is convenient for you—so we can work together on some of

---

8 Gershwin refers to his tour with the Leo Reisman Orchestra celebrating the tenth anniversary of *Rhapsody in Blue*.

the spirituals for Scene 2, Act I. Perhaps when the weather grows a little warmer you will find time to do this. I cannot leave New York to go South as I am tied up with the radio until June 1st; then I have a two-months' vacation—which time I shall devote entirely to the opera. Of course I would prefer you to come North to stay with me long before June 1st and we could do a lot together.

I saw *4 Saints in 3 Acts*, an opera by Gertrude Stein and Virgil Thomson, with a colored cast. The libretto was entirely in Stein's manner, which means that it has the effect of a 5-year-old child prattling on. Musically, it sounded early 19th century, which was a happy inspiration and made the libretto bearable—in fact, quite entertaining. There may be one or two in the cast that would be useful to us.

Hoping you and your wife and child are 100% well and looking forward to seeing you soon, I am

As ever,

George G.

March 2nd. 1934

Dear George:

I was very glad to hear from you. I have been hearing you on the radio, and the reception was so good it seemed as though you were in the room. In fact, the illusion was so perfect I could hardly keep from shouting at you "Swell show, George, but what the hell is the news about PORGY!!!!" It is a good show. You have managed to give it a charming informality, and, in spite of the brevity, a definite impress of your own personality.

I am naturally disappointed that you have tied yourself up so long in New York. I believe that if you had gotten down for a reasonably long stay and gotten deep into the sources here you would have done a bigger job. I am not criticizing your decision. I know well what an enormously advantageous arrangement the radio is, and I know, also, how this tour of yours and the broadcasts are rolling up publicity that will be good business for us when the show opens, only I am disappointed. There is so much more here than you have yet gotten hold of. Anyway, this can be offset to a great extent by my going on and working with you, and I shall do this, availing myself of your invitation, and stopping with you with pleasure. I don't know now just when I can go. It will take some adjustments here, but it will possibly be around the middle of April. I'll let you know promptly as my plans shape.

I am happy that you like the work sent in on Act 2. Here is the third scene. Hope that goes over with you too. I think that I have managed to get the lyrical parts to conform to the rhythm of ordinary speech, and also the idiom, and what I have hoped to do is to ease these passages in so that there will be no consciousness of a break in the flow, and no feeling of a set song in the conventional operatic sense.

I got fragments of the Gertrude Stein opus over the radio, and had a marvelous reception of Merry Mount.[9] I was relieved at the last one. From the advance ballyhoo I thought something revolutionary was coming that might steal our thunder, but it seemed to me to be pretty much the conventional thing.

As for the script from now on, I am sort of at a deadlock. The storm scene must stand about as is with very few cuts in dialog. Musically it must be done when we are together. It must carry itself on the big scene when Crown sings against a spiritual, and I can't do the lyrics until I get your ideas as to time. Then I am doing a lyric for Porgy just before the curtain as he gets ready to drive out for Bess. Have you any thoughts about any of this last section of play?

I hope mightily that you have plenty of time now that you are giving to the work. Munsell has been after me as to dates. I feel that it is terribly important that we get it readied for summer rehearsal and early opening. Frankly it is financially quite important to me, as I have been letting everything else go, counting on it for early fall. If it is going to be late, I will have to get at something else, myself, to carry me over. Reassure me about this some time. Also, please, reassure the Guild.

I am going to ask Rosamund Johnson to get in touch with you and ask for an appointment and bring a girl to sing for you.[10] I think she has the exact quality for Clara. Also I want you to talk to Rosamund about working for you. I think he is first class.

8 March 1934

Dear DuBose:

I was happy to get your letter with the 3rd Scene of Act I enclosed. I think it is a very interesting and touching scene, although a bit on the long side. However, I see one or two places that do not seem terribly important to the action and which could be cut. You must make sure that the opera is not too long as I am a great believer in not giving people too much of a good thing and I am sure you agree with this.

---

9 "Merry Mount" refers to the opera by American composer Howard Hanson produced by the Metropolitan Opera in 1933.

10 Heyward is referring to Abbie Mitchell. Gershwin probably knew of her, however, since she was married to Will Marion Cook.

I went to see Mr. Munsell the other day and told him a bit about the opening of the opera. He seemed very excited about it—in fact he asked me to come upstairs and tell some of the other Directors what I told him. They all seemed very interested but I must say that Lawrence Langner came through with some pretty stupid remarks. I have heard from several sources that he is on the dull and thick side so I shall probably have to ask him in the future to keep out of my way. Munsell was charming and I believe he has written to [Paul] Robeson to find out whether he is available. I see in the papers where [Jules] Bledsoe—my choice for Crown—has made a sensational hit in the opera *Emperor Jones* in Amsterdam.[11]

I am working as much as I can on our opus and I am finding it very interesting. I am skipping around—writing a bit here and a bit there. It doesn't go too fast but that doesn't worry me as I think it is all going to work out very well.

I would like to write the song that opens the 2nd Act, sung by Jake with fish nets, but I don't know the rhythm you had in mind—especially for the answers of the chorus, so I would appreciate it if you would put dots and dashes over the lyric and send it to me.

I am delighted that you will find it convenient to come up and spend some time with me as I believe more work can be done during that time than in any other way.

Ira and I have worked on some words to music in the very opening, in Jazzbo Brown's room while the people are dancing, and I finished it up with a sort of African chant.

I am looking forward to seeing you next month. Hoping you and your family are well, I am

Sincerely,

George

5 November 1934

Dear DuBose:

I was happy to receive your letter and find that you were in complete accord with my views on the date of production of "Porgy." There are so many many details involved that even for early production next season you would find there would not be too much time.

I am planning to see Mr. Munsell in about a week to discuss a few things. First, I would like to set a tentative date for rehearsals. Second, I would like to have auditions started during January or February so that those people we

---

11 Gershwin is referring to American composer Louis Gruenberg's opera based on Eugene O'Neill's play.

choose for parts can be learning the music and save us so much time. I do hope that you can come to New York for these auditions as your knowledge of certain types will be of value in picking the characters.

I had a long talk with Ernst Lubitsch when he was here at the apartment the other evening after I played him a few bits of the opera. He gave me some interesting slants, such as having the scenery just a bit off realism with very free use of lighting to enhance dramatic events. These ideas of Lubitsch's coincide with my feeling—how about yours?

I am off to Emil Mosbacher's place in the country this afternoon to get some work done on Scene 2, Act 3. I am going to try to finish all the music to the opera as soon as I can and then I want to go over the whole thing very carefully for any possible changes. I shall keep you informed of any ideas I have.

Ira has written the lyrics for Porgy and Bess' first duet and I really think that this bit of melody will be most effective.

Incidentally, I start and finish the storm scene with six different prayers sung simultaneously. This has somewhat the effect we heard in Hendersonville as we stood outside the Holy Rollers Church.

If I should go to Florida in January I shall surely stop in and see you.

I hope that you and your wife and child are in the best of health,

Sincerely,

George

17 December 1934

Dear DuBose:

I haven't heard from you in some time and hope you and your family are well.

There are just a few little things that have happened which I would like to tell you about. Theresa Helburn came up for lunch the other day with Sam Behrman to hear some of the Porgy music and I must say they were most enthusiastic and excited. Also, I played some of the music for Deems Taylor whose judgement I respect highly, and he was so enthusiastic and flattering that I blush to mention it. If the opera is so successful as these people think we have an exciting event ahead of us.

I spoke of possible producers and think the Guild leaned rather heavily toward Mamoulian. They feel that he knows more about music than any other producer and might do a beautiful thing with the musicalization of the book. They feel that John Houseman might be somewhat inexperienced to handle so huge a task. Hearing the music gave them quite a different impression than they had. I told them that you are prejudiced a little against Mamoulian and that you would rather have someone else. They seemed surprised at that as they had thought the two of you had worked without friction.

Here is an exciting piece of news: I heard about a man singer who teaches music in Washington and arranged to have him come and sing for me on Sunday several weeks ago. In my opinion he is the closest thing to a colored Lawrence Tibbett I have ever heard. He is about six feet tall and very well proportioned with a rich booming voice. He would make a superb Crown and, I think, just as good a Porgy. He is coming to sing for me again during Christmas week. I shall ask the Guild to take an option on his services.[12]

Emil Mosbacker [*sic*] is taking a house in Florida the middle of January and if I go down with him I will try to stop off for a day or two with you as I did last year. I am very anxious to see you and play you more of the music. Also will try to persuade you to come North while we are casting as I think your opinion would be invaluable at that time.

Please write to me and let me know what you are doing and how you and your family are.

Sincerely,

George

55   *"George Gershwin Arrives to Plan Opera on* Porgy*" (1933)*

Gershwin made two trips to South Carolina to meet with Heyward and absorb the environment as background for his score. The briefer, less well known first visit occurred in 1933 when he traveled to Charleston—the trip he refers to in his letter dated November 25, 1933, to Heyward.

George Gershwin, the outstanding composer of jazz music, is spending several days in Charleston obtaining atmosphere for an operatic version of DuBose Heyward's *Porgy*. Mr. Gershwin arrived yesterday and is stopping at the Fort Sumter hotel. He probably will be here until Wednesday.

"I felt that I should come to Charleston and see what it's like and study the Negroes as best I can," Mr. Gershwin said.

Opera is a new field for Mr. Gershwin, but he said he was glad to get the opportunity of putting *Porgy* to music. Yesterday afternoon he and Mr. Heyward went to a negro church and listened to the singing.[1]

---

12 Gershwin is referring to Todd Duncan, then a voice instructor at Howard University.
SOURCE *Charleston News and Courier*, December 4, 1933.
1 The correct capitalization of the word "Negro" is often neglected in periodicals of this era.

"I'm sure that even Mr. Heyward was surprised at the primitiveness of this particular service and it gave me a lot to think about," Mr. Gershwin said.

Mr. Heyward is going to conduct the composer around the city. They plan to arrange to hear as much negro music as possible and Mr. Gershwin also is anxious to listen in on some of the fish and vegetable hucksters.

Mr. Gershwin had just roused from a nap when he was seen last night. He still hadn't had his supper and he was a bit hungry, but more than that, he was eager for suggestions as to where he best could see the real Negroes of the South Carolina Lowcountry. He is on his way to Palm Beach, where he plans to rest for about a month before going out on a thirty-night tour of thirty cities.

"It will be a while yet before I can get down to real work on *Porgy*, but I want to absorb as much as I can so that I will have plenty of time to think about it," he said. It probably will be about eight or nine months before he completes his work, which is being done for the Theater Guild. This morning Mr. Gershwin plans to play a round of golf at the Charleston Country Club. He said that he isn't much of a golfer, but enjoys getting out to play. He has scored as low as 80 but wouldn't bet that he would break 100 today.

Mr. Gershwin gained his first great fame as a composer with his *Rhapsody in Blue*. Later his *Concerto in F* for the New York Symphony society added to his prestige. He has written the music for numerous musical comedies and revues. He did all the composing for George White's *Scandals* from 1920 through 1924. He was the composer of *Of Thee I Sing*, the only musical show ever to win the Pulitzer Prize.

Mr. Gershwin has done only one moving picture, *Delicious*, in which Janet Gaynor played the lead, but he believes that there is a definite place for music in talking pictures and expects its rapid development.

The theater is making somewhat of a comeback in New York now, he said. He explained that more real hits have resulted this year than in many years, and he does not believe the theater is going into extinction. The hard times, he guessed, have caused theatrical producers to be more careful of their standards and this probably accounts for the unusual percentage of hits in a year in which not a great many shows have been produced.

But it is on the subject of jazz music that Mr. Gershwin becomes emphatic.

"There can be no question but that jazz is the first real American music," he said. "When you look into any other kind you find the influence of some other country, but not so in jazz."

He declared that jazz will live, probably with many variations, but always retaining its basic syncopation.

"I have tried, myself, to do something more than just a song," he said. "I've tried to grasp the real spirit of our people. I've wanted to do something that would last. *Rhapsody in Blue* will celebrate its tenth anniversary soon, but I'm looking for something more."

Mr. Gershwin probably will find it. He is only thirty-five years old. He began composing as a boy, working in a music store. His first song was published in 1917, when he was nineteen years old. He wrote *Rhapsody in Blue* while touring as a pianist with Paul Whiteman.[2]

Mr. Gershwin said that he is delighted with what he has seen of Charleston and expects to visit here again before *Porgy* is finally completed.

56   Brooks Atkinson and Olin Downes: "Porgy and Bess, *Native Opera, Opens at the Alvin; Gershwin's Work Based on DuBose Heyward's Play*" (1935)

These two *New York Times* reviews have often formed the basis for later investigations of the critical reception of *Porgy and Bess*. The fact that the paper chose to place reviews by its chief music (Downes) and drama (Atkinson) critics side-by-side speaks to the importance of the *Porgy and Bess* premiere on the American musical scene at the time.

"Dramatic Values of Community Legend Gloriously Transposed in New Form with Fine Regard for Its Verities," by Brooks Atkinson

After eight years of savory memories, *Porgy* has acquired a score, a band, a choir of singers and a new title, *Porgy and Bess*, which the Theatre Guild put on at the Alvin last evening. DuBose and Dorothy Heyward wrote the original lithograph of Catfish Row, which Rouben Mamoulian translated into a memorable work of theatre dynamics. But *Porgy and Bess* represents George Gershwin's longing to compose an American folk opera on a suitable theme. Although Mr. Heyward is the author of the libretto and shares with Ira Gershwin the credit for the lyrics, and although Mr. Mamoulian has again mounted the director's box, the evening is unmistakably George Gershwin's personal holiday. In fact, the volume of music he has written during the last two years on the ebony fable of a Charleston rookery has called out a whole

---

2 This statement is, of course, incorrect. George Gershwin never "toured" with Paul Whiteman nor had he even performed with Whiteman and his Palais Royale Orchestra before the premiere of the *Rhapsody in Blue* in February 1924.

SOURCE *New York Times* (October 11, 1935), 30.

brigade of Times Square music critics, who are quite properly the masters of this occasion. Mr. Downes, soothsayer of the diatonic scale, is now beating his brow in the adjoining cubicle. There is an authoritative ring to his typewriter clatter tonight.

In these circumstances, the province of a drama critic is to report on the transmutation of *Porgy* out of drama into music theatre. Let it be said at once that Mr. Gershwin has contributed something glorious to the spirit of the Heywards' community legend. If memory serves, it always lacked glow of personal feeling. Being a fairly objective narrative of a neighborhood of Negroes who lived a private racial life in the midst of a white civilization, *Porgy* was a natural subject for theatre showmanship. The groupings, the mad fantasy of leaping shadows, the panic-stricken singing over a corpse, the evil bulk of the buzzard's flight, the screaming hurricane—these large audible and visible items of showmanship took precedence over the episode of Porgy's romance with Crown's high-steppin' gal.

Whether or not Mr. Gershwin's score measures up to its intentions as American folk opera lies in Mr. Downes' bailiwick. But to the ears of a theatre critic Mr. Gershwin's music gives a personal voice to Porgy's loneliness when, in a crowd of pitying neighbors, he learns that Bess has vanished into the capacious and remote North. The pathetic apprehension of the "Where's My Bess" trio and the manly conviction of "I'm on My Way" adds something vital to the story that was missing before.

These comments are written by a reviewer so inured to the theatre that he regards operatic form as cumbersome. Why commonplace remarks that carry no emotion have to be made in a chanting monotone is a problem in art he cannot fathom. Even the hermit thrush drops into conversational tones when he is not singing from the topmost spray in a tree. Turning *Porgy* into opera has resulted in a deluge of casual remarks that have to be thoughtfully intoned and that amazingly impede the action. Why do composers vex it so? "Sister, you goin' to the picnic?" "No, I guess not." Now, why in heaven's name must two characters in an opera clear their throats before they can exchange that sort of information? What a theatre critic probably wants is a musical show with songs that evoke the emotion of situations and make no further pretensions. Part of the emotion of a drama comes from the pace of the performance.

And what of the amusing little device of sounds and rhythms, of sweeping, sawing, hammering and dusting, that opens the last scene early one morning? In the program it is solemnly described as "Occupational Humoresque." But any music hall would be glad to have it without its tuppence-colored label. Mr. Mamoulian is an excellent director for dramas of ample proportions. He is not subtle, which is a virtue in showmanship. His crowds are arranged in masses that look as solid as a victory at the polls; they move with simple unanimity, and the rhythm is comfortably obvious.

Mr. Gershwin knows that. He has written the scores for innumerable musical shows. After one of them he was presented with the robes of Arthur Sullivan, who also was consumed with a desire to write grand. To the ears of a theatre critic there are intimations in *Porgy and Bess* that Mr. Gershwin is still easiest in mind when he is writing songs with choruses. He, and his present reviewer, are on familiar ground when he is writing a droll tune like "A Woman Is a Sometime Thing" or a lazy darky solo like "I Got Plenty o' Nuttin'," or made-to-order spirituals like "Oh, de Lawd Shake de Heavens," or Sportin' Life's hot-time number entitled "There's a Boat That's Leavin' Soon for New York." If Mr. Gershwin does not enjoy his task most in moments like this, his audience does. In sheer quality of character they are worth an hour of formal music transitions.

For the current folk opera Sergei Soudeikine has prepared Catfish Row settings that follow the general design of the originals, but have more grace, humor and color. In the world of sound that Mr. Gershwin has created, the tattered children of a Charleston byway are still racy and congenial. Promoting *Porgy* to opera involves considerable incidental drudgery for theatregoers who agree with Mark Twain that "classical music is better than it sounds." But Mr. Gershwin has found a personal voice that was inarticulate in the original play. The fear and the pain go deeper in *Porgy and Bess* than they did in penny plain *Porgy*.

"Exotic Richness of Negro Music and Color of Charleston, S.C., Admirably Conveyed in Score of Catfish Row Tragedy," by Olin Downes

George Gershwin, long conspicuous as an American composer with a true lyrical gift and with original and racy things to say, has turned with his score of *Porgy and Bess* to the more pretentious ways of the musical theatre. The result, which vastly entertained last night's audience, has much to commend it from the musical standpoint, even if the work does not utilize all the resources of the operatic composers, or pierce very often to the depths of the simple and pathetic drama.

It is in the lyrical moments that Mr. Gershwin is most completely felicitous. With an instinctive appreciation of the melodic glides and nuances of Negro song, and an equally personal tendency to rich and exotic harmony, he writes a melody which is idiomatic and wholly appropriate to the subject. He also knows the voices. He is experienced in many phases of the theatre, and his work shows it. His ultimate destiny as an opera composer is yet to be seen. His native gifts won him success last night, but it appears in the light of the production that as yet he has not completely formed his style as an opera composer.

The style is at one moment of opera and another of operetta or sheer Broadway entertainment. It goes without saying that many of the songs in the score of *Porgy and Bess* will reap a quick popularity. Many of them are excellent, as we have a right to expect of Mr. Gershwin. But that is the least important thing about this work. There are elements of a more organic kind in it. Here and there flashes of real contrapuntal ingenuity combine themes in a manner apposite to the grouping and action of the characters on the stage. In ensemble pieces rhythmical and contrapuntal devices work well. Harmonic admixtures of Stravinsky and Puccini are obvious but not particularly disconcerting. Sometimes the spicy harmonies heighten felicitously the color of the music. There is effective treatment of the "spiritual." No one of the "spiritual" melodies is actually Negro in origin. They are all Mr. Gershwin's invention. He makes effective use of them, not only by harmony sometimes "modal" but by the dramatic combination of the massed voices and the wild exhortations of individual singers.

It must be admitted that in spite of cuts there are still too many set songs and "numbers" which hold back the dramatic development, and the treatment of passages of recitative is seldom significant. The songs were welcomed. Porgy's "I got plenty of nuttin'" held up the show, while all the inhabitants of Catfish Row beat time for it. Clara's lullaby, "Summer Time," sets early a melodic pace that is fairly maintained in the lyrical moments of the score. The prayer of Serena for Bess is eloquent, original, and the most poetical passage in the whole work. The duets of Porgy and Bess are more obvious and savorous of Puccini.

The performers had much that was uncommonly interesting, particularly to a reviewer accustomed to the methods of the opera stage. These methods are usually as out of date as the dodo. Operatic acting and stage management have too often been fit subjects for ridicule. When it came to sheer acting last night certain operatic functionaries should have been present. If the Metropolitan chorus could ever put one-half the action into the riot scene in the second act of *Meistersinger* that the Negro cast put into the fight that followed the crap game, it would be not merely refreshing but miraculous. And when did Isolde wave a scarf more rhythmically from the tower than those who shook feather dusters and sheets from the windows to accompany Porgy's song? Or Hans Sachs cobble more rhythmically to Beckmesser's Serenade than the shoemaker on the doorstep? What could excel the beautiful precision of the tremolo of the shoe-shiner?

As individual and collective acting, these and many other things were admirable. There were magnificent effects of choral song and action. Other groupings were often astonishingly conventional in the operatic manner, and thus contrary to dramatic purpose. This was probably due to the sectional character of the score, but why should the pathetic and tragically helpless Porgy be given the position and the air of the strutting opera baritone?

Admitted the instinct of Negroes to dance, did the inhabitants of Catfish Row set themselves in centrifugal patterns along the floor and wiggle hands and toes like the ladies who are auxiliary to a soloist's performance in a revue? Of course this was amusing. So was the capital clogging of Sportin' Life in the forest scene. He was a rare fellow, with magnificent clothes. There were a hundred diverting details in the spectacle. What had become of the essential simplicity of the drama of *Porgy?* Let Mr. Atkinson answer.

The cast provided some excellent singing. None of the vocalists fell short of musicianship and expressiveness. The Porgy, Todd Duncan, has a manly and resonant voice, which he uses with eloquent effect. The fresh tone, admirably competent technic, and dramatic delivery of Anne Brown as Bess was a high point of interpretation. Miss Elzy's Serena was equally in key with her part, and distinguished by truly pathetic expression. Musically this was a very eloquent interpretation by soloists and chorus. Smallens conducted with superb authority and spirit.

57 *George Gershwin: "Rhapsody in Catfish Row: Mr. Gershwin Tells the Origin and Scheme for His Music in That New Folk Opera Called 'Porgy and Bess'"* (1935)

Since the opening of *Porgy and Bess* I have been asked frequently why it is called a folk opera. The explanation is a simple one. *Porgy and Bess* is a folk tale. Its people naturally would sing folk music. When I first began work on the music I decided against the use of original folk material because I wanted the music to be all of one piece. Therefore I wrote my own spirituals and folksongs. But they are real folk music—and therefore, being in operatic form, *Porgy and Bess* becomes a folk opera.

However, because *Porgy and Bess* deals with Negro life in America it brings to the operatic form elements that have never before appeared in opera and I

SOURCE *New York Times* (October 20, 1935), X, 1–2.

have adapted my method to utilize the drama, the humor, the superstition, the religious fervor, the dancing and the irrepressible high spirits of the race. If, in doing this, I have created a new form, which combines opera with theatre, this new form has come quite naturally out of the material.

The reason I did not submit this work to the usual sponsors of opera in America was that I hoped to have developed something in American music that would appeal to the many rather than to the allured few.

It was my idea that opera should be entertaining—that it should contain all the elements of entertainment. Therefore, when I chose *Porgy and Bess*, a tale of Charleston Negroes, for a subject, I made sure that it would enable me to write light as well as serious music and that it would enable me to include humor as well as tragedy—in fact, all of the elements of entertainment for the eye as well as the ear, because the Negroes, as a race, have all these qualities inherent in them. They are ideal for my purpose because they express themselves not only by the spoken word but quite naturally by song and dance.

Humor is an important part of American life, and an American opera without humor could not possibly run the gamut of American expression. In *Porgy and Bess* there are ample opportunities for humorous songs and dances. This humor is natural humor—not "gags" superimposed upon the story but humor flowing from the story itself.

For instance, the character of Sportin' Life, instead of being a sinister dope-peddler, is a humorous, dancing villain, who is likable and believable and at the same time evil. We were fortunate in finding for that role a young man whose abilities suit it perfectly, John W. Bubbles, or, as he is known to followers of vaudeville, just plain Bubbles, of Buck and Bubbles. We were equally fortunate in finding Todd Duncan for the role of Porgy and Anne Brown for the role of Bess, both of whom give to the score intense dramatic value. We were able to find these people because what we wanted from them lies in their race. And thus it lies in our story of their race. Many people questioned my choice of a vaudeville performer for an operatic role but on the opening night they cheered Bubbles.

We were fortunate, too, in being able to lure Rouben Mamoulian, a great director, back from Hollywood to stage the production. It was Mr. Mamoulian who staged the original production of *Porgy* as a play. He knew all of its value. What was even more valuable, he knew opera as well as he knew the theatre and he was able to bring his knowledge of both to this new form. In my opinion, he has left nothing to be desired in the direction. To match the stage in the pit we obtained Alexander Smallens, who has directed the Philadelphia and Philharmonic Symphony Orchestras and who has conducted more than 150 operas and who has been invaluable to us.

I chose the form I have used for *Porgy and Bess* because I believe that music lives only when it is in serious form. When I wrote the *Rhapsody in Blue* I took "blues" and put them in a larger and more serious form. That was twelve years ago and the *Rhapsody in Blue* is still very much alive, whereas if I had taken the same themes and put them in songs they would have been gone years ago.

No story could have been more ideal for the serious form I needed than *Porgy and Bess*. First of all, it is American, and I believe that American music should be based on American material. I felt when I read *Porgy* in novel form that it had 100 per cent dramatic intensity in addition to humor. It was then that I wrote to DuBose Heyward suggesting that we make an opera of it.

My feelings about it, gained from that first reading of the novel, were confirmed when it was produced as a play, for audiences crowded the theatre where it played for two years. Mr. Heyward and I, in our collaboration on *Porgy and Bess*, have attempted to heighten the emotional values of the story without losing any of its original quality. I have written my music to be an integral part of that story.

It is true that I have written songs for *Porgy and Bess*. I am not ashamed of writing songs at any time so long as they are good songs. In *Porgy and Bess* I realized I was writing an opera for the theatre and without songs it could be neither of the theatre nor entertaining, from my viewpoint.

But songs are entirely within the operatic tradition. Many of the most successful operas of the past have had songs. Nearly all of Verdi's operas contain what are known as "song hits." *Carmen* is almost a collection of song hits. And what about "The Last Rose of Summer," perhaps one of the most widely known songs of the generation? How many of those who sing it know that it is from an opera?

Of course, the songs in *Porgy and Bess* are only a part of the whole. The recitative I have tried to make as close to the Negro inflection in speech as possible, and I believe my songwriting apprenticeship has served invaluably in this respect, because the songwriters of America have the best conception of how to set words to music so that the music gives added expression to the words. I have used sustained symphonic music to unify entire scenes, and I prepared myself for that task by further study in counterpoint and modern harmony.

In the lyrics for *Porgy and Bess* I believe that Mr. Heyward and my brother Ira have achieved a fine synchronization of diversified moods—Mr. Heyward writing most of the native material and Ira doing most of the sophisticated songs. To demonstrate the range of mood their task covers, let me cite a few examples.

There is the prayer in the storm scene written by Mr. Heyward:

Oh, de Lawd shake de Heavens an' de Lawd rock de groun',
An' where you goin' stand, my brudder an my sister,
When de sky come a-tumblin' down.

Oh, de sun goin' to rise in de wes'
An' de moon goin' to set in de sea
An' de stars goin' to bow befo' my Lawd,
Bow down befo' my Lawd, Who died on Calvarie.

And in contrast there is Ira's song for Sportin' Life in the picnic scene:

It ain't necessarily so,
It ain't necessarily so,
De t'ings dat yo' li'ble
To read in de Bible,
It ain't necessarily so.

Li'l David was small, but oh my!
Li'l David was small, but oh my!
He fought big Goliath
Who lay down an' dieth.
Li'l David was small, but oh my!

Then there is Mr. Heyward's lullaby that opens the opera:

Summer time, an' the livin' is easy,
Fish are jumpin', an' the cotton is high.
Oh, yo' daddy's rich an' yo' ma is good-lookin',
So hush, little baby, don't yo' cry.

One of these mornin's you goin' to rise up singin',
Then you'll spread yo' wings an' you'll take the sky.
But 'til that mornin' there's a nothin' can harm you
With Daddy an' Mammy standin' by.

And, again, Ira's song for Sportin' Life in the last act:

There's a boat dat's leavin' soon for New York
Come wid me, dat's where we belong, sister.
You an' me kin live dat high life in New York.
Come wid me, dere you can't go wrong, sister.

I'll buy you de swellest mansion
Up on upper Fi'th Avenue,
An' through Harlem we'll go struttin',
We'll go a-struttin',
An' dere'll be nuttin'
Too good for you.

All of these are, I believe, lines that come naturally from the Negro. They made for folk music. Thus *Porgy and Bess* becomes a folk opera—opera for the theatre, with drama humor, song and dance.

58   Todd Duncan: From an Interview by Robert Wyatt (1990)

Several taped interviews exist of members of the original production team of *Porgy and Bess* collecting their thoughts decades later. The two interviews presented here—with the original Porgy, Todd Duncan, and with the original Bess, Anne Brown—have not appeared in print previously.

I had been doing quite a lot of singing in New York and, although I was teaching at Howard University at the time, people in New York still remembered me. I had heard about the new Gershwin opera *Porgy* but had no interest in it at all. My training had been strictly classical and I simply had no interest in any show business stuff. But when I received a phone call from George Gershwin, well, it was pretty difficult to say no. So up to New York I went on the train one day. I sang an old Italian aria that day, "Lungi dal caro bene." Well, number one, he didn't understand because he thought I was going to sing "Shortnin' Bread" or "Ol' Man River" or some Negro spiritual—something "niggery," you know. That's what he thought.

But I sang what I loved and what I wanted to sing. And so I had a big stack of music, I didn't know what he'd want to hear. And then I asked him to play and he says, "Well, where is your accompanist?" I didn't know that I was supposed to pay five bucks and bring an accompanist. And I said, "Well, can't you play?" "Well," he said, "I play a little bit." And I said, "If you can't, I'll play for myself." Oh, he loved to tell that story! He'd used to tell it at all the parties and he would say, "I fell in love with that man then." He was so honest and so true. He stopped me after twelve measures of "Lungi dal caro bene"—twelve measures!

SOURCE Todd Duncan, interview by Robert Wyatt, February 2, 1990. Transcribed from an audio recording in the editor's collection.

And he said, "Will you go around there? Do you know this by memory?" "Of course I know it by memory, I sing everything by memory," I replied rather indignantly. He said, "Look straight in my eyes. Don't look anywhere else, look straight in my eyes." I sang the same twelve measures and he stopped once again! So, I'm thinking, "What is wrong with this man? Why won't he just let me sing this aria?" And he said, "Will you be my Porgy?" Now guess what I had the nerve to say? I didn't say, "Yes, I'll be glad to be your Porgy." Guess what I said? I said, "Mr. Gershwin, I have to hear your music first." Oh, he loved it! He just loved it! He then said, "Well, we can arrange that. Could you come back next week?" I thought a bit and then said that I could return if he could pay for the train fare for both my wife, Gladys, and myself. When he asked how much I would need, I managed a quick calculation. Knowing that the train fare was $18 round trip and that if I asked for $25 we could also go out for sandwiches, I asked for $30 so I could have a $5 bill to stick in my pocket. And that was the beginning of an exciting time in our lives.

The next weekend we went up to New York early in the morning. At the theater we met some foppish man in striped pants whom I took an instant dislike to. Going up in the lift together, he asked, "Who are you? Are you going to George's?" And I said, "Yes, yes we are." To which he replied, "Well, you'd better be damned good. George has made us all come out of the country to come hear this new genius he's just found. The entire Theatre Guild board will be here today so you'd better be good—damned good."[1]

Well I was, and I sang even more beautifully that day because I was so mad at that unpleasant man. I sang a lot for those people: opera, lieder, French songs, Negro spirituals. And then we ate while George and Ira talked about the opera. We were sitting everywhere—on chairs, couches, and on pillows on the floor when he started out with the opening [imitating the trumpets with his voice] and I said to myself, "Oh, my God. Gee, this junk!" And then he segued with [hums the orchestral opening of "Summertime"]. And Gladys was sitting here, I was here and George Gershwin was over there and Ira was over there. And Ira with his rotten voice starts [horribly off pitch] "Summertime, and the living is easy." And he [George] looked up at me and smiled. Then George sang, "Fish are jumpin'" with Ira finishing the verse, "And the cotton is high." Then George [now a raspy, guttural voice imitation, worse than Ira's], "Oh your daddy's . . ." But when he got to the second verse I could have wept. I said to myself, "Well this is so beautiful. Where did this man get this from?" I just couldn't get over it. And then he went into the next

---

1 The man referred to here is Lawrence Langner of the Theatre Guild. (See selection 54, March 8, 1934, letter from Gershwin to Heyward.)

part where Porgy's theme enters. It was like the royal gates opened. I said to myself, "This is so graphic." And he had me hooked from then on. I was very skeptical before this day.

Rehearsals began shortly after that. I negotiated a leave of absence from Howard University, and Gladys and I took an apartment near the theater. I learned my part quickly since I was a good reader and could play the piano well. My mother was a piano teacher, the best in Danville, Kentucky, where I was born, and she taught me from back before I can even remember. I learned the piano first and began singing later. Well, Anne Brown already lived in New York since she was studying at the Juilliard School. And we would rehearse our parts quite often. We knew that this was going to be an important opera and we were professionals; we wanted to be musically sound in order to be more focused on the stage direction.

It was a wonderful cast, highly educated, highly trained. We never had the trouble casts do these days, you know, moral troubles, morale troubles. You know the last song, "There's a Boat dat's Leavin' Soon for New York" when they were sniffing that happy dust? Well, we didn't know what it was! After the show we'd say, "What's he talking about?"

Of course, Bubbles knew what it was. He was a bit of a scoundrel, but a nice scoundrel; certainly a talented one. But he simply couldn't learn his part and it was holding us all back. He didn't read music at all; had to learn everything by rote. Smallens got so frustrated with him coming in wrong that he complained to Gershwin to replace him. Well, George Gershwin was not about to do that. Bubbles was an important entertainer, a big draw. So Gershwin taught him to dance his part; taught him everything—all the notes, all the rhythms, all the cues—with his feet. It was brilliant. And when he learned to dance it, he never made a mistake after that. He had to dance it. But he had no education and certainly no musical education, and when you talked about a major or a minor third or a perfect fourth or go up the scale, well he didn't know what you were talking about, even if you'd sing it. But if he got the rhythm, and would pat it out and let him dance it, he got it. He would never miss. He caused problems in the rehearsals because he wanted to use his own rhythms. He wasn't accustomed to sticking to what's on the page.

There were two or three in the cast who had difficulty. I'm not going to name them now; I think that would be unsporting of me. But one lady, who would always say haughtily, "I'm very sorry," she would say, she would make mistakes every day and Alexander Smallens would get so disgusted and he almost broke his baton! Every time she would come in wrong! You know, several of Gershwin's rhythms are rather tricky, and she would make the mistake and she would be so bravado, "I'm sorry!" So that's what we named her: president of the I'm Sorry Club.

I had only one problem with Gershwin's folk opera: singing the entire show on my knees. I had to train, yes I did. I had to learn by just keeping on the floor all the time and practicing. That was when I became very interested in posture. Because, you know, crawling around is taxing. I would take two steps with my knees and then two more and I was out of breath. And I couldn't sing! So that was when I really learned about vocal posture. I even sang on my back and that used to bring the house down; boy, it sure did! I sang "I Got Plenty o' Nuttin'" on my back lying down, and then I would rise up and they just wouldn't let me stop. I used my knees all the time, never the little cart like they do now. I wore pads on my knees, still have them upstairs in a drawer. And now I have terrible problems with my knees. I've always wondered if that was the cause.

I loved singing the role of Porgy and after Gershwin had heard me sing, he tailored the part for my voice. Some of the music had already been written but once he knew my sound, everything just seemed to fit so well. You know, the Porgys these days don't always make the grade. I'm going to say this to you and I know it's ungracious of me, but I think I owe it to posterity at this time to make this statement. It seems that the Porgys that I've heard really don't know who Porgy is. They've not gone into the depth of who the character is; they don't know the man himself. And when they sing "I Got Plenty o' Nuttin'" they think it's a buffoon song or a blackface "step-and-fetch-it" song. It's not that at all. It is very deep philosophy and I got it from the composer himself. It is making fun of very wealthy white people. I got this from George Gershwin's own mouth when he said to me, "Todd, you're not singing what we're after. This is a bitter song and you have to sing it with tongue-in-cheek; you have to sing it smiling all the time. Because what you're doing is making fun of us. You're making fun of people who make money and to whom power and position is very important."

"We just labored in pain over these words," Gershwin told me, and the point is this: [Gershwin sang the lyrics "I got no lock on the door, that's no way to be. They can steal the rug from the floor, that's okay with me"] . . . "The things that I prize are not money and not power and not being president, and not having an army, not having a great big automobile. The things that *I* prize are the stars and the sun and the moon." So when the next verse starts off with these words, "I got de sun, I got de moon, got de deep blue sea," and when the song ends, "I got my Lord, I got de sun, I got de moon, I got de waters," well then you have just told the audience what really is important to you, to the composer, to the lyricist and to Porgy. And also to me, Todd Duncan, as an artist and a Negro man. It became my credo: I got love, and I got God, and I got my song. So the things that really matter in life under God are things that you can't buy: like love, like the sea, like the sun and the moon. So I don't have to lock my door. I got my gal, I got my lord and I got my song. I own them. And I own the moon and the seas. And there are a lot of people on this earth that don't own or even appreciate them. They don't plant any beautiful flowers, they don't enjoy flowers, they don't even look at flowers. Well, Porgy did. He was very smart and his very first lines as he comes out on the stage, [he sings], "Evenin' ladies, hello boys! Luck been ridin' high with Porgy today. I got a pocket full of the Buckra money." In other words, he's been down in front of the courthouse and he's got a lot of the white people's money in his pocket.

People have no idea what that song is about yet they just love it. Now how do I know that? Well, I had so many southerners from Mississippi, from Georgia, come backstage to tell me, "I understand that song, Mr. Duncan. That's a wonderful song. When you hear it at first you don't know at first what you're talking about, but I understand. Thank you for singing it."

Yes, I loved singing that role. And I did it thousands upon thousands of times. And what was I paid to play Porgy? Well, that's a good question. Very cheap in relationship to fees these days. I started out with $400 a week. Very cheap. Today I would start out with $5,000. But in 1935, $400—that was good money. It would have taken me a whole month to make that much teaching school at Howard University. But the next time I did the show, in 1943, my salary was a lot higher.

The morale of the cast was pathetic when we closed in New York after only 128 performances; it was truly pathetic. Very sad. There is speculation as to its failure and I have my own answer, one which I don't know whether is right or not; but there are a lot of people—press and others—who agreed with me. George Gershwin had never had a failure on Broadway, a real flop. But there was a Jewish following which was significant on Broadway at the time, and they didn't like it that George had gone "high-fallutin'." He had gone and written an *opera* and they were not about to come. The opera people, those who went to the Metropolitan Opera, felt that George Gershwin was Tin Pan Alley and Broadway and how dare he! And then the papers, so many of the press wrote that this is not opera. Some called it musical comedy, some folk opera; they called it everything: musical drama, musical comedy, music theater, operetta. They called it everything. But George Gershwin insisted on calling it folk opera. He insisted on it and that was in lights. If it had been done as a show or done at the Met—and that means every four or five days—you would not have to sing every night. You must remember this: I sang it every night! And these singers now, they sing one performance and then they have to rest. [Laugh] Now they have to have three or four Porgys for one production. I was doing eight performances a week although I had in my contract that I could take off one of the matinees. They begged me not to take a Saturday matinee, however, so I usually took off the Wednesday matinee. That's when singers were singers. I was no genius, just a damned hard worker. My priority is music—that is my breakfast, it's my dinner, my lunch, it's my sleep. It's my song; it's my love. Music is the stuff that keeps me going.

There were many wonderful things about those months in New York. Perhaps the best was working with such a first-rate cast. Anne Brown has remained my friend these past fifty-plus years. She lives in Norway but comes to visit her sister each year and always stops by for a meal and talking. She couldn't put up with the racial situation in this country and fell for some Scandinavian man who swept her off her feet. But she kept singing and can still do it today, just like I can. And then there was the work with Rouben Mamoulian. What an artist! He did all the Garbo movies in Hollywood. And, of course, the work with George and Ira Gershwin.

There was a time when I got so angry at George Gershwin that I told him that we were going to have to go into the alley and settle something like men. For the first few weeks of rehearsal, he used to spend a lot of time with my wife while they both listened to rehearsals. I could see them talking and laughing and having a great time. And you know of Gershwin's reputation with women! Well, I told him that if he had any ideas about spending time with Gladys that we would have to settle it with our fists. He was so stunned! He said, "Todd, you do have a most beautiful wife and she is lovely to talk with. But I know that you are happily married and love her so much. I would never take advantage of either of you." And I could tell by the way that he spoke that while looking me in the eyes that he really meant it. And that was that.

And then there was the opening night party and oh, what a party. Condé Nast threw a fandango at his apartment and there were two orchestras in the living room, one at one end and the other was on the other end. One was Paul Whiteman's Orchestra. The ladies were all beautifully dressed and they'd just flop down on the floor. That was the first night that I saw Josephine Baker. I'll never forget her. She was there that night and all of those men—eight, ten—anytime, wherever she was, there were eight or ten men wiggling rings around her. I'll never forget her that night. I told her about that night when I met her in Israel years later and we went into the river of Jordan—"Well, this reminds me of the other time I saw you at the Condé Nast party." But she said, "I remember you most in California, in Los Angeles, when I came to your concert that night." We had been in Capernaum, in a beautiful restaurant on the Sea of Galilee, and there were our two managers, mine and hers, and we were in this big limousine. I asked to go to five or six places that Jesus had gone to, and I knew where I wanted to go; I knew where it was because I had studied it. Well, I wanted to collect some water from the Sea and there was only this beer bottle available. So that's what I brought back with me and, do you know, we've used that water to baptize four children.

The most difficult part of *Porgy and Bess* was the official cast recording, when Lawrence Tibbett and Helen Jepson were hired to do the RCA record. Remember that this was at a time, 1935, when Tibbett was considered the greatest baritone in the world. One afternoon I looked up and there he was in the rehearsal, sitting back there in the back rows. It puzzled me and I simply couldn't understand: why was Lawrence Tibbett coming to hear me sing? And so I figured that he had heard about my singing and was interested in me. This happened for several days in a row and I began to feel so honored. He came almost every day to rehearsals, for about three weeks or something like that. What he was doing, of course, was listening to how I did the role. But I can tell you this, and you can write it anytime you want to because it's the truth. We weren't able to do the recording then but we did eight or nine months later. Well, Jack Kapp [president of Decca records] said to me, "Well, you don't need to worry" (he told me this about five years later). He said, "Your records have sold more than all of the Porgys put together." And he said, "You and Bing Crosby have made me a millionaire!"

When George Gershwin hired me to play Porgy, he was looking for a person, not just a voice. He called for me to come out to Los Angeles in 1937 and I sang there with the Los Angeles Symphony. I was the only one. And that's when he had that big party at the Trocadero, a famous nightclub out on the Strip in Beverly Hills; he bought the whole place out. At four o'clock in the morning, he showed me into his house and he said, "I have some new music that I'm working on and you're going to be starring in this show and you're going to be a comedian." And I said, "I'm no comedian!!" He says, "Yes you are!" And then he said, "Todd, I don't mean that kind of comedian. You brought Porgy to life and you made him a living, breathing person and you did it through comedy." I said, "Did I?" And he said, "Yes, you made people laugh. That's money. Every composer knows that if you can make the audience laugh that means it will bring in other people." He never told me what kind of show it was going to be and I never heard anything about it because in five months he was dead. He made a lot of money in Hollywood but he didn't like it. The main thing he wanted to do, the last time I saw him, was to leave Hollywood. He really hated it there.

Anne and I sang at his memorial service at the Hollywood Bowl; it was a difficult performance for me. And then I came home and taught at Howard for another two years. They actually wouldn't let me officially resign for ten years! But with the thrill of *Porgy and Bess* in my blood and a strong feeling about singing recitals as well as opera, I set off on my career. I had a contract with Columbia Management for many years, until I retired, made Hollywood films [*Syncopation* and *Unchained*], premiered two other big shows [*Cabin in the Sky* and *Lost in the Stars*] played award-winning roles in *Show Boat* and Cole Porter's *The Sun Never Sets* and did lots and lots of singing, all over the world—two-thousand concerts in twenty-five years, and on five continents. Sang at the White House for three different presidents: Roosevelt, Eisenhower, Johnson. Now had I not met George Gershwin, things would have been different for me. In what ways I'll never know. He was the type of musician that you loved to be with. He was a genius, that man was. A real genius.

59 Anne Brown: From an Interview by Robert Wyatt (1995)

The composition of *Porgy and Bess* had just begun when I met George Gershwin. Now the Metropolitan Opera wanted a work by George Gershwin and made him a generous offer to which George Gershwin said, "No, thank you." He knew that the greatest success of his opera depended on being sung and acted by black people. And that would have been impossible at the racist Metropolitan Opera at that time. I was still a music student at the Juilliard School when I saw a notice in a New York newspaper that George Gershwin was interviewing singers, dancers, and actors, both classically trained as well as jazz musicians, for the opera he was in the process of writing. I decided to make contact with him at once. The Theatre Guild had commissioned the work and would be the producers: *the* Theatre Guild—that was top quality in the theatrical world. Rouben Mamoulian, Hollywood director, was to instruct the people and Alexander Smallens was to conduct. I wrote a letter to George Gershwin that same evening and two days later received a phone call asking me to come for an audition.

Several days later I found myself standing in the foyer of his apartment, bending over to look under the coatrack for a place to put my boots. "What are you looking for?" he asked politely. And then one of those crazy ideas popped into my head. I said without thinking, "Your roller skates!" George

SOURCE Anne Brown, interview by Robert Wyatt, March 15, 1995. Transcribed from an audio recording in the editor's collection.

Gershwin was quiet for a few moments and then he laughed. He threw back his head and he roared. "How did you know about my roller skates?" he said, still laughing. "Well, I read, you know." He laughed again. "It's been many years," he said, "since I had a pair of roller skates on my feet. I'm an old man now. So I play tennis and golf and I even box occasionally, for exercise." Then he said, "By the way, did you ever roller-skate?" And then I told him about my own passion for roller-skating—how many hours each week from the age of nine until I left my hometown in Baltimore, I skated.

And so there I was, standing beside his Steinway after having slung my wet boots under the coatrack. I sang a French aria by Massenet, several German lieder, Russian songs in English, even a Gershwin melody. And George Gershwin was full of praise. And then he asked me to sing a Negro spiritual. Well, unless one is nearly as old as I am and has lived in the United States before the Second World War and understood the insidious damage racial prejudice can afflict on both the victim and the racist, it may be difficult to understand my reaction at that moment. I said, "Well, weren't you satisfied with what I sang?" And he said, "Yes, of course, it was lovely—beautiful." "But why do people always ask Negro singers to sing spirituals as if that is the only thing that they should be singing and not German lieder or French arias." I was very much on the defensive. George Gershwin simply looked long at me and he said, "Ah huh, I understand." And I realized that he *did* understand and then I wanted more than anything else to sing a spiritual for him. How dumb I had been! Wasn't this to be an opera about Negroes? "I didn't bring any accompaniment for a spiritual," I said, "but I could sing one without accompaniment if you would like." "Oh, yes, please do," he said. So I sang a spiritual, "A City Called Heaven." And when I finished I knew that I had never sung it better nor would I ever sing it better. Instead of the half hour I had expected to be there, I stayed nearly two hours. George played as much of *Porgy and Bess* as had been written, including "Summertime," with which I was completely fascinated. He sang all the parts himself and then he asked me to sing "Summertime." It was not a difficult melody and it just rolled out of my throat, and he was very pleased. And then I went home.

Several days later his secretary rang up and said that Mr. Gershwin would like me to come and sing for his brother, Ira, and for his mother. Ira was the shy, quiet one but he praised my singing and kept nodding his head to his brother—in approval, I supposed. His mother said nothing, not even, "Very nice." She was, well, she was rather arrogant, a doting mother who was interested only in her son, not even her *two* sons. I didn't like her very much.

The following week I was asked to come again to sing for the directors of the Theatre Guild. As the producers, they would have a certain influence on

the final selection of the singers. And for weeks afterwards there were sessions with George Gershwin. He would personally call sometimes and say,
"Annie, I've just finished music for Clara. I want you to come and sing it for
me." (After meeting my mother and hearing her call me Annie, he always
called me Annie.) This went on week after week. "I'm a guinea pig," I
thought of it. But I was happy to be that. Sometimes others were there but
more often just George Gershwin, and we sang different songs, and duets,
and trios as soon as the ink was dry on the paper. And it was very good training for my sight-reading. And then one day during this period, George Gershwin said, "Annie, how would you like to sing the role of Bess?" I had
suspected for some time that he would say just that. Even so, it came as a surprise. "Bess is, in the original story, a very black woman," he said. "But I cannot see any reason why my Bess shouldn't have a *café au lait* complexion. Can
you?" "No, no," I answered quickly. And gave him big hug. Then I asked him,
"What will you do if the Theatre Guild insists on engaging another singer for
the Bess role?" "They'll have to do it over my dead body," he said. "Don't
worry, Annie, George Gershwin will have the last word."

And so rehearsals began. George was present at almost every rehearsal.
He sat alone often in the dark theater wearing his hat and an old tweed sport
jacket, and sometimes cracking and eating peanuts. And occasionally smoking a thick cigar. Other times he was as elegant as any prince. He was certainly a man with many faces. Some days he sat together with other
musicians, journalists, friends, and admirers. At the rehearsals George occasionally complained that many of the people in the cast had unfortunately
been born in the north. Everyone laughed at this since many of us had not
even *visited* the south. Some of us were college students and didn't know the
dialect of the southern Negro. Now that was a bit unfair, that criticism,
because the Gullah black man had a very special dialect with many African
words. As it happened, Gershwin and Heyward were able only to use a few
terms of this dialect in the opera. And with the passage of time these passages have been practically eliminated.

I was quite confident in my ability to do the role of Bess and I loved being
on the stage. Bess was somewhat foreign to my experience and background,
of course, and when I think about it now, I think that the very first days of
rehearsals and then perhaps even in the performances I must have been a
very schoolgirlish Bess. But of course it developed as time went on. I became
bolder bit by bit and although I never thought of myself as sexy, I don't really
think of Bess as sexy. I think of her as a—how shall I describe it—as an earthy
woman for one thing. And she was weak in one sense and she was strong in
another sense: she was strong for Porgy and she was weak for Crown. And

she was a person who was easily swayed—like when Sportin' Life came along with the dope and Porgy had been taken away to jail—and she was still swept away with that. I don't think that Bess really could stand to be lonely. Those characteristics were the ones I thought of rather than her being a flirt or a slut or anything of that kind.

Emotionally, of course, I had a lot to learn and I did learn a great deal, especially from Rouben Mamoulian who directed. He was such a brilliant man and he helped me without actually saying how he wanted the character of Bess to be, which was, I believe, difficult for a director to do—to try to bring it out of the actor. Of course, I believe that everyone has everything inside of him and if you can just get your finger on it and get it out, the person himself can do it; or the director can help you do it. But that's the way to create an actress or the art of teaching someone to act.

Alexander Steinert worked with us on the music and he was a very good coach. He was a wonderful piano player, and he had the feeling of the music and a certain authority there. He was the coach who rehearsed the parts we didn't know. I knew my score almost perfectly when I came to the first rehearsal because I had the score and worked on it in Baltimore during my summer vacation from Juilliard, where I was still a student. Todd knew his role perfectly, absolutely, and the parts that were a little difficult we worked through them and sang through them with Steinert.

During the actual stage rehearsals, we were coached by Alexander Smallens. He was a fine conductor but, well, he wasn't a patient man, really. I always thought he played the score too fast, for the most part [she hums the opening Jazzbo Brown music], and we made jokes about it because he lived in Connecticut and he had to make a train each night. "Oh, he doesn't want to be late tonight!" And he would go through the score like a house afire! Gershwin would sometimes play for rehearsals and then the tempi were right. But you know, Gershwin was a strange man. He never objected to changes in his music. When Ruby Elzy, for example, embroidered her prayer with all sorts of ornamentation, he smiled and said, "That's wonderful, keep it in." Not only that, people who sang "Summertime" in the jazz version—even back in the beginning—he never objected as long as you were singing *Gershwin* music; regardless of how you handled it, how you treated it, it was okay. That's a characteristic which not so many composers have.

George's piano playing was simply spectacular. When I went to his apartment—and it was very often in that year leading up to the time when he went south in the summer—he would play through the music. Then I would eat lunch with him, and he would sometimes, once or twice, invite me into his bed. Of course, I never went there. After lunch he would play the whole opera over again on his Hammond organ! And make all sorts of variations on the different themes. He would sing and he would ask me to sing; we had fun! His voice was like a nutmeg grater—husky—but he got the melody over. The pitch was perfect but the quality of the sound was really not pleasing. And his chin shook, his whole head shook a little when he sang. He was so proud of this music, it was his baby. It also expressed his acceptance of all forms, his love for the elements of the rhythm and the harmonies of black men.

Shortly after rehearsals had begun, George invited me to have lunch with him at a little café across from the Alvin Theatre. Once there he told me with a very serious face that the opera by George Gershwin would henceforth be known as *Porgy* and *Bess*. He also told me that he had changed the last act at my request. "How's that?" I answered in surprise. "Well, from the beginning you have harassed me to find a place for Bess to sing "Summertime." "It's the most beautiful melody in the whole opera," I said, "I love it." "Just keep still and listen now. I composed a trio for Lily and Serena and Maria for that spot in Act III but I have decided to drop the trio and let you sing your favorite melody. It's very logical; I don't know why I didn't think of it before. Are you happy now, Miss Brown?" he said. I wouldn't allow myself to cry in front of him so I said nothing.

I remember so well that day—after weeks of rehearsals on the stage of the Alvin Theatre—when we had the first full orchestral rehearsal of the finished opera with soloists and chorus on the stage of Carnegie Hall, hired by the Theatre Guild for just that purpose. When the echoes of the last chords of *Porgy and Bess* had disappeared into the nearly empty hall, we were—all of us—in tears. It had been so moving. Todd Duncan turned to me and said, "Do you realize, Anne, that we are making history?" George Gershwin stood on the stage as if in a trance for a few minutes. Then, seeming to awaken, he said, "This music is so wonderful, so beautiful that I can hardly believe that I have written it myself."

I think that no one—other than his family and those strictly connected with the opera—had a closer association and contact with George Gershwin while he was writing *Porgy and Bess* than I did. Maybe Kay Swift did but that was from another point of view. He used me as a guinea pig and he tried everything and he would ask me, "Is this too high for a baritone?" "No, no, not if he doesn't stay up there too long," I would say. "How's this, should I change this note?" "No, no. As a matter of fact, I'd like to do it higher," would be my answer. I even made a few changes in "I Loves You Porgy," notes which fit my voice better and he would say, "That's good, let's use that." I was hired long before Todd was. And it was not Olin Downes who recommended Todd Duncan, it was Abbie Mitchell. I know because I was there and I heard Abbie

Mitchell say, "Have you heard Todd Duncan sing?" And George said, "No." Well, then she said, "Well, he would make a perfect Porgy." And George said, "Give me his name and address. I'll get in touch with him right away." I met her there in New York, at the rehearsals but I had heard her before. She was fifty-two years old then, when she played Clara and sang "Summertime."

The opening in Boston was spectacular, and remember, this was the full four-hour version. The response from the audience was tremendous, an ovation which some people said lasted almost a half an hour. Many people were in tears at the end. Only the critics argued about the work's form: whether it was an opera or a musical or even a folk opera, as Gershwin had called it. Already they had begun to question the validity of this as opera and Virgil Thomson—the New York critics came to Boston—had lots of opinions. When it opened in New York ten days later, the reactions in the audience were—if possible—even stronger and the critics were still arguing among themselves. Rouben Mamoulian said, "My God, you Americans are nuts. Why don't you stop fighting over a name and just enjoy the masterpiece?" And we were all so disappointed when they cut out certain things. Of course, Todd was terribly disappointed when they took out "The Buzzard Song." Do you know why Gershwin wrote that? He heard Todd Duncan sing Mussorgsky's "Song of the Flea" and he said to me, "I'm going to write a song for Porgy like the "Song of the Flea." You know he laughs in the "Buzzard Song?" Maybe he never told that to Todd. He admitted it quite frankly.

We had a wonderful cast and I was friendly with many of them. I especially liked J. Rosamund Johnson, a man who was an authority on many topics. He only had a small part which he was very good in, after he learned his part musically. He was also a coach with the chorus. He might have worked with Bubbles because Bubbles needed a lot of work. You know, he sang by rote, he couldn't read notes. He learned best if you could tap it first. Bubbles put the moves on me, like all the others. But I just laughed at him. There was no question there! But we got along beautifully and on stage he would do that (leer at her body) and then look with a sly look, an *extra* look at me. I thought it was fun! He smoked marijuana all the time and gave it to some of the girls in the chorus. Those things I wasn't part of. I was married at the time—my first marriage—and I went home after the performances and after the rehearsals.

Oh yes, of course there was the fiasco surrounding the "cast" recording of *Porgy and Bess*. We were all so young in the business that we knew that there was simply nothing to be done about it. And we accepted it. We didn't like it, of course, but we understood that it was a business thing. They want to sell their records right away and so they want to have names. None of us in the original cast had any names at that point. Gershwin said, "I would prefer that you and Todd would sing these parts but I don't have much to say about it. This is business." He, in a sense, apologized for it. But the records didn't sell very well. Poor Lawrence Tibbett! He never got the feel of the dialect or the inflection in the voice needed to sing an effective Porgy, he simply never got it. We were conscious that people were very often sitting in on the rehearsals but we didn't always know who they were. Decca should be ashamed of themselves for giving us so little money! They did not pay royalties but simply gave us a one time payment of—oh I don't remember—I believe that my check was for $1,000. And they made millions on that recording! I understand that when the record first came out that each shop was required to take a minimum of 10 records. And there were thousands upon thousands of record shops who sold these records. I think they made a million dollars in the first cutting and it sold well for a very long time. And now when I want one of these CDs I must pay 12 dollars and a half for one of them. I think it's terrible. I asked Leopold [Godowsky] if there wasn't some way that he could get them to send me 10 copies, and he said that they are the stingiest people in the world.

But back to the actual production. It was magical yet suddenly, and very suddenly, the magic was over. Closing the show was sad, we felt we should have gone on much longer, that it should have continued. Later, Todd and I would have our first disagreement: about who first said that we would refuse to sing at the National Theater in Washington, D.C.; I insist that I said first. The minute I read the itinerary I said, "Well, I'm not going to sing at the National Theater in Washington. Its a segregated theater." And I can remember as if it were yesterday that the other members who stood around me, particularly Matthews who sang Jake, they said, "You can't refuse. Who do you think you are? This is your first experience on the stage and you think you can say where you will sing and where you will not? Well, you'll be blacklisted for the rest of your career." And I said, "I don't give a damn. I'll do something else. I don't have to sing. I'm not going to sing in Washington." Well, I don't know exactly what happened but soon Todd and I together were saying it. Todd hired a secretary and wrote a lot of letters to a lot of people, something which I didn't do. I let the others do all the dirty work! And then George Gershwin came over that same evening and he asked, "Did you really say that?" "Yes, I won't sing, not even your opera. I won't sing in the National Theater." And he said, "All right, Annie. We'll see what we can do."

The Theatre Guild and management came together and the policy was changed for that one week. The following week Ethel Waters appeared there in a play—I forget what it was called—and the policy was the original one: no blacks were allowed. And it was twenty years before it changed! And fifty years before the opera was presented at the Metropolitan. I was so very confident after I got the role of Bess that I knew that if I had refused to sing and couldn't do any Broadway shows—I didn't do any others anyway—well, tough! I was offered the role of Carmen in *Emperor Jones* a few weeks later for a big salary. And I refused it, telling them that I had signed a contract with an impresario to go on a long concert tour with Schubert and Brahms and Debussy—classical and romantic music—and that I wanted to do that. I didn't want to be stamped as only Bess.

Several years later, when George Gershwin was in Hollywood, I received short notes and a postcard now and then from him, and he wrote one time that he was tired of Hollywood and wished to return to New York to write another opera. And that was one of the last messages I got from him. When I heard that he had a brain tumor and was going to be operated on, I was in New York. I remembered one time when I went to his apartment—oh, two years before—and he had a headache and he kept doing this [rubs her head vigorously] while saying, "I have such a headache." And I said, "Well, I'm sorry. I can go home." "No, no, I've been playing golf and I was hit in the head with a golf ball." Now I never saw this written anywhere. He continued to rub his head and he continued to massage it even after we began to rehearse. I have often wondered whether that blow by a golf ball had caused a tumor. You know that if you have an injury on your head and it goes in instead of out, it can fasten itself.

George Gershwin, to me, was a loveable big brother but that sounds so silly. I know that he was really interested in both me and my voice. Each night he would come to the theater before the performances, come to my dressing room first saying, "Hi, Annie how are you? Is everything all right?" That was normal. I knew that he approved and liked what I did with the role. You know, it's really strange when I look back on it. How many years ago was that? Sixty years? The influential members of the troupe—Mamoulian, Smallens, even the two stage managers—they would often go out together but they never invited Todd and me. They never invited any members of the cast. But George, he would come to my house, come to our parties, and always the first thing he did was to sit down at the piano and begin to play. And that he would do for the whole evening!

He was simply crazy about music, especially his own; he was extremely proud of his musical gifts. I remember one story he told me about a "shouting" contest at a church gathering in Charleston. After it was over, and he had "out-shouted" the best of them, an old man clapped him on the back and said, "By God, you can sure beat out them rhythms, boy. I'm over seventy years old and I ain't never seen no po' little white man take off and fly like you. You could be my own son."

My fondest memories of him were the times the two of us would have lunch alone in his apartment. We dined with friends and cast members in restaurants frequently but never alone, except the time when he told me I would be his Bess. At his home, he had a manservant and George would say to him, "How about getting lunch up for Miss Brown and me?" And then we would sit down and have lunch and talk about everything. He had his idiosyncrasies, as we all do, he was complicated! He was a very complicated person. And do you know the only thing that he feared? He was afraid not to be the person he was supposed to be.

VI. LAST YEARS: HOLLYWOOD (1936–1937)

The steep arch of Gershwin's rise to prominence is ironically matched by the unexpected suddenness of his early death. Following the completion of *Porgy and Bess*, the Gershwins sold their New York residences and moved west to settle in Hollywood and begin writing a series of film scores for RKO. Once there, Gershwin met up with many of his Broadway cronies, made new friends, and reveled in the sunny atmosphere, even if he was never completely comfortable with the Hollywood system. The following series of articles and letters chronicles this last period of his life.

Garson provides a succinct overview of Gershwin in Hollywood from the
time of his arrival in August 1936 to the moment of his death in July of the
following year.[1]

With *Porgy and Bess* running at the Alvin Theater, and no new projects in
sight, Gershwin felt tired and restless. His digestive system, what he called his
"composer's stomach," was continuing to bother him, and perhaps as a reaction from the tension and excitement of creating and launching his opera, he
seemed drained and at odds. He decided to go off for a four-week holiday in
Mexico, hoping to get some ideas from the native music for a new composition. Although Gershwin found no source of inspiration, the vacation
helped, nevertheless, to refresh him. On his return, the *Porgy and Bess* cast
greeted him at the dock with a serenade—a nice welcome, and one that further helped restore his spirits. He was ready for work, and it seemed
inevitable that he should respond when Hollywood beckoned.

Gershwin had already had one experience with the "talkies," and not a
particularly happy one, back in 1930, when he and Ira did the score for *Delicious,* a meaningless trifle, for Fox Film Corporation. Despite such popular
stars as Janet Gaynor and Charles Farrell, it was a rather bad picture, and the
critics blasted it. The Gershwins fled back to the arms of Broadway. The only
redeeming consequence was the *Second Rhapsody,* which had been expanded
by Gershwin from some background music used briefly in the film.

Now, in 1936, things again began inauspiciously. RKO wanted the Gershwins to do the score for an Astaire-Rogers musical. But Hollywood measures
prestige in terms of a "hit," and the Gershwins hadn't had a hit since *Of Thee
I Sing* five years before. While Irving Berlin and Jerome Kern had been writing songs for the successful cycle of Astaire-Rogers films, Gershwin had been
busy with composing *Porgy and Bess.* It was suggested that writing an opera

SOURCE In Isaac Goldberg, *George Gershwin: A Study in Arminian Music* (New York: Frederick Ungar Publishing, 1958).

1 Edith Garson was the wife of Gershwin biographer and writer Edward Jablonski and, like her
husband, an intimate friend of Ira Gershwin.

had caused Gershwin to go highbrow (anathema in Hollywood), and part of the reason for his return to the coast was his desire to prove that he had not lost his hit-writing ability. "Am not highbrow. Have written hits before and expect to write them again," he emphatically wired his agent.

After much wiring back and forth between the coasts (mainly dickering about money), George and Ira arrived in California in early August 1936, and immediately stepped into the chaos of picture-making. When shooting of the film *Shall We Dance* began, there was practically no story—only a general idea involving Rogers and Astaire. The Gershwins were expected to furnish songs for undetermined spots, with the plot being worked out as they went along. As the shooting schedule stretched out, the strain affected all concerned. Although George, as a Broadway veteran, was used to the changes and cutting that occurred in a musical before opening night, the lack of overall planning was somewhat new to him. The title song was written only after someone decided to change the name of the film from *Watch Your Step* to *Shall We Dance*. Then for the big ballet finale, nobody seemed quite to know what they wanted Gershwin to do. An extended number of a Latin American nature that he had composed was simply discarded. At one time another arranger was given the job of re-working the ballet, but Nathaniel Shilkret, director of the studio orchestra, found the rework impossible. After a morning's fruitless rehearsal with the orchestra he stalked out of the studio. Finally, Gershwin, Shilkret, Robert Russell Bennett, and even Ira, whose lyrics were not required for the sequence, worked till three in the morning and completed the ballet.

Despite the treatment, Gershwin managed to make some points in a short instrumental interlude, "Walking the Dog," a charming joke on overblown Hollywood scoring. He used six instruments instead of the usual lush, full orchestra. And George and Ira together turned out such memorable songs as "They Can't Take That Away From Me," "Slap That Bass," "They All Laughed," and "Let's Call the Whole Thing Off."

Almost simultaneously, the brothers worked on *A Damsel in Distress* for Astaire, but this time with Joan Fontaine as the leading lady. Again they provided a superior score: "A Foggy Day," "I Can't Be Bothered Now," "Things Are Looking Up," "Nice Work if You Can Get It," "Sing of Spring," and the excellent quasi madrigal, "The Jolly Tar and the Milkmaid."

Meanwhile, the new Gershwin ménage, West Coast version, was going full blast. George, with Ira and his wife, Leonore, had rented a typical extravaganza of a house, complete with swimming pool and tennis court, at 1019 North Roxbury Drive, in Beverly Hills. There the social days and nights kept them all busy while things were slowly grinding along at the studio. There was the usual round of dinners and parties, both at the Gershwins' and at the homes of producers, stars, songwriters, and other cronies, both new and old. The athletic George golfed and played tennis and enjoyed taking long hikes with Tony, his wire-haired terrier. A weekly tennis partner was neighbor Arnold Schoenberg, the composer, whom George much admired. Others in his circle included Harold Arlen, E. Y. "Yip" Harburg, Moss Hart, Lillian Hellman, Edward G. Robinson, Harry Ruby, Oscar Levant. It was a congenial, lively group, but as the months wore on, from 1936 into 1937, George began to grow restless again, and resentful of the languorous, stultifying atmosphere of Hollywood itself. For Ira, the warm, sunny climate, the slower pace were ideal. He had never been inclined to jump about from one place to the other or to feel prodded into action by the kind of nervous energy that was always close to the surface with George; Ira in fact, began to talk of settling permanently in Beverly Hills, while George talked more frequently of getting back to New York, to Broadway and to serious composing again. He and DuBose Heyward were considering another collaboration, and he had also contacted Lynn Riggs (author of *Green Grow the Lilacs,* which eventually was to become the basis for Rodgers and Hammerstein's *Oklahoma!)* about doing a libretto for an opera; he thought, too, of doing a string quartet (possibly influenced by his association with and admiration for Schoenberg); and other works that he mulled over in his mind included a symphony or a ballet. Anything, in other words, in the larger more serious forms, that could expand what he felt was his growing musical maturity. None of these plans seemed to materialize. When he wasn't working, it seemed he was partying or playing in the sun. The restlessness continued to grow, and perhaps for the first time, consciously, a feeling of loneliness. The piano playing, the improvising, the concerts, the composing—all the things that had been plunged into with such fervor in the past, in part to allay loneliness for the young man in a hurry, either were not attempted or did not suffice. Almost belatedly, he turned to romance (although there had been many a woman in his life before) as a means of filling the void. Most of his attachments, as in the past, resulted in no more than short-lived interludes with a series of attractive women. When he met Paulette Goddard, however, he felt that he had at last found what he had been seeking. His unsuccessful wooing of her was still another blow, not only to his ego, but to his spirits in general.[2]

A new assignment came along, and again he started in to work. This time it was for Samuel Goldwyn; he and Ira were to do the songs for *The Goldwyn*

---

2 The main reason Gershwin was unable to successfully "woo" Goddard was because she was secretly married to Charlie Chaplin at the time.

Follies, one of those lavish screen revues, with Vera Zorina, Kenny Baker, Edgar Bergen and Charlie McCarthy, Helen Jepson, Bobby Clark, and the Ritz Brothers. George Balanchine had been brought to Hollywood to do the choreography, while nine songs were planned for George and Ira to do.

It was during this period, though he looked tan and healthy, that Gershwin began to grow increasingly restless, and in turns, despondent and jumpy. Physical check-ups showed nothing wrong, and doctors and close friends agreed that it was nerves, and that the feeling would pass. In June, however, while working on the Goldwyn film, Gershwin began to complain of headaches, and on occasion seemed to be physically drained and exhausted. There had been two brief, ominous episodes earlier, but they had been ignored. One occurred in February 1937, when Gershwin appeared with the Los Angeles Philharmonic in an all-Gershwin program. While at the piano, he experienced, for a fraction of a minute, a blackout, and missed a few bars. Later he recalled that during this moment he had the sensation of smelling burned rubber. A similar experience—the slight momentary loss of consciousness and the smell of burned rubber—repeated itself in April, while Gershwin was in a barber shop in Beverly Hills. But until June, when he began to complain of the headaches, and his irritability and fatigue began to show, there was no hint of anything wrong. Even then no one thought there was any physiological basis for his complaints.

When, early in June, Gershwin complained of a violent headache, a Los Angeles psychoanalyst was called in. The analyst, however, disagreed with Gershwin's own theory of overwork as the cause, insisting that the patient's illness was not mental but physical in nature. Gershwin was then referred to a medical doctor, whom he consulted for the first time on June 9. According to the doctor's records, as reported in an article in the *Eye, Ear, Nose & Throat Monthly* of May 1958, Gershwin's major complaints were early morning headaches and daily momentary dizzy spells, the latter covering a three-month period. There was also the strange, disagreeable sense of smell. A physical examination showed no abnormalities, but it was decided nonetheless to call in a neurologist for consultation. Except for the finding that the sense of smell of one nasal passage was impaired, all other tests proved normal.

A few weeks later, with Gershwin's headaches and dizzy spells continuing, the doctors decided to have him enter Cedars of Lebanon Hospital for more extensive examinations. The possibilities of a brain tumor were considered, but Gershwin laughed it off, still feeling that his condition was due to exhaustion and overwork. From June 23 to June 26, X-rays, blood tests, and other diagnostic procedures all proved negative; Gershwin opposed a spinal tap when it was suggested, however, saying it would be too painful.

He returned home under the care of a nurse, and remained in constant contact with both a medical doctor and a psychoanalyst. But the situation seemed to grow worse. He began to lose coordination now and then, spilling water when he drank, dropping things, and suffering more and more frequently the blinding, painful headaches. There was still the possibility that psychological rather than physical factors were the basis of his condition, and finally the doctor decided to isolate Gershwin for complete seclusion and rest. Gershwin moved into a smaller house nearby, where telephones and visitors could not reach him. Except for the doctors, who continued to search for a possible brain tumor, no one except Ira and Leonore, who visited him for brief periods several times a day, was allowed to see him. The new set-up seemed to be doing some good. Gershwin slept a great deal, complained less about his headaches, occasionally discussed songs with Ira, and even managed to play the piano for short spells.

Then, a few days after the move—on Friday, July 9—there was a sudden and rapid deterioration. That morning he was still able to play the piano. But at about five o'clock in the afternoon he became drowsy and fell into a deep sleep, which worsened into a coma. Actually, he never awoke from this sleep.

He was rushed to the hospital, and there examined by a neurosurgeon. Now the evidence was there: reflexes gone, and all the other symptoms pointing suddenly and definitely to a brain tumor.

The doctors decided that immediate surgery was necessary, and suggested calling in Dr. Walter E. Dandy, one of the country's top brain specialists. This touched off a dramatic and frantic search for the doctor, who could not be found at his home, office, or hospital, but was vacationing, it turned out, on a yacht cruising somewhere in Chesapeake Bay. In desperation the White House was called to help locate him, and that afternoon (it was now Saturday) two government destroyers were dispatched down the Chesapeake to find the yacht. Like something out of the very movies for which Gershwin had been writing, the yacht was found, and the doctor came roaring in with motorcycle escort to Cumberland, Maryland. There, in a three-way telephone conversation, the Los Angeles doctor authorized Dr. Dandy to come to the Coast for the operation, while simultaneously arrangements were made with a friend in New York for a private plane to stand by in readiness at the Newark airport for the doctor's flight west. He was rushed by another private plane to the Newark airport.

While these hurried arrangements were being made, another noted California surgeon was flown in for consultation. When he arrived, Gershwin's pulse was found to be so low that an immediate operation was deemed imperative; it would be impossible to wait for Dr. Dandy. Gershwin was then wheeled into the operating room for preliminary surgery to locate the exact position of the tumor. This operation lasted an hour and a half, after which Gershwin spent another two and a half hours in the X-ray room. During this time Dr. Dandy had arrived at Newark airport, only to be told of the new developments which would make it too late for him to continue his flight to California. However, an open line was kept for him so he could follow the progress of the operation by phone.

Gershwin was then returned to the operating room for the major operation, which lasted four hours. The doctors reported that he suffered from a cystic degeneration of a tumor on a part of the brain that could not be touched. It was their opinion that even if it had been possible to remove the tumor, the pattern of the sudden and complete attack indicated that it would have recurred, and quickly.

By now it was morning. Leonore, when she heard the news, couldn't bear to tell Ira, and said instead that George was all right, badly in need of rest more than anything else. Max Dreyfus telephoned just then from New York, anxious to hear news of George. In a daze, Ira told him, "George will be all right, Max. The operation was a success. There is nothing to worry about." He did not know that George had never regained consciousness and was already dead. He had died, at the age of 38, at 10:35 A.M. on July 11, 1937.

61   Isabel Morse Jones: "Gershwin Analyzes Science of Rhythm" (1937)

After Gershwin had settled on the West Coast in August 1936, he made a number of friends in the artistic community there beyond those in the immediate orbit of Hollywood. Part of this resulted from his insatiable desire to learn new things, and the differences between southern California and New York City presented these in abundance. The title of this article is wonderfully thirties-ish but rather hyperbolic given its content. In it, Gershwin begins to recognize that new phase of jazz known as swing that he did not live to see reach full flower.

If the American scene means anything at all in music, George Gershwin looms as one of the leading lights. Not yet 40 years of age, he has won races which finished in two widely separated but equally exacting fields, Tin Pan Alley and Carnegie Hall. Having conquered New York, he has obeyed Horace

SOURCE *Los Angeles Times* (February 7, 1937), III, 5.

Greeley and come West but not to settle down. From this vantage point of Hollywood and riches, he is out to discover new worlds.

If he has formulated any creed in his varied life from Grand Street, New York, through the length and breadth of Broadway to an *American in Paris*, it is that his particular kind of happiness exists only when he is finding out something that he didn't know before. Playing his piano concerto and conducting the orchestras at Seattle, San Francisco, and Wednesday and Thursday with the Los Angeles Philharmonic, Gershwin has found a new world here and it delights him. He says it frees his musical intuitions and enlarges his subjective mind, his composing mind.

Contrary to expectations, Gershwin is not a dyed-in-the-wool New Yorker. He gave up his famous modern penthouse without a qualm and embraced the Hollywood hills with enthusiasm. A five-mile walk on the dirt roads back of his Beverly Hills house of white stucco is now his setting-up exercise, and he comes in tanned and ravenous, ready for a tussle with the studio, a Ping-Pong bout or an argument over the twelve-tone scale with Schoenberg, or even interviewers. Polished off by several years of association with admiring society, Gershwin's sophisticated poise is almost invulnerable but his genuine sincerity saves him from the hard shell covering.

Pausing to analyze some of his own work, Gershwin has found definite laws of rhythm as mathematical and precise as any science. He will show you beautifully intricate patterns on a graph paper that proves swing music to be fundamental in the highest sense. As he explains it, the relationship between five different rhythms in one long undivided phrase makes rhythms such as the Americans love absolutely inevitable and basic with those of Cuba and the Congo.

Believing in the response from the middle listener whose musical mind lies between the man who knows nothing and the one who knows too much, Gershwin thinks the reason more men react to his music is its inevitability of rhythm. True rhythm, possible to prove mathematically correct, attracts their emotions and their intellect, in his opinion. He pioneered in the *Rhapsody in Blue* but he does not consider himself revolutionary but evolutionary.

He confesses to a preference for the word "swing" and has always hated the word "jazz." If music really swings it is right, and obvious syncopation is not necessarily swing music, according to Gershwin. When asked if he would rather have a swing band play his music than a regular symphony orchestra, he said the best orchestra for him would be a combination of the two: a young, rhythmically responsive but highly trained orchestra. He likes to conduct.

A day or two before Alexander Smallens arrives here to direct the two Los

Angeles concerts, Gershwin will take over a preliminary rehearsal. The program consists of *An American in Paris*, the *Concerto in F*, excerpts from *Porgy and Bess* with Todd Duncan, the six-foot baritone whom Gershwin wrote the second and third acts around, and the inevitable and right *Rhapsody in Blue*. *Porgy and Bess* is at present his favorite, without doubt. He has the full company score piled up within reach in his entrance hall and would get it out and produce it at the drop of a hat.

One of his most treasured compliments is the remark of Rosamund Johnson, the eminent Negro composer, that George Gershwin is a Lincoln for he has set Negro music free in *Porgy and Bess*.[1] He aimed to make *Porgy and Bess* natural Negro music and, according to them, he has succeeded. He knew instinctively that the Negro singer could not be restricted beyond a certain point without losing power. There is a certain five-point prayer in *Porgy* that illustrates Gershwin's genius in that direction. It is scored so that the singers can improvise as Gershwin knew they would in any case, because Negroes are artists and can't do anything the same way twice.

62   Nanette Kutner: "Radio Pays a Debt" (1936)

> Nanette Kutner became Gershwin's personal secretary following his arrival on the West Coast, the renewal of a friendship originating in New York. Here Kutner speaks about the role of Gershwin's 1934 radio shows (*Music by Gershwin*, on NBC in the spring and CBS in the fall) in underwriting the production costs of *Porgy and Bess*.[1]

"If it were not for radio, there mightn't have been a *Porgy and Bess*."

The words were spoken in the deep full voice of George Gershwin. He continued: "Last year some people criticized me because I went on the air for Feen-a-mint. They said that if I broadcast at all, I should have a more dignified sponsor.

"I'm glad to take this opportunity to answer what seems to me an utterly stupid objection. As far as I'm concerned, there is no difference between the

---

1 Given his years of stage experience (working most notably with Bob Cole and his brother James Weldon Johnson) and by all accounts, J. Rosamund Johnson (1873–1954) was among the most respected members of the original production team for *Porgy and Bess* (he created the small role of Lawyer Frazier). The comments to which Jones refers can be found in Johnson's "Emancipator of American Idioms," in Merle Armitage, ed., *George Gershwin* (New York: Longmans, Green and Company, 1938), 65ff.

SOURCE *Radio Stars* (February 1936).
    1 For sample recordings taken from his radio programs, see *Gershwin Performs Gershwin: Rare Recordings 1931–1935* (Ocean City, N.J.: MusicMasters 5062-2-C, 1991).

labels of a cathartic, a toothpaste, or an automobile. A sponsor *pays* me to broadcast my music to millions. That's the main issue. It may sound commercial. And it is! I'm not ashamed of being commercial-minded. Why should I be ashamed? It's a means to an end. Let me tell you," and he waved a forefinger, "it was just because I was paid by a sponsor that I could afford to take the time to do the one thing I've always wanted to do—compose an opera."

I looked at him admiringly. I have known George Gershwin a good many years. During that time he has steadily gained in competence, in social position, in success, in maturity, but he has lost none of his original enthusiasm.

I remembered a day, nine years ago, when, with his boyish, see-what-I've-got-here manner, he handed me a book.

"Read it. I want to do an opera out of this," he had said. The book was *Porgy*. And George Gershwin said that to me even before *Porgy* became a successful Theatre Guild drama.

At the time I wasn't impressed. I didn't really know Gershwin. The Gershwin who can frankly and accurately appraise himself, his abilities and ambitions; the Gershwin who is a combination of nerves, of emotion and sheer level-headedness, of steel and intuition, an intuition so great that when he wrote his first long piece, although he knew he could take several of its themes and transpose them into quick money-making songs, he refused to be tempted. He felt that the piece in its entirety would live. He was right. For the past twelve years, ever since George Gershwin played it with Paul Whiteman's orchestra during that gentleman's first memorable jazz concert at Carnegie Hall, no one has topped the *Rhapsody in Blue*. And for music lovers it has lost none of its magnetism.

When Gershwin confided his operatic ambition, I was but dimly aware of these facts. The previous week Vincent Youmans had also told me he intended writing an opera. The next day another composer publicly made the same vow. An opera to a composer is what the great American novel is to a newspaperman. It's the big thing they're always going to do . . . someday. Only they never do it.

Gershwin did.

And you can't just sit down and dash off an opera. It meant a lot to George Gershwin. It meant not being side-tracked by big commercial projects. It meant giving up his painting. It meant giving up many amusements. It meant spending a hot summer on Folly Island near Charleston. It meant going abroad, not to sun himself on the Riviera, but to study counterpoint. It meant constant building . . . building. Although *An American in Paris* was a gratifying success, to Gershwin it was merely a step toward his goal—the opera. This meant more and more work, and study with Joseph Schillinger, the musicologist who made him concentrate on modern harmony.

Then after that, Gershwin considered himself ready to begin the actual composing, which took *two years more.*

With justifiable pride he showed me the finished published score—five hundred and sixty pages, the original of which he has had photostated. And he showed me the orchestration he did himself, seven hundred pages of closely written music, and in his own hand.

No wonder Gershwin is furious when people doubt that he does his own orchestrations.

"I have only one answer to that—every orchestra in America employs two men who do the orchestrations, so why shouldn't I be considered competent to do my own?"

He stared again at the many pages.

"Radio has done a lot for me," he said softly. He paused. Then, "I agree that radio can kill a popular song faster than any other medium. For the present I am restricting the *Porgy* music. However, I shall shortly release two of the dance tunes, and the songs have already gone to a gifted few—to Everett Marshall, to Conrad Thibault, to Jane Froman, and to Lawrence Tibbett.

"Yes, radio does a lot to kill the sale of a song. But, in its way, it has repaid me. Because I made money from my broadcasts I could afford *not* to write a Broadway show, which, of course, takes much time and effort, and thus I could work on my opera.

"Besides, I feel that radio has educated the public musically to the point where they can thoroughly enjoy an opera. Radio never hurt symphony concerts and operas because they can't be played thirty times a night. Instead, radio brought the finest music to people who never before had had the chance to hear it. I believe that in music everyone possesses natural good taste. Radio helped to develop that taste. It has readied the American public for opera. And I'm grateful.

"Why, do you know," and in spite of his opinion regarding good taste, Gershwin seemed amazed, "*Porgy* is a financial success!"

We were seated in the workroom on the second floor of his duplex apartment. There are a great many rooms in the Gershwin home, a living-room with two pianos and many paintings, including a Rousseau. There is an English den and a modern dining-room and bar, and a great hall, and a studio where he can paint. There are many chairs and sofas, statues and tables. But there is something about the little workroom that is distinctly Gershwin. You feel that here he spends most of his waking hours. Here is an overturned ashtray, a stain on the carpet, and from the wall hangs a Bellows prize-fight scene brought from the house in which Gershwin lived ten years ago.

A piano stands near the windows. As he talked, Gershwin, not a light man, was seated upon it, and when he grew excited over *Porgy's* success, he bounced. The piano creaked.

"You're not Helen Morgan," I reminded him.

"But I wrote 'The Man I Love!'"

Composer of the most discussed opera of the day, George Gershwin still is proud that he wrote a popular song. You like him for this.

"I hope some of the *Porgy* songs will be popular; I hope they'll be sung from coast to coast. I'm glad I can write a popular song, so long as it's a good song. Songs are entirely within the operatic tradition. *Carmen* is practically a collection of song hits, and how many know that 'The Last Rose of Summer' came from an opera?"

He went on to tell me more about *Porgy.* How he found the cast himself, most of them never having acted before.

"But they were right—so right for their parts."

And he hopes to bring *Porgy and Bess* to the air.

"In a sort of musical serial built around the main characters. I'm working out the deal now. I hope it goes over so I can stick around New York and study."

While in New York he goes daily to a psychoanalyst.

"I'm a great debunker. I'm always searching for the truth. Psychology is like taking a college course. People who can't face themselves can never go on. I want to know myself so I can know others. I'm interested in one thing—life. I want to find its spark of truth, and have it come through my music."

His mood changed. Grabbing my hand he raced me into the studio.

"Look—my first painting in two years—DuBose Heyward."

Gershwin, because he knows people, had managed to catch on canvas Heyward's gentle expression.

Then back into the workroom where he showed me the desk upon which he writes his orchestrations.

"I designed it. See, it's on wheels. I can move it anywhere. You press this—a pencil sharpener jumps out. Here's the ink!"

He was all enthusiasm, just as he was years ago when he exhibited two autographed pictures, one of Charles Chaplin, the other of the Duke of Kent, inscribed: "To George . . . from George."

I stared at him. Here was no long-haired, arty looking genius. Here was a very modern young man, one who cares for the things this age offers, for fast motor cars and a game of golf; one who is glad to be sponsored not by a king or an art lover, but by the medium that is attuned to his time—radio. Gershwin's music is as modern as broadcasting itself. That is why it can speak for America and that is why it can reach out, touching the people of today. Of this I am convinced.

63   Alec Wilder: "A Foggy Day" (1972)

The zany movie musical *A Damsel in Distress* featured Fred Astaire with a leading lady other than Ginger Rogers—this time the ingenue Joan Fontaine. With a screenplay by P. G. Wodehouse and the antics of comedians Gracie Allen and George Burns, the movie also had many memorable tunes: "The Jolly Tar and the Milkmaid," "Things Are Looking Up," and "Nice Work if You Can Get It." But no tune was as popular as "A Foggy Day," danced to and sung by Astaire.

A Damsel in Distress was a film released on November 19, 1937. Gershwin had died on July 11th. So this and *The Goldwyn Follies*, released in 1938, were the last productions, either on Broadway or in Hollywood, over which Gershwin could have exercised creative control. Therefore, these films are, I feel, the last works of his that should be considered.

"A Foggy Day," from the first of them, is certainly one of the most famous Gershwin songs, and contains one of his brother's best-known lyrics. It's truly extraordinary how constant is Gershwin's use of repeated notes. They are more usually to be found in rhythm songs, but are seldom absent, even in a tender ballad like this. For example, the very first three notes are repeated. And the notes accompanying "I viewed the" and "The British" are repeated.

In any type of song but a romantic ballad, Gershwin's angularity may produce the most effective result. But the proof that there are no hard and fast rules is "A Foggy Day." For in it there is no step-wise writing, and there are many leaps of fourth and fifth intervals. Yet, it remains a most tender and moving, a far from aggressive, song.

I should make it clear that I do not view the repeated note songs with alarm. "A Foggy Day," for instance, has a heartbreak quality, not one note of which would I change. Right away I am captured by the *e* flat accompanying the word "day." And I am given, as a dividend, the avoidance of the cliché of the diminished chord. The bass line of the first four measures has been done to death by popular songwriters. Perhaps its most attractive use has been in Harold Arlen's "Stormy Weather."

But Gershwin uses, instead of the diminished chord, a minor sixth chord, which is much more winning. And he remains consistent, by moving up another minor third in the melody in his second phrase, to *a* flat, and also up a fifth again at the end of the phrase.

SOURCE   Alec Wilder, *American Popular Song: The Great Innovators, 1900–1950* (New York: Oxford University Press, 1972; repr. 1990), 157–58.

At the end of the *B* section (the song is *A-B-A-C*), the drop to the *d* in the cadence is truly gentle and loving. It's as personal as the revelation of a secret. And this is followed by the truly chilling wedding of the word "suddenly" with the two *f*'s and the *d*.

He then winds it up by extending the last section two measures longer than is customary, in the course of which he writes a pastoral, vulnerable, childlike phrase to go with the beautifully resolving lyric.

The elegant verse resolves on a tonic chord, as might a chorus, whereas verses usually reach a dominant seventh in preparation for the tonic of the beginning of the chorus. Gershwin was uncannily right to resolve the verse. It suggests a deep breath.

64 *George Gershwin: Letters to Zenna Hannenfeldt (1936)*

Gershwin's letters to his New York secretary, Zenna Hannenfeldt, offer a glimpse inside his management of the administrative aspects of his

SOURCE DLC [GC].

career. These particular letters primarily concern the settling of his finances in New York and the westward shipping of items, most notably his art collection.

August 24, 1936

Dear Miss Hannenfeldt:

You will understand not having heard from me sooner when I tell you that we have gone practically crazy trying to find a house in which to live and work. For two weeks we looked at all available houses but found nothing that suited our needs, and you can understand that that is not a very good situation for creating melodies. However, the day before yesterday we found one that will serve beautifully. The furniture leaves a little to be desired, but it has a swimming pool and tennis court. We move in this Friday. The address is 1019 No. Roxbury Drive, Beverly Hills.[1]

Did you find that piano copy of the Spanish song? If you did, please have it copied without that title and I will mail you the lyric that fits it. Let me know if this is done as I want the piano copy to go, eventually, to Mr. Vincent Minnelli. He wants the song for Beatrice Lillie.

I found my tune book in one of the suit cases that Paul brought out with him.[2]

There isn't much more at the moment to tell you except that I opened an account this morning with the Bank of America and made out a check for $7500.00 as deposit. I will send you the stub of this and other checks I have made out so you can keep your accounts complete.

I may want you to have sent to me a half dozen or so of my paintings to put up in the house we rented. I will let you know which pictures I want sent and you can get in touch with Budworth Company, who are very experienced in shipping pictures so they will not be damaged in any way.

I hope you are keeping well and enjoying your evenings in the country. Please keep me informed, regularly, as to what goes on in the big city. I will write you again, soon.

Sincerely,

George Gershwin

P.S.

I am enclosing statement from Douglas Gibbons & Co., Inc., dated Aug. 1, 1936 in the amount of $583.34.

1 The Roxbury address that Gershwin cites was shared by George, Ira, and Ira's wife, Leonore, in 1936–37; Ira and Leonore bought the house next door (1021) in 1940 and lived there the rest of their lives.

2 "Paul" refers to Paul Mueller, Gershwin's valet, who drove Gershwin's Buick automobile, packed with some personal effects and Gershwin's dog, Tony, cross-country for him. Mueller had performed a similar service when Gershwin traveled to Folly Island in 1934 with Henry Botkin.

I have mailed the following checks, together with invoices, direct from here:

Ch. 3881—dated Aug. 19, 1936–The Museum of Modern Art—$1.05
Ch. 3882—dated Aug. 21, 1936–Crawford-Emanuel Cig. Co.—$24.83

September 2, 1936

Dear Miss Hannenfeldt:

Well, we are finally settled in our new house and love it. The swimming pool and tennis court are the envy of our less fortunate Hollywood friends. Paul and his wife are here busy getting the house into shape and, I imagine, enjoying the California climate as much as everybody else.

Tony had to be taken to the veterinary yesterday because he has developed eczema and will have to be in the dog hospital for a couple of days until they check it.

Ira, Leonore, and myself are in fine health, which about concludes small news, with possible exception of the fact that my Buick broke down somewhere near Colorado Springs on the way out and I had to send $166.00 to have a new inside put into it. Incidentally, I will send you the stubs of all the checks I have made out as soon as I get through paying some of the bills which have accrued since my arrival.

The new house can use some paintings and I was thinking of having some of mine sent out. I wish you would investigate right away the best way to have about a dozen pictures sent out here. Get the various prices by rail and boat. Find out how much the extra insurance while pictures are en route would be and all other details. The pictures that I am considering having sent are the following:

Picasso's	Absinthe Drinker
Pascin's	Girl with Cat
Gauguin's	Self-Portrait
Utrillo's	Fishermen Houses
Modigliani's	Portrait of Doctor
	Woman's Head
Rousseau's	Isle De La Cité
Derain's	Road Through the Forest
Gershwin's	Portrait of Grandfather
Sequiro's	Mexican Children
Segonzac's	Landscape
Thomas Benton's	Burlesque
Chagall's	Rabbi
	Slaughter House
Max Jacob's	Religious Festival

I believe Budworth Company, the picture shippers, are considered the most reliable, as they moved my collection to Chicago and back one time—so I would contact them.[3] Also, the Modern Museum might give you some information on this.

There isn't much more to write about at this moment, so I will close. Hope that you are in good health and getting plenty of riding in the country these days.

Please let me know about all the music you send down to Harms and to Chappell so I can lay my hands on them any moment that I might need them.

All good wishes,

George Gershwin

65   George Gershwin: Letters to Mabel Schirmer (1936–1937)

Unlike the matter-of-fact tone of his 1928 letter to his friend Mabel Schirmer (see selection 32), these letters reveal more of Gershwin as he details both his activities and many of his inner feelings during the last months of his life. There is perhaps no better window on his world at this time than that which he himself provides here. While some of the references have been obscured with time, one clearly comes away from these heartfelt notes with a personal sense of the man, his hopes, his joys, and his fears.

September 1, 1936

Dear Mabel:

I have been wanting to write you for a long time but, what with trying to find a house for two and a half weeks and being greeted every night by our many friends who are out here—and California sunshine—I just haven't gotten down to it. In fact, I wrote my first letter to Zilboorg only last night.[1]

We finally found a house that is really lovely. It is in Beverly Hills and has many charming things about it, not the least of which are a swimming pool and a tennis court. It is a nice spacious, cheery house with a fine workroom.

---

3 In 1933 Gershwin loaned his entire art collection (forty-nine oils, seventeen water colors, lithographs, drawings, and three sculptures) to the Art Club of Chicago for the "Exhibition of the George Gershwin Collection of Modern Paintings."

SOURCE DLC [GC].

1 "Zilboorg" refers to psychoanalyst Dr. Gregory Zilboorg, whom both Schirmer and Gershwin had been seeing for some time (as had Kay Swift and her husband, James Warburg). The whereabouts of Gershwin's letter to him are unknown. In addition to their interest in such therapy, Schirmer and Gershwin had something else in common—both had studied piano with Charles Hambitzer.

The living room is very large, white walls and a fine Steinway piano. The furnishings aren't all to our taste but then—you can't have everything, can you?

Ira and I have been doing a little work on some songs, but we haven't really begun to dig in. We are waiting for the script to be put into better shape.[2] However, with the little start that we have, we feel quite confident that we won't be stuck.

We've had some very gay times out here already with the Jerome Kerns, Sam Behrmans, Moss Hart, Oscar Levant, Harpo Marx, Yip Harburg and dozens of others of our old cronies. Would certainly be lovely if you could also be here.

Have you seen Kay? I haven't written to her nor have I heard from her. I should like to know if you ever see her.[3]

What's happening around town these days? How are you and the Doctor getting along? Have you seen Emily and Lou?[4] Please write to me, telling me all that goes on in little old New York. Ira and Leonore join me in sending love to you—I'm giving you an extra kiss besides.

Yours,

George

September 18, 1936

Dear Mabel,

What a sweet and warm letter you wrote. It was like a tonic—you know, even tonics are needed out here in God's country.

I saw Gus Schirmer out here and of course we spoke about you—and "of course" you came out on top as—"of course" you always do.

I miss you very much, Mabel, and wish it were possible for you to come out here. This place is just full of people you know and who love you. Of course, there are depressing moments, too, when talk of Hitler and his gang creep into the conversation. For some reason or other the feeling out here is even more acute than in the East.

I wrote to Em and Lou the other day and told them how much they are being missed by the Gershwins. Incidentally, Lou shot an eighty-three at golf the other day, which is quite remarkable.

---

2 Gershwin is referring to the film *Shall We Dance?*, the brothers' first project upon arriving in Hollywood.

3 "Kay" refers to Kay Swift. Although the two had not been communicating, friends shared news of each to the other.

4 "Emily and Lou" refers to the Paleys.

We have seen your nephew, Donald Pleshette, quite a few times and I must say he's a nice-looking and well-behaved boy.[5]

Our work is going along slowly because the script for the picture is not completely finished, however, with the few songs that we have, we feel that we will be ready with our part.

I saw *Swing Time* out here and liked the picture very much. Although I don't think Kern has written any outstanding song hits, I think he did a very creditable job with the music and some of it is really delightful. Of course, he never really was ideal for Astaire, and I take that into consideration.

Otto Klemperer is playing the "Music for Orchestra and Baritone" by Ernst Toch, next week. It is a concert given by the American Guild for German Cultural Freedom—and I shall be there.[6] Will write you about it.

There is a lot more to tell you, but I can't tell you everything at once so I'll wait for you to write me a nice newsy letter. Hoping you are happy and well,

With love,

George

October 18, 1936

Dear Mabel,

The fact that I don't write to you more frequently doesn't mean that I don't think about you often—it simply means that I'm not very business-like about answering letters.

Nevertheless, here I am again writing to you to tell you that everything out here is about the same as it was, except that last week we had a taste of the beginning of the rainy season. Hollywood is a place of great extremes—when it rains, it pours—when it's cloudy, it's cloudy the whole day—and when the sun shines, well, you know all about that.

It looks as though the three Gershwins will be out here for a longer period than they first anticipated. Samuel Goldwyn is constructing a contract right now for our services for a picture to start around the fifteenth of January. And, now, RKO has piped up with talk of their option, which was originally in our agreement. They would like us to start on the next Astaire picture shortly after this contract is over. If Goldwyn doesn't have a story ready for us in about three weeks, he may put his date back so we could do the next Astaire vehicle, otherwise we go to work for Goldwyn on that date.

Naturally, I miss New York and the things it has to offer quite a good deal,

---

5 Schirmer's maiden name was Mabel Pleshette.

6 Emigré Ernst Toch (1887–1964) was among the more notable fellow serious composers that Gershwin met up with on the West Coast.

and will probably miss it more as time goes on, but I must say that California has many very delightful advantages; for example, I am writing this letter on October 28, sitting in a pair of shorts with no top, in a hot sun around our pool. That sounds almost like a moving picture scenario, but it's true. We play quite a lot of tennis and the work so far seems easy. So you see, California has much to offer to the Gershwins.

I have agreed to do several concerts out here; the first taking place in Seattle on December 15, and in San Francisco on January 15, 16, and 17. Also, probably in Los Angeles late in January.

Ernst Toch and his family are out here in a house in Santa Monica. We met the other night at the big anti-Nazi meeting which was held here. It was quite an impressive affair with many speakers, including Eddie Cantor, Gifford Cochran, and several others.

How are you these days? I wish you would write me of the important events that are happening in your life. Who you are seeing mostly these days—How the analysis is going—etc., etc. Do you see much of Emily? Have you seen anything of Kay? I think about her a great deal and wonder if she is all right. Have you seen my mother recently? She is planning to come out, but in usual Gershwin fashion is taking a long time to make up her mind.

Ira and Lee are in fine health and spirits. Lee, sun-worshiper that she is, is getting to look like an Indian squaw.

Why don't you come out and loll around our pool with us? I'd love to see you again, darling. You'd better make up your mind to take your vacation out here.

We all send our love to you—and here's an extra big hug from me.

Yours,

George

February 9, 1937

Hello, Mabel:

I know I've been pretty naughty in not writing you lately, but I assure you I've been much busier than I've been naughty. What—with my concert tour—with two performances tomorrow night and Thursday night in Los Angeles—with one Astaire picture in production and another one to be written, you can see that your Georgie boy has had little time for correspondence. I'm sorry that you can't be here to witness the excitement that is going on about the two concerts here in Los Angeles. You know, I have brought out Alexander Smallens to conduct and Todd Duncan to sing and they tell me that they've seen nothing like the excitement for a concert in years. My friend, Arthur Lyons, is taking a room at the Trocadero and has invited about 250 people to come in after the concert.[7] He's going to great trouble to decorate the room and there will be two orchestras—one American and one Russian. I wish I could send a magic carpet for you, Emily, and Lou so you could all be here for the occasion.

You were right in your letter in stating that Kay seemed in good spirits and happy. She has written me about a new relationship which has developed between herself and some fellow I know, which seems to have done the trick for her. I am very happy for her sake that she was able to adjust herself so soon. Keep this information to yourself, please.

The rainy season seems to be about over and I think once again we might expect some of the renowned sunshine that will be most welcome I can assure you.

My mother seems to be in better health out here than she was in the East and for that I am very happy.

Did you see Frankie and Leo in New York when they came back from Mexico?

There isn't much more to write about now and I will write again after the concerts.

Yours,

With love, George

April 20, 1937

Dear Mabel,

I am lying comfortable on a chaise lounge with a new gadget, which I have just bought, on my head. You would probably scream with laughter if you could see me. The machine is a new invention put out by the Crosley Radio Company and has been recommended by several people out here as a positive grower of hair. It's an entirely new principle and you know me for new principles.[8]

While relaxing I thought of you so called in my secretary to take down a few words to you. I wonder how you are and what you are doing—how you are enjoying your new job and if you are ever planning to take a vacation. It would be so good to see you again. Hollywood continues about the same except that the weather is really getting nice again after its worst winter in many years.

Our first Astaire picture *Shall We Dance* is practically ready for public gaze

---

7 Lyons was the Gershwins' agent in Hollywood.
8 It is not clear if this device in any way exacerbated Gershwin's brain tumor.

and if you turn on your radio you will hear the songs from it achieving a rather quick popularity. Our second Astaire opus must be finished in three weeks and then with one week's vacation we start in working for Samuel Goldwyn, so you can see that collaborators Gershwin have been extremely active and shall continue to be until the middle of September. After that, maybe New York for a few months. How is the old burg these days? I would love a long letter from you with all the news you can possibly dish out.

My mother is on her way back to New York via the Pan-Pacific boat "Pennsylvania," which at this moment is somewhere in the vicinity of the Panama Canal. It's quite an adventure for her as this is the first boat she has been on, believe it or not, since she came to America. She wired us that she was having a wonderful time. She arrives in New York in about a week and perhaps you will see her then and she will give you all the news from Hollywood.

Dear, sweet, Mabel, take an hour out of your busy day and write me everything and try and get into the habit of doing it often as I really would appreciate it. With my love to you and al the best from Ira and Lee,

As always,

George

66   *George Gershwin: Letter to Emily Paley (1937)*

Tuesday, Mar. 16, 37.

I've been wanting to write you for some time to tell you how happy your letter made me. What a great person you are dear Em. So generous, so understanding, so beautiful. Your yearly letter from Miami has gotten to be a necessity. It nearly always comes when I am a little below par & always does the trick of cheering me in an important way.

I talked about you with another member of the "Emily Paley Society" last night. It was at Eddie Robinson's house & Gladys was the one.[1] She loves you & admires you so between us we had a wonderful time. The whole evening was memorable. Stravinsky was the guest of honor & was charming. He asked if he & Dushkin[2] could play for the group. They played

SOURCE DLC [GC].

   1 The actor Edward G. Robinson was a member of the Greenwich Village crowd that regularly brought the Gershwin brothers, the Strunsky sisters (Emily and Leonore), Mabel Pleshette, Lou and Herman Paley, and others together for Saturday evening festivities of amusement, music, and lively conversation.

   2 Samuel Dushkin (1891–1976) was a wealthy and gifted violinist who commissioned Stravinsky to write the *Concerto in D* (1931) and the *Duo Concertante* (1931–32) for him. Dushkin and Gershwin collaborated on *Short Story*, published by B. Schott in 1925, which transformed two of Gershwin's piano novelettes into a minor work for violin and piano.

seven or eight pieces superbly. Stravinsky & mother got on famously. Isn't Hollywood wonderful? Gladys sat me next to the most glamorous & enchanting girl in the west. Paulette Goddard. She is a really exciting creature. Gladys knows my taste better than I thought. The whole evening was grand, what with those pictures, Stravinsky, Miss P.G., Frank Capra & thoughts & talk about you.

Our Astaire picture No. I is being completed this week & perhaps in another week comes the sneak preview. It looks good.

Ira & I have started some songs for the next Astaire opus & have a couple of promising beginnings.

We are all in good health & looking forward to the time when you & Lou are out here with us. Won't that be fun? Give my love to Lou & take an extra large portion for yourself. Ira, Lee & Mother send their love along also. There's a lot more to tell you but I have to get ready now to be photographed for the magazine *Life*. They want Kern, Berlin & me to adorn their pages.

Please tell Lou to write me all the news & you do the same.

As ever & always,

George

67   George Gershwin: Letter to Henry Botkin (1937)

Along with Ira and several of his friends, Gershwin's cousin, the painter Henry Botkin (1896–1983), helped encourage the composer's interest in the fine arts and tutored him as he taught himself. He later served as Gershwin's adviser and buyer of his collections of French Impressionist paintings, drawings, and watercolors. As can be seen in this letter, Botkin also assisted the Gershwin brothers with their East Coast business affairs.

May 17, 1937

Dear Henry,

I'm glad to know that you are getting better from your recent illness. I hope by the time this reaches you, you are a completely well man.

Many thanks for your letter which arrived today with enclosed clippings. Ira and I are more than pleased with the reaction of the critics of the important New York papers. The climax to all this will come when you push one, or maybe two, of our songs up high in the first ten on the *Hit Parade*, which evidently has a very important standing out here in Hollywood.

SOURCE DLC [GC].

I am sending some photostatic piano copies of the new songs from Astaire's next vehicle. There are nine in number, but two are written in the old English style for atmosphere and score construction. The reason we were so generous in the number of songs was that we wanted to give Pandro Berman an extra song or two in case he needed it as Ira and I will be on the *Goldwyn Follies* for the next four or five months. Incidentally, Pandro Berman is simply crazy about "Things Are Looking Up" and "A Foggy Day"—and "I Can't Be Bothered Now." There are four others, however, that have distinct possibilities; they are, "Nice Work If You Can Get It," "Put Me to the Test," "Pay Some Attention to Me," and a little English comedy song called "Stiff Upper Lip." When the proper time comes I will let you know how the songs shape up in the production. In the meantime, please have them copyrighted in my name and then put them away where nobody can see them as it will be at least several months before they can be made public.

I asked Selma to send me the orchestration of "Wake Up, Brother, and Dance," which I received this morning, so I could hear it played out here as I am thinking of possibly using it in the *Goldwyn Follies*.

Please write to me letting me know that you've received the new songs and also about the possibility of some of the *Shall We Dance* numbers getting onto the *Hit Parade*. I would like you to go to work on this right away.

I guess that's about all just now, Henry. Ira joins me in sending best wishes to you with the hope that you are once again in fine health.

Sincerely,

George

68   *George Gershwin: Letter to Rose Gershwin (1937)*

May 19, 1937

Dear Mom,

I'm in my office and just received your sweet letter and am hastening to dictate an answer to you. I have been meaning to write you a long letter, but with all of the excitement of finishing the second Astaire picture and starting on the new *Goldwyn Follies* you can imagine what a hectic period it must be.

We are now settled in a very nice studio at the Goldwyn lot and Ira and I are working very hard trying to get some new songs started. We really should be taking at least a month's vacation after finishing two pictures for Astaire,

SOURCE   DLC [GC].

but unfortunately our contracts came one on top of the other and we have to work harder than ever to get a good start on the next and I hope the last picture for some time.

We are all feeling well, as is Harry Botkin who is living with us. Incidentally, his exhibition opened on Monday and was a big success. I think his pictures have improved tremendously in the last year and believe that he is on the way to becoming one of our most important American painters. I am sure he will sell some of his pictures and if he decides to settle down here he could have quite a lot of pupils who are interested in painting.

I'm glad your boat trip turned out so well and also that you arrived in New York in time for some good weather. Now all you need is someone to look after the entertainment side of your life and I'm sure you will be very happy.

After the Goldwyn picture is finished we are planning to come back to New York and stay for a while and then I might take a trip to Europe. Ira and I will be ready for a good vacation after we are through here as it really has been a year of a great deal of labor.

I'm glad to hear that Frankie is going to Europe once again in June as I know how much she enjoys the occasional trips that she takes.

You asked in your letter about Miss P. There is nothing new to tell you about her. I see her less frequently than I did. She seems very well and asks about you often. There is a possibility of her appearing in the picture *Gone With The Wind*. That's about all the news there is to tell about her.[1]

Some of the pictures that I took of you turned out pretty well and I shall mail them to you in a day or so.

How is brother Arthur these days? I am glad to hear that he is writing a lot of tunes and I hope that he can find a market for some of them. It is also good to hear that Kate and Abe are doing well.[2] How is Grandma these days? Give her my love—in fact, give my love to the whole family and especially to you and Arthur. Ira and Lee also send their love to you both. Please take good care of yourself and have a fine time these lovely Spring days. I promise that I will write more often in the future.

Your loving son,

George

---

1 Miss P. refers to Paulette Goddard who was, by this time, no longer romantically involved with Gershwin. She was seriously considered for the role of Scarlett O'Hara which, of course, went to Vivian Leigh.

2 Gershwin is referring to his mother's sister, Kate Wolpin, and her husband.

69 *George Gershwin: Letter to Rose Gershwin (1937)*

His last known letter to his mother in retrospect is chilling since it was written little more than a month before his death. He intimates that he is not
feeling well but is hopeful that the outcome will be positive. Neither Gershwin nor his doctors knew that his condition was as grave as it was.

June 10, 1937

Dear Mom,

It was a most pleasant surprise to get your nice fat letter with so much
news in it. Your writing is certainly improving and if you don't watch out
some Hollywood studio will sign you up—I think I've got something there
because the only thing the Gershwin family lacks is a book writer and it
would be simply wonderful if the posters read—Book by Rose
Gershwin—Lyrics by Ira Gershwin—Music by George Gershwin—and we've
got to get Arthur in somewhere, so let's say—Entire Production staged by
Arthur Gershwin.

There isn't a lot of news to write you about out here in Hollywood. Ira
and I continue to work hard on the *Goldwyn Follies* and as you can imagine it
is tough after just finishing two other pictures; however, we will keep on
working and the chances are that we will turn out a good job. I have had
quite enough of Hollywood and can't wait until the Goldwyn picture is finished, so that I can go to New York and possibly to Europe.

Of late I haven't been feeling particularly well. Yesterday I put myself in the
hands of a Dr. Segall and he is going to try to find out the reason for the slight
dizziness I get every once in a while. He examined me yesterday and told me
not to worry about it as he was convinced that it was nothing of a serious
nature but that he would like to investigate it further to make sure about the
cause of it. I will keep you informed as to the progress the Doctor makes.

70 *George A. Pallay: Letter to Irene Gallagher (1937)*

George Pallay was a cousin of the Paleys and the brother of the newspaper
writer Max Abramson (see selection 8). A resident of California, he and
Gershwin spent time together during the Gershwin brothers' two working
stints in Hollywood and wrote frequently when they lived on opposite

SOURCE DLC [GC].
SOURCE DLC [GC].

coasts. Although their relationship was sometimes strained (Todd Duncan mentioned that Pallay was a bit too persistent in spending time with Gershwin in 1936–37), their letters are invaluable resources as they often used each other as confidants. Irene Gallagher was a friend of Pallay and the secretary of Max Dreyfus, the long-time head of the T. B. Harms Company, publisher of Gershwin's music as early as 1918.

Dear, dear Irene:

The tragedy of George's passing and your nearness to him impels me to write you a sort of report of events prior and after. And I can report the same to you because everything is authentic by reason of the fact that I was or tried to be of assistance prior and especially during the period when the danger commenced.

I was present on the operating floor and watched part of the operation. The family designated me to keep them posted while they waited three floors below. Strict orders forbade them. I should have said anyone but Arthur Lyons and myself to be present.

But to go back: in November of last year George once remarked that while once sitting in a barber chair he had had a dizzy spell for a second. Then at this Philharmonic concert here he had a second dizzy spell for a second. This was in February during his conducting of the *Porgy and Bess* singing chorus. Then three or four times since then, on the tennis court, or while reading. In all he just mentioned these spells casually.

Four weeks ago he seemed unhappy and a bit moody. He was critical of things, people, and events. I was around him constantly and he always spoke his heart out to me. Then he complained of headaches and fatigue. Immediately doctors examined him at home very thoroughly, as thorough as a home examination can be. Every part of him was checked and found O.K.

Even then a big neurologist examined his head for possible symptoms and declared, "no indication of any symptom of brain disease."

Because his headaches continued we decided to take him to a hospital where the fullest examination was made. X-rays, eye specialist, lung specialist, brain specialist, etc. All found no symptom of any organic or physical illness. All agreed that his condition showed every proof of a nervous affliction, perhaps self-induced by worry, overwork, or general emotional geographic unhappiness or something.

Immediately the greatest psychoanalyst was employed to search out the cause of this apparent mental illness. The man was the best in America. He studied and studied George. George worked with him hard to co-operate but the headaches continued. Yet all during these headaches there was no change from normal to subnormal of pulse, appetite, temperature, respiration, blood pressure, etc. Just headaches. And each day physical doctors examined George watching his physical reactions for improvement or unimprovement.

All during this period there were days when he indicated [he was] on the way to recovery: this by fewer headaches, moments of cheerfulness, clear thinking, planning for his comfort and work. Always most optimistic of not only his recovery but the fact that nothing physical was the matter.

He slept most of the day and night that doctors or meal time permitted and the headaches were relieved by sedatives.

Then came Friday the ninth of July. At four P.M. I cajoled the doctors to let me see him and Ira and myself went into his room. Oh yes, he had a male nurse all during his bedded condition. This nurse was the assistant to the psychoanalyst. He slept near George and was never out of sight for a moment. He and Paul! The reason no one was allowed to see George is because visitors and their layman conversation would destroy the work of the doctor. This since every expert agreed that this was all mental (remember that the first time in the hospital every scientific means employed by the best doctors failed to disclose the slightest ever indication of anything organic. He was tested in taste, sight, smell, hearing, touch, memory and all down the line).

So Friday at four P.M. Ira and I found George asleep and this sleep was described as the first one without pills to relieve headaches. This indicated his possible quick recovery. At seven P.M. when he was escorted to the bathroom he suddenly shook and trembled all over. He was bedded immediately and his eyes seemed to swell. Doctors, brain and otherwise rushed to the house, removed him after examination to the hospital at midnight, and then the symptoms showed definitely that somewhere in the head physical illness was present. In fact, it was the psychiatrist who first discovered that it was physical and not mental, because it was the first time that the illness manifested itself to give forth the symptoms that science is aware of.

The belief was a brain tumor. Midnight pictures failed to disclose where it was located. To locate the tumor air had to be pumped into the brain so an X-ray picture would "take."

Because of the seriousness of the operation, of course, the family wanted the greatest in the world. The doctors all agreed that Dr. Dandy of Johns Hopkins was the best. Saturday early we were advised. After phoning that Dandy could not be located until Monday because he was on a yachting trip. Then I insisted that if Dandy was alive I'd reach him. I phoned the home and got word that he was a guest of Gov. [Harry W.] Nice of Maryland. I phoned the Gov. and learned that they were on Gov. Nice's yacht in Chesapeake Bay. The governor's secretary assured me that short wave broadcast by the Maryland police to the boat would be employed. Then I phoned Emil Mosbacher, told him the life and death importance of getting Dandy. He got the White House secretary McIntire and McIntire ordered out the Navy.

Well, they reached Dandy and Dandy phoned and I spoke to him after the doctors here asked his co-operation. He agreed and chartered a plane to Newark where he would change to a special plane for here.

At that time it all indicated that no emergency was necessary. Meanwhile Dr. Nafzinger of Berkeley University was located at Lake Tahoe. He was due to arrive at L.A. at nine P.M. Saturday. This was the time that Dandy was brought ashore and phoned me at the Gershwin house.

When Nafzinger arrived, seven or eight doctors went into further consultation, and while Lee and Ira were present at the hospital, I was at the house handling Dandy's arrangement for arrival and transportation.

Dr. Nafzinger, Rand and all the rest realized that an emergency operation was necessary, because he could not live until Dandy arrived. And so Rand and Nafzinger started to prepare George for the operations at eleven P.M. Saturday.

There was no way to head off Dandy for he was by then in the air bound for Newark but would arrive at one-thirty our time in Newark. So I got Mosbacher in New York and he stopped Dandy.

George was taken to the operating room at twelve-thirty Saturday night our time.

I was installed at a desk ten feet away from the room. The family was forced to wait on the fourth floor, and their only contact were their phone talks to me. Of the twenty or twenty-five people co-operating in the work I was able to talk constantly with the nurses, interns, doctors, etc. Of course I asked thousands of questions. At one-thirty A.M. they had completed the first part of the operation, which was only to pump air into the brain. Then they took him downstairs to the X-ray room. They returned at three A.M. with him and then started the removal of the tumor. They couldn't locate the tumor in its exact brain location for removal until the final X-ray with air in the brain.

Well Irene, as they brought him back to begin the chance-in-a-million operation the doctor in charge waved his hand and shook his head to me in hopelessness, but stopped and whispered that if the tumor was soft and not hard a small chance remained.

The anguish of the family downstairs was indescribable. I reported for all to pray that it would be soft and not hard. Then at four-thirty great cheerfulness seemed to spread over the doctors as they viewed a formation known as a cyst. The cyst was the size of a small grapefruit full of pus, etc. They lanced it, emptied it and burned its membrane down, down, down and then discovered the root of the tumor embedded deep in the brain. It was too deep to cut further or remove. The cyst was the result of or rather the degeneration of the tumor, and degeneration began Friday late and flamed up like a volcano from there on. This is important to understand: that human science could not detect, suspect, locate, or diagnose George's condition until the tumor degenerated and caused the cyst to grow. With the degeneration of the tumor and the growth of inflammation or cyst, this latter growth gave forth the symptoms that science can recognize.

We felt better that it appeared as a cyst only, for this was better than a tumor. But as I say, further cutting disclosed the embedded tumor. At six-fifteen we all returned to the house. All were of the belief that George had a chance. I could not get myself to tell them that it was all hopeless. I did tell Lee Gershwin that even if he lived we could expect at its best that George's left side of face and arm, side and leg would be forever paralyzed; that he'd never be able to play again. That this was at its best, even if he lived. But he could not live because too much brain was destroyed and besides the tumor would grow again in a year; that while George was paralyzed and even living, it was a living death. When it was all over, I told all what I had told Lee before George died.

George's strong condition to withstand the horrors of his operation was the talk of the assemblage. Of course they had two blood transfusions and injected glucose and sugar into his veins while they operation was in progress etc. In fact, at seven A.M. our time when they took him to his room, his pulse and respiration rallied wonderfully. Then at nine-ten A.M. his temperature started, breathing became difficult, and at death at ten-twenty-five A.M. his temperature was a hundred and seven. In fact the doctors told me that his heart beat for twenty or thirty seconds after he stopped breathing. Death was the result of paralysis of his respiratory organs, caused of course from cutting the brain nerves which direct these functions.

Unbeknown to all is the fact that any and every doctor who was in the case or suggested, was personally checked on thru by Dr. Rudolph Marx. Ask my brother Max how and why Dr. Marx is the most dependable one for me to check others' reputations with. Marx assured me as each name was previously mentioned to him how great each one was in his particular field. So I want you to know that the best possible was obtained and everything human was done.

We are all worried about Ira and his mother. What and how Ira will react in his life losing George is our main concern and out here everyone will do all possible to keep and assist Ira.

Paul Berman said he would try to make a permanent team of Ira and Jerome Kern.

Sam Goldwyn told Ira to choose any composer he wanted if he cared to complete the *Follies*.

Irene dear, George's songs for *Damsel in Distress* are wonderful. The *Shall We Dance* score is nothing by comparison. The five songs completed for the *Goldwyn Follies* are terrific. A few need verses which were never completed. The titles of the five songs for Goldwyn are "I Was Doing All Right," "Just Another Rhumba," "Love Walked Right In," "I Love to Rhyme" and "It's Very Clear." (This is his last musical work.) Also there are a number of phrases in his musical workbook, an old unpublished prelude was being considered for a title. Ira called it "Sleepless Night."

I have written this letter to you because I know how close you and Max Dreyfus were to George and if Mr. Dreyfus' health permitted perhaps he would care to know the full truth of everything as I know it. Having been entrusted with the care and loving duty that I tried to fulfill in my own small way.

Irene darling, what can any of us say? How can we express what we feel? It's so awful, so terrible, so . . . oh God.

You know me, Irene, and no one knows what my love for George was because I felt uplifted when I was near him. And there is no one left in the world who can give me this one thing that was vital to my very character.

There is lots more to talk about, details of things, people, George's last pleasures, hopes, viewpoints, ideas, plans, etc. But all this must wait until I see you.

I hope you are well and also Mr. Dreyfus. Tell him I have something of interest to tell regarding George's secret to me of an unusual idea, a musical idea that George planned on furthering when he went to Europe.

I am fatigued now so I will close with lots of love to you, Irene. Write me, honey, if you have any questions or if there is anything I can do.

Lovingly,

George Pallay

P.S. You can read this letter to my brother Max. I haven't the strength to repeat this awful tale verbally or in writing. Excuse running short of paper.

VII. OBITUARIES AND EULOGIES

Gershwin was one of those rare figures who actually had the opportunity to witness his own iconization. The tenor of his eulogies continued the tone of many press reports during his lifetime, pointing to the uniqueness of his gifts and contributions and to his importance on the American musical scene. Throughout the selections below, one can also discern the shock, horror, and sense of loss that accompanied the news of his death. Several of the reports are detailed news accounts of the memorial events that were hastily organized in his honor. Ira's poignant letter to his mother embodies his sorrow at losing his younger brother and music teammate.

In a series of almost daily reports, *Variety*, the chronicle of show business, provided among the most detailed accounts of the situation, preparations, and services following Gershwin's death. In this article, *Variety* documented the drama surrounding the memorial services held for Gershwin on opposite coasts.

NY Mourners Defy Rain

New York, July 15.—Pounding rain did not prevent a turnaway attendance at Temple Emanu-El for the George Gershwin funeral services this afternoon. Temple's auditorium was packed to its 3,000 capacity and more than 1,000 persons were turned away.

As if the heavens had stopped weeping, those entering during downpour emerged an hour later under clearing skies following pronouncement of the eulogy by Rabbi Stephen Wise and prayer by Rabbi Nathan A. Perilman.

Cream of the nation's song fashioners were among the honorary pallbearers. Their names read like a Who's Who of the radio, stage, screen, politics, finance, and the arts.

Cavalcade of Gershwin radio memorial programs was capped by today's tribute to the 38-year-old composer.

Interment was in Mount Hope cemetery, Yonkers.

American Society of Composers, Authors & Publishers has offered to Ira Gershwin full cooperation and use of member talent for completion of music assignment on *The Goldwyn Follies* halted by Gershwin's death.

George and Ira Gershwin had completed five of the nine scheduled numbers for the Goldwyn musical. Indications are that Ira will probably compose the other four alone.

"Coincident with Services Held in New York Yesterday"

Coincident with services held in New York yesterday afternoon at Temple Emanu-El, memorial exercises were conducted yesterday morning at 10

SOURCE "Coincident with Services Held in New York Yesterday," *Variety* (July 16, 1937): 37.

o'clock in Temple B'nai B'rith, Wilshire Boulevard, for George Gershwin, American composer who died here last Sunday. Nearly a thousand persons attended, including leading executives, stars, composers, and writers of the picture industry.

The memorial program was arranged by a committee of the American Society of Composers, Authors & Publishers, consisting of Sigmund Romberg, chairman; Jerome Kern, Oscar Hammerstein, 2nd; Irving Berlin, Moss Hart, and L. Wolfe Gilbert.

Eulogy to Gershwin—the man and composer—was delivered by Hammerstein. Rabbi Edgar F. Magnin also paid tribute to Gershwin's contribution to music. Hammerstein said: "Our friend wrote music, and in that mould he created gaiety and sweetness and beauty. And 24 hours after he was gone his music filled the air and triumphant accents proclaimed to the world of men that gaiety and sweetness and beauty do not die.

"A genius differs from other men only in that his immortality is intangible. What he thought, what he felt, what he meant has been crystallized in a form of expression, a form far sturdier than the flesh and sinew of men. But lesser beings than geniuses leave their marks upon this earth, and it as this lesser being that George Gershwin's friends knew him and loved him.

"We remember a young man who remained naive in a sophisticated world. We remember a smile that was nearly always on his face, a cigar that was nearly always in his mouth. He was a lucky young man, lucky to be so in love with the world, and lucky because the world was so in love with him. It endowed him with talent. It endowed him with character. And, rarest of all things, it gave him a complete capacity for enjoying all his gifts.

"It was a standing joke with us that George could not be dragged away from a piano. He loved to play the piano. He played well and he enjoyed his own playing. How glad we are now that some divine instinct made him snatch every precious second he could get at that keyboard, made him drink exultantly of his joy-giving talent, made him crowd every grain of gratification he could get into his short, blessed life.

"Maybe the greatest thing he left us is this lesson: Maybe we take the good things of life too much for granted. Maybe we took George too much for granted.

"Some will want a statue erected for him. He deserves this. Some will want to endow a school of music in his name. He deserves this. But his friends could add one more tribute in his honor. They could try to appreciate and be grateful for the good things in this world, in his honor. They could try to be kinder to one another—and this would be the finest monument of all."

Honorary ushers were: Louis Alter, J. Kiern Brennan, Sidney Clare, David

Diamond, Dave Dreyer, Gus Edwards, Arthur Freed, Mack Gordon, Lew Pollack, Frederick V. Bowers, Jimmy HcHugh, Albert Von Tilzer, Charles Tobias, Herbert Stothart, Oscar Rasbach, Philip Cohen, Jose Gorney, Gus Kahn, Walter Donaldson, Johnny Green, Sam Coslow, Bernie Grossman, Harry Revel, Ralph Rainger, Sid Silvers, Nathaniel Shilkret, Richard Whiting, R. H. Burnside, Victor Young, Jack Yellen, and Eddie Ward.

72 Arnold Schoenberg: *"George Gershwin"* (1938)

Schoenberg (1874–1951) and Gershwin may seem unlikely colleagues, but they were friends, despite the great different in their ages and their music. Each appreciated something in the other that he knew he did not possess. Many observers were unaware of the depth of their friendship, for along with the Filene family of Boston, Gershwin had helped to secure Schoenberg's passage from Europe when he fled the Nazis in 1933. Once Gershwin settled on the West Coast they resumed their contacts. An even closer friendship was established when the two composers began to share a common passion: tennis. Neighbor Schoenberg was a frequent visitor at the 1019 Roxbury Drive court in Beverly Hills, trekking there to challenge the Gershwin brothers, Harold Arlen, Jerome Kern, or Yip Harburg to a sometimes not-so-friendly game.

Many musicians do not consider George Gershwin a serious composer. But they should understand that, serious or not, he is a composer—that is, a man who lives in music and expresses everything, serious or not, sound or superficial, by means of music, because it is his native language. There are a number of composers, serious (as they believe) or not (as I know), who learned to add notes together. But they are only serious on account of a perfect lack of humor and soul.

It seems to me that this difference alone is sufficient to justify calling the one a composer, but the other none. An artist is to me like an apple tree: When his time comes, whether he wants it or not, he bursts into bloom and starts to produce apples. And as an apple tree neither knows nor asks about the value experts of the market will attribute to its product, so a real composer does not ask whether his products will please the experts of serious arts. He only feels he has to say something; and says it.

It seems to me beyond doubt that Gershwin was an innovator. What he

SOURCE In Merle Armitage, ed., *George Gershwin* (New York: Longmans, Green and Company, 1938), 97–98.

has done with rhythm, harmony and melody is not merely style. It is fundamentally different from the mannerism of many a serious composer. Such mannerism is based on artificial presumptions, which are gained by speculation and are conclusions drawn from the fashions and aims current among contemporary composers at certain times. Such a style is a superficial union of devices applied to a minimum of idea, without any inner reason or cause. Such music could be taken to pieces and put together in a different way, and the result would be the same nothingness expressed by another mannerism. One could not do this with Gershwin's music. His melodies are not products of a combination, nor of a mechanical union, but they are units and could therefore not be taken to pieces. Melody, harmony and rhythm are not welded together, but cast. I do not know it, but I imagine, he improvised them on the piano. Perhaps he gave them later the finishing touch; perhaps he spent much time to go over them again and again—I do not know. But the impression is that of an improvisation with all the merits and shortcomings appertaining to this kind of production. Their effect in this regard might be compared to that of an oration which might disappoint you when you read and examine it as with a magnifying glass—you miss what touched you so much, when you were overwhelmed by the charm of the orator's personality. One has probably to add something of one's own to reestablish the first effect. But it is always that way with art—you get from a work about as much as you are able to give to it yourself.

I do not speak here as a musical theorist, nor am I a critic, and hence I am not forced to say whether history will consider Gershwin a kind of Johann Strauss or Debussy, Offenbach or Brahms, Lehar or Puccini. But I know he is an artist and a composer; he expressed musical ideas; and they were new—as is the way in which he expressed them.

73   Olin Downes: "Hail and Farewell: Career and Position of George Gershwin in American Music" (1937)

Fans and friends, critics and musicians—all were shocked by Gershwin's early death. People, especially those in the music industry, responded by trying to understand and appreciate his importance. Following the paper's reporting of the event, the *New York Times* offered this reflection by its chief music critic, Olin Downes, who had covered every major premiere of Gershwin's career since *Rhapsody in Blue*. He knew Gershwin, and he knew his music.

SOURCE   *New York Times* 86 (July 18, 1937): X, 5.

No other American composer had such a funeral service as that held last Thursday for George Gershwin. Not a MacDowell, not a Chadwick, not a Stephen Foster or Dan Emmett or John Philip Sousa received such parting honors. Authors, editors, playwrights, and critics; national figures of the stage, the screen, the radio, the ballet; celebrated musicians, from Paul Whiteman to Walter Damrosch, composers as well as executants, gathered to say hail and farewell. This was eloquent of the place Gershwin held in the public esteem.

His immense success was due to his own great and indisputable talent and also to the period in American music. Some could read in this success and in the popular support of Gershwin a significant sign of the times. Popularly speaking, at least, Gershwin was the musical man of the hour. His rise to fortune was a Horatio Alger epic of Grand Street. As a boy he lived, played, fought, rose from poverty via the coop of a song-plugger in a music shop to the rank and fortune of the most widely known American composer. In that capacity, at the height of his reputation, he was busily producing, at one and the same time, light operas and orchestral works bid for by famous symphonic organizations. He was a public figure on two sides of the water, and all the concomitants of spectacular success were his.

He also benefited by the fact that metropolitan society was changing its ways, as, indeed, our ideas and manners were changing, the while that the conditions of urban life replaced the prevalently agricultural environment of the American of the former century. The day that saw a singing waiter make millions in music and eventually wed the daughter of a millionaire saw also the metamorphosis of the boy of immigrant parentage into a cosmopolite, who was sought by managers, interviewers, photographers, impresarios—yes, and young women of Park Avenue, who languished and leaned over the piano as George played. All this, and much more, happened to him, in the Babylonic epoch when everybody was so gay and everything so flush and amusing. He relished it, too, in an unbelievably naive and simple way!

Gershwin had precisely the gift to delight and entertain. He was a born melodist, with a native instinct for exotic harmonic effects and the rhythmical ingenuity that usually pertain to musicians of his experience and kind. His way of playing the piano was maddeningly his own. He could never write down his accompaniments as he played them, although the edition of selected songs which appeared some six years ago had affixed to them a series of laughably appropriate embroideries on the melody for the keyed instrument. How original, felicitous and piquant were the best of the songs! How he could hit off verses, preferably by his brother Ira! "Swanee," "Stairway to Paradise," "Sentimental Oriental Gentlemen Are We," "Virginia," "Lady Be Good"—these were inimitable miniatures. It need not be claimed that George had studied the laws of prosody with a scholar's passion. No. But he had the feeling of words, as the vaudevillian values them, and his musical style was the one tonal investiture for Ira's texts.

There is no need now to expatiate upon the details of the *Rhapsody in Blue,* but its consequences were many. One of them, which may not have worked out for the composer's best good, was that well-meaning critics and musical friends talked earnestly with George, and found him more than willing to attempt serious, even symphonic composition. He had shown that he could write a theme susceptible of symphonic treatment, granting that he could summon the necessary technique and structural power—a thing that he was not completely able to do. At the same time, he had shown dazzling possibilities in a new and original treatment of the outworn form of the piano concerto.

It is said that when Gershwin accepted the order of Damrosch and the New York Symphony to write a concerto in three movements he went out and bought a textbook to find out what a concerto was! He made an astonishingly good attempt at the big form. It is a technical growth, but not a creative evolution. Essentially Gershwin sang one song. It is of the city, the music hall, the mechanical age. Granted poetry in the concerto's slow movement: it is the peace of the twilight outside the stage door. The doorkeeper puffs his cigar in the hot summer evening, he sees blue and yellow electric lights, hears the echoes of the street, and the hum of the approaching elevated. It is city music, topical music, free of introspection or problems, written in a gay, thoughtless decade. It is sensuous, amorous and of a racy idiom, but it unfolds no broader horizon.

The best of the other orchestral works was undoubtedly *An American in Paris,* with the exhilarating hilarity of the "walking themes," and the unity of the impression augmented by amusing and personally devised instrumentation. The composition gets no farther than the earlier works; it reveals no new artistic or emotional ground. Gershwin strove in certain compositions toward the higher realms of composition. He looked into the promised land, and pointed a way—one way—that a greater musician might follow.

As it was, he displayed the immense virtues of his defects as a crafts man, his lack of musical background, his youthful ignorance of symphonic usage and tradition, and the environment which fortunately was not that of a standardized institution of musical learning, following with comfortable routine the century-old traditions of other lands and peoples than ours. Gershwin was free of that. He talked, musically speaking, the language that his countrymen and generation knew.

This, admittedly, was a dialect used by the less cultured of the populace, but it was a patois that everyone understood, and one upon which a creative artist could genuinely build. Gershwin used the idiom in his own way. Others, such as Henry F. Gilbert and John Alden Carpenter, had approached the same issue through the medium of grander forms and complicated style. They were not widely understood. Gershwin was far enough from the bottom and near to the top to foreshadow an era that will spring from the people and sublimate their expression, but in a way that reflects the individuality of the thinker and artist.

No doubt Gershwin was materially aided in his career by the intense desire of his countrymen to see something of that sort happen in the development of an American music. It is also to be remembered that at least until the turn of the century few Americans took the study or cultivation of good music seriously. The man in the street passed Carnegie Hall distrustfully. A chap that composed was likely to be a "high-brow" or sissified, or both. The general popular acceptance, and indeed astonishing enthusiasm for great music by Bach and Wagner and Debussy and Strauss, to say nothing of a Bloch or Sibelius or Stravinsky, is a very recent thing. It was only in Gershwin's generation that the American people as a whole took with ardor to good music. He came on the scene just at the time to be a connecting link between the "serious" and "popular" composers of America. It was a highly desirable development. And here is a point for consideration: the process, too often imitative, with our schooled composers, of imitating foreign models, versus another process, which is one of normal growth through creative energy and power of assimilation, on the part of our most gifted composers of light music. The conservatory student kneels before Mozart, Beethoven, Brahms, Wagner, Schumann, or Strauss and it will be hard, indeed, for him to proceed in his work independently of these models.

But the man in Tin Pan Alley, of meager technical knowledge at best, writes the melody that comes into his head, writes to please. While he is doing that there comes into his ear a chord he has heard in a work by a classic master, and he finds he can profitably incorporate that progression in one of his songs. He does not imitate, he absorbs. The chances are all for the composer who grows upward rather than for the gentleman who condescendingly holds out a hand to people outside his circle, and who seems to fear anything savoring of common expressions. But they are good for native art. Doubtless the author of the *Rhapsody in Blue* was overrated, just as he and his ilk had in preceding days been grossly and snobbishly undervalued. It may soberly be said that the *Rhapsody in Blue* has had a strong and lasting influence for the good upon American composers.

They do tell the very amusing story, which can perfectly well be true, of

Gershwin's asking Stravinsky to teach him composition, whereas Stravinsky is supposed to have asked, blandly, "What is your income per year?" When Gershwin, somewhat embarrassed, said he supposed it was in the neighborhood of $100,000 per annum, Stravinsky said, "Then I think you'd better teach me composition!" We shall certainly expose ourselves to contumely when we say that we would prefer one of the representative Gershwin's songs to many of the later compositions of Igor Stravinsky. This despite the fact that Stravinsky almost invariably succeeds in putting down on paper what he wants there, thus carrying out to the last tone his musical conception. Gershwin could not do this, perhaps could not even harbor a conception that would require vast skill to realize. It remains that, as Debussy said, there is one music, which may inhabit a waltz or a symphony. Gershwin was in rapport much of the time, and in his own way, with that magic. Sometimes he conveyed it in a way that made him a pioneer of importance. This writer finds his expression limited, emotionally, imaginatively, stylistically. It is fundamentally popular music, jazz music and music which has intrigued the whole world. This writer has had jazz scraped and blared into his face in Tiflis. It is a music of a new color and it has given to the art new energy. Its elementary structures of jazz, its banalities, its defects in any amount you please, do not stultify its vitality and its wide appeal. It gained a new consideration with Gershwin, and Gershwin, in turn, contributed individual genius to the form. When the tumult and shouting are over—and already they are subsiding—he will have a secure place in the American tonal art.

74   Irving Berlin: "Poem" (1938)

Gershwin's mentor, composer-lyricist Irving Berlin (1888–1988), penned the following poem on the occasion of the memorial services after Gershwin's death.

> I could speak of a Whiteman rehearsal
> At the old Palais Royal when Paul
> Played the Rhapsody that lifted Gershwin
> From the "Alley" to Carnegie Hall.
> I could dwell on the talent that placed him
> In the class where he justly belongs,

SOURCE In Merle Armitage, ed., *George Gershwin* (New York: Longmans, Green and Company, 1938), 78.

But this verse is a songwriter's tribute
To a man who wrote wonderful songs.

His were tunes that had more than just rhythm,
For just rhythm will soon gather "corn,"
And those melodies written by Gershwin
Are as fresh now as when they were born.
As a writer of serious music,
He could dream for a while in the stars,
And step down from the heights of Grand Opera
To a chorus of thirty-two bars.

And this morning's Variety *tells me*
That the last song he wrote is a hit,
It's on top in the list of best sellers,
And the air-waves are ringing with it.
It remains with the dozens of others,
Though the man who composed them is gone;
For a songwriter's job may be ended,
But his melodies linger on.

75 Jerome Kern: "Tribute" (1938)

Like Berlin's piece, Jerome Kern's brief reflection was written soon after
Gershwin's death. Perhaps no one was a greater influence on Gershwin
than Kern (1885–1945), who was like a musical father figure for the
younger composer.

There never was anything puny or insignificant about the life, work, or opinions of George Gershwin.

He lived, labored, played, exulted, and suffered with bigness and gusto. It
was some other contemporary, definitely *not* George, who was the subject of
Thomas Mann's observation, "Why does he make himself so little? Surely, he
is not that big."

There is not much that this unpracticed pen can add to the volumes
already written in critical survey of George's work; yet one utterance may be
recorded which came from the heart of the man and is illustrative of his

SOURCE In Merle Armitage, ed., *George Gershwin* (New York: Longmans, Green and Company, 1938), 120.

stature. It came at the crossroads of his career, long after his dissatisfaction with Broadway musical comedy; even after he had unfolded his pinions and lifted himself into the realm of serious music: "Do you think," he asked with naïveté, "that now I am capable of grand opera? Because, you know," he continued, "all I've got is a lot of talent and plenty of *chutzpah*."

It was then that these ears realized that they were listening to a man touched with greatness.

76   *"Gershwin Left $341,089 Estate to His Mother; 'Rhapsody in Blue' Appraised at 'Greatest Value' and Opera Rights of 'Nominal Interest' to the Residue"* (1938)

George Gershwin, the late Broadway composer who is said to have done more to direct the trend of American music than any other composer, left a gross estate of $430,841 and a net estate of $341,089, according to a transfer-tax appraisal filed yesterday in Surrogates' Court. Mr. Gershwin died on July 11, 1937, in Hollywood, following an emergency operation for the removal of a brain tumor. He was thirty-eight years old.

The residuary value of his musical works, which ranged from Tin Pan Alley songs to *Rhapsody in Blue*, was appraised at $50,125. This value, according to the appraisal papers, was based on earnings derived by the company from his works during the five years preceding his death.

The residuary value of *Rhapsody in Blue* was appraised at $20,000. According to an affidavit by A. M. Wattenberg, music publishing company official, this was rated "as the outstanding work of the decedent and is of the greatest value to the estate."[1] His score of *An American in Paris* was appraised for residuary value at $5,000; *Of Thee I Sing*, $4,000, and his *Concerto in F*, written for the New York Symphony Society in 1925 at $1,750.

The appraisal papers listed as of only "nominal interest" to the estate the performing rights in his opera, *Porgy and Bess*, which the Theater Guild brought to New York in 1935. Henry W. Spitzer, of the music publishing firm of Chappell & Co., said in an affidavit that separate compositions written for the opera probably will sell in small quantities for years. The volumes of the score were valued at $20.

SOURCE   *New York Herald Tribune* (September 27, 1938).
    1 Files from the Wattenburg firm are in DLC [GC].

"If You Want 'Em, You Can't Get 'Em," composed by Mr. Gershwin with Murray Roth in 1916, was described as probably the composer's first published song. "It never had any demand" the affidavit said, and was published solely to give the composers "a little boost."

Mr. Gershwin had taxable insurance and cash in banks in New York and California amounting to $228,811, of which $122,427 represented bank accounts. He owned $141,615 in securities, chief among them being $41,271 in United States Treasury notes. Funeral and administration expenses were $50,941, and debts, $38,810.

The composer died intestate, and his mother, Mrs. Rose Gershwin, of 25 Central Park West, was listed as the sole beneficiary.

77   *Ira Gershwin: Letter to Rose Gershwin (1937)*

Forming an epilogue to George's last letter to his mother (see selection 69), Ira's notes here are poignant and sad, written from the perspective of the survivor having to face the world he has known in a wholly new way.

July 31, 1937

Dear Mom,

The trip was very smooth—in fact, I actually slept for five hours.[1]

As you can imagine, I've been kept busy every minute. The first thing to settle was the Memorial Concert. There were two groups working against each other, one—the ASCAP which wanted to run one at the Shrine Auditorium—the proceeds to go to a scholarship fund—the other group was the Hollywood Bowl organization which wanted the proceeds of their concert to go to themselves as there is usually a deficit at the end of the season just as at the Lewisohn Stadium. I knew that two concerts within a couple of weeks of each other would be at cross purposes so I told the various committees they ought to try to get together this way: that ASCAP hire the Hollywood Bowl and the Los Angeles Symphony and run the entire concert and the Bowl organization cooperate and get 25% of the proceeds for their deficit. So far they have bowed to my judgment in every respect and I'm hoping there will be no more trouble.

The *Goldwyn Follies* is something else again. My understanding was that I'd come out here and work from 4 to 6 weeks trying to dig up possible tunes

SOURCE DLC [GC].
    1 Ira is referring to his trip back to the West Coast following Gershwin's funeral in New York.

from those George left behind to finish the score. Well, it now develops that Goldwyn thought he was hiring Duke to help *me* finish the score and that he doesn't want to pay any more money than he has to. Yesterday I gave Duke a lead sheet of a waltz of George's to go ahead with for a dance that Balanchine wanted. Today I called Duke and explained the situation and he agreed not to work on the waltz, but would put in one of his own.[2]

As you probably know, George and I signed a contract as a *team*, so that when George was through I was through. Goldwyn wants me to come to work Monday to help Balanchine and Duke on an idea for the opening. I told Lyons to ask for at least two weeks' guarantee for me, but I couldn't even get that. His (Goldwyn's) attitude is that I ought to be able to finish it in a week—if it takes longer or if there is any other work to be done, *he* wants to be the judge and at the moment he won't guarantee anything. What I imagine has happened is that he is not ready with his book, also that the actors' salaries start in a week or so and the picture is going to cost him much more than he bargained for, and he has come to a realization that he may not need any new songs because after all most pictures do not have more than five songs (which he already has). So I'll probably go to see him, but frankly I've found him a great disappointment, to put it mildly, and personally I don't care if I go on with it at all, but I'll keep you informed if anything happens. Incidentally, when he told Lyons he was worried about the *American in Paris* because the ballet that was rehearsing seemed to be too highbrow, Lyons gladly released him from the agreement because he (Lyons) felt more money could be had for the work some future day.

I packed a trunk with suits, shoes, etc. and will send it by freight Monday. You'll probably get it in two weeks. The gold cigarette case, Paul tells me, is in the warehouse along with the two silver articles with the signatures on them. You will also find in the trunk about 50 photographs which you can distribute to those of your friends who desire them.

Sunday, August 1st.

Because of constant interruptions, I couldn't finish this letter yesterday.

Friday I spoke with Marshall Taylor on the telephone and he will cooperate with Alexander and Rosenthal and help them in any course they think best. Paul [Mueller] is staying on for the month of August. Naturally I am trying to cut down expenses but I didn't want to let Paul go just at this minute.

---

2 Duke is Vladimir Dukelsky or Vernon Duke, composer of "April in Paris" and other song hits. (See selection 80.)

Also I sent my usual monthly checks to Grandma, Aunt Mary, and Barney. Vincente Minnelli is through at Paramount and leaves for New York sometime the coming week. I'll give him the key to the trunk and a few trinkets, which he will deliver to you, as I don't want them lost in the mails.

Well, Mom, this is about all I can think of at the moment. My love to you and keep well. Don't worry about things but try to have a good time. Love to Frankie and Arthur and remember me to the rest of the family.

Leonore, Lou, and Emily send their love.

I.

VIII. AS TIME PASSES

Because Gershwin's music has remained a potent force throughout the twentieth and into the twenty-first century, most musicians and composers of his time and since have had something to say about him. Some of the more notable and revealing essays follow.

78   *"Music by Slide Rule"* (1944)

The following article represents a sly attack on Gershwin's fitness as a composer. It claims essentially that via his study of Schillinger's "method" Gershwin was able to discover some sort of magic formula or a crutch by which he could continue to compose. It implies that he could not have done so otherwise and that by using this method, he wrote music of a lesser quality. Ira Gershwin's pointed response in the following entry in this volume serves as rebuttal enough.

At a composer's conference at the New School for Social Research a few years ago, a Russian named Joseph Schillinger demonstrated his theories of composition by playing a new work of his own. Of what style, he asked his listeners, did the piece seem reminiscent? After hearing that it had been inspired by everybody from Mozart to Debussy, he told his audience that he had converted into music a newspaper graph of Wall Street stock prices. The same thing, he told his fellow composers, could be done with telephone numbers or the silhouette of the Manhattan skyline—it was simply a matter of mathematics.

"My belief," Schillinger once wrote, "is that because music has been created by intuitive or trial-and-error method and there has never been any scientific investigation of the resources, there is more new unexploited material in forms in music than in any other field subjected to scientific investigation. More is known about the weather than about music."

Following this belief, Schillinger approached music as a pure science. He drew graphs of passages by Bach, Mozart, Beethoven, and Wagner to determine whether reason or whimsy had dictated their compositions. He decided in favor of reason. He then proceeded to expand and systematize their procedures, feeling that the composers had arrived at them by coincidence and that their fullest possibilities had never been explored.

Schillinger also applied these scientific principles to art. He designed combinations of geometric figures, proportions, and color so successfully that he

SOURCE *Newsweek* 24 (September 24, 1944): 80–82.

was offered a job as textile designer. A fastidious dresser, he applied the same ideas to his clothes. From the skin out, he matched in color harmony. Beyond this, and the fact that he was an avid mountain climber, little else is known about Schillinger the man. The Schillinger System was almost his whole life.

He proved his pudding commercially. George Gershwin, for example, came to Schillinger in desperation. He had written hundreds of songs; he feared he had run dry. From Schillinger he got what he needed: innumerable new combinations and uses for the same old notes. *Porgy and Bess* was written during his Schillinger period—a three-lesson-a-week, four-and-a-half-year study which ended only at Gershwin's death in 1937.[1]

Other Schillinger students ranged from the tall, scholarly Rt. Rev. Msgr. L.H. Bracken (former conductor of the Catholic Diocesan Choristers of Brooklyn), to the short, jazzy Toots Mondello. Lyn Murray and Paul Lavalle from radio were also followers, as were Benny Goodman and Glenn Miller, who, incidentally, wrote "Moonlight Serenade" as a Schillinger exercise. To those who had to produce compositions and arrangements fast and in quantity, the Schillinger System was a boon. The permutations of some note combination like D, E, G, A turned out to be endless. Those that sounded like a rusty riveting machine could simply be thrown out.

But Schillinger died in 1943. What he had taught personally (at $10 a half hour) was left up to seven authorized teachers who included Jess Crawford, the organist, and Ted Royal, one of Broadway's best-known arrangers. There was ample evidence last week, though, that his name will not be forgotten for some time. In Cleveland, where the newly organized Society for Aesthetics met as a part of the huge convention of the American Association for the Advancement of Science, Dr. Jerome Gross, a prominent Cleveland surgeon, concert violinist, and disciple of Schillinger, gave a brief memorial on his late teacher's work.

And in New York, where other Schillinger pupils were making plans for a Schillinger Society, the composer-mathematician's estate revealed that Carl Fischer, Inc., was publishing a two-volume set of the Schillinger System.[2] To come out in the early part of 1945, the set will sell at $30. Whether it will eventually revolutionize music—as zealots claim—is a question. Whether it can help you, too, to become a composer with the aid of a slide rule is also a moot point. But that's what you pay your $30 for.

---

1 Gershwin had stopped studying with Schillinger well before his death—probably in mid-1936, prior to his departure for the West Coast.

2 See Joseph Schillinger, *The Schillinger System of Musical Composition*, 2 vols. (New York: Carl Fischer, 1941–1942). The set was reprinted in an edition by Lyle Dowling and Arthur Shaw in 1978.

79 Ira Gershwin: *"Gershwin on Gershwin"* (1944)

In direct response to the previous *Newsweek* piece, Ira Gershwin strives to set to rest the claims that his brother George was somehow lacking in inspiration following his early successes. His studies with Joseph Schillinger (like his taking up painting a few years previously) were not an attempt to restart a compositional energy that had run dry; more probably Gershwin turned to Schillinger (as he did to other diversions) as a means to develop his technique, a point Vernon Duke also takes up in selection 80.

In *Newsweek*, September 25 [1944], the Schillinger System is discussed. I have nothing against the system.

But I do object to a couple of the writer's statements. When he says "George Gershwin, for example, came to Schillinger in desperation. He had written hundreds of songs; he feared he had run dry," he goes in for a stratospheric flight of musical fancy. I collaborated with my brother, on and off, for some twenty years and never did he (or I, or anyone else, for that matter) feel he had "run dry."

Certainly my brother was a pupil of Schillinger's. He had an unquenchable thirst for study and undoubtedly learned a good deal from the system. But if the writer of the article wished to give the impression that *Porgy and Bess* wouldn't have had quite the same value or integrity or acclaim if George hadn't studied, say, "Rhythmic Groups Resulting From the Interference of Several Synchronized Periodicities" with Schillinger, he's musically misinformed. Lessons like these unquestionably broaden musical horizons, but they don't inspire an opera like *Porgy and Bess* or a symphonic piece like *Concerto in F.*

80 Vernon Duke: *"Gershwin, Schillinger, and Dukelsky: Some Reminiscences"* (1947)

Composer Vernon Duke, né Vladimir Dukelsky (1903–1969), was Gershwin's peer in several ways. Both were of Russian-Jewish heritage, both Americanized their names, both wrote art music as well as popular music, and both studied with Joseph Schillinger. Gershwin's friend Duke offers

SOURCE (79) *Newsweek* 24 (October 23, 1944): 14.

SOURCE (80) *Musical Quarterly* 33 (January 1947): 102–15. The article contains the following footnote at its beginning: " 'Vernon Duke' is the pseudonym used by Vladimir Dukelsky for his works in a lighter vein." Apparently Gershwin had suggested this to him.

reminiscences that thus contain more authority than anyone else's regarding the role of Schillinger and his method in Gershwin's compositional
development.[1]

Beginning with the *Piano Concerto* commissioned by Walter Damrosch,
Gershwin was on his own as an orchestrator. There are still a good many
doubting Thomases who claim that this work and *An American in Paris* were
orchestrated by Daly, Grofé, or "a host of other experts." Along with several
others, I can vouch for the fact that, except for musical comedy scores,
George orchestrated every note he wrote after the *Rhapsody*.

What was George's orchestration like in those pre-Schillinger days? Brilliant in spots, adequate in others, but on the whole top-heavy and with too
much doubling and padding. Both the Concerto and the overlong *American in
Paris* contain much sparkling sound, and even some pretty dazzling fireworks
(inspired by Ravel and early Stravinsky), yet the overall effect is not altogether
what the composer intended. The music itself was partly to blame; the
themes sounded like 32-bar choruses bridged together with neo-Lisztian passages; of real thematic development there was but little, and the codas were
either too lengthy or too abrupt. These youthful faults were less noticeable in
the *Rhapsody*, but only because Gershwin had been less preoccupied there
with workmanship and construction, not because its material was more
spontaneous, as is generally believed. The themes of the two later works,
both melodically and harmonically, are richer and more pungently Gersh-
winesque than those used in the *Rhapsody*.

Gershwin's trouble was the well-known "growing pains." His material
was proving too overpowering and taxing for the limitations of hastily
acquired technique; the legendary Gershwin facility was getting to be somewhat of a boomerang. His 1926 trip to Paris was a rich if bewildering experience. George met Ravel, Stravinsky, Milhaud, Poulenc, and Auric and made
quite a stir—particularly with Ravel, who adored his piano playing. Wiener
and Doucet played the *Rhapsody* with a worse than mediocre Paris orchestra
whose idea of jazz was the Folies Bergère.

I took Serge Diaghilev to a gala concert conducted by Vladimir Golschmann at which Dimitri Tiomkin played the Gershwin *Concerto*. Diaghilev,
who was eager to add an American ballet to the Ballet Russe repertory, was
distinctly disappointed, and so was Prokofieff, to whose home I brought

---

1 Numerous attempts have been made to discern Schillinger's influence on Gershwin's compositions.
For a rigorous and useful analysis, see Paul Nauert, "Theory and Practice in *Porgy and Bess*: The Gershwin-
Schillinger Connection," *Musical Quarterly* 78 (Spring 1994): 9–33.

Gershwin the next day. "His piano playing is full of amusing tricks, but the music is amateurish," was Prokofieff's stern verdict. Gershwin's success in London was more pronounced. He was already favorably known there as the composer of *Primrose, Tell Me More*, and *Lady, Be Good!* and his salon successes recalled those of Thalberg and Liszt in the previous century.

Gershwin, with his top-notch material and awkward groping to give it shape, couldn't help realizing his shortcomings. "The European boys have small ideas but they sure know how to dress 'em up," George admitted to me after listening to a virtuoso piece by Honegger.

On his return to the U.S.A., George was teeming with musical projects. I am not familiar with the circumstances that led to the choice of *Porgy and Bess* as a libretto for George's first and only opera. He once wrote a one-act melodrama called *135th Street*, full of blues and spirituals, for an all-colored cast. This was an early and rather crude effort although it contained much good stuff. George was always admired by the Negroes and had a special understanding and liking for them. When he sang at his piano, his full lips and the peculiarly strident "reedy" quality of his voice, plus the acrobatic goings-on on the keys, gave his performance a curiously Negroid quality. Spirituals and blues held an enduring fascination for Gershwin, particularly as stage material. Before he met Schillinger, we held interminable nocturnal discussions on the subject of the proposed opera. George was still under the sway of the Wagnerian formula, which I held—and still hold—to be completely anti-theatrical. I insisted on the old Italian approach, with separate numbers, duets, trios, and ensembles. What emerged was a distinct compromise; it is generally acknowledged that the separate numbers are superior to the somewhat amorphous stretches of music that hold them together.

Gershwin did not go to Schillinger for the purpose of getting him to help with *Porgy*. George met Schillinger through Joseph Achron, the late composer and violinist, and apparently what he was then seeking was fresh vistas, which would enable him to write fresher songs. It was Schillinger's impression that Gershwin was at the end of his very short rope as a technician—not as a composer.

Shortly afterwards, on visiting Gershwin in his Riverside Drive apartment at 75th Street, I found the piano and the writing table cluttered up with exercises dictated by Schillinger. George, who always resembled a child with a new toy—he took an amazing delight in the simplest pleasures and discoveries—now finally had found a toy that was real fun and would also yield great dividends, an unheard-of combination. I was pretty skeptical at first, when confronted with pitch scales, units, etc. These terms had an anti-musical sound and meant nothing to my unmathematical ear. George was indignant

at my skepticism. "You just don't understand," said he. "I used to do all kinds
of things—harmony and counterpoint, I mean—did them correctly, too, but
didn't even know what I was doing! It was pure instinct and—well, I guess,
some talent!" That last remark was pure Gershwin. "Why, I once wrote a
whole 32-bar chorus in canon and if someone told me it was a canon I'd
laugh right in his face. Remember the scale tune?" The scale tune was one of
George's lesser songs which was particularly dear to him because you could
play the whole E-flat major scale to it in counterpoint six times, and wind up
with the lowest notes of the piano at the end of the chorus. "You see, I never
knew why I was doing all these things—I thought they were just parlor tricks.
They always went great at parties. Now they'll go right into my music!" continued George excitedly. One day he played the ingenious "crap game" fugue
from *Porgy*, his face beaming: "Get this—Gershwin writing fugues. What will
the boys say now?"

"The boys" could be divided into two separate groups. The first group
consisted of the "lowbrows" of the Broadway stage and song publishers' ret-
inues. The second group—almost entirely hostile—was composed of musicians and writers of modern music who were patronizing at best and openly
scornful as a rule. Both groups, with some dissenters, had one idea in common. They felt that George should stay on Broadway, and regarded his
Carnegie Hall escapades with suspicion or somewhat prejudiced curiosity.

His studies with Schillinger and the successful completion of the *Porgy and
Bess* score caused the raising of the "highbrows" eyebrows. To the "lowbrows" the very words "Grand Opera"—by which strange term all operatic
composition is still known in our country—were like the end of their world,
and a plunge into the deep and frightening beyond.

I went to Boston with George for the tryout. At the orchestra rehearsal he
beamed with delight at the well-organized sounds that emerged from the pit.
I was sitting quietly in a seat in the last row of the orchestra when George
startled me by suddenly appearing from the back and grabbing me by the
shoulder. "Get this!" he whispered fiercely. "Just listen to those overtones!"
The overtones were there all right, but what was infinitely more important,
clear orchestral writing was there too. The tunes we all listened to around
George's piano—"Summertime," "It Ain't Necessarily So," "I Got Plenty of
Nuttin'," were now clothed in appropriate orchestral garb and shone with a
new and dazzling brilliance. The "Schillinger slavery" brought an unexpected
freedom to George's musical utterances. The critics in New York, both musical and dramatic, wrote at great length but not too enthusiastically about the
overstuffed Guild production, falling between two schools, etc. Again the
"lowbrows" and the "highbrows" found themselves agreeing—they all loved

the songs, and weren't so sure about the recitatives and the stretches of incidental music. But George knew. The opera was there and the music was
right—not only in subject matter but also in presentation. That *Porgy* has
come to stay was proved but recently. Some cuts and livelier stage direction
helped, although Gershwin would have winced at the inexplicably fast tempos. Gershwin and his teacher Schillinger—who both died in their
prime—were vindicated posthumously.

Another Schillinger-inspired work, almost completely unknown today
(and it certainly descries a speedy revival) is the witty variations on "I Got
Rhythm" for piano and orchestra, containing a number of devices recommended by Schillinger and deftly and ingeniously applied.

Gershwin's case illustrates the evolution of a splendidly gifted songwriter
into an accomplished and resourceful composer. His example is a significant
lesson to his songwriting contemporaries. Not every songwriter has the stuff
of a composer in him—and a good many won't bother about finding out.

81 Leonard Bernstein: "Why Don't You Run Upstairs and Write a Nice Gershwin Tune?" (1955)

Probably no commentary by another composer has done more to shape
the posthumous view of Gershwin than Leonard Bernstein's musing here,
which he cast in the form of a dialogue between himself and a professional
manager. Bernstein (1918–1990) not only struggles with the many similari-
ties between himself and Gershwin, he uses Gershwin's example for a
cathartic effect, as his subsequent compositional activities demonstrated.

*(Through the windows of the English Grill in Radio City we can see the ice skaters
milling about on the rink, inexplicably avoiding collision with one another. One cannot look at them for more than a few seconds, so dazzling are they as they whirl and
plummet in the white winter sunlight.*

*The shirred eggs are gone from our plates, and the second cup of coffee offers the
momentary escape from the necessity of conversation. My lunch date with PM is one
of those acid-forming events born of the New York compulsion to have lunch with
one's business associates, at all costs, "sometime," as if the mere act of eating
together for ninety minutes were guaranteed to cement any and all relations, however
tenuous.*

PM is what is known in the trade as a Professional Manager, that unlucky soul

SOURCE Leonard Bernstein, *The Joy of Music* (New York: Simon & Schuster, 1978), 52–62.

whose job it is to see that the music published by his firm actually gets played. This involves his knowing, more or less intimately, an army of musical performers and some composers. He must once have been a large man, I think; powerful and energetic. He must have had young ideas and ideals. He must have gloried in his close associa-tion with the giants of the golden age of popular song-writing. But the long years have wearied him and have reduced his ideas to formulas, his ideals to memories, his persuasive powers to palliatives. Still, he knows and loves two generation's worth of American popular music, and this gives him his warmth, his zeal, his function in life. I like him.

But why has he asked me to lunch? We have ranged all the immediately available subjects, and I feel there must be something in particular he wants to bring up, and can't. Everyone in the Grill seems to be talking, earnestly or gaily; only we remain chained to an axis of interest terminating at one pole in the skating rink and at the other in a cup of coffee. Again the skaters: back to the coffee. Compulsively, I break the silence.)

LB: How's business? *(This is inane, but he looks up gratefully. It must have helped somehow.)*

PM: Business? Well, you know. Sheet music doesn't sell the way it did in the old days. It's all records now. The publisher isn't so much a publisher any more. He's an agent. Printing is the least—

LB *(Climbing on with excessive eagerness)*: But that ought to make good busi-ness, oughtn't it? The main thing is owning the music, the rights—

PM: Sure; but owning the music doesn't guarantee that we sell it. Take the music from your new show, for instance.

LB *(To himself)*: So this is why he's invited me to lunch. But pretend inno-cence. *(Aloud):* What about the show?

PM *(Kindly)*: How's it going?

LB *(As though this were just another subject)*: Fine. I caught it two nights ago. Seemed as fresh as ever.

PM *(Carefully)*: Very, very strange about that show of yours. It's a big suc-cess, the public enjoys it, it's been running for five months, and there's not a hit in it. How do you explain it?

(The bomb has dropped. The pulse has quickened.)

LB: How do *I* explain it? Isn't that your job to know? You're the man who sells the songs to the public. A hit depends on a good selling job. Don't ask me. I'm just the poor old composer.

PM: Now don't get excited. If you had been in this business as long as I have, you'd know that there are two sides to everything. There's no point in laying the blame here or there. A hit is the result of a combination of things: a good song, a good singer to launch it, thorough exploitation, and lucky timing. We can't always have all of them together. Now in your case we've made one of our biggest efforts. I can't remember when we've—

LB: All right, I get it. You just weren't handed good material. I don't need a map. I don't write commercial songs, that's all. Why don't you tear up my contract?

PM: Really, LB, you are in a state of gloom today. I didn't ask you to lunch to upset you. We all want to do our best for that score; it's to our mutual advantage. I just thought we might talk a bit about it, quietly and constructively, and maybe come up with something that might—

LB: I'm sorry. I'm somewhat sensitive about it. It's just that it would be nice to hear someone accidentally whistle something of mine, somewhere, just once.

PM: It's understandable.

LB: And I thought there were at least three natural hits in the show. You never hear the songs on the radio or on TV; there are a few forgotten recordings; one is on Muzak, I believe. It's a little depressing, you must admit.

PM: Now come on. Think of all the composers who don't have hits, and don't have hit shows either. You're a lucky boy, you know, and you shouldn't complain. Not everyone can write "Booby Hatch" and sell a million records in a month. Why, I remember George always used to say—

LB: George who?

PM: Gershwin, of course. What other George is there?

LB: Ah, but now you're talking about a man who really had the magic touch. Gershwin made hits, I don't know how. Some people do it all the time, like breathing. I don't know.

PM *(Plunging in)*: Well, now that you mention it, it might not be a bad idea for you to give a little thought now and then to these things. Learn a little from George. Your songs are simply too arty, that's all. You try too hard to make them what you would call "interesting." That's not for the public, you know. A special little dissonant effect in the bass may make *you* happy, and maybe some of your highbrow friends; but it doesn't help to make a hit. You're too wrapped up in unusual chords and odd skips in the tune and screwy forms. That's all only an amusing game you play with yourself. George didn't worry about all that. He wrote tunes, dozens of them, simple tunes that the world could sing and remember and want to sing again. He wrote for people, not for critics. You just have to learn how to be simple, my boy.

LB: You think it's so simple to be simple? Not at all. I've tried hard for years. After all, this isn't the first time I'm hearing this lecture. A few weeks ago a serious composer-friend and I were talking about all this, and we got boiling mad about it. Why shouldn't we be able to come up with a hit, we said, if the standard is as low as it seems to be? We decided that all we had to do was to put ourselves into the mental state of an idiot and write a ridiculous hillbilly tune. So we went to work, sure we could make thousands by simply being simple-minded. We worked for an hour and then gave up in hysterical despair. Impossible. We found ourselves being "personal" and "expressing selves"; and try as we might, we couldn't seem to boil any music down to the feeble-minded level we had set ourselves. I remember that at one point we were trying like two children, one note at a time, to make a tune that didn't even require any harmony, it would be that obvious. Impossible. It was a revealing experiment, I must say, even though it left us with a slightly doomed feeling. As I say, why don't you tear up my contract? *(I drain the already empty coffee cup.)*

PM *(With a touch of the basketball coach)*: Doom, nothing. I'll bet my next week's salary that you can write simple tunes if you really put your mind to it. And not with another composer, but all by yourself. After all, George was just like you, highbrow, one foot in Carnegie Hall and the other in Tin Pan Alley. He wrote concert music too, and was all wound up in fancy harmony and counterpoint and orchestration. He just knew when to be simple and when not to be.

LB: No, I think you're wrong. Gershwin was a whole other man. No connection at all.

PM: You're only being modest, or pretending to be. Didn't that critic after your last show call you a second Gershwin, or a budding Gershwin, or something?

LB *(Secretly flattered)*: That's all in the critic's mind. Nothing to do with facts. Actually Gershwin and I came from opposite sides of the tracks, and if we meet anywhere at all it's in my love for his music. But there it ends. Gershwin was a songwriter who grew into a serious composer. I am a serious composer trying to be a songwriter. His was by far the more normal way: starting with small forms and blossoming out from there. My way is more confused: I wrote a symphony before I ever wrote a popular song. How can you expect me to have that simple touch that he had?

PM *(Paternally)*: But George—did you know him, by the way?

LB: I wish I had. He died when I was just a kid in Boston.

PM *(A star in his eye)*: If you had met him you would have known that George was every inch a serious composer. Why look at the *Rhapsody in Blue,* the *American in—*

LB: Now PM, you know as well as I do that the *Rhapsody* is not a composition at all. It's a string of separate paragraphs stuck together—with a thin paste of flour and water. Composing is a very different thing from writing tunes, after all. I find that the themes, or tunes, or whatever you want to call them, in the *Rhapsody* are terrific—inspired, God-given. At least four of them, which is a lot for a twelve-minute piece. They are perfectly harmonized, ideally proportioned, songful, clear, rich, moving. The rhythms are always right. The "quality" is always there, just as it is in his best show-tunes. But you can't just put four tunes together, God-given though they may be, and call them a composition. Composition means a putting together, yes; but a putting together of elements so that they add up to an organic whole. *Compono, componere—*

PM: Spare us the Latin. You can't mean that the *Rhapsody in Blue* is not an organic work! Why, in its every bar it breathes the same thing, throughout all its variety and all its change of mood and tempo. It breathes America: the people, the urban society that George knew deeply, the pace, the nostalgia, the nervousness, the majesty, the—

LB:—the Tchaikovsky sequences, the Debussy meanderings, the Lisztian piano-fireworks. It's as American as you please while the themes are going on; but the minute a little thing called development is called for, America goes out the window and Tchaikovsky and his friends march in the door. And the trouble is that a composition *lives* in its development.

PM: I think I need some more coffee. Waiter!

LB: Me too. I didn't mean to get started on all this, and he's my idol too, remember. I don't think there has been such an inspired melodist on this earth since Tchaikovsky, if you want to know what I really feel. I rank him right up there with Schubert and the great ones. But if you want to speak of a *composer*, that's another matter. Your *Rhapsody in Blue* is not a real composition in the sense that whatever happens in it must seem inevitable, or even pretty inevitable. You can cut out parts of it without affecting the whole in any way except to make it shorter. You can remove any of these stuck-together sections and the piece still goes on as bravely as before. You can even interchange these sections with one another and no harm done. You can make cuts within a section, or add new cadenzas, or play it with any combination of instruments or on the piano alone; it can be a five-minute piece or a six-minute piece or a twelve-minute piece. And in fact all these things are being done to it every day. It's still the *Rhapsody in Blue.*

PM: But look here, that sounds to me like the biggest argument yet in its favor. If a piece is so sturdy that whatever you do to it has no effect on its intrinsic nature, then it must be pretty healthy. There must be something there that resists pressure, something that is real and alive, wouldn't you say?

LB: Of course there is: those tunes. Those beautiful tunes. But they still don't add up to a piece.

PM: Perhaps you're right in a way about the *Rhapsody*. It was an early work, after all—his first attempt to write in an extended form. He was only twenty-six or so, don't forget; he couldn't even orchestrate the piece when he wrote it. But how about the later works? What about the *American in Paris*? Now that is surely a well-knit, organic—

LB: True, what you say. Each work got better as he went on, because he was an intelligent man and a serious student, and he worked hard. But the *American in Paris* is again a study in tunes, all of them beautiful and all of them separate. He had by that time discovered certain tricks of composition, ways of linking themes up, of combining and developing motives, of making an orchestral fabric. But even here they still remain tricks, mechanisms borrowed from Strauss and Ravel and who knows where else. And when you add it all up together it is still a weak work because none of these tricks is his own; they don't arise from the nature of the material; they are borrowed and applied to the material. Or rather *appliqué* to it, like beads on a dress. When you hear the piece, you rejoice in the first theme, then sit and wait through the "filler" until the next one comes along. In this way you sit out about two-thirds of the composition. The remaining third is marvelous because it consists of the themes themselves; but where's the composition?

PM *(A bit craftily)*: But you play it all the time, don't you?

LB: Yes.

PM: And you've recorded it, haven't you?

LB: Yes.

PM: Then you must like it a lot, mustn't you?

LB: I adore it. Ah, here's the coffee.

PM *(Sighing)*: I don't understand you. How can you adore something you riddle with holes? Can you adore a bad composition?

LB: Each man kills the thing he loves. Yes, I guess you can love a bad composition. For noncompositional reasons. Sentiment. Association. Inner meaning. Spirit. But I think I like it most of all because it is so sincere; it is trying so hard to be good; it has only good intentions.

PM: You mean you like it for its faults?

LB: No. What's good in it is so good that it's irresistible. If you have to go along with some chaff in order to have the wheat, it's worth it. And I love it because it shows, or begins to show, what Gershwin might have done if he had lived. Just look at the progress from the *Rhapsody* to the piano concerto, from the concerto to—

PM *(Glowing)*: Ah, the concerto; there is a masterpiece.

LB: That's your story. The Concerto is the work of a young genius who is learning fast. But *Porgy and Bess:* there the real destiny of Gershwin begins to be clear.

PM: Really, I don't get it. Doesn't *Porgy* have all the same faults? I'm always being told that it's perhaps the weakest composition of all he wrote, in spite of the glorious melodies in it. He intended it as a grand opera, after all, and it seems to have failed as a grand opera. Whenever a production of *Porgy* really succeeds, you find that it's been changed into a sort of operetta. They have taken out all the "in-between" singing and replaced it with spoken lines, leaving only the main number. That seems to me to speak for itself.

LB: Oh no; it speaks only for the producers. It's a funny thing about *Porgy*: I always miss the in-between singing when I hear it in its cut form. Perhaps it is more successful that way; it certainly is for the public. It may be because so much of that recitative seems alien to the character of the songs themselves, instead recalling *Tosca* and *Pelléas*. But there's a danger of throwing out the baby with the bath. Because there's a lot of that recitative that *is* in the character of the songs and fits the opera perfectly. Do you remember Bess's scene with Crown on the island? Bess is saying *(Singing)*:

> "It's like dis, Crown,
> I's the only woman Porgy ever had—

PM *(Joining in rapturously)*:

> "An' I's thinkin' now,
> How it will be tonight
> When all these other niggers go back
> to Catfish Row."

LB and PM *(With growing excitement)*:

> "He'll be sittin' and watchin' the big front gate,
> A-countin' 'em off waitin' for Bess.
> An' when the last woman—"

(The restaurant is all eyes and ears.)

PM *(In a loud whisper)*: I think we are making a scene.

LB *(In a violent whisper)*: But that's just what I mean! Thrilling stuff, isn't it? Doesn't it point the way to a kind of Gershwin music that would have reached its own perfection eventually? I can never get over the horrid fact of his death for that reason. With *Porgy* you suddenly realize that Gershwin was a great, great theater composer. He always had been. Perhaps that's what was wrong with his concert music: it was really theater music thrust into a concert hall. What he would have done in the theater in another ten or twenty

years! And then he would still have been a young man! What a loss! Will
America ever realize the loss?

PM (*Moved*): You haven't touched your coffee.

LB (*Suddenly exhausted*): It's gotten cold. Anyway, I have to go home and
write music. Thanks for lunch, PM.

PM: Oh, thank you for coming. I've enjoyed it. Let's do it again, shall we?
We have so much to talk about.

LB (*With a glance at the skating rink*): Like what, for instance?

PM: Well, for one thing, that show of yours. Very strange. It's a big success, the public enjoys it, it's been running for five months, and there's not a
hit in it. How do you explain it?

82   Duke Ellington: "George Gershwin" (1973)

> Gershwin left behind no firsthand comments regarding his great contem-
> porary Duke Ellington (1899–1974), which is not thoroughly surprising
> since he rarely had anything to say about his contemporaries, especially
> those with whom the comparison to himself may have required defense.
> While at times self-conscious, Gershwin was rarely defensive publicly.
> Instead, he erred on the side of exuding confidence in what he was doing.
> Ellington's remarks have been referred to several times in the Gershwin lit-
> erature as a means to apply later social sensibilities to complex social
> questions, namely those revolving around the role of race in American
> music. In truth, Gershwin and Ellington seem to have respected each
> other, as is clear from Ellington's brief remarks here.[1]

When I saw the movie based on the life of George Gershwin, I remember
feeling a little annoyed about the way it depicted an aspect of him I certainly
never encountered. He was shown as a man and artist of temperament who
was somewhat rude at times.

I never heard of this in his lifetime, and I was very close to many people
who were as close to him as they could be, and they could not recall this side
of him either.

He was not the kind of guy who would be in Row A, ready to take the
bow on opening night. In fact, when several of his most successful shows

---

SOURCE Duke Ellington, *Music Is My Mistress* (New York: Doubleday, 1973), 104.

1 Other remarks associated with Ellington concerning *Porgy and Bess* have been the subject of more
concern. See Mark Tucker's discussion of these comments, and problems about their attribution, in his *The
Duke Ellington Reader* (New York: Oxford University Press, 1993), 114ff. Also recall that Gershwin and
Ellington worked together on *Show Girl* in 1929.

opened, he could be seen dressed like a stagehand, who could get in the front or backstage door. In a sports shirt, with no tie, he would humbly take his place in the standing-room area. If you didn't know him, you would never guess that he was the great George Gershwin.

He once told Oscar Levant that he wished he had written the bridge to "Sophisticated Lady," and that made me very proud.

83 Wayne Shirley: "George Gershwin: yes, the sounds as well as the tunes are his" (1998)

Once again, Gershwin's ability to orchestrate his own music is discussed, this time by a scholar who, as a librarian and researcher at the Library of Congress, has the entire Gershwin Collection at his fingertips.

It happens every time you have a discussion about Gershwin the orchestral composer—the writer of *An American in Paris* as opposed to the writer of *Girl Crazy* or "Love Is Here to Stay." Someone says earnestly "but did he do his own orchestration?" Or, categorically, "But somebody else had to score it for him." And yet in the Library of Congress there are bound volumes of Gershwin manuscripts of the orchestral scores of all his concert works later than *Rhapsody in Blue*, and of *Porgy and Bess*. All the orchestrations are in Gershwin's own hand. (If you believe that Gershwin copied out the scoring of others in his own hand to fool musicologists—a race of people I doubt he knew existed—I invite you to copy out any ten pages of the full score of *An American in Paris* and ask yourself whether you would be willing to copy out the remaining 84 for any reason at all. If you still believe this, take a look at the scores themselves, which show many signs of decisions and revisions: not at all fair copies.) No other composer has his or her ability to score challenged in the same way. Why will we not believe that Gershwin scored his own music?

Actually, there are many reasons. Gershwin's Broadway scores were orchestrated by others, as is traditional in that genre. (Even Victor Herbert, whom current wisdom cites as scoring his own operettas, turned much of the routine work over to his amanuensis Harold Sanford [you read it first in *Opus!*].) Several of Gershwin's concert works are published in versions "revised by" or "orchestrated by" someone else. Robert Russell Bennett's Symphonic Picture of *Porgy and Bess* is much performed at pops concerts. Rescorings by Bennett of arias from *Porgy and Bess* are so often performed on

SOURCE *Schwann Opus* (Fall 1998): 6a–11a.

the concert stage that at least one major singer of the role of Bess has categorically stated that "Robert Russell Bennett orchestrated *Porgy and Bess.*"
What is the real state of affairs?

To start with something everyone knows: Gershwin did not orchestrate
the *Rhapsody in Blue.* The scoring was done by Paul Whiteman's chief
arranger Ferde Grofé. Gershwin's early music studies had brought him safely
past the two bugaboos of the novice orchestrator—Transposing Instruments
and the Alto Clef—but in the last months of 1923, when he began work on the
Rhapsody, he had no practical experience in orchestration. Nor, with February
12, 1924, set as the date for the first performance, was there time to learn. And
the special sound of the Paul Whiteman band—the sound Whiteman relied
on in selling his music—was the product of experienced orchestrators: if
Gershwin had been interested in scoring the *Rhapsody*—which he was
not—Whiteman would not have let him do it. It was ten years later, with the
"I Got Rhythm" Variations, that Gershwin first approached the problems of
scoring for the Whiteman-style band; and even then he did it very cautiously.

By the time it was decided to rescore the *Rhapsody in Blue* for symphony
orchestra (I am here condensing a somewhat more complex story), Gershwin
was certainly capable of orchestrating the *Rhapsody*; but the sound of Grofé's
orchestration had become wedded to the piece. Gershwin and his editor,
Frank Campbell-Watson (whom we shall meet in a less complimentary role
later in this story), rightly decided to let Grofé do the symphonic version. So
Gershwin's most famous piece does appear in a dress devised by others.

For his next concert work—the *Concerto in F* of 1925—Gershwin took on
the composer's responsibility for scoring as well as writing a work for the
concert hall. It was a responsibility he never laid down. He got himself some
preliminary experience by scoring two numbers for his London show *Primrose* (September 1924). The *Primrose* numbers he scored tentatively, in pencil:
the *Concerto in F* and all his later concert works, he scored in pen.

The manuscript full score of the *Concerto in F,* unlike the scores of Gershwin's later concert works, shows a few spots where conductor Walter Damrosch or amanuensis William Daly made minor suggestions for changes in
instrumentation. But the score in general—190 pages of it—is in Gershwin's
hand (save for the piano part, which he turned over to a copyist). It is a cautious hand—not the assured flowing hand with which he was to write out the
full score of *Porgy and Bess*—but it's unmistakably his.

The scoring of the *Concerto in F* is likewise cautious and straightforward.
Occasionally it is awkward; sometimes it is quite beautiful (especially the second movement—the luminous opening; the raffish strummed strings under
the piano's first entry). Gershwin was proud of the scoring: Roger Sessions

told the story that when he complimented Gershwin on the *Concerto in F* the composer replied "Yes. And I orchestrated all of it." (Until you've heard your own orchestration—the one aspect of a musical creation that you simply cannot tell until you hear it live—you can't hear everything that's in that answer.)

Three years and one European trip later came *An American in Paris* (1928). The orchestral score, again in Gershwin's most fastidious ink hand is on his own personalized score paper, a facsimile of his signature at the bottom of each page. (Grofé had similar paper. There is a drawer in the desk Gershwin designed, now in the Gershwin Room in the Library of Congress, made especially to hold such paper; indeed the desk itself is designed for the process of scoring.)

The scoring is far more elaborate than that of the *Concerto in F*: this is the George Gershwin who has chatted with Maurice Ravel. *An American in Paris* establishes Gershwin as an orchestrator of high competence: he is now ready to score whatever he composes. (One homely detail reminds us that he is still not quite used to orchestration: for in the first 19 pages the English horn has one flat more, not one flat less, than the instruments in C. Gershwin adjusts this by means of accidentals; it is corrected in the published score.) He continued to turn his Broadway scores over to orchestrators, and would do the same with his film scores: this was part of the tradition. And he would continue to worry about his scoring.

The published score of *An American in Paris* bears the note "Revised by F Campbell-Watson." Many of the revisions involve the saxophone parts, which switch instruments in Gershwin's manuscript but remain a trio of alto, tenor, and baritone—easier for orchestral players—in the published score. Some of the other changes are improvements (the flute runs between cues 3 and 7 have been moved up an octave); some seem merely fussy; none involves any basic change in Gershwin's texture.

Gershwin's next concert work, the *Second Rhapsody* of 1931, would seem to be the main witness for Gershwin's non-scoring of his concert works: the published score says "arranged by Robert McBride." Yet Gershwin did score the *Second Rhapsody*: indeed the photograph of Gershwin in the *New Grove Dictionary of Music and Musicians* shows him examining the orchestral score with Serge Koussevitzky. (An odd choice of photographs, but that's another story.) His scoring of the *Second Rhapsody* is darker and heavier than that of *An American in Paris*—a Rouault to a Dufy.

Gershwin once said to his editor Frank Campbell-Watson that he was unhappy with the orchestration and hoped to rescore the work. (Perhaps he was seeking an excuse for the failure of the *Second Rhapsody* to achieve the success of its predecessors.) After Gershwin's death Campbell-Watson, needing to publish the piece, solved the problem of Gershwin's dissatisfaction in the least satisfactory way: by giving the work to another musician to rescore. McBride did not work from Gershwin's full score: he started anew from the published two-piano score, which is essentially a version of Gershwin's pre-orchestration sketch. Thus Gershwin's additions in the orchestral score (clarinet countermelody at cue I is a good example) went entirely by the board. McBride was a competent if not particularly interesting musician—the one compact disc containing his work in the current issue of *Opus* gives a good idea of his abilities and limitations. His orchestration of the *Second Rhapsody* is lighter and more transparent than Gershwin's, which oddly has a negative effect on the piece. In Gershwin's own orchestration, used by Michael Tilson Thomas on CBS MK 39699, the *Second Rhapsody* is a dark-hued piece of the right length; in the McBride version it is a lighter piece which is several minutes too long—a watercolor trying for the size of an oil.

Quickly through the two least-performed of Gershwin's orchestral pieces: the *Cuban Overture* of 1932—again, there is a detailed orchestral score in Gershwin's hand—remains unpublished in orchestral score. The *"I Got Rhythm" Variations* of 1934, written for Gershwin's tour with a jazz band raising money for *Porgy and Bess*, marks the first time Gershwin had scored for the kind of ensemble which gave the premiere of the *Rhapsody in Blue*. The published full score bears the note "revised by William C. Schoenfeld." (G. Schirmer's current rental catalog ups the ante to "orchestrated by William C. Schoenfeld.") In fact Schoenfeld's "revision" consists of separating the parts for clarinets/bass clarinets from those for the saxophones: in Gershwin's scoring both sets of instruments were covered by a single set of "wind men" in the jazz-orchestra tradition. Schoenfeld's revision makes the work available for standard orchestras, who are willing to hire a set of saxophone players but who do not want to ask their first-chair clarinet to play saxophone (or E-flat clarinet, or bass clarinet for that matter); but it is hardly a rescoring.

This brings us to 1935 and *Porgy and Bess*. Charles Schwartz's 1973 biography of George Gershwin quotes a letter to Gershwin's teacher Joseph Schillinger—Gershwin, like Schubert and Bruckner, continued taking lessons in composition long after he became an established composer—in which Gershwin remarks that the scoring of Act II of *Porgy* "goes slowly," and in a new paragraph, proposes that, being back in New York, he "take some lessons" from Schillinger. Schwartz, never adept at reading human documents, claims that this shows that Gershwin had Schillinger's help in scoring *Porgy*. At the least it seems to show that Schillinger did not help in the scoring of Act I. (Gershwin scored Act I Scene 2—the hit scene in the play—first then went back to score Act I Scene 1, then scored the rest of the show in the order in which it is performed.) But to anyone with experience in writing out orchestral score or parts, this letter suggests only that Gershwin, scoring a work which lasted over six times as long as anything he'd scored before, found the job time-consuming; and—new paragraph, new subject—that he would be willing to take further lessons in the Schillingeresque techniques of composition which had, in fact, had some impact on *Porgy and Bess*. (The opening of Act II Scene 3 is the classic example of Schillingerian "expansion" as the Catfish Row theme is distorted to reflect Bess's feverish mind.) We have Gershwin's notebooks for his studies with Schillinger in 1935: they contain almost nothing on orchestration.

Schillinger's theories of orchestration—which, in contrast with his mathematical theories of musical transformation, stressed simplicity—did have their influence on *Porgy and Bess*, whose score is clearer and less heavy than that of the *Second Rhapsody*. (It is possible that Gershwin's dissatisfaction with the orchestration of the *Second Rhapsody* comes from a session where he showed the work to Schillinger and Schillinger criticized the elaborateness of the scoring.) But this is not "scoring help": this is the interaction between two musicians.

In fact the 557 pages of orchestral score of *Porgy and Bess* represent Gershwin's orchestration at its most assured. (Just think of "Summertime": the opening descending clarinet arpeggio; the shifting string harmonies which form the accompaniment; the English horn obbligato to the first verse; the murmurous violin accompaniment to the second verse; the tranquil final cadence.) Even the hand—Gershwin's informal hand with its downstemmed notes backwards rather than the careful, best-behavior hand of his previous orchestral scores—radiates a new confidence in scoring. (Agreed, it also radiates the knowledge that he has a full three hours of music to score.) If you have ever heard *Porgy and Bess* onstage, or if you have any recording of the full opera, from the 1951 Lehman Engel to the most recent all-digital version, it's this score you have heard. Perhaps it is abbreviated—Engel's classic recording uses the score as it was circulated for European performance in the 1940s, with more cuts than we are used to today—but basically it's as Gershwin scored it.

And yet. If you go to a symphony or pops concert in which something is sung from *Porgy and Bess*, you will almost certainly hear it in a version arranged by Robert Russell Bennett. All the rental excerpts for voice and orchestra come in arrangements by Bennett: the only way to get Gershwin's original orchestration is to rent the parts for the entire opera. (G. Schirmer, the rental agent, is extremely cooperative; the parts are handsome and accurate; but harried orchestra librarians put their faith in the tried-and-true.) Audiences who hear their *Porgy and Bess* in concert, and who read their programs with any interest (and intermissions can be long) will notice that arranger credit.

Bennett came by his proprietorship of *Porgy* honestly. He was an orchestrator for Gershwin's Broadway and film scores; his versions for singer and symphony orchestra of such Gershwin tunes as "Embraceable You" are models of unassertive pops-orchestra scoring. And after Gershwin's death, when Fritz Reiner wanted to do an orchestral suite from *Porgy and Bess,* he approached Bennett to do a "symphonic picture" of the opera.

Bennett's Symphonic Picture of *Porgy and Bess* is as legitimate a work as, say, Rodion Shchedrin's *Carmen* Suite. It no more suggests that Gershwin didn't score *Porgy and Bess* than Shchedrin's suite suggests that Bizet didn't score *Carmen.* (The scoring is, in fact, quite different from Gershwin's: these cannot be two scorings by the same person.) Bennett's arrangements of orchestral accompaniments for the main vocal numbers in *Porgy* are much harder to justify, but they can be explained in terms of the music business: when orchestras wanted a Gershwin show tune, the publisher hired an orchestrator; so they hired an orchestrator for the *Porgy* "tunes" as well. (Bennett himself considered Gershwin to be an amateur orchestrator; he doubtless thought of himself as helping Gershwin along.) Why they continue to be used—well, singers and players are used to them, and by now the legend that Gershwin did not orchestrate *Porgy and Bess* is widespread enough so that the orchestra librarian does not question it.

How important is all this? After all, the *Rhapsody in Blue,* which Gershwin did not orchestrate, is an icon of twentieth-century music in a way that no other Gershwin's orchestral works—not even, quite, *An American in Paris*—is. And we respect other works in the classical music tradition which were not scored by their composer—*The Tales of Hoffmann* (Offenbach died before he could orchestrate it) comes to mind. But readers of *Opus* tend to see the scoring of a work as part of its creation, and to think of composers who do not do their own orchestration as somehow amateurs. (Both Schumann and Chopin are regularly criticized for their awkward scoring, and conductors regularly revise their scores: but what would we feel if they had not established to the best of their ability the sound they wanted?) Perhaps all of this will be useful to readers of *Opus:* the next time you hear *An American in Paris* or the *Concerto in F* or *Porgy and Bess* you can know that not only the tunes and the harmonies but the sounds themselves are Gershwin's. Gershwin also had a gift for the kind of music which flowers in arrangements by others—

the great popular songs and the shows which contain them. But we should not deny him his ability as a concert composer as well. Close your eyes and think of the greatest American tragic aria, "My Man's Gone Now": the pulsing, rhythmic horns-strings-and-piano introduction with the woodwind wails above; the weird keening choral background; the orchestral counterthemes and fills; the final timeless wail. All these—instruments as well as voices—are pure Gershwin. As are the thousand other magical moments of the Gershwin concert works after the *Rhapsody in Blue.*

CHRONOLOGY

1895
July 21—Russian-born Rose Bruskin and Morris Gershovitz marry in New York; they
have three sons (Ira, George, and Arthur) and a daughter (Frances); the family name
is changed from Gershovitz to Gershwine to Gershvin to Gershwin

1896
December 6—Ira Gershwin [IG] (né Israel Gershovitz or Israel Gershvin) born in
New York in the family home, a building at the corner of Hester and Eldridge Streets
on Manhattan's Lower East Side

1898
September 26—George Gershwin [GG] (né Jacob Morris Gershvin or Jacob Morris
Gershwine) born in Brooklyn, N.Y.; the family now lives at 242 Snediker Avenue in
that borough

ca. 1900
The Gershwins move back to Manhattan; GG grows up on the Lower East Side

March 14—Arthur Gershwin born in New York; the family now lives at 91 Second
Avenue in Manhattan

1906
December 6—Frances "Frankie" Gershwin born in New York on IG's tenth birthday

1908
GG meets Maxie Rosenzweig (violinist Max Rosen)

1909
GG begins to keep a musical scrapbook (now in the Gershwin Collection at the
Library of Congress [DLC (GC)]

ca. 1910–1912
GG begins piano lessons with neighborhood teachers: Kate Wolpin (his aunt), a Miss
Green, and a Mr. Goldfarb

ca. 1912–before 1918
GG studies piano with Charles Hambitzer

1913

September—GG enters the High School of Commerce; he writes his first tunes, "Since I Found You" and "Ragging the Traumerei," both unpublished songs with lyrics by Leonard Praskins

ca. 1913–1915

GG begins to take an interest in the Yiddish musical theater, frequenting the National Theater on Second Avenue

1914

GG quits high school to become a piano-pounder at Remick's on West 28th Street; there he meets the Astaires and Herman Paley (1879–1955), a former student of Edward MacDowell; during this time GG submits songs to Remick manager Mose Gumbel for publication but they are rejected for their "sentimentality"; GG stays at Remick's until March 17, 1917

1915

GG begins recording piano rolls for the Standard Music Roll Company in East Orange, N.J.

1916

March 1—GG signs a contract with the Harry von Tilzer Publishing Company for "When You Want 'Em, You Can't Get 'Em, When You Got 'Em, You Don't Want 'Em" (lyrics by Murray Roth), his first published song

June 22—*The Passing Show of 1916* opens at the Winter Garden Theatre in Manhattan and runs for 140 performances; GG provides "Making of a Girl," written with Sigmund Romberg, and "My Runaway Girl" (not used)

ca. 1916–1917

GG meets ragtime pianist Charles "Luckey" Roberts, with whom he perhaps studies; he also makes contact with James P. Johnson; Eubie Blake reports hearing about a "very talented ofay piano player" (presumably GG) from Johnson and Roberts

after ca. mid–1916

GG frequents Barron Wilkin's nightclub on 7th Avenue and 135th Street in Harlem, which features James Reese Europe's band; GG begins his first "tunebook"

1917

ca. January—Remick's publishes "Rialto Ripples," a collaboration between GG and Will Donaldson, a songwriter at Remick's

March 17—GG leaves Remick's; meets Will Vodery, through whom he secures a job as house pianist at Fox's City Theatre, a vaudeville house on 14th Street; after a first-night fiasco, GG quits without pay

ca. July–November 4—GG works as rehearsal pianist for Victor Herbert and Jerome Kern's *Miss 1917* at the Century Theatre, New York City; he meets Herbert, Kern, P. G. Wodehouse, and Lew Fields at this time

September 3—GG (under pseudonym George Wynne) accompanies singer Rita Gould at Proctor's 58th Street Theatre

November 5—GG is retained by the Century after *Miss 1917* opens, serving as accompanist for Sunday afternoon concerts there

December—"You Are Not the Girl," the Gershwins' first collaboration is written; no longer extant

December 18—GG receives a contract from Remick's for "Yoo-oo, Just You" (Irving Caesar), which is interpolated into *Hitchy-Koo of 1918*; GG's first song in a Broadway musical

1918
Gatherings in Greenwich Village with Emily (Strunsky) and Lou Paley, Leonore Strunsky, Mabel Pleshette (Schirmer), Josefa Rosanska, and the Gershwin brothers occur often

February 10—GG signs a songwriting contract (at $35/week, with $50 advance, and a 3 cents royalty on each new song) with Max Dreyfus of T. B. Harms; GG probably meets Harms house arranger Albert Sirmay around this time

June 6—*Hitchy-Koo of 1918* opens at the Globe Theater in New York City (68 performances)

September—Harms publishes its first GG song, "Some Wonderful Sort of Someone" (Schuyler Greene)

October 24—*Ladies First* opens at the Broadhurst Theater in New York City (164 performances); GG provides "The Real American Folk Song (Is a Rag)," the Gershwins' first song in a musical, and "Some Wonderful Sort of Someone"

December 9—*Half Past Eight* opens at the Empire Theater, Syracuse, N.Y.; closes after 5 days. GG provides four songs

ca. 1918–ca. 1921
GG studies composition (harmony and orchestration) with Edward Kilenyi; early notebooks from this period are in DLC [GC]

ca. 1919
GG composes *Lullaby*, for string quartet, probably as part of a composition exercise for Kilenyi; first published in 1968

by 1919
GG meets Robert Russell Bennett, who lives with the Gershwin family for a time prior to his marriage; Bennett remains an important confidant for GG throughout GG's career

1919
February 6—*Good Morning, Judge* opens at the Shubert Theater, New York City (140 performances); GG provides "There's More to the Kiss Than the X-X-X" (Irving Caesar) and one other song

March 2—GG produces "O Land of Mine, America" (Michael E. O'Rourke) as an entry in a national anthem contest sponsored by the *New York American*; they receive 2nd prize; the song is published in the Sunday edition of the paper (March 2); the contest judges are Irving Berlin, John Golden, John McCormack, John Philip Sousa, and Josef Stransky

May 12—*The Lady in Red* opens at the Lyric Theater, New York City (48 performances); GG provides a revised version of "Some Wonderful Sort of Someone" and one other song

May 26—*La, La Lucille*, GG's first complete Broadway show, opens at the Henry Miller Theatre, New York City (104 performances)

Before October—GG meets critic and writer Carl Van Vechten and plays his as-yet-unpublished "Swanee" for him; Van Vechten becomes an important advocate

December 27—*Morris Gest Midnight Whirl* opens at the Century Grove (atop the Century Theater), New York City (110 performances); GG provides six songs

early 1920s
GG composes *Three-quarter Blues* (a.k.a. "Irish Waltz") for piano solo; first published in 1967

1920
Al Jolson incorporates "Swanee" into his traveling revue *Sinbad*; the song becomes GG's biggest-selling hit

February 2—*Dere Mabel* begins a tryout run in Baltimore but closes before reaching Broadway; score includes the Gershwins' "Back Home" and also incorporates "Swanee," "Yank-Kee" (Irving Caesar), and one other song

April 5—*Ed Wynn's Carnival* opens at the New Amsterdam Theater, New York City (64 performances); GG provides one song

June 7—George White's *Scandals of 1920* opens at the Globe Theater, New York City (318 performances); GG provides the complete score, which includes "Scandal Walk" and other songs

August 31—*The Sweetheart Shop* opens at the Knickerbocker Theater, New York City (55 performances); includes "Waiting for the Sun to Come Out," GG and IG's (as "Arthur Francis") first published song as a team

September 27—*Piccadilly to Broadway*, with a score by GG, Vincent Youmans, William Daly, and others, and lyrics by IG and others, opens and tours extensively, but does not reach Broadway

September 29—*Broadway Brevities of 1920* opens at the Winter Garden Theater, New York City (105 performances); GG provides "Spanish Love" (Irving Caesar) along with two other songs

1921
May 3—*Two Little Girls in Blue*, lyrics by IG (his first complete Broadway score), music by Vincent Youmans, opens at the George M. Cohan Theatre, New York City (228 performances)

May 21—*A Dangerous Maid*, score by GG/IG (Arthur Francis), tries out in Atlantic City, later closing in Pittsburgh; the brothers' first full score together, it includes the song "Boy Wanted"

July 11—*Scandals of 1921* opens at the Liberty Theater, New York City (97 performances); score includes "South Sea Isles"

Summer—GG takes two summer courses at Columbia University with Rossetter G. Cole, studying music history ("19th-century Romanticism in Music") and "Elementary Orchestration"

November 7—*The Perfect Fool* opens at the George M. Cohan Theater, New York City (256 performances); GG provides "My Log-Cabin Home" (Irving Caesar and B.G. DeSylva) and one other song

1921–1926
GG keeps a notebook (5 pp., "early notebook," in DLC [GC])

1922
February 20—*The French Doll* opens at the Lyceum Theater, New York City (120 performances); GG provides "Do It Again" (B. G. DeSylva), which was featured 40 years later in the film *Thoroughly Modern Millie*

February 20—*For Goodness Sake* opens at the Winter Garden, New York City (73 performances); the Gershwins provide songs and Fred and Adele Astaire are featured, thus the show represents the first professional collaboration between the two sets of siblings

July 6—*Spice of Life* opens at the Winter Garden, New York City (73 performances); GG provides one song, "Yankee Doodle Blues" (Irving Caesar and B. G. DeSylva)

GG and B. G. DeSylva offer the idea of *Blue Monday* to George White, who rejects it due to the complications posed by blackface; White returns to GG and DeSylva for *Blue Monday*

ca. August—GG and B. G. DeSylva write *Blue Monday* in five days; it was orchestrated by Will Vodery

August 21—*Blue Monday* tries out in New Haven as part of the *Scandals of 1922* (4 performances)

August 28—*Blue Monday* (Act II of George White's *Scandals of 1922*) opens at the Globe Theater (closes after the first night); *Scandals of 1922* also includes "I'll Build a Stairway to Paradise" (B. G. DeSylva and IG)

December—*Our Nell*, with a score by GG and William Daly, and lyrics by Brian Hooker, opens at the Nora Bayes Theatre, New York City (40 performances); GG and Daly become friends during this collaboration; Daly remains an important confidant until Daly's death in 1936; score includes "Innocent Ingenue Baby," "Madrigal," "The Cooney County Fair," and "We Go to Church on Sunday," among others

1922–1924
GG keeps a notebook (31 pp., "red tune book," in the DLC [GC])

1923
GG studies with Rubin Goldmark (a student of Dvořák)

January 14—*The Dancing Girl* opens at the Winter Garden, New York City (126 performances); GG provides one song, "That American Boy of Mine" (Irving Caesar)

February 1—GG sails to England to complete work on *The Rainbow*; GG in London, his first trip abroad; *The Rainbow* opens at the Empire Theater, London

ca. April 28—GG leaves Paris for New York City

June 18—*Scandals of 1923* opens at the Globe Theater, New York City (168 performances)

August 28—*Little Miss Bluebeard* opens at the Lyceum Theater, New York City (175 performances); GG provides a single song

August 30—GG completes a "prelude" or "novelette" in G-major (1-page pencil holograph, dated "Aug. 30, 1923," now in DLC(GC)

September 25—*Nifties of 1923* opens at the Fulton Theater, New York City (47 performances); GG provides two songs, including "Nashville Nightingale" (Irving Caesar)

November 1—GG appears in concert at Aeolian Hall with soprano Eva Gauthier in the American portion of her "Recital of Ancient and Modern Music for Voice;" GG had been introduced to Gauthier through their mutual friend Van Vechten

December 20—*Sweet Little Devil* (as "The Perfect Lady") begins its tryout in Boston

before 1924
GG studies conducting with Artur Bodanzky

ca. 1924
GG composes *Impromptu in Two Keys* for solo piano; first published in 1973

1924
January 4—Paul Whiteman announces his "An Experiment in Modern Music"

January 7—GG dates the beginning of his two-piano manuscript for *Rhapsody in Blue*

January 21—*Sweet Little Devil* (B.G. DeSylva) opens at the Astor Theater, New York City (120 performances)

ca. January 25—GG completes the two-piano version of *Rhapsody in Blue*

January 29—GG and Gauthier repeat their recital program in Boston

February 12—*Rhapsody in Blue* premiered, GG pianist, with the Paul Whiteman Orchestra, Paul Whiteman, conductor, at Aeolian Hall, New York City

March-April—GG keeps a notebook (20 pp., labeled March–April 1924, now in DLC [GC])

March 7—February 12 program repeated at Aeolian Hall

April 21—GG plays *Rhapsody in Blue* at Carnegie Hall

May 15—GG on tour with *Rhapsody in Blue*, beginning in Rochester, N.Y., then in Pittsburgh, Cleveland, and Indianapolis

June 10—GG records an abridged *Rhapsody in Blue* with the Whiteman Orchestra

June 30—*Scandals of 1924* opens at the Apollo Theater, New York City (192 performances); GG's fifth and last *Scandals*

July 8—GG travels to London to begin work on *Primrose*

September 11—*Primrose* (Desmond Carter, Ira Gershwin) opens at the Winter Garden Theater, London

October–November—GG and IG work on a musical for Fred and Adele Astaire entitled *Black-Eyed Susan* (becomes *Lady, Be Good!*)

December 1—*Lady, Be Good!* opens at the Liberty Theater, New York City (330 performances), the Gershwins' first complete score together; includes "Fascinating Rhythm," "Little Jazz Bird," "Oh, Lady Be Good!," "The Half of It, Dearie, Blues"; six songs, including "The Man I Love," are cut

late 1924
GG and Samuel Dushkin arrange two GG's piano "novelettes" into *Short Story* for violin and piano

1924–1925
GG keeps a notebook of themes (15 pp., now in DLC [LC])

1925
January—GG pens "Preludes, Jan. 1925" on a manuscript book; begins a prelude in g-minor (1 p., pencil holograph, dated "Jan. 1925," now in DLC [GC])

January 7—GG meets Igor Stravinsky in New York City at a pre-American debut party for Stravinsky held by violinist Paul Kochanski; GG begins a notebook entitled "Preludes," which includes ideas for solo piano pieces

February 8—GG and Samuel Dushkin premiere *Short Story* at the University Club, New York City

April 13—*Tell Me More* opens at the Gaiety Theatre, New York City (32 performances)

May 26—GG in London; revised version of *Tell Me More* opens at the Winter Garden, London

July–September—GG works on the "sketch score" for *Concerto in F* (dated "July–Sept. 1925")

July 20—*Time* magazine features GG on the cover, the first American composer to receive this notoriety

November 10—GG completes the full score for *Concerto in F*

December 3—*Concerto in F* premieres, with GG, pianist, the New York Symphony Orchestra, Walter Damrosch, conductor, Carnegie Hall

December 28—*Tip-Toes* opens at the Liberty Theatre, New York City (194 performances)

December 29—*135th Street* (reworking of *Blue Monday*) is presented as part of White-man's "Second Experiment in Modern Music," Carnegie Hall

December 30—*Song of the Flame* opens at the Forty-fourth Street Theatre, New York City (219 performances); score by GG and Herbert Stothart (Oscar Hammerstein II and Otto Harbach)

1926
April—GG sails to England

April 14—Revised version of *Lady, Be Good!* opens at the Empire Theatre, London; score now includes three new songs

April 19–20—GG makes recordings for Columbia from the *Lady, Be Good!* score with stars from the show

July 6—GG records songs from *Tip-Toes*

Summer—GG travels to Paris, where he hits upon the idea for a symphonic work that will become *An American in Paris*

August 31—London version of *Tip-Toes* opens at the Winter Garden Theatre

September—GG reads DuBose Heyward's novel *Porgy* and writes to the author

September 14—IG marries Leonore Strunsky

November 8—*Oh, Kay!* opens at the Imperial Theater, New York City (256 performances)

December 4—GG appears in recital with Marguerite d'Alvarez (1892–1953) at the Hotel Roosevelt, New York City; premieres five piano preludes

1927
January 16—GG and d'Alvarez repeat their program in Boston; Boston reviewers report "five" preludes (contradicting the majority of Gershwin biographers)

April 21—GG makes the first electrical recording of *Rhapsody in Blue* for RCA Victor, with the Whiteman Orchestra

April 25—GG's first attempt at a watercolor, a still life

July 25—GG's first outdoor concert, before an audience of 16,000 at the Lewisohn Stadium, NY

September 5—*Strike Up the Band* (first version, book by George S. Kaufman) begins tryout in Philadelphia; closes after 2 weeks, prior to Broadway opening

October—GG and IG work on songs for *Smarty* (becomes *Funny Face*)

October 10—*Porgy*, the play by DuBose and Dorothy Heyward, opens at the Guild Theatre, New York City; GG subsequently attends

November 8—*Oh, Kay!* opens at His Majesty's Theatre, London

November 22—*Funny Face*, starring the Astaires, opens at the Alvin Theatre, New York City (250 performances)

late 1920s
GG studies composition with Wallingford Riegger and Henry Cowell

1928
January—GG executes sketches for *An American in Paris*, dated "January 1928"; "sketch score" (two-piano version) dated "Jan.–Aug. 1, 1928"

January 10—*Rosalie* (IG and P. G. Wodehouse) opens at the New Amsterdam Theatre, New York City (335 performances)

March 7—GG meets Maurice Ravel at a party given by Eva Gauthier; Maurice Ravel attends a performance of *Funny Face,* and the two composers travel to Harlem to hear jazz

March 10—GG, IG, Leonore Gershwin, and Frankie Gershwin board the *Majestic* for London, to begin a European trip during which GG meets [Alban] Berg, [Nadia] Boulanger, [Serge] Prokofiev, [Noel] Coward, [Franz] Lèhar, [Darius] Milhaud, [Maurice] Ravel, [William] Walton, and [Kurt] Weill, among others

March 25—The Gershwins arrive in Paris

March 27—GG and his friend Josefa Rosanska (another student of Edward Kilenyi whom Gershwin had met in 1919, and who would later marry Rudolf Kolisch) meet with the Kolisch Quartet in the Majestic Hotel; the quartet performs Schubert and Schoenberg

April 3—GG shops with Mabel Schirmer along the Avenue de la Grand Armée, where they select four taxi horns that GG plans to use in his *An American in Paris*

April 23—The Gershwins arrive in Berlin; GG meets Kurt Weill

April 28—The Gershwins arrive in Vienna; GG meets Franz Léhar and Alban Berg

June 8—GG records the *Preludes for Piano* and the famous E-major section of *Rhapsody in Blue* for Columbia Records in London

June 13—The Gershwins sail home from Southampton aboard the *Majestic*; they arrive on June 18

August 1—GG completes the two-piano version of *An American in Paris*

November 8—*Treasure Girl* opens at the Alvin Theatre, New York City (68 performances)

November 12—GG records four songs for Columbia Records, New York City

November 18—GG finishes the orchestration for *An American in Paris*

December 13—*An American in Paris* premieres, with New York Philharmonic Orchestra, Walter Damrosch, conductor, Carnegie Hall

1929
GG and IG take neighboring penthouse apartments at 33 Riverside Drive

February—*An American in Paris* recorded for RCA Victor, New York City, Nathaniel Shilkret conducting

June—GG and IG work on *Show Girl*

July 2—*Show Girl* opens at the Ziegfeld Theater, New York City (111 performances)

October 30—GG signs a contract with the Metropolitan Opera to produce an opera based on S. Ansky's Yiddish play *The Dybbuk*; the project fails when it is learned that the rights already have been assigned to Italian composer Lodovico Rocca, whose *Il Dibuk* is produced in Milan in 1934

1930
January 14—*Strike Up the Band* (second version, book by Morrie Ryskind) opens at the Times Square Theater, New York City (191 performances); GG conducts on opening night

July—GG begins his "Girl Crazy" notebook (47 pp.) which remains in use until 1932; it also contains material for *Of Thee I Sing* and *Let 'Em Eat Cake*; it is now in DLC [GC])

October 14—*Girl Crazy* opens at the Alvin Theatre, New York City (272 performances); GG conducts on opening night

November 1—Frankie Gershwin marries Leopold Godowsky II, musician (son of pianist Leopold Godowsky) and co-inventor of the Kodachrome process

November 5—GG, IG, and Leonore Gershwin leave by train for Hollywood, staying there in a house formerly owned by Greta Garbo

1931
ca. January 15—GG works on a "Manhattan Rhapsody" for the upcoming and nearly complete film *Delicious*, music that serves as the basis for *Second Rhapsody*

February 22—GG, IG, and Leonore return to New York from Hollywood by train

March 14—GG completes the full score for *Second Rhapsody*

May 23—GG completes additional details of *Second Rhapsody*

December 3—After much delay, *Delicious* (Fox) is released, the Gershwins' first film score

December 26—*Of Thee I Sing* opens at the Music Box Theatre, New York City (441 performances); book by George S. Kaufman and Morrie Ryskind; GG conducts opening night

1932–ca. August 1936
GG studies composition (harmony and counterpoint) with Joseph Schillinger

ca. 1932
GG's "Schillinger notebook-A" (92 pp.) and "B" (80 pp.), both now in DLC [GC])

1932
January—GG completes the "sketch score" for *Cuban Overture*

January 29—*Second Rhapsody* premiere, GG as soloist with the Boston Symphony Orchestra, Serge Koussevitzky, conductor, Symphony Hall, Boston late March—GG recontacts DuBose Heyward about setting *Porgy*

March 27—*Girl Crazy*, first film version (RKO), starring Bert Wheeler, Robert Woolsey, Eddie Quillan, and Arline Judge, released

May 2—Random House publishes a limited edition version of *George Gershwin's Songbook*, signed by GG and illustrator Alajalov, including an inserted edition of the song "Mischa, Yascha, Toscha, and Sascha"

May 14—Morris Gershwin dies in New York

June 1—IG, Kaufman, and Ryskind awarded the Pulitzer Prize for *Of Thee I Sing*, the first musical to be awarded the prize for drama; the committee felt that GG's music was ineligible for a literary award so his name was not included

ca. June—GG, IG, and Leonore travel to Cuba

GG completes *Cuban Overture* (on title page: "Rhumba"; on spine: "Original Orchestration Manuscript, July–August 1932"); now in DLC [GC]

August 16—*Rhumba* (a.k.a. *Cuban Overture*) premieres in New York's Lewisohn Stadium, Albert Coates, conductor

September—Simon & Schuster publishes the trade edition of *George Gershwin's Songbook*

December 2—*Pardon My English* tries out, Philadelphia

1933
GG moves to a duplex apartment at 132 East 72nd Street in Manhattan; IG and Leonore take an apartment across the street at 125 East 72nd Street

January 20—*Pardon My English* opens at the Majestic Theatre, New York City (46 performances)

February 20—*Pardon My English* closes

October 22—*Let 'Em Eat Cake* (sequel to *Of Thee I Sing*) opens at the Imperial Theater, New York City (90 performances)

October 26—Contract signed with Theatre Guild for *Porgy* (opera)

December—GG visits Dorothy and DuBose Heyward in Charleston, S.C.; later in the month, in Palm Beach, GG sketches "Summertime"

1933–1937
GG's last tunebook—96 pp., now in DLC [GC]

1934
January 6—GG completes the full score for *Variations on "I Got Rhythm"*

January 13–February 10—GG tours the United States and Canada with the Leo Reisman Orchestra, covering 28 cities in 29 days, on a tour celebrating the 10th anniversary of *Rhapsody in Blue*

January 14—*"I Got Rhythm" Variations* premieres, GG with the Reisman Orchestra, Charles Previn, conductor, Symphony Hall, Boston

February 19—GG begins twice-weekly (15 minutes, Mondays and Fridays) *Music by Gershwin* radio program for NBC for $2,000 per week

Late February—GG begins composition of *Porgy*, with "songs and spirituals"— for Act I

May 31—Final *Music by Gershwin* broadcast of the first season

Summer—GG at Folly Island, S.C. works on the *Porgy* score

September 23—Second season of *Music by Gershwin* begins, now an hour-long Sunday broadcast on CBS

Fall—GG begins orchestrating *Porgy*

December 23—Second season of *Music by Gershwin* ends

GG and Kay Swift are guests at the White House, where GG plays for President Franklin Delano Roosevelt

1935
Bill Daly's transcription of *An American in Paris*, for solo piano, is published by Harms

Summer—Kay Swift divorces husband Paul Warburg, hoping to marry GG

August 26—*Porgy* stage rehearsals begin in New York

September 2—GG completes full score for *Porgy and Bess*; concert version is performed at Carnegie Hall

September 30—*Porgy and Bess* Boston tryout; good reviews

October 10—*Porgy and Bess* opens at the Alvin Theatre, New York City (124 performances); mixed reviews

ca. 1935
GG's last "black notebook"—11 pp. in GG's hand, remainder in the hand of Kay Swift, now in DLC [GC]

ca. 1936
GG's "Schillinger notebook-C" (80 pp.) now in DLC [GC]

1936
January 21—Orchestral suite from *Porgy and Bess* (later retitled *Catfish Row Suite* by IG) premieres, Philadelphia Orchestra, Alexander Smallens, conductor, Academy of Music, Philadelphia

April 21—An exhibition of some of GG's paintings by the Society of Independent Artists in New York

May 14—Agent Arthur Lyons arranges for the Gershwins to score an Astaire-Rogers picture, *Watch Your Step* (becomes *Shall We Dance*)

June 26—The Gershwins sign a contract with RKO for two films (*Shall We Dance?* and *A Damsel in Distress*)

July—GG and Kay Swift agree to end their relationship

August 8—GG, IG, and Leonore fly from Newark to Los Angeles to begin work for RKO, renting a house at 1019 North Roxbury Drive, Beverly Hills

Fall—GG develops friendships with émigrés Arnold Schoenberg and Ernst Toch, among others

December 25—*The Show Is On* opens at the Winter Garden Theater, New York City (237 performances); GG and IG provide a single song, "By Strauss"

1937
February—Friends begin to notice uncharacteristic lapses in GG's playing

May 7—*Shall We Dance* (RKO) is released; GG completes score for *A Damsel in Distress* (released posthumously)

May 12—GG and IG begin work on *The Goldwyn Follies* (Goldwyn-United Artists)

June 9—GG experiences a dizzy spell; medical examination reveals nothing

June 23–26—GG at Cedars of Lebanon Hospital, Hollywood; refuses to have a spinal tap taken

July 4—GG leaves 1019 North Roxbury Drive, for rest and quiet at vacant home of lyricist Yip Harburg

July 9—GG slips into a coma and is rushed to Cedars of Lebanon Hospital

July 10—Physicians, suspecting a brain tumor, decide on "energetic surgical intervention," a five-hour operation

July 11—GG dies of a brain tumor in Hollywood on Sunday, at 10:35 A.M.

July 15—Funeral service held at Temple Emanu-El in Manhattan; interment occurs at Mount Hope Cemetery in Hastings-on-Hudson, N.Y.; a simultaneous memorial service is held at Temple B'nai B'rith in Hollywood

August 9—Gershwin Memorial Concert, Lewisohn Stadium, New York City

September 8—Gershwin Memorial Concert, Hollywood Bowl, Los Angeles

November 19—*A Damsel in Distress* is released

1938
February 23—*The Goldwyn Follies* (MGM) is released; GG's unfinished score completed by Vernon Duke and IG

IG provides lyrics for a posthumous song, "Dawn of a New Day" (completed with the assistance of Kay Swift), which becomes the "official march" of the 1939 New York World's Fair

1940
September 17—*Strike Up the Band*, film version (MGM) by Busby Berkeley is released; stars Judy Garland and Mickey Rooney and features Paul Whiteman and his orchestra

1941

July 16—*Lady, Be Good!*, film version (MGM), is released, starring Eleanor Powell, Ann Sothern, and Robert Young

1943

November—MGM produces the second film version of *Girl Crazy*, starring Judy Garland and Mickey Rooney

1945

June 26—*Rhapsody in Blue*, film biography (Warner Brothers), released in Hollywood; opens the following day in New York City

1947

November 11—*The Shocking Miss Pilgrim*, film (Twentieth Century Fox), is released, starring Betty Grable, Dick Haymes, Anne Revere, and Gene Lockart; score consists of unpublished Gershwin songs

1948

December—Rose Gershwin, mother of GG and IG, dies in New York City

1951

August 29—*An American in Paris*, film (MGM), is released; directed by Vincente Minnelli; stars Gene Kelly, Leslie Caron, Oscar Levant, and Georges Guetary

1957

February 13—*Funny Face*, film (Paramount), is released; stars Fred Astaire and Audrey Hepburn

1959

IG publishes his *Lyrics on Several Occasions*; contains first publication of "The Real American Folk Song (Is a Rag)"

"Just Another Rhumba" is published

July 1—Film version of *Porgy and Bess* (Samuel Goldwyn for Columbia Pictures) is released; stars Dorothy Dandridge (vocals by Adele Addison) and Sidney Poitier (vocals by Robert McFerrin)

1960

Promenade, for piano solo (later orchestrated) is published

1964

December 16—*Kiss Me Stupid*, film (United Artists) is released; stars Dean Martin and Kim Novak, directed by Billy Wilder; uses GG's "All the Livelong Day (and the Long, Long Night)," "I'm a Poached Egg," and "Sophia"

1965

December 1—*When the Boys Meet the Girls*, third film version (MGM) of *Girl Crazy*, is released; stars Connie Francis, Liberace, Louis Armstrong, and Herman's Hermits

1967
"Hi-Ho," *Merry Andrew*, and *Three-Quarter Blues* are published

1968
Lullaby for String Quartet is published

"Dear Little Girl," used in the film *Star*, is published

1971
Two Waltzes in C, piano solo, is published

1973
Impromptu in Two Keys, piano solo, is published

1981
November 20—Arthur Gershwin dies in New York City

1982
April 7—revival of *Porgy and Bess* opens at Radio City Music Hall, New York City (45 performances

1983
May 1—*My One and Only*, incorporating Gershwin standards into a new story, opens at the St. James Theatre, New York City (767 performances)

August 17—IG dies in Beverly Hills

June 5—Name of Broadway's Uris Theatre changed to the George and Ira Gershwin Theatre

1991
August 20—Leonore Strunsky Gershwin dies in Beverly Hills, at the home she and IG had shared since 1940

1992
February 19—*Crazy for You*, incorporating Gershwin songs from *Girl Crazy* and from other shows and films into a new story, opens at the Shubert Theatre, New York City (1,622 performances)

1998
Gershwin centennial celebrations around the world

Pulitzer committee votes GG a special Pulitzer Prize for his body of work; award accepted by Frances Gershwin Godowsky

June 4—GG and IG received a star on the Hollywood Walk of Fame

1999
January 18—Frances "Frankie" Gershwin Godowsky dies in New York City

SELECTED BIBLIOGRAPHY

Adams, Franklin P. "The Conning Tower; The Diary of Our Own Samuel
    Pepys." *New York Herald Tribune*, October 11, 1935; DLC [GC].
————. *The Diary of Our Own Samuel Pepys (1911–1934)*. New York: Simon & Schuster,
    1935.
Alpert, Hollis. *The Life and Times of Porgy and Bess: The Story of an American Classic.*
    New York: Alfred A. Knopf, 1990.
Armitage, Merle, ed. *George Gershwin.* New York: Longmans, Green, 1938. Reprint,
    New York: Da Capo Press, 1995.
————. *Gershwin: Man and Legend.* New York: Duell, Sloan & Pearce, 1958.
"The Arts Club of Chicago, Exhibition of the George Gershwin Collection of Mod-
    ern Paintings." Exhibition catalogue, November 10–25, 1933; DLC [GC].
Arvey, Verna. "George Gershwin Through the Eyes of a Friend." *Opera and Concert* 13
    (April 1948): 10–11, 27–28.
Astaire, Fred. *Steps in Time.* New York: Harper, 1959.
Behrman, Samuel Nathaniel. *People in a Diary: A Memoir.* Boston: Little, Brown, 1972.
————. "Troubadour." *New Yorker*, May 25, 1929, 27–29.
Block, Geoffrey. "Gershwin's Buzzard and Other Mythological Creatures." *Opera
    Quarterly* 7 (Summer 1990): 74–82.
Blumfeld, Larry. "Fascinatin' Vision." *Jazziz*, December 10, 1998, 58.
Bolcolm, William. "A serious composer with Broadway Style." *New York Times*,
    August 30, 1998, II, 1.
Brown, Anne. *Sang fra frossen gren.* Oslo: A. Aschehoug, 1979.
Campbell, Frank C. "The Musical Scores of George Gershwin." *Library of Congress
    Quarterly Journal of Current Acquisitions* 11 (May 1954): 127–39.
————. "Some Manuscripts of George Gershwin (1898–1937)." *Manuscripts* 6 (Winter
    1954): 66.
Carnovale, Norbert. *George Gershwin: A Bio-bibliography.* Westport, Conn.:
    Greenwood Press, 2000.
Carp, Louis, M.D. "George Gershwin—Illustrious American Composer: His Fatal
    Glioblastoma." *American Journal of Surgical Pathology* (October 1979): 473–78.
Cerf, Bennett. "In Memory of George Gershwin (September, 1898–July, 1937)." *Satur-
    day Review of Literature* 26 (July 17, 1943): 14–16.
Chasins, Abram. "Paradox in Blue." *Saturday Review of Literature* (February 25, 1956):
    37, 39, 64–66.
Crawford, Richard. "It Ain't Necessarily Soul: Gershwin's 'Porgy and Bess' as a Sym-
    bol." *Yearbook for Inter-American Musical Research* 8 (1972): 17–38.

————. "Gershwin's Reputation: A Note on *Porgy and Bess.*" *Musical Quarterly* 65 (April 1979): 257–64.

Crawford, Richard, and Wayne Schneider. S.v. "Gershwin, George," in *The New Grove Dictionary of American Music* (1986).

Crouch, Stanley. "An Inspired Borrower of a Black Tradition." *New York Times*, August 30, 1998, II, 4, 17.

Deering, Ashby. "Brothers as Collaborators." *Morning Telegraph*, February 1, 1925, theatre section, 1.

DeLong, Thomas A. *Pops: Paul Whiteman, King of Jazz.* Piscataway, N.J.: New Century Publishers, 1983.

DeSantis, Florence Stevenson. *Gershwin.* New York: Treves Publishing, 1987.

Dizikes, John. *Opera in America: A Cultural History.* New Haven, Conn., and New York: Yale University Press, 1993.

Dunne, F. P. "Gershwin Shelves Jazz To Do Opera; Tin Pan Alley's King Composing One for Metropolitan; Based on 'The Dybbuk'; At Kahn's Request, He Admits, Saying He'll Be Back." Unidentified clipping, after December 1928; DLC [GC].

Durham, Frank. *DuBose Heyward: The Man Who Wrote Porgy.* Columbia: University of South Carolina Press, 1954.

Ewen, David. *George Gershwin: His Journey to Greatness.* Englewood Cliffs, N.J.: Prentice Hall, 1970.

Floyd, Samuel A., Jr., ed. *Black Music in the Harlem Renaissance: A Collection of Essays.* Contributions in Afro-American and African Studies, Number 128. Westport, Conn.: Greenwood Press, 1990.

Gershwin, George. "The Composer in the Machine Age [1930]." In *Revolt in the Arts,* edited by Oliver M. Saylor. New York: Coward-McGann, 1931. Reprinted in *George Gershwin,* edited by Merle Armitage, 225–30. New York: Longmans, Green, 1938.

————. "Does Jazz Belong to Art? Foremost Composer of Syncopated Music Insists on Serious Appraisal." *Singing* 1 (July 1926): 13–14.

————. "Fifty Years of American Music: Younger Composers, Freed from European Influences, Labor Toward Achieving a Distinctive American Musical Idiom." *The American Hebrew,* November 1929, 47.

————. "Introduction." In *Tin Pan Alley: A Chronicle of the American Popular Music Racket,* by Isaac Goldberg, vii–xi. New York: John Day, 1930.

————. "Introduction." In *George Gershwin's Songbook.* New York: Simon & Schuster, 1932.

————. "Jazz Is the Voice of the American Soul." *Theatre Magazine,* June 1926, 52B.

————. "Making Music." *New York Sunday World Magazine,* May 4, 1930.

————. "Mr. Gershwin Replies to Mr. Kramer." *Singing* 1 (October 1926): 17–18.

————. "Our New National Anthem: Broadway's Most Popular Modern Composer Discusses Jazz as an Art Form." *Theatre Magazine,* May 1925.

————. "The Relation of Jazz to American Music." In *American Composers on American Music,* edited by Henry Cowell, 186–87. Palo Alto, Calif.: Stanford University Press, 1933. Reprint, New York: Frederick Ungar, 1962.

————. "Rhapsody in Catfish Row: Mr. Gershwin Tells the Origin and Scheme for His Music in That New Folk Opera Called 'Porgy and Bess.'" *New York Times,* October 20, 1935, X, 1–2.

Gershwin, George, and Joan Foster. "Melody Shop Formulas: The Elusiveness of Tunes and Ways of Trapping Them." *Musical America* (1926); DLC [GC].

"Gershwin Goes Political After Chats With Rivera; Composer Returns From Mexico Impressed by Radical Thinkers." *New York Post*, December 17, 1935.

Gershwin, Ira. "Gershwin on Gershwin." *Newsweek*, October 23, 1944, 14.

———. Letter to Max Dreyfus [typescript, dated August 20, 1959]. Kay Swift Archive at Gilmore Music Library, Yale University.

———. *Lyrics on Several Occasions; A Selection of Stage & Screen Lyrics Written for Sundry Situations; and Now Arranged in Arbitrary Categories. To Which Have Been Added Many Informative Annotations & Disquisitions on Their Why & Wherefore, Their Whom-for, Their How; and Matters Associative.* New York: Alfred A. Knopf, 1959.

———. *The Complete Lyrics of Ira Gershwin.* Edited by Robert Kimball. New York: Alfred A. Knopf, 1993.

———. "Which Came First?" *Saturday Review*, August 29, 1959, 31–33, 45.

———. "Words and Music." *New York Times*, November 9, 1930.

"Gershwin Plans." *Time*, April 14, 1930, 26.

"Gershwin Plans Serious Works." *New York Times*, July 15, 1926, 21.

"Gershwin Takes Up Painting as Aid to Music: Jazz Composer Finds Brush Inspiring When Muse of Orpheus Deserts Him." *New York Herald Tribune*, May 19, 1929, I, 9.

Gilbert, Steven E. "Gershwin's Art of Counterpoint," *Musical Quarterly* 70 (1984): 423–56.

———. *The Music of Gershwin.* Composers of the Twentieth Century. New Haven, Conn., and London: Yale University Press, 1995.

Gilman, Lawrence. "Mr. George Gershwin Plays His New Jazz Concerto With Walter Damrosch." *New York Herald Tribune*, December 4, 1925, 19.

Goldberg, Isaac. "All about the Gershwins: Principally George, Incidentally Ira." *Boston Evening Transcript*, December 21, 1929, 3–4.

———. "George Gershwin and Jazz: A Critical Analysis of a Modern Composer." *Theatre Guild Magazine* 7 (March 1930): 15–19, 55.

———. *George Gershwin: A Study in American Music.* New York: Simon & Schuster, 1931. Reprint, with a supplement by Edith Garson, New York: Frederick Ungar, 1958.

———. "If Not Back to Bach, Then On to Lincoln." *Boston Evening Transcript*, May 10, 1930, IV, 5–6.

———. "Music by Gershwin." *Ladies' Home Journal*, February 1931, 12; March 1931, 20; April 1931, 25.

———. *Tin Pan Alley: A Chronicle of the American Popular Music Racket*, with an introduction by George Gershwin. New York: John Day, 1930. Reprint, with a supplement by Edward Jablonski, New York: Frederick Ungar, 1961.

———. "What's Jewish in Gershwin's Music?" *B'nai B'rith Magazine* 50 (April 1936): 226–27, 247.

Graham, Sheila. "Gershwin Rhapsodic Over 'Single Bliss'." *Los Angeles Examiner*, September 29, 1935.

Haas, Robert Bartlett, ed. *William Grant Still and the Fusion of Cultures in American Music.* Los Angeles: Black Sparrow Press, 1972.

Hajdu, David. "Rhapsody in Black and White." *New York Times Magazine*, October 25, 1998, 52.

Halle, Kay. "The Time of His Life." *Washington Post*, February 5, 1978, F, 1–5.

Hamm, Charles. *Yesterdays: Popular Song in America*. New York: W.W. Norton, 1979.

———. "The Theatre Guild Production of *Porgy and Bess.*" *Journal of the American Musicological Society* 40 (Fall 1987): 495–532.

Haven, Charles. "Even Gershwin Was Bailed Out by a Comedien." *Boston Sunday Post*, January 7, 1934, II, 6.

Hellman, Lillian. *An Unfinished Woman*. Boston: Little, Brown, 1969.

Heyward, Dorothy, and DuBose Heyward. *Porgy, A Play in Four Acts*. New York: Doubleday, Doran, 1927.

Heyward, DuBose. *Porgy*. Decorated by Theodore Nadejen. New York: George H. Doran, 1925.

———. "Porgy and Bess Return on Wings of Song." *Stage*, October 1935, 34–42.

Hitchcock, H. Wiley. "Who Loves You Porgy?" In *Approaches to the American Musical*, edited by Robert Lawson Peebles. Exeter, England: University of Exeter Press, 1995.

Howard, John Tasker. *Our Contemporary Composers: American Music in the Twentieth Century*. New York: Thomas Y. Crowell, 1941.

Hyland, William G. "The Best Songwriter of Them All." *Commentary*, October 1991, 35–42.

Hyman, Dick. "Gershwin, Piano Player." *Jazziz*, December 1, 1998, 52–54.

Jablonski, Edward. "Gershwin on Music." *Musical America*, July 1962, 32–35.

———. "George Gershwin." *HiFi/Stereo Review* 12 (1967): 49.

———. "The Making of Porgy and Bess." *New York Times*, October 21, 1980.

———. *Gershwin*. New York: Doubleday, 1987.

———, editor. *Gershwin Remembered*. London: Faber and Faber, 1992. Reprint. Portland, Ore.: Amadeus Press, 1992.

Jablonski, Edward, and Lawrence D. Stewart. *The Gershwin Years*. Introduction by Carl Van Vechten. Garden City, N.Y.: Doubleday, 1973.

Jacobi, Frederick. "The Future of Gershwin." *Modern Music* 15 (November–December 1937): 3–7.

Johnson, Hall. "Porgy and Bess—a Folk Opera." *Opportunity* XIV (June 1936): 24–28.

Johnson, John Andrew. "Gershwin's 'American Folk Opera': The Genesis, Style, and Reputation of *Porgy and Bess* (1935)." Ph.D. diss., Harvard University, 1996.

Jones, Isabel Morse. "Gershwin Analyzes Science of Rhythm; Swing Music Fundamental Because It Follows Mathematical Rules, Says Noted Pianist and Composer." *Los Angeles Times*, February 2, 1937.

Kashner, Sam, and Nancy Schoenberger. *A Talent for Genius: The Life and Times of Oscar Levant*. Los Angeles: Silman-James Press, 1994.

Keller, Hans. "Rhythm: Gershwin and Stravinsky." *Score and I.M.A. Magazine* 20 (June 1957): 19–31.

Khachaturian, Aram. "Homage to George Gershwin." *Masses and Mainstream*, November 1955, 24–25.

Kilenyi, Edward. "George Gershwin as I Knew Him." *Etude* 68 (October 1950): 11–12, 64.

———. "Gershwiniana: Recollections and Reminiscences of Times Spent with My Student George Gershwin." Unpublished, 89-page typescript written ca. 1963; DLC [GC].

Kimball, Robert, and Alfred Simon. *The Gershwins*. New York: Atheneum, 1973.

Kraft, Robert. *Dialogues and a Diary*. Berkeley: University of California Press, 1982.

Kresh, Paul. *An American Rhapsody: The Story of George Gershwin*. Jewish Biography Series. New York: Lodestar Books and E. P. Dutton, 1988.

Lawrence, Gertrude. *A Star Danced*. Garden City, N.Y.: Doubleday, 1945.

Levant, Oscar. "My Life, Or the Story of George Gershwin." In *A Smattering of Ignorance*. New York: Doubleday, Doran, 1940.

Levine, Henry. "Gershwin, Handy and the Blues." *Clavier*, October 1970, 10–20.

Lindsay, Howard. "That Summer at Folly Beach: George Gershwin Wrote Most of 'Porgy and Bess' in 1934." *Charleston News and Courier Sunday Magazine*, January 18, 1964.

Maisel, Arthur. "Talent and Technique: George Gershwin's *Rhapsody in Blue.*" In *Trends in Schenkerian Analysis Research*, 51–69, edited by Allen Cadwallader. New York: Schirmer Books, 1990.

Mellers, Wilfrid. *Music in a New Found Land: Themes and Developments in the History of American Music*. London: Barrie & Rockliff, 1964. Reprint, New York: Oxford University Press, 1987.

Merman, Ethel, and Pete Martin. *Who Could Ask for Anything More*. New York: Doubleday, 1955.

Montgomery, Mike. "George Gershwin Piano-Rollography." *Record Research*, March–April 1962, 3–4.

Mordden, Ethan. *Opera in the Twentieth Century: Sacred, Profane, Godot*. New York: Oxford University Press, 1978.

———. *Broadway Babies*. New York: Oxford University Press, 1983.

Morrow, Edward. "Duke Ellington on Gershwin's 'Porgy.'" *New Theatre*, December 1935, 5–6.

Nauert, Paul. "Theory and Practice in *Porgy and Bess:* The Gershwin-Schillinger Connection." *Musical Quarterly* 78 (Spring 1994): 9–33.

Nichols, Beverley. "George Gershwin, or, a Drunken Schubert." In *Are They the Same at Home? Being a Series of Bouquets Diffidently Distributed*. New York: Doubledaly, Doran, 1927.

O'Hara, John. "An American in Memoriam." *Newsweek*, July 15, 1940, 34.

Oja, Carol J. "Gershwin and American Modernists of the 1920s." *Musical Quarterly* 78 (Winter 1994): 646–68.

———. *Making Music Modern: New York in the 1920s*. New York: Oxford University Press, 2000.

Osgood, Henry. "The Jazz Bugaboo." *The American Mercury*, November 1925, 328–30.

Page, Tim. "Gershwin, Porter and Rodgers Scores Found." *New York Times*, November 20, 1982, 1, 17.

Payne, Robert. *Gershwin*. London: Robert Hale, 1960.

Pessen, Edward. "The Great Songwriters of Tin Pan Alley's Golden Age: A Social, Occupational and Aesthetic Inquiry." *American Music* 3 (Summer 1985): 180–97.

Peyser, Joan. *The Memory of All That: The Life of George Gershwin*. New York: Simon & Schuster, 1993.

Prokofieff, Serge. "Music in America." *Carnegie Hall Program*, October 31, 1965: 5–7.

Riis, Thomas L. *Just Before Jazz*. Washington, D.C.: Smithsonian Institution Press, 1989.

Rorem, Ned. "Living with Gershwin: Thoughts on the American Melodist." *Opera News* 49 (March 16, 1985): 10–18, 46.

Rosenberg, Deena. "A Gershwin Musical Meant More Than Good Tunes." *New York Times*, June 11, 1978, 39.

———. *Fascinating Rhythm: The Collaboration of George and Ira Gershwin*. New York: Dutton, 1991.

Rosenfeld, Paul. "George Gershwin." In *Discoveries of a Music Critic*. New York: Harcourt, Brace, 1976.

Rothstein, Edward. "George Gershwin's Heav'nly Lan'." *New Republic*, March 18, 1985, 28–32.

Saylor, Oliver, ed. *Revolt in the Arts*. New York: Brentano's, 1930.

Schiff, David. *Gershwin: Rhapsody in Blue*. Cambridge: Cambridge University Press, 1997.

———. "Misunderstanding Gershwin." *Atlantic Monthly*, October 1, 1998, 100.

Schillinger, Joseph. *Kaleidophone: Pitch Scales in Relation to Chord Structures*. New York: M. Witmark & Sons, 1940.

———. *Schillinger System of Musical Composition*. 2 vols. New York: Carl Fischer, 1941–1942. Reprint, Lyle Dowling and Arthur Shaw, eds. New York: Da Capo Press, 1978.

Schneider, Wayne Joseph, ed. *Gershwin Studies*. New York: Oxford University Press, 1999.

Schuller, Gunther. "Jazz and Classical Music." In *The New Edition of the Encyclopedia of Jazz*, edited by Leonard Feather, 497–99. New York: Bonanza, 1960.

Schwartz, Charles. *George Gershwin: His Life and Music*. Indianapolis: Bobbs-Merrill, 1973

Seldes, Gilbert. "The Gershwin Case." *Esquire* 2 (October 1934): 108, 130.

Shirley, Wayne D. "Porgy and Bess." *Quarterly Journal of the Library of Congress* 31 (April 1974): 97–107.

———. "Reconciliation on Catfish Row: Bess, Serena, and the Short Score of *Porgy and Bess*." *Quarterly Journal of the Library of Congress* 38 (Summer 1981): 14, 165.

———. "Notes on George Gershwin's First Opera." *Institute for Studies in American Music Newsletter* 11 (May 1982): 8–10.

———. "Scoring the *Concerto in F*: George Gershwin's First Orchestration." *American Music* 2 (Summer 1984).

———. "George Gershwin Learns to Orchestrate." *Sonneck Society Bulletin* 16 (Fall 1990): 101–2.

Simon, Paul. "Highbrows and Hits: A Fertile Compound." *New York Times*, August, 30, 1990: II, 1, 28.

Spaeth, Sigmund. "Spaeth Recalls Prophetic Tip To a Shy Youngster, Gershwin." *New York Herald Tribune*, March 28, 1942.

Standifer, James A. "Reminiscences of Black Musicians." *American Music* 4 (Summer 1986).

Starr, Lawrence. "Towards a Re-evaluation of Gershwin's *Porgy and Bess*." *American Music* 2 (Summer 1984): 25–37.

———. "Gershwin's 'Bess, You Is My Woman Now': The Sophistication and Subtlety of a Great Tune." *Musical Quarterly* 72 (1986).

———. "Ives, Gershwin, and Copland: Reflections on the Strange History of American Art Music." *American Music* 12 (Summer 1994): 167–87.

Swain, Joseph. *The Broadway Musical: A Critical and Musical Survey.* New York: Oxford University Press, 1990.

———. "Gershwin's 'Bess, You Is My Woman Now': The Sophistication and Subtlety of a Great Tune." *Musical Quarterly* 72: 4 (1986): 429–48.

Teachout, Terry. "The Fabulous Gershwin Boys." *Washington Post,* January 10, 1992.

Thomson, Virgil. *"Porgy* in Maplewood." *New York Herald Tribune,* October 19, 1941. Reprint, Thomson, *The Musical Scene.* New York: Alfred A. Knopf, 1945.

———. *Music with Words: A Composer's View.* New Haven, Conn.: Yale University Press, 1989.

"Thousands Attend Gershwin Funeral." *New York Times,* July 16, 1937.

Tucker, Mark Thomas. *The Duke Ellington Reader.* New York: Oxford University Press, 1993.

Van Vechten, Carl. "The Great American Composer." *Vanity Fair,* April 1917.

"The William Grant Still Reader: Essays on American Music," Edited by Jon Michael Spenser. *Black Sacred Music* 6 (Fall 1992): 1–277.

Winer, Deborah Grace. "Kid Sister." *Opera News,* February 1, 1986, 35, 46.

Wodehouse, Artis. "Gershwin's Solo Piano Disc Improvisations." *Clavier,* October 1988.

Woollcott, Alexander. "George the Ingenuous." *Hearst's International Cosmopolitan,* November 1933, 32–33, 122–23.

Wyatt, Robert. "The Seven Jazz Preludes of George Gershwin: A Historical Narrative." *American Music* 7 (Spring 1989): 68–85.

Youngren, William. "Gershwin, Part 1: *Rhapsody in Blue." New Republic,* April 23, 1977.

———. "Gershwin, Part 2: *Concerto in F." New Republic,* April 30, 1977.

———. "Gershwin, Part 3: *An American in Paris." New Republic,* May 7, 1977.

———. "Gershwin, Part 4: *Porgy and Bess." New Republic,* May 14, 1977.

Zimel, Heyman. "George Gershwin." *Young Israel,* June 1928, 10–11.

CREDITS

The following publishers and individuals have generously given permission to reprint articles and excerpts from longer works:

"George Gershwin" from *Music Is My Mistress* by Duke Ellington. Copyright © 1973 by Duke Ellington, Inc. Used by permission of Doubleday, a division of Bantam Doubleday Dell Publishing Group, Inc.

"Hollywood—An Ending" by Edith Garson Jablonski (d. 1979) in *George Gershwin: A Study in American Music* by Isaac Goldberg, reprinted by Frederick Ungar Publishing in 1958. Permission to reprint this chapter was granted by Edward Jablonski.

"Lady, Be Good!" from *Ira Gershwin: The Art of the Lyricist* by Philip Furia, copyright © 1996 by Philip Furia. Used by permission of Oxford University Press, Inc.

"That Certain Feeling" and "A Foggy Day" from *American Popular Song: The Great Innovators, 1900–1950* by Alec Wilder, edited by James T. Maher, copyright © 1972 by Alec Wilder. Used by permission of Oxford University Press, Inc.

Excerpt from *William Grant Still: A Study in Contradictions* by Catherine Parsons Smith. Copyright © 2000 by Catherine Parsons Smith. Used by permission of University of California Press. All figures that appear in *William Grant Still: A Study in Contradictions* are courtesy of William Grant Still Music.

"Gershwin on Gershwin" by Ira Gershwin. From *Newsweek* (September 24) © (1944) Newsweek, Inc. All rights reserved. Reprinted by permission.

"George Gershwin: yes, the sounds as well as the tunes are his" by Wayne Shirley from *Schwann Opus* (Fall 1998) Schwann Publications, Inc. All rights reserved. Reprinted by permission.

"George Gershwin's 'I Got Rhythm'" in *The American Musical Landscape* by Richard Crawford. Copyright © 1973 by Richard Crawford. Used by permission of University of California Press.

"George Gershwin, An American Composer" by Carl Van Vechten from *Vanity Fair* (March 1925). All rights reserved. Reprinted by permission.

"Someone to Watch Over Me" in *American Popular Ballads of the Golden Era, 1924–1950* by Allen Forte. Copyright © 1995 by Allen Forte. Used by permission of Princeton University Press.

"The Gershwins in Britain" by James Ross Moore in *New Theatre Quarterly* (February 1994). All rights reserved. Reprinted by permission.

"The Ewe Lamb of Widow Jazz" by Abbe Niles in *New Republic* (December 1926). All rights reserved. Reprinted by permission.

"Gershwin, Schillinger, and Dukelsky" by Vernon Duke in *Musical Quarterly* (January 1947). Reprinted by permission of Kay Duke Ingalls for the Estate of Vernon Duke.

"Tribute" by Jerome Kern in *George Gershwin*, Merle Armitage, editor. Reprinted by permission of the Betty Kern Miller Literary Trust.

INDEX

NOTE: *References to "Gershwin" indicate George Gershwin. Other members of the Gershwin family are differentiated by use of their first names.*

Aarons, Alex, 52–53, 60, 65–68, 72, 194
Abramson, Max, 39, 263
Achron, Joseph, 291
Aeolian Hall, 45–49, 49–51, 83, 125
African American cultural influence
  American Jews and, 124n
  Arvey on, 23–24
  "borrowings" from black music, 149,
    150–52, 152n, 154
  Dalrymple on, 41
  dance, 205, 217
  Downes on, 50
  in film, 107n
  Gershwin and, 90, 93, 115, 217–18, 291
  Goldberg on, 29
  Gullah Negroes, 184, 200, 230
  "I Got Rhythm" and, 167–72
  language and dialect, 230
  Negro sermons, 185
  performers, 196, 200–201, 207, 209–10,
    211, 221–28, 228–36, 239, 249
  Samuel Chotzinoff on, 84
  Smith on, 147–56
  songs and spirituals, 99, 193–94, 205–7,
    211–13, 216, 229, 246
Afro-American Symphony, 147, 150, 151
"Ain't It a Shame?," 77
Albert Hall, 96
Alda, Frances Jeanne, 46
Aldrich, Richard, 78
"Alexander's Ragtime Band," 77, 116, 125
"All Coons Look Alike to Me," 77, 116
Allen, Gracie, 250
Alvin Theater, 196, 232
America (Bloch), 117–18

American Association for the
  Advancement of Science, 288
American Hebrew, 114
An American in Paris
  Bernstein on, 298
  Daly on, 176
  Downes on, 112–14, 276
  Dukelsky on, 290
  Dupree on, 128
  early sketch, 317
  estate value, 280
  film, 7, 322
  Gershwin on, 117, 119–22
  Jacobi on, 188–89
  Jones on, 245, 246
  Kutner on, 247 48
  Langley on, 173–75
  orchestration, 301, 302–3, 306
  origin, 316
  premiere, 317
  reviews, 177, 282
  Schirmer's contribution, 109
  solo-piano version, 320
  Taylor on, 110–11
  two-piano version, 317
The American Language (Mencken), 66
American Masters (television series), xiii
American Mercury, 123, 124
American music, 114–19, 121. *See also*
  African American cultural influence;
  jazz
The American Musical Landscape (Crawford),
  155n
American Society of Composers, Authors
  & Publishers, 271–72

Ames, Florenza, 145
Ansky, S., 16
Antheil, George, 28, 119, 126
"Anthropology," 170
anti-Semitism, 172
"Apple Honey," 165
Arden, Victor, 65, 72, 161
Arlen, Harold, 241, 273
Armitage, Merle, xiii–xiv
art collection
    Botkin's works, 262
    Harkins on, 141–42
    Kutner on, 248–49
    Levant on, 11
    museum exhibition, 254n
    shipping, 252–54
    Woollcott on, 182–83
art music, 123–30
articles and reviews. *See also* obituaries and
        eulogies
    "American Music" question, 44–45
    Benchley, 137–38
    Bernstein, 293–300
    Chotzinoff, 82–84
    Crawford, 156–72
    Daly, 175–76
    Downes, 112–14, 177–78
    Duke (Dukelsky), 289–93
    Dupree, 123–30
    Ellington, 300–301
    Garson, 239–44
    Gershwin, xii, 94–98, 98–100, 119–22,
        133–36, 217–21
    Gershwin (Ira), 289
    on Gershwin's background, 145–46
    on Gershwin's estate, 280–81
    Gilman, 85–87
    Harkins, 138–43
    Jacobi, 186–90
    Jones, 244–46
    Kutner, 246–49
    Langley, 172–75
    Niles, 101–2
    on *Porgy and Bess*, 213–17
    Ruhl, 143–45
    Shirley, 301–7
    South Carolina visit, 211–13
    Still, 151
    Swain, 193–201
    Taylor, 110–11

    Van Vechten, 77–82
    Whiteman concert, 49–51
    Woollcott, 179–84
Arvey, Verna, 20–25, 150–51, 154
Associated Recorded Program Service,
    152n
Astaire, Adele, 4, 58, 65, 70, 72–73
Astaire, Fred
    A Damsel in Distress, 250
    Ira Gershwin on, 58–59, 72–73
    on John Bubbles, 15
    Lady, Be Good!, 4–5, 65, 67, 70–72, 157n
    Shall We Dance, 16, 240
Atkins, Harry, 81, 217
Atkinson, Brooks, 198, 213–15
atonalism, 20–21
auditions, 211, 221–22, 229
Auric, Georges, 290
Austin, William, 157, 157n

"The Babbitt and the Bromide," 58
"Babes in the Woods," 103
Bach, Johann Sebastian, 100, 120, 277
"Back Home," 312
"Bad Bad Men," 74
Bailey, Bill, 29
Baker, Josephine, 226
Baker, Kenny, 242
Balakirev, Mili, 34
Balanchine, George, 242
Balfe, Michael William, 34
ballad-operas, 57
banjos, 147n
Barber of Seville, 187
Barrymore, Ethel, 143
Bartok, Bela, 78
Bauer, Harold, 34
Bayes, Nora, 5, 7–8, 39, 40
Be Yourself, 74
The Beauty Prize (Wodehouse), 53
bebop, 167–72. *See also* jazz
Bechet, Sidney, 165, 165n
Beethoven, Ludwig van, 167, 198, 277
Beethoven Symphony Orchestra, 32
The Beggar's Opera (Gay), 57
Behrman, Sam, 210, 255
Belcher, George, 60
Bell, Clive, 123, 130
Bellini, Vincenzo, 58

Benchley, Robert, 137–38
Bennett, Robert Russell, 11, 176, 301–2,
    305–6, 311
Berg, Alban, 17
Bergen, Edgar, 242
"Berkeley Square Kew," 54
Berlin, Irving
    "American Music" question, 45
    associated with jazz, 108
    Astaire-Rogers films, 239
    Carl Van Vechten on, 78
    eulogy for Gershwin, 278–79
    Gershwin on, 100, 119, 136
    influence of, 116
    James Ross Moore on, 56
    jazz and, 123
    at memorial service, 272
Berman, Pandro, 261
Berman, Paul, 267
Bernstein, Leonard, 293–300
"Bess, You Is My Woman Now," 188
The Big Charade, 62
"Bill Bailey," 77
biographers of Gershwin, xi–xiv
Black, Frank, 8
Black Belt, 82
Black-Eyed Susan, 67, 315. *See also* Lady, Be
    Good!
"Blah, Blah, Blah," 108
Blake, Eubie, 149–50, 154
Blakey, Art, 171
Bledsoe, Jules, 209
Bloch, Ernest, 117–18, 277
Bloomfield-Zeisler, Fannie, 34
Blore, Eric, 56
"Blow Top," 165
Blue Monday, 37, 41, 87–89, 194, 313
blues music, 29, 84, 156
Blues Rhythm Orchestra, 160n
Bodini, Jean, 43
Bolton, Guy, 53, 66–67, 103, 177, 194
"Bon-Bon Buddy," 77
Bordoni, Irene, 56
Boris Goudonov, 100
Boston Symphony Orchestra, 177–78
Botkin, Henry, 11, 141, 184, 260–61, 262
Boulanger, Nadia, 5
"Boy Wanted," 55, 56, 313
Bracken, L. H., 288
Brahms, Johannes, 18, 118, 277

Bring on the Girls (Bolton and Wodehouse),
    53
British Broadcasting Corporation (BBC),
    xiii
Broadway Brevities, 312
Broun, Heywood, 46
Brown, Anne Wiggins
    Duncan on, 223, 226
    Gershwin on, 218
    on Gershwin's personality, xi–xii
    interview, 228–36
    reviews, 217
Bruskin, Rose, 28
Bubbles, John W., 15, 218, 223, 233
Budworth Company, 252, 254
Burleigh, Harry T., 151n
Burns, George, 250
Busoni, Ferruccio, 34
Butterfield, Billy, 104n
"The Buzzard Song," 233
"By Strauss," 321
Byas, Don, 164

Campbell-Watson, Frank, 302–4
Campion, Thomas, 57
"Can This Be Love?" (Swift), 21
"Can't We Be Friends?" (Swift), 21
Cantor, Eddie, 257
Carmen, 125, 199, 219, 249, 306
Carnegie Hall, 6, 82–84, 88, 177
Carpenter, John Alden, 126, 277
Carter, Desmond, 53, 54
cartoons, 60
Caruso, Enrico, 94
cast recordings, 227, 233–34
casting and auditions, 211, 221–22,
    229
Catfish Row theme, 305
Cedars of Lebanon Hospital, 242
Charleston, South Carolina, 211–13
Charleston (dance), 84, 93, 102, 111
Charlie Chan at the Opera, 16
Charlot's Review, 56
Chopin, Frederick, 32, 100, 101, 306
Chotzinoff, Samuel, 21, 82–84, 174
chronology of Gershwin's life and works,
    309–23
cinema, 133. *See also* films
Circus Day (Taylor), 88, 100, 126

"A City Called Heaven," 229
"Clap Yo' Hands," 103, 107n, 189
Clark, Bobby, 138, 242
classical music, 48. *See also specific composers and works*
classification of Gershwin music, 199–201
Clements, Dudley, 145
clubs, 84n, 227
Cochran, Gifford, 257
collaboration
    Arvey on, 21–22
    Bolton, 54
    Downes on, 275–76
    Dushkin, 315
    Heyward (DuBose), 201–11
    Ira Gershwin, xiii, 54–55, 57–62, 65, 108, 189, 275–76
    Levant on, 10–11
    lyric-writing and, 57–62
    musical comedies, 194–95
    Shall We Dance, 16
    Swift on, 6–7
comedic music, 47
composition process. *See also* collaboration
    Bernstein on, 298
    Gershwin on, 119–22, 133–36
    Harkins on, 140
    Langley on, 172–75
    Levant on, 15–16
    Schillinger's system, 287–88, 291–92
    Stravinsky's influence, 277–78
Concerto in F
    associated with jazz, 99
    Bernstein on, 298
    Crawford on, 156
    Dalrymple on, 42
    Downes on, 112
    Dukelsky on, 290
    estate value of, 280
    Frankie Gershwin on, 5
    Gershwin on, 91, 94, 98, 117
    influences on, 16
    Ira's defense of, 289
    Jacobi on, 187, 188–89
    Jones on, 246
    Langley on, 173
    Levant on, 12
    orchestration, 22, 302–3
    performances, 5, 13
    release date, 63

    reviews, 82–84, 177
    scoring, 302–3, 315
    Swift on, 6–7
    vernacular style, 127
confidence of Gershwin, 5, 8–9, 194
Confrey, Zez, 27
Connie's Inn, 84n
Converse, Frederick, 126
Conway, Jack, 66
Coolidge, Elizabeth Sprague, 17
"The Cooney County Fair," 313
Copland, Aaron, 28, 118, 126, 129, 163n
correspondence
    Abramson, 39–41
    Botkin, 260–61
    on Gershwin's death, 263–68, 281–83
    Hannenfeldt, 251–54
    Heyward (DuBose), 201–11
    Ira Gershwin, 42–44, 72–74, 185–86
    Paley, 184–85, 259–60
    Rose Gershwin, 178–79, 261–62, 263
    Schirmer, 108–9, 254–59
    as source on Gershwin, xii
    Van Vechten, 52
"Cotton Tail," 165, 170
Count Basie, 165, 167
counterpoint, 24
Coward, Noel, 53
Cowell, Henry, 27–28
Crawford, Cheryl, 197
Crawford, Jess, 288
Crawford, Richard, 155n, 156–72, 157n
crime, 30
Crosley Radio Company, 258
Crowninshield, Frank, 46
Cuban Overture
    counterpoint in, 24–25
    experimentation, 131
    Levant on, 11
    premiere, 319
    scoring, 318
    Shirley on, 304
cultural influences on music, 121, 124. *See also* African American cultural influence
curiosity of Gershwin, 14–15, 22

Dalrymple, Dolly, 41–42
d'Alvarez, Marguerite, 52, 95–96, 101, 102–3

Daly, William
  friendship with Gershwin, 9, 19, 140
  Furia on, 69
  Langley on, 174–75
  Levant on, 13
  orchestration, 290
  response to Langley, 175–76
  scoring suggestions, 302
  Smith on, 102–3
Damrosch, Walter
  An American in Paris, 113–14
  Arvey on, 21
  Chotzinoff on, 83–84
  concert patronage, 46
  Concerto in F, 7, 85–89, 276
  Gershwin on, 91
  scoring suggestions, 302
  works commissioned, 25–27
A Damsel in Distress
  contract, 320
  Frances Gershwin on, 5
  Gershwin contributions, 240, 268
  participants, 250
  scoring, 321
dance
  Charleston, 84, 93, 102, 111
  Chotzinoff on, 84
  Downes on, 51
  Fred and Adele Astaire, 4
  Gershwin and, 4, 91, 93, 94
  Ira Gershwin dance numbers, 71–72
  jazz and, 94, 129–30
  Lady, Be Good!, 71
The Dancing Girl, 314
Dandy, Walter E., 243–44, 265
A Dangerous Maid, 55, 65, 313
Daniel Jazz (Gruenberg), 118
Dashiell, Allen, 16n
Davis, Miles, 170
"Dawn of a New Day," 321
De Koven, Reginald, 28
De Lerma, Dominique-René, 150n
"Dear Little Girl," 322
death of Gershwin, 228, 243–44, 263–68,
  281–83, 321
Debussy, Claude, 32, 101, 277–78
Decca Records, 234
Delicious (film)
  Gershwin contract, 107–8
  Gershwin contributions, 212, 239

Levant on, 10
"Manhattan Rhapsody," 318
Second Rhapsody and, 173n, 177
Dere Mabel, 312
DeSylva, B. G. "Buddy," 41, 54, 140, 194
Diaghilev, Serge, 290
Dial, 123
Die Meistersinger, 18, 87, 187, 216
Dillingham, Charles, 92
d'Indy, Vincent, 178
"Do It Again," 8, 26, 313
documentaries on Gershwin, xiii
Don Redman and His Orchestra,
  165n
Donaldson, Walter, 58, 136
"Don't Be That Way," 165
Doucet, Charles-Camille, 290
Dowland, John, 57
Downes, Olin
  on *An American in Paris,* 112–14
  Brown on, 232
  Gershwin eulogy, 274–78
  on *Porgy and Bess,* 198, 215–17
  on *Second Rhapsody,* 177–78
  on Whiteman concert, 49–51
Draak, Tom, 145
Dreiser, Theodore, 27
Dresser, Louise, 5
Dresser, Paul, 27
Dreyfus, Max, 81, 142, 244, 264, 268
Duke, Vernon (Vladimir Dukelsky), 282,
  289–93
The Duke Ellington Reader (Tucker), xii
Dukelsky, Vladimir. *See* Duke, Vernon (Vla-
  dimir Dukelsky)
dummy titles, 60–61
Duncan, Todd
  Brown on, 231, 232–33
  Gershwin on, 218, 257
  interview, 221–28
  Jones on, 246
  on opening night, 197
  on Pallay, 264
  reviews, 217
Duo Concertante, 259n
Dupree, Mary Herron, 123–30
Dushkin, Samuel, 259n, 315
Dvořák, Antonin, 115
The Dybbuk (Ansky), 16, 318

Ed Wynn's Carnival, 312
education of Gershwin
  composition lessons, 311, 317, 318
  conducting studies, 314
  formal training, 30, 309–10
  Goldberg on, 28
  high school, 310
  introduction to music, 31–32
  music history, 313
  musical intuition, 35
  self-education, 22
Einstein, Albert, 122
Eliot, T. S., 123
Ellington, Duke
  Gershwin's influence on, 104n, 165–67, 170
  on Gershwin's personality, 300–301
  impact of Gershwin on, 17
  on *Porgy and Bess*, 200
Elliot, Jane, 40
Elzy, Ruby, 217, 231
embellishment, 130, 156. *See also* jazz
"Embraceable You," 157n, 306
Emperor Jones, 209, 235
Engel, Carl, 126n, 127, 129, 199
Engel, Lehman, 195, 305
enthusiasm of Gershwin, 247
Escape, 142
estate of Gershwin, 252, 280–81
Europe, 20, 119. *See also* travels
Evening Post, 108
"Everybody Step," 100
Ewen, David, 197
"An Experiment in Modern Music," 314
experimentation in music, 48, 121
Eye, Ear, Nose & Throat Monthly, 242

Falla, Manuel de, 18
Falstaff, 187
fame, 5–6
family life of Gershwin. *See also specific
    individuals*
  childhood, 27–35, 80, 275
  extended family, 39n
  Frankie Gershwin on, 4–5
  Gershwin's correspondence on, 178–79
  Gershwin's travels and, 44
  Goldberg on, 28
  musical talent and, 92
Farrar, Geraldine, 187

Farrell, Charles, 239
"Fascinating Rhythm"
  composition, 26
  inspiration for, 55
  Jacobi on, 189
  in *Lady, Be Good!*, 315
  origins, 68–70
  "rhythm" terminology, 157–60n
  "Syncopated City" and, 68
father. *See* Gershwin, Morris
Fields, Benny, 88
Fields, Herbert, 62
films, 7, 107n, 107–8. *See also specific titles*
finances and estate of Gershwin, 252,
    280–81
Finck, Heinrich, 187
Fine and Dandy (Swift), 21
Finley Club, 34–35
Fitzgerald, Ella, 103, 171–72
Fitzgerald, F. Scott, 65, 71
Fliver Ten Million (Converse), 126
"A Foggy Day," 56, 240, 250–51, 261
folk music, 217. *See also* African American
    cultural influence
Folly Island, South Carolina, 247, 320
Fontaine, Joan, 240, 250
For Goodness Sake, 313
Forsyth, Cecil, 18
Forte, Allen, 103–7
The Fortune Teller, 27
"Four Little Sirens We," 54–55
Four Serenades, 126
Fox Movietone Company, 107–8, 145–46
Francis, Arthur, 53, 55
Frank, Waldo, 123
Freedley, Vinton, 53, 58–59, 65–67, 72, 194
The French Doll, 313
Friar's Society Orchestra, 157n
"From the Land of Blues," 153
From the New World (Dvořák symphony),
    151n
Froman, Jane, 161, 248
funeral, 275
Funny Face, 4, 58, 316, 317, 322
Furia, Philip, xiii, 65–72
futurism, 117

Gallagher, Irene, 263–68
Galli-Curci, Amelita, 46, 135

Galloway, Hunter, 22
Galsworthy, John, 142
Garden, Mary, 187
Garland, Bob, 140
Garland, Judy, 161
Garson, Edith, 239–44
Gauthier, Eva, 78–79, 124–25
Gaxton, William, 144–45
Gaynor, Janet, 212, 239
Geddes, Norman Bel, 67
George Gershwin (Armitage), xiii
George Gershwin (Goldberg), 161n
George Gershwin's Songbook, xii, 142, 156, 319
George White's *Scandals. See* Scandals
Gershwin, Arthur, 12, 30, 262, 309, 323
Gershwin, Frances ("Frankie"). *See*
    Godowsky, Frances Gershwin
Gershwin, George — Note: As George
    Gershwin is the subject of the work,
    please find additional information
    throughout the index. *See also*
    personality traits of Gershwin
  birth, 27, 309
  childhood, 27–35, 80, 275
  chronology of life and works, 309–23
  death, 228, 243
  health problems, 138–39, 180, 235, 239,
    242–43, 264–67, 321
  social life, 4, 6–7, 10, 13, 21, 30, 52, 140–41,
    240–41, 255, 259n, 259–60
Gershwin, Ira
  Arvey on, 22
  at auditions, 222–23, 229
  birth, 30, 309
  collaboration, xiii, 54–55, 57–62, 65, 108,
    189, 275–76
  dance numbers and, 71–72
  death, 323
  Delicious lyrics, 177
  family life, 92
  Gershwin's death and, 243–44, 265, 267
  on Gershwin's personality, 3
  Goldberg on, 30, 34
  Goldwyn Follies, 261
  Harkins on, 140
  "I Got Rhythm," 157, 160, 162
  Lady, Be Good!, 66, 72–74
  Luce on, 25–27
  lyric credits, 53
  marriage, 10

penthouse apartment, 141–42
Porgy and Bess, 209, 210, 213, 219–21
Primrose, 53
reviews, 260
rhyme schemes, 70
Shall We Dance, 240
show attendance, 150–51
"Syncopated City," 68
travels, 179, 241, 253, 257
Woollcott on, 183
Gershwin, Leonore
  death, 323
  Gershwin's death, 243–44, 267
  Oscar Levant on, 10
  travels, 179, 253, 257
Gershwin, Morris, 13–14, 30–31, 66–67, 92,
  309
Gershwin, Rose
  at auditions, 229
  background, 28
  correspondence, 261–62
  Gershwin's death and, 267, 280–81
  marriage, 309
  travels, 258, 259
Gershwin (Jablonski), xiii–xiv
Gershwin Remembered (Jablonski ed.), xiii,
  xiv
The Gershwin Years (Jablonski and Stewart),
  xiii
The Gershwins (Kimball and Simon), xiii
ghost writing, 24
Gilbert, Henry F., 277
Gilbert, L. Wolfe, 272
Gilbert, William S., 53
Gillespie, Dizzy, 170
Gilman, Lawrence, 85–87, 174
Girl Crazy
  Crawford on, 157
  film, 319
  Garland recording, 161
  Gershwin conducting, 318
  "I Got Rhythm" and, 163
  Levant on, 10
  orchestration, 301
  Smith on, 147
  Still and, 155
Glaenzer, Jules, 46
Glazounof, Alexandre, 34
Glenn Miller Orchestra, 163–64
Glière, Reinhold Moritzovich, 34

Gluck, Alma, 44, 46
"Goat Sammy," 193. *See also Porgy and Bess*
Goddard, Paulette, 241, 262n
Godowsky, Frances Gershwin
    birth, 30, 309
    concert patronage, 46
    death, 323
    on Gershwin's personality, 3–6
    marriage, 318
    on "Syncopated City," 68
    travels, 262
Godowsky, Leopold, 3, 234
Godowsky, Leopold, II, 318
Goetz, E. Ray, 56
Goldberg, Isaac, xii, xiv, 27–35, 124, 183
Goldmark, Karl, 33
Goldmark, Ruben, 33, 81, 115–16, 143
Goldwyn, Samuel, 241, 256, 259, 268, 281–82
The Goldwyn Follies
    Gershwin contributions, 241–42, 261, 263,
        268, 321
    Ira Gershwin on, 281–82
"Golliwogg's Cakewalk," 77, 101
Golschmann, Vladimir, 290
Gone with the Wind, 262
Good Morning, Judge, 93, 311
Good News, 160
Goodman, Benny, 157, 165, 288
Goossens, Eugene, 23
Gordon, Jeanne, 46
Gorman, Ross, 50
Götterdämmerung, 187
Gottschalk, Louis Moreau, 34
Grand Street Follies, 65
"The Great American Composer" (Van
    Vechten), 78
Great Depression, 131
Green, Stanley, 195–96
Greenwich Village Follies, 65
Grey, Clifford, 42
Grofé, Ferde
    "A Tone Journey," 88
    Arvey on, 22
    Gershwin on, 100
    Goldberg on, 27
    Langley on, 174–75
    orchestration, 290, 302
    Rhapsody in Blue orchestration, 49
Gross, Jerome, 288
Grossmith, George, 53

Gruenberg, Louis, 118
Guild Theatre, 15
Guinan, Tex, 66
Gullah Negroes, 24, 184, 200

Hackett, James K., 181
Hadley, Henry, 88–89
Haggin, B. H., 129
"The Half of It, Dearie, Blues," 71, 189, 315
Half Past Eight, 311
"Hallelujah!" (Still), 147, 148
"Hallelujah Chorus," 126
Hambitzer, Charles, 32–33, 34, 80
Hamilton, David, 199
Hamm, Charles, 150n, 198
Hammerstein, Oscar, 272
Hammett, Dashiell, 180
Handy, W. C., 151
"Hang on to Me," 72
Hannenfeldt, Zenna, 251–54
Harburg, E. Y. "Yip," 241, 255, 273
Harkins, John, 138–43
Harlem, 87, 194
Harling, W. Franke, 126
harmony, 33, 80–81, 162, 216, 248
Harris, Marion, 97
Hart, Charles, 88
Hart, Edward, 102–3
Hart, Moss, 241, 255, 272
Hawkins, Erskine, 167
Heifetz, Jascha, 21, 44, 46, 92
Helburn, Theresa, 210
Hellman, Lillian, 241
Heming, Percy, 53
Henderson, Fletcher, 165, 167
Hendersonville, South Carolina, 210
Henson, Leslie, 53, 56
Herald Tribune, 138
Herbert, Victor, 27, 45, 46–47, 50, 174, 301
"Here Comes a Sailor," 29
Herman, Woody, 165
Hevonpaa, Sulo, 145
Heyward, Dorothy, 184, 194, 213–14
Heyward, DuBose
    Arvey on, 24
    correspondence with Gershwin, 201–11
    Gershwin on, 219–21
    Gershwin's visits with, 184, 185–86, 211–13
    influence of *Porgy*, 193

Porgy and Bess collaboration, 195, 213–14, 230, 241
    portrait, 249
"Hiawatha," 77
Hicklin, Margery, 53
"High Hat," 189
Hill, Edward Burlingame, 125
Hindemith, Paul, 78
Hines, Earl, 167
Hinton, Milt, 170
Hirsch, Lou, 14
Hit Parade, 260, 261
Hitchy-Koo of 1918, 311
H.M.S. Pinafore, 125
Hodges, Johnny, 167
Hofmann, Josef Casimir, 92
Hollywood, California, 227–28, 235, 237, 256
Holy Rollers Church, 210
homes and residences of Gershwin
    art collection displayed, 252–55
    California, 240–41
    family and, 22
    Frances Gershwin on, 4
    Harkins on, 141–42
    Kutner on, 248–49
    Levant on, 14–16
    variety, 30–31
Honegger, Arthur, 17, 119
Horne, Lena, 103
Houseman, John, 210
Howard, Francis, 88
Hulbert, Claude, 53
humor, 13, 34
Humoresque (Dvořák), 31
Hurst, Fannie, 46
Hutcheson, Ernest, 33

"I Can't Be Bothered Now," 240, 261
"I Got Plenty of Nuttin'," 16, 199, 215–16, 224, 292–93
"I Got Rhythm"
    Crawford on, 156–72
    harmonic structure, 162, 162n, 167
    "I Got Rhythm" Variations, 131, 302, 304, 319
    instrumental version, 165n
    as jazz standard, 161–65
    melody, 164
    recordings, 158–60, 164, 171–72
    Schillinger's influence, 293

Smith on, 147–56
Still and, 155n
"I Love To Rhyme," 268
"I Loves You Porgy," 232
"I Make Hay While the Sun Shines," 56
"I Was Doing All Right," 268
"I Was So Young, and You Were So Beautiful," 26, 81, 93
"I Won't, I Will," 56
"I Won't Say I Will," 26
idioms of American music, 118
"If You Want 'Em, You Can't Get 'Em," 281
Il Trovatore, 187
"I'll Build a Stairway to Paradise," 8, 26, 81, 275, 313
"I'm on My Way," 214
imagery in music, 119–22
imitation, 136
Immerman, Connie, 84n
Immerman, George, 84n
Impromptu in Two Keys, 314, 323
improvisation, 124, 164
"In a Sentimental Mood," 104n
"Innocent Ingenue Baby," 313
innovation in music, 273–74
inspiration in music, 133–36
interviews, 138, 221–28
"Isn't It Wonderful," 54
Istar Variations, 178
"It Ain't Necessarily So," 16, 61, 188, 289–93
"It's Very Clear," 268

Jablonski, Edward, xiii–xiv, xiv, 54
Jacobi, Frederick, 186–90
Janis, Elsie, 5
jazz
    arrangement, 163
    art music and, 123–30
    Arvey on, 20
    bebop, 167–72
    Concerto in F, 85–86
    concerts, 47
    conducting, 90–91
    critiques, 101–2, 127–28
    dance, 94, 129–30
    defining, xi, 98–100, 123–24
    Downes on, 278
    Dupree on, 123–30

jazz (*continued*)
    evolution of, 45–46
    Gershwin and, 75, 89–91, 91–94, 94–98,
        116–18, 120–21, 123–30, 212–13
    Goldberg on, 35
    harmonization in, 162n
    "I Got Rhythm," 161–72
    influences, 84, 116–17
    Jacobi on, 187–88
    Jazz Age, 65–68, 71, 83
    "jazz rage," 126
    journal articles on, 123
    Langley on, 173
    as "performer's music," 171
    player status, 163n
    popularity of, 78
    rhythm, 96, 100, 120, 223–24
    scoring, 47–48, 79–80
    singing, 94–98, 224
    standards, 161–65
    swing music, 244–45
"Jazz Music of Today" (Hill), 125
Jazz Piano Concerto (Copeland), 118
Jazz Records A-Z (Rust), 160n
Jazz Symphony (Antheil), 126
The Jazz Tradition (Williams), 164n
"Jenny," 59
Jepson, Helen, 227, 242
Jessel, Léon, 172n
Johnson, Hall, 200
Johnson, J. Rosamund, 208, 233, 246, 246n
"The Jolly Tar and the Milkmaid," 240, 250
Jolson, Al, 39, 93–94, 97, 202–3, 312
Jones, Isabel Morse, 244–46
Joplin, Scott, 156
"Jurgen," 82
"Just Another Rhumba," 268, 322

Kahn, Otto, 46
Kapp, Jack, 227
Kaufman, George, 181, 195
Kaufman, Harry, 19, 137
Kaufman, S. Jay, 46
Kaye, Danny, 59
Kearns, Allen, 75
Kern, Jerome
    Furia on, 66
    Gershwin on, 97, 136
    Gershwin's death and, 267, 279–80

jazz associated with, 124
    on *Ladies First*, 39
    Langley on, 174
    at memorial service, 272
    Moore on, 53
    Show Boat origins, 193
    Smith on, 103
    social life, 255, 273
    songs for film, 239
Kilenyi, Edward, 33, 80
Kimball, Robert, xiii
King, Charles, 93
King, Mollie, 93
The King and I, 54
Kiss Me Stupid, 322
Kitchin, Karl, 46
"Kitten on the Keys," 126n
Klemperer, Otto, 256
Kolodin, Irving, 196, 199
Koussevitsky, Serge, 177–78, 303
Kramer, A. Walter, 98–100, 175
Kreisler, Fritz, 46
Krupa, Gene, 157
Kutner, Nanette, 246–49

La, La Lucille, 37, 60, 65, 93, 312
La Bohème, 10
"La Maxixe," 110–11, 113
Ladies First, 7–8, 39–41, 157n, 311
Lady, Be Good!
    collaboration, 37
    dancing, 4
    "Fascinating Rhythm," 157n
    film, 321
    Furia on, 65–72
    Gershwin on, 94, 97
    Harkins on, 142
    Ira Gershwin on, 59
    lyrics and rhythms, 65–72
    musical numbers, 73–74
    premiere, 63, 315
    success, 56, 65, 291
"Lady, Be Good," 26, 189, 275. *See also* "Oh,
    Lady Be Good"
The Lady in Red, 312
Langley, Allan Lincoln, 172–75, 175–76
Langner, Lawrence, 209
language, 65–72. *See also* lyrics
"The Last Rose of Summer," 219, 249

Lavalle, Paul, 288
Lawrence, Gertrude, 56, 59, 103–4, 108
League of Composers, 125
Ledermann, Minna, 186
Lennox, Vera, 53
Leo Reisman Orchestra, 156–57
Les Adventures du Roi Pausole (Honegger), 17
Les Noces (Stravinsky), 18
Let 'Em Eat Cake, 18, 181, 189, 195, 318–19
"Let's Call The Whole Thing Off," 240
Levant, Oscar
   friendship with Gershwin, 140, 241, 255
   on Gershwin, 7–19
   Woollcott on, 180–81
Levee Land (Still), 23, 150–51
Lewis, Sinclair, 123
Lewisohn Stadium, 11–12
Lhevinne, Josef, 34
Library of Congress, xiii, 154
Liebling, Leonard, 44, 46
A Light for Saint Agnes (Harling), 126
Lillie, Beatrice, 252
Lincoln, Abraham, 23
Liszt, Franz, 32, 34
"Little Jazz Bird," 315
Little Miss Bluebeard, 56, 314
"Little Rhythm, Go 'Way," 69
"Livery Stable Blues," 45–46, 47, 50, 125
"Liza," 156, 189
"Loch Lomond," 29
London, 43–44
"Looking for a Boy," 55, 75
Lopez, Vincent, 125, 125n
Los Angeles Philharmonic, 5
Los Angeles Symphony, 227
"Love Is Here to Stay," 301
"Love Nest," 14
"Love Walked Right In," 268
Lowell, Amy, 96
Lubitsch, Ernst, 210
Luce, Henry, 25
Luis Russell and His Orchestra, 157
Lullaby for String Quartet, 37, 311, 322
Lunceford, Jimmie, 165, 167
Luther, Frank, 161
Luther, Martin, 57
Lyons, Arthur, 258, 264, 282
lyrics
   "Boy Wanted," 55
   dummy titles, 60–61

"Fascinating Rhythm," 68–70
   Ira Gershwin on, 57–62
   Lady, Be Good!, 66–67
   "Little Rhythm, Go 'Way," 69
   "Looking for a Boy," 55
   lyricism, 199–200
   misconceptions about songwriting,
      133–36
   "Oh, Lady Be Good," 68
   Porgy and Bess, 205–6, 208, 213, 219, 224–26
   Primrose, 53
   royalties, 186
   Strike Up the Band, 137
   vocal writing, 199
Lyrics on Several Occasions (Ira Gershwin),
   xiii, 55, 57, 322
Lyrische Suite, 17

"Ma Blushin' Rosie," 77
Maazel, Lorin, 197
MacDonald, Jeanette, 75, 115
Macedonia Church, 24
Machine Age, 119–22
"Madrigal," 313
The Magistrate, 93
Magnin, Edgar F., 272
"Making of a Girl," 310
Mamoulian, Rouben
   Brown on, 228, 231, 233, 235
   Duncan on, 198, 226
   friendship with Gershwin, 15
   Gershwin on, 218
   Porgy and Bess reviews, 210, 213–15
"The Man I Love," 103, 137, 189, 249
"Manhattan Rhapsody," 318
Mann, Thomas, 279
"Maple Leaf Rag," 156
Marsalis, Wynton, 171
Marshall, Everette, 248
Martin, Mary, 161, 161n
Marx, Harpo, 255
Marx, Rudolph, 267
Massenet, Jules Emile Frederic, 34
mathematics and music, 14, 287–88
Matthews, Ralph, 200
"May Day" (Fitzgerald), 71
"Maybe," 107n
McBride, Mary Margaret, 45–49
McBride, Robert, 303–4

McCarthy, Charlie, 242
McCormack, John Francis, 46
McGowan, Jack, 88
McIntyre, O. O., 46
Medtner, Nicolai Karlovich, 34
"Meet the Boys," 88
Mellers, Wilfrid, 196–97
Melody in F (Rubinstein), 29
"Memo to Musicologists" (Arvey), 151n
memorial services for Gershwin, 228,
    271–73, 281
"The Men Behind American Music" (Still),
    151
Mencken, H. L., 66, 123
Mengelberg, Willem, 173
Merman, Ethel, 160–61, 162–63
The Merry Widow, 87
Metropolitan Opera, 228, 235
"Mexican Dance," 43
Meyer, Joseph, 69
Meyerbeer, Giacomo, 58
Milhaud, Darius, 290
Miller, Glenn, 157, 163–64, 288
Miller, Jack, 32
Miller, Marilyn, 41
Mills, Florence, 23
"Mine," 189
Minnelli, Vincent, 252, 283
Miss 1917, 81, 310
Mitchell, Abbie, 232–33
Modern Music, 123, 186
Mondello, Toots, 288
Monk, Thelonious, 170
"Moonlight Serenade," 288
Moore, James Ross, 52–56
Moore, Victor, 144–45
"Moose the Mooche," 168
"The Mophams," 56
Moran, Lois, 145
Morris Gets Midnight Whirl, 312
Mosbacher, Emil, 205, 210, 211, 266
mother. *See* Gershwin, Rose
*The Mother, The Maid, and the Mistletoe
    Bough* (Bellini), 58
movies, 282
Mozart, Wolfgang Amadeus, 18, 198, 277
Mueller, Paul, 184, 252n, 282
Murray, Lyn, 288
Music by Gershwin, 320
"Music for Orchestra and Baritone," 256

Music for the Theater (Copeland), 118
Musical America, 123, 125
musical background of Gershwin, 26, 28–31
The Musical Courier, 44
Musical Quarterly, 123, 127
"musical slang," 128
Musikalisches Wochenblatt, 128n
Mussorgsky, Modest Petrovich, 34, 100, 233
"My Life, Or the Story of George Gersh-
    win" (Levant), 7
"My Log-Cabin Home," 313
"My Man's Gone Now," 307
"M.Y.T. Sascha," 74

"Narcissus and Ophelia," 78
"The Nashville Nightingale," 26, 103, 314
Nast, Condé, 226
Nation, 123
Native American music, 115
"Naughty Baby," 54, 55
Navarro, Fats, 170
Negro Rhapsody, 115–16
New Amsterdam Theatre, 9
*New Grove Dictionary of Music and
    Musicians,* 303
New Orleans Rhythm Kings, 157n
New Republic, 123, 127
New York City, 8
New York Herald Tribune, 101
New York Philharmonic, 173–74
"New York Rhapsody," 173n
New York Symphony Orchestra, 9, 92,
    173–74
New York Times, 49–51, 78, 198–99, 213, 274–78
New York Town Hall, 164
New York World, 41
The New Yorker, 137–38, 174
Newman, Ernest, 74, 82, 99, 102
Newsweek, 289
Nice, Harry W., 165
"Nice Baby!," 75
"Nice Work If You Can Get It," 240, 250,
    261
Nichols, Red, 157
Nifties of 1923, 314
night life, 140
nightclubs, 84n, 227
Niles, Abbe, 101–2, 127
Noguchi, Isamu, 67–68

"Nola," 125n
Norma (Bellini), 58
The Nun, The Dun, and the Son of a Gun, 58

"O Land of Mine, America," 312
obituaries and eulogies, 269, 271–83
O'Dea, June, 145
Of Thee I Sing
   composition process, 140
   estate value of, 280
   Ira Gershwin on, 62
   Jacobi on, 189–90
   musical influences, 18
   opening, 318
   premiere, 145
   Pulitzer Prize, 212, 319
   Ruhl on, 143–45
   as "satirical operetta," 195
   success, 65, 212, 239, 319
   Woollcott on, 181
Offenbach, Jacques, 187, 190, 306
"Oh, de Lawd Shake de Heavens," 215
Oh, Kay!, 56, 94, 103–7, 107n, 316
"Oh, Lady Be Good!," 67, 70, 315
"Oh Lord, I'm On My Way," 23
Ohman, Phil, 65, 72, 161
"Oil Well," 74
"On the Banks of the Wabash," 27
135th Street, 87–89, 128, 194, 291, 316
opera
   ballad-operas, 57
   compared to musicals, 198
   defining, 197
   folk opera, 217–22, 225–26
   Metropolitan Opera, 228, 235
   "Opera Ala Afro-Americana," 41
   operatic acting, 216
   satirical operetta, 195
"Opera Ala Afro-Americana," 41
Opportunity, 200–201
Opus, 306
orchestration
   Dalrymple on, 42
   Daly on, 175–76
   Kutner on, 248
   Langley on, 174–75
   Moore on, 54
   Porgy and Bess, 204
   Rhapsody in Blue, 100

Schillinger's influence, 289–93
Second Rhapsody, 177
   Shirley on, 301–7
   Still on, 150n
Orchestration (Forsyth), 18
Ornstein, Leo, 34, 117, 118
"An Oscar for Treadwell," 168
Our Nell, 65, 313

Pacific No. 231 (Honegger), 119
Paderewski, Ignace Jan, 13
painting, 4, 11, 141–42, 182–83, 252. *See also*
   art collection
Palais Royal Orchestra, 125
Paley, Emily, 53, 259–60
Paley, Lou, 39, 53
Pallay, George A., 39, 263–68
"Papa Loves Mama," 98–100
"The Parade of the Wooden Soldiers," 172n
Pardon My English, 319
Parker, Charlie, 167–70
parties, 52
Passcaglia (Bach), 100
The Passing Show of 1916, 310
Paul Fried and His Rhythmicians, 160n
Paul Whiteman Band, 79, 124, 226, 247
"Pay Some Attention To Me," 261
Pepper, Art, 170
The Perfect Fool, 313
"The Perfect Lady," 314
performance, 11–13, 18, 146, 171. *See also spe-*
   cific works
Perilman, Nathan A., 271
personality traits of Gershwin
   Arvey on, 22–23
   Brown on, xi–xii, 236
   childhood delinquency, 30
   confidence, 5, 8–9, 194
   curiosity, 14–15, 22
   Downes on, 275
   Ellington on, 300–301
   enthusiasm, 247
   Frankie Gershwin on, 5
   Goldberg on, 28
   humor, 13, 34
   lack of pretense, 180
   relationships, 4, 6–7, 10, 30, 181–82
   sincerity, 245
   sophistication, 28

Peterson, Oscar, 103
Peyser, Joan, 104n
The Philharmonic Society, 34
phonographs, 17, 122
photography, 52
physical appearance of Gershwin, 7
Piano Concerto in F. See Concerto in F
piano lessons, 30
Piano Solo by George Gershvin, 35
Piano Sonatas (MacDowell), 115
Piccadilly to Broadway, 312
Pittsburgh Symphony Orchestra, 27
plagiarism, 149, 150–52, 152n, 154
Pleshette, Donald, 256
politics, 143–45, 201
"Pomp and Circumstance," 126
popular music, 86–87, 135, 277–78, 293–300.
        See also jazz
Porgy and Bess
    Atkinson on, 213–15
    audience, 225
    Bernstein on, 298–99
    Brown on, 228–36
    cast, 209–10, 211, 221–28, 228–36, 239,
        249
    character development, 224–25, 230–31
    composition begun, 320
    cut for length, 208
    dialogue, 204
    Downes on, 215–17
    Duncan on, 221–28
    estate value, 280
    film, 322
    Gershwin on, 217–21
    Goldberg on, xii, 217–21
    Heyward collaboration, 195, 201–11,
        213–14, 230, 241
    influences, 15, 18
    Ira's defense of, 289
    Jacobi on, 188–89
    Jones on, 246
    literature on, 191
    lyrics, 210, 230
    naming of, 232
    opening, 233, 320
    orchestration, 204, 301–2, 304–5, 320
    performances, 5, 264
    production team, 246n
    reception, 239–40
    recordings, 227, 233–34

rehearsals, 223–24, 224–25, 226, 230–32,
        320
    "Resistance Hymn," 61
    salaries, 225
    schedule, 202–3
    Schillinger's influence, 292
    scoring, 305
    social and political implications, 201
    songs, 230
    success, 291
    Suite from, 5
    Swain on, 193–201
    Swift's contributions to, 6
Porgy (Heyward), 247, 316
Porter, Cole, 16
Poulenc, François, 290
Powell, Bud, 170
Preludes for Piano, 6, 101–2, 102n, 128, 188,
        317
press and media, 138. See also specific publica-
        tions
The Pretty Druidess (Bellini), 58
Primrose
    Ira Gershwin on, 74
    Moore on, 53–57
    opening, 315
    orchestration, 302
    release date, 63
    scoring, 54, 65
    success, 291
Prokofieff, Sergei, 290–91
Promenade, 322
Provine, Dorothy, 103
psychoanalysis, 14–15, 264
publicity, 207
Puccini, Giacomo, 216
Pulitzer Prize, 195, 212, 319
Punch, 60
"Put Me To the Test," 261
"Put Your Arms Around Me Honey, Hold
        Me Tight," 29

Quintet (Ornstein), 117

Rachmininoff, Sergei, 44, 46, 92, 188
racism, 229
Radin, Oscar, 8
radio, 122, 133, 207, 246–49

Raff, Joachim, 34
"Ragging the Träumerei," 80, 310
ragtime
    Berlin and, 116–17
    Gershwin on, 93
    Goldberg on, 35
    "I Got Rhythm" and, 157
    influence of, 101
    Niles on, 127
Rain or Shine, 151, 154, 156
The Rainbow, 42, 65, 314
Ralston, Bert, 43
Rapee, Arno, 9
"Rashana," 152–53
Ravel, Maurice, 18, 78, 145, 290, 303, 317
"The Real American Folk Song (Is a Rag),
    157n, 311, 322
"Recital for Ancient and Modern Music for
    Voice" (Gauthier), 314
"Red Cross," 168
Red Nichols and His Five Pennies, 157
Reel, Olive, 32
rehearsals, 92, 223–24, 224–25, 226, 230–32,
    320
Reiner, Fritz, 19, 175, 305–6
religious affiliations of Gershwin, 23–24
Remson, Walter, 152n
Requiem, 187
"Resistance Hymn," 61
Revelers, 97
Rhapsody in Blue
    anniversary tour, 319
    Bernstein on, 296–98
    Crawford on, 156
    critiques, 74, 99
    Downes on, 112
    film, 7, 108, 322
    Gershwin on, 89, 94, 97, 117, 120, 219
    influence of, 83, 276, 277
    inspiration for, 26–27, 134
    Jacobi on, 188–89
    jazz association, 99, 213
    Jones on, 245, 246
    Kutner on, 247
    Langley on, 172–75
    Levant on, 8–9
    orchestration, 22, 54, 100, 301–2, 304, 306
    performances, 5, 12, 13, 65, 102–3, 126
    premiere, 37, 314
    recordings, 316, 317

release date, 63
reviews, 44–45, 47, 50–51, 81–82, 177
success, 25, 49, 81
tour, 314–15
two-piano version, 314
Van Vechten on, 78–79
Whiteman on, 45–49
Rhapsody in Rivets, 173n, 177
Rhumba, 174
rhyme schemes, 70
"The Rhythm Rag," 160n
"Rialto Ripples," 310
Rich, Freddie, 157, 161
Riesenfeld, Hugo, 124
Riggs, Lynn, 241
Rimsky-Korsakoff, Nikolay, 34, 100
Ring, Blanche, 138
Ripples, 9
Ritz Brothers, 242
Roach, Max, 167
Roaring 20s (television program), 103
Robert le Diable (Meyerbeer), 58
Robertson, Dick, 157
Robeson, Paul, 209
Robey, George, 43
Robinson, Bill, 23
Robinson, Edward G., 241, 259n
Robison, Willard, 152, 160n
Robison and His Deep River Orchestra,
    160n
Rodgers, Richard, 16, 28, 54
Rogers, Ginger, 16, 240
Rollins, Sonny, 170
Romberg, Sigmund, 272
Roosevelt, Franklin Delano, 320
Roosevelt recital series, 101–2
Rosalie, 65, 317
Rosanoff, Marie, 21
"Rose of Madrid," 82
Rosen, Max (Maxie Rosenzweig), 26, 31, 34,
    80
Rossini, Gioacchino Antonio, 187
Roth, Murray, 281
Royal, Ted, 288
Rubinstein, Anton, 29
Rubinstein, Beryl, 41–42
Ruby, Harry, 181–82, 241
Ruhl, Arthur, 138, 143–45
Russell, Luis, 157
Russell, Robert, 240

Russian school of music, 34
Rust, Brian, 160n
Ryskind, Morrie, 131, 137, 195

"St. Louis Gal," 84
St. Louis Rhythm Kings, 160n
salaries, 146
"Sam and Delilah," 189
Sampson, Edgar, 165
Sanborn, Pitts, 46
Sanford, Harold, 301
Sapelnikoff, Vassily, 34
satire, 143–45
The Savoy Orchestra, 43
SaxÜbung (Parker), 167
"Scandal Walk," 312
Scandals
    African American influence, 194
    Dalrymple on, 41–42
    Gershwin on, 43
    Gershwin songs for, 81, 313
    Ira Gershwin on, 74
    opening, 314, 315
    "Scandal Walk," 312
    success, 37, 63
    Woollcott on, 179
Schillinger, Joseph
    composition method, 287–88, 289, 290n,
        304–5
    Duke on, 289–93
    influence of, 15, 24–25
    Kutner on, 248
    lessons with Gershwin, 318
    Levant on, 14
Schirmer, Gus, 255, 305–6
Schirmer, Mabel, 108–9, 254n, 254–59
Schirmer, Robert, 109n
Schoenberg, Arnold, 17, 19, 118, 241, 273–74
Schoenfeld, William C., 304
Schubert, Franz Peter, 18, 122
Schuller, Gunther, 162, 162n
Schwartz, Arthur, 70
Schwartz, Charles, 304
scoring, 47–48
    Arvey on, 24
    Concerto in F, 302–3, 315
    Cuban Overture, 318
    A Damsel in Distress, 321
    Downes on, 50

    jazz and, 47–48, 79–80
    Porgy and Bess, 305–6
    Primrose, 54, 65
    Rhapsody in Blue, 79
    Second Rhapsody, 303–4
    Of Thee I Sing, 140
Second Rhapsody
    Downes on, 177–78
    experimentation in, 131
    influences, 18
    Langley on, 173–74
    Levant on, 11
    naming of, 173n
    performances, 12
    Porgy and Bess compared, 305
    premiere, 318
    scoring, 303–4
    source of, 239
Seeley, Blossom, 88
Segal, Vivienne, 81
segregation, 234
Seldes, Gilbert, 46
Selwyn, Edgar, 16
semisymphonic arrangement, 48
"Sentimental Oriental Gentlemen Are
    We," 275
Serenades (Herbert), 48, 50
Sessions, Roger, 302–3
"Shag," 165n
Shall We Dance
    collaboration on, 16
    contract, 320
    Damsel in Distress compared, 268
    Frankie Gershwin on, 5
    Gershwin on, 258–59, 261
    schedule for, 240
"Shaw 'Nuff," 170
Shchedrin, Rodion, 306
Sheehan, Winnie, 140
Shilkret, Nathaniel, 240
Shirley, Wayne, 301–7
The Shocking Miss Pilgrim, 22, 322
Short, Hassard, 59
Short Story, 259n, 315
Show Boat, 193, 197
Show Girl, 318
The Show Is On, 321
Shuffle Along, 150–51, 154, 156
Shumlin, Herman, 203
Sibelius, Jean, 277

signification, 156
Silver Linings, 43
Simon, Alfred, xiii
Sinatra, Frank, 103, 104
Sinbad, 39, 93–94, 312
"Since I Found You," 35, 310
sincerity of Gershwin, 245
"Sing In Spring," 240
"Sing Me Not a Ballad," 62
Singing, 94, 98–100, 101
singing associated with jazz, 94–98,
    224
"The Sirens," 54–55
Sixth Symphony, 187
slang, 66, 72
"Slap That Bass," 240
slavery, 156
"Sleepless Night," 268
Sloan, Dodge, 186
Sloane, A. Baldwin, 39, 40
Small, Paul, 161, 223
Smallens, Alexander
    Brown on, 228, 231, 235
    Duncan on, 198
    friendship with Gershwin, 15
    Gershwin on, 218, 257
    Los Angeles concerts, 245–46
    reviews, 217
Smattering of Ignorance, 7
Smith, Alfred E., 143
Smith, Catherine Parsons, 147–56
Smith, Harry B., 39, 40
Smith, Queenie, 75
social life of Gershwin
    Arvey on, 21
    in Beverly Hills, 240–41, 255, 259–60
    Greenwich Village, 259n
    Harkins on, 140–41
    Levant on, 10, 13
    relationships, 4, 6–7, 10, 30
    Van Vechten on, 52
Society for Aesthetics, 288
"Some Far-Away Someone," 54
"Some Wonderful Sort of Someone," 311,
    312
"Somebody Loves Me," 26, 55
"Someone to Watch Over Me," 103–7
"Something About Love," 40
Song of the Flame, 37, 316
"Song of the Flea," 233

Songbook, 131, 147
songwriting, 57–62. *See also* lyrics
"Sophisticated Lady" (Ellington), 301
sophistication of Gershwin, 28
Soudeikine, Sergei, 215
"soul," 91–94, 96
"South Sea Isles," 313
"Spanish Love," 312
Spanish Prelude, 22
Spazler, Karl, 128n
Spice of Life, 313
spirituals, 99
Spitzer, Henry W., 280
sports and athletics
    childhood games, 28–29
    golf, 186, 241, 255
    Jones on, 245
    roller skating, 229
    tennis, 17, 241, 257
Sprague, Carleton, 102–3
Stabat Mater, 187
"Stairway to Paradise." *See* "I'll Build a
    Stairway to Paradise"
"Steeplechase," 168–69
Stein, Gertrude, 207–8
Steinert, Alexander, 16, 231
Stewart, Donald Ogden, 21
Stewart, Lawrence D., xiii, xiv
Stewart, Slam, 164
"Stiff Upper Lip," 261
Still, Judith Ann, 149, 150n
Still, William Grant, 20, 23, 147–56, 155n
Stitt, Sonny, 170
Stokowski, Leopold, 46, 100
"Stomp It Off," 165
Stone, Fred, 9
"Storm Music," 24
Straton, John Roach, 95–96
Strauss, Johann, 190, 277
Strauss, Richard, 113, 118
Stravinsky, Igor
    composition lessons, 277–78
    debut party, 315
    Gershwin on, 118, 259–60
    influence on Gershwin, 17–18, 145, 216,
        290
Strike Up the Band
    Benchley on, 137–38
    composition, 37
    film, 321

Strike Up the Band (continued)
    Levant on, 9, 10
    Moore on, 52–56
    opening, 318
    in Philadelphia, 316
    as "satirical operetta," 195
    Selwyn and, 16
    success, 131
"Strike Up the Band," 29, 135
structure of *The Gershwin Reader*, xii–xiii
Strunsky, Emily, 39
Sullivan, Arthur Seymour, 29, 34, 187, 190,
    215
"Summertime"
    Brown on, 229, 231–33
    composition, 16
    Duncan on, 222–23
    early work on, 319
    music critics on, 199
    orchestration, 305
    performances, 18
    reviews, 216
    Schillinger's influence, 289–93
Swain, Joseph, 193–201
"Swanee"
    composition, 26
    Downes on, 275
    Gauthier performance, 125
    Gershwin on, 93–94
    Harkins on, 143
    Jacobi on, 187
    success, 25, 39, 43
    Van Vechten on, 81, 312
"Sweet and Low-Down," 75
Sweet Little Devil, 65, 74, 314
The Sweetheart Shop, 312
Swift, Kay, 6–7, 20–25, 232
swing era, xi
*The Swing Era: The Development of Jazz 1930-
    1945* (Schuller), 162n
swing music, 165, 167–72, 244–45
Swing Time, 256
"Syncopated City," 68
syncopation, 124, 245

T. B. Harms Company, 81, 142
The Tales of Hoffmann, 306
"Tango," 80
Tatum, Art, 103, 164n, 164–65

Taylor, Deems
    "An American in Paris: Narrative Guide,"
        110–11, 113, 174
    Chotzinoff on, 82
    "Circus Day," 88, 100, 126
    concert patronage, 46
    Gershwin on, 210
Taylor, Marshall, 282
"Tchaikovsky," 59
technology and music, 122
Tell Me More, 55, 63, 72, 75, 291, 315
Temple B'nai B'rith, 272
Temple Emanu-El, 271
"That American Boy of Mine," 314
Thatcher, Heather, 53, 56
Theatre Guild, 196, 213, 222, 228–30, 234
Theatre Magazine, 92
thematic development, 188–89
"There's a Boat That's Leavin' Soon for
    New York," 215, 223
"There's More to the Kiss Than the X-X-X,"
    311
"They All Laughed," 240
"They Can't Take That Away From Me,"
    240
"They Didn't Believe Me," 97, 99–100
Thibault, Conrad, 248
"Things Are Looking Up," 240, 250, 261
Thomas, Michael Tilson, 304
Thompson, Fred, 67
Thompson, Oscar, 129
Thomson, Virgil, 163n, 201, 207, 233
Thoroughly Modern Millie, 313
Three-Quarter Blues, 312, 322
Tibbett, Lawrence, 227, 234, 248
Time, 138, 315
Tin Pan Alley
    Gershwin on, 136
    Gershwin's contributions, 71
    Goldberg on, 35
    impact on Gershwin, 183, 277
    jazz associated with, 124
    musical forms, 162
*Tin Pan Alley: A Chronicle of the American
    Popular Music Racket* (Goldberg), xii
Tiomkin, Dimitri, 290
Tip-Toes, 55, 63, 75–77, 97, 315–16
titles for songs, 60–61
"To a Wild Rose," 126
tobacco use, 140

Toch, Ernest, 256, 257
Tod und Verklarung (Strauss), 113
Tombes, Andrew, 75
Tommy Dorsey Orchestra, 104n
"A Tone Journey" (Grofé), 88
transposing music, 80–81
travels
    Adirondacks, 203
    Arvey on, 26
    California, 17, 227–28, 235, 237, 239–44,
        253, 256–57, 262, 318, 320–21
    England, 317
    Europe, 52–56, 108–9
    Frankie Gershwin on, 5
    Gershwin family, 179
    Gershwin on, 43, 94, 97
    Gershwin's valet, 252n
    Harkins on, 142
    Havana, Cuba, 179
    Levant on, 13, 16–17
    South Carolina, 184–85, 185–86, 205–6,
        210, 211–13, 319, 320
    White House, 320
Treasure Girl, 317
Trocadero nightclub, 227
"Trumpets of Belgravia," 62
Tucker, Mark, xii
Twain, Mark, 215
"The Twenties Are Here to Stay," 56
Two Little Girls in Blue, 61, 312
Two Waltzes in C, 323

"Under the Bamboo Tree," 77

Van Hoogstraten, Willem, 26–27
Van Vechten, Carl, 46, 52, 77–82, 101, 138
Vanity Fair, 78, 138
Variety, 66, 271–73
vaudeville, 71, 146
Vaughan, Sarah, 103
Venice International Festival of Contempo-
    rary Music, 19
Verdi, Giuseppe, 187, 219
vernacular, 72
"Views and Reviews" (Engel), 127
"Virginia," 275
*Vocal Selections by Chas. Rose and George
    Gershvin*, 35

vocals, 94–98. *See also* lyrics
Vodery, Will, 20, 24, 150n
"Volga Boatman's Song," 126
Von Tilzer, Harry, 93

Wagner, Richard, 34, 277
"Wait a Bit, Susie," 55
"Waiting for the Sun to Come Out,"
    312
"Wake Up, Brother, and Dance," 261
Walker, James J., 143, 144
"Walking the Dog," 240
walking themes, 110–11, 113, 276
"Walküre," 114
waltzes, 99
Watch Your Step, 240, 320
Waters, Ethel, 23, 234
Watson, Henry, Jr., 75
Wattenberg, A. M., 280
Wayburn, Ned, 81
"We Go to Church on Sunday," 313
Webb, Chick, 165, 167
Weekly Dispatch, 43
Weill, Kurt, 59, 75
"What'll I Do," 99
"When Buddah Smiles," 129
When the Boys Meet the Girls, 322
"When Toby Is Out of Town," 56
"When You Ain't Got No Money You
    Needn't Come Around," 77
"When You Want 'Em You Can't Get
    'Em," 93, 310
"Where's My Bess," 214
White, George, 37, 41, 81. *See also* Scandals
Whiteman, Paul
    "American Music" question, 44–45
    Arvey on, 26
    Chotzinoff on, 84
    Downes on, 49
    Duncan on, 226
    "An Experiment," 45–49
    Gershwin on, 96
    jazz associated with, xi, 65, 108,
        124
    Kutner on, 247
    on "musical slang," 128–29
    135th Street, 87–89, 194
    orchestration, 302
    Van Vechten on, 78–79

Whiting, Margaret, 104, 104n
"Who Cares," 189
Who Could Ask For Anything More? (Swift),
    21
"Why Was I Born?," 75
Wilder, Alec, 75–77, 104, 163, 250–51
William Grant Still: A Study in Contradictions
    (Smith), 147–56
William Tell, 32, 187
Williams, Martin, 164n
Wilson, Dooley, 149
Wilson, Teddy, 103
Winchell, Walter, 66
"Wintergreen for President," 62, 143
Wise, Stephen, 271
Wodehouse, P. G., 53, 56, 66, 103, 250
"A Woman Is a Sometime Thing," 215
"Wonderful How Love Can Understand,"
    74
Woodland Sketches (MacDowell), 115
Woollcott, Alexander, 179–84

Wozzeck, 17
Wyatt, Robert, 221–28, 228–36

"Yank-Kee," 312
"Yankee Doodle Blues," 26, 313
"Yeah Man," 165, 165n
"Yes, We Have No Bananas," 126
"You Are Not The Girl," 311
"You-oo, Just You," 93, 311
You'd Be Surprised, 43
Youmans, Vincent, 61, 247
Young, Lester, 167
Youngren, William, 201

*Zez Confrey's Modern Course in Novelty Piano
    Playing* (Confrey), 126n
Zilboorg, Gregory, 254n
Zimbalist, Efrem, 44
Zorina, Vera, 242